LAWRENCE
OF ARABIA

"T. E." FROM A DRAWING BY AUGUSTUS JOHN

LAWRENCE
OF ARABIA

BY

B. H. LIDDELL HART

ILLUSTRATED

WITH MAPS AND PHOTOGRAPHS

A DA CAPO PAPERBACK

Library of Congress Cataloging in Publication Data

Liddell Hart, Basil Henry, Sir, 1895-1970.
  [Man behind the legend]
  Lawrence of Arabia / by B. H. Liddell Hart.
      p.   cm. — (A Da Capo paperback)
  Reprint. Originally published: The man behind the legend. New
York: Halcyon House, 1937.
  ISBN 0-306-80354-2
  1. Lawrence, T. E. (Thomas Edward), 1888-1935. 2. World War,
1914-1918 — Middle East. 3. Great Britain. Army — Biography. 4.
Soldiers — Great Britain — Biography. I. Title.
D568.4.L45L5   1989
940.4′15′0924   88-38465
[B]   CIP

This Da Capo Press paperback edition of *Lawrence of Arabia* is an unabridged
republication of the edition published in New York in 1935, originally entitled
Colonel Lawrence: The Man Behind the Legend. It is reprinted by arrangement with the
Estate of B. H. Liddell Hart.

Published by Da Capo Press, Inc.
A Subsidiary of Plenum Publishing Corporation
233 Spring Street, New York, N.Y. 10013

PREFACE

This book has changed its form as it has progressed. I began it with the idea of writing an historical sketch of the Arab Revolt in which T. E. "Lawrence" would naturally fill a large corner. My purpose was to clear away the dust of legend that has covered this peculiarly interesting episode of the World War, and to put it in perspective, bringing out its relation to the main campaign and to the history of irregular warfare. Also I desired to establish the true proportions of Lawrence's personal achievement—which I expected to be less than legend conveyed.

But as my study went further and deeper my picture changed. The events that had significance were seen to have their source in his action, and, still more, in his conception. The others faded into insignificance. I saw that there was a truth greater than its superficial suggestion in his deprecatory comment that his part—"was only synthetic. I combined their loose shower of sparks into a firm flame: transformed their series of unrelated incidents into a conscious operation."

Although he was here speaking only of his relations with the Arab chiefs I have gradually come to see that it should be applied to the whole.

But for him the Arab Revolt would have remained a collection of slight and passing incidents. Through him it had an important bearing on the course of outer events both during and since the war. Also on the course of warfare.

I found him growing more distinct as the background faded, until the Arab Revolt became an emanation of him. Thus I was compelled to recast the book and to make it primarily a study of him.

I have, however, kept the original form of the opening chapters, while diminishing their content, because it may help to convey the gradual sense of how he grew out of the Revolt as the Revolt was growing out of him.

Those who are not interested in the events that led up to the Revolt may prefer to skip Book II (Chapters ii, iii, and iv). For their convenience a brief historical summary is provided as an introduction to Book III.

My grateful thanks are due to the numerous participants in the campaign, and to others with first-hand knowledge of earlier and later events covered in this book, who have generously assisted me with their evidence in checking and supplementing that of documentary records. Also for the facilities afforded me in regard to such records.

Beyond these sources of information I have been fortunate in that T. E. Shaw (sometime Lawrence) has provided me with many notes and comments that help to explain his ideas and actions, as well as the course of events. These have been of special value. My indebtedness is increased by the astonishing patience he has shown in submitting to prolonged and repeated cross-examination on questions of fact. But I would make it clear that he has no part in the opinions I express or the judgments I have formed.

In seeking evidence from many sources I have found two sharply contrasted currents of opinion as to Lawrence's achievement, character, and qualities of leadership. One is overwhelmingly favourable, the other disparagingly sceptical. Such a difference of view is to be expected about any outstanding figure: the remarkable feature of this case lies in the contrast of the composition of the two groups. For it is significant that the first includes all those who for long periods were in close contact with Lawrence and his work in the Arab campaign; although they have an extraordinary diversity of type and outlook they are linked in a common admiration for Lawrence and an unstinting testimony to his transcendent powers. The second current of opinion, I have observed, is composed of men who had only a fleeting contact with Lawrence, or, more often, a hearsay acquaintance with his activities. Usually their adverse attitude is discovered, on deeper examination, to have its roots in a dislike of the cause for which he strove: the man is castigated merely as a symbol.

Thus it is clear which of the two currents must have the greater influence with anyone who is trying to form an historical judgment —even if the first were not confirmed by analysis of events.

B.H.L.H.

CONTENTS

BOOK I

PERSONAL PROLOGUE

CHAPTER   PAGE

   I   THE "CRUSADER" 3

BOOK II

HISTORICAL PROLOGUE

  II "THE SICK MAN" 23
 III THE LIFE-LINE 34
 IV THE UNDERCURRENT 42

BOOK III

THE ARAB REVOLT

      INTRODUCTION TO BOOK III 55
    V THE TOCSIN RINGS 58
   VI MEN OR A MAN 77
  VII THE WEDGE 93
 VIII SPREADING RIPPLES 114
   IX MARTIAL REVERIES 124
    X SPREADING THE INFECTION 140
   XI STRATEGY FULFILLED 154
  XII A NEW HORIZON 164
 XIII SECURING THE BASE 174
 XIV LEVERAGE ON PALESTINE 188
  XV A "REGULAR" CAMPAIGN 210
 XVI MORE AND MORE REGULAR 224
 XVII THE FINAL STROKE—PREPARATION 248
XVIII THE FINAL STROKE—EXECUTION 265
 XIX THE ROAD TO DAMASCUS 279

vii

CONTENTS

BOOK IV
AFTER

CHAPTER		PAGE
XX	TROUBLES OF A MAN WITH A CONSCIENCE	307
XXI	THE "SEVEN PILLARS OF WISDOM"	323
XXII	FULFILMENT	330
XXIII	POSTSCRIPT	354
	THE MAN OF REFLECTION	374
	THE MAN OF ACTION	380
	THE MESSAGE	390
	INDEX	391

LIST OF ILLUSTRATIONS

"T. E." from a drawing by Augustus John . . . . . *Frontispiece*

FACING PAGE

The Kaaba, Mecca 102

Dawn in Nakhl Mubarak (Feisal's encampment) December, 1916 . 102

Feisal's army coming back into Yanbo. December, 1916 118

The triumphal entry into Aqaba. July 1917 118

Feisal's Ageyl bodyguard. January, 1917 122

Captain Lawrence, early in 1917 134

Outside Feisal's tent at Wejh 142

Railway Raiding Party. Newcombe on left; Hornby on right . . . 182

Lawrence amid the results of a raid 182

The "Blue Mist" in Wadi Ithm 222

Lawrence's "Ghazala," and foal 222

"Tulips" exploding on the railway near Deraa 222

Ja'far Pasha and Sherif Nasir at Shobek 222

Lawrence, at Aqaba 230

Azraq 254

Aqaba 326

Lawrence on arrival at Damascus 358

MAPS

The Near and Middle East 24

The Hejaz Railway 34

Arabia, Syria and Mesopotamia 42

Turkey's Life-Line 56

The Hejaz 58

The Northern Theatre 140

'Aqaba-Ma'an Zone 154

'Amman-Der'a Zone 164

Battle of Tafila 216

The Palestine Campaign 224

BOOK I

PERSONAL PROLOGUE

CHAPTER I

THE "CRUSADER"

THE County of Carnarvon in North Wales points like an arm into the Irish Sea. At the armpit lie the villages of Portmadoc and Tremadoc, close beneath the foothills of Snowdon. This resemblance, which catches the map-gazing eye, offers a convenient method of indication. It is also an apt symbol for the career of one who was born here on August 15th, 1888. History hardly offers a clearer case of a man born for a mission, of a life moving along a path pointed out by fate—even though twists in its course may have hid the direction.

He was of mixed race. His father's family were Elizabethan settlers from England, favoured in gaining land in County Meath by Walter Raleigh, a connexion. During three hundred years of Irish domicile they never married into Ireland, but chose their wives from intruders such as themselves, from England, from Holland even. His mother was Island Scottish in feeling and education, but her parentage was part English, part Scandinavian. The sympathy of his home was Irish, all the stronger for being exiled. Wales had no share in him, after his first year.

The friends of his manhood called him "T.E.," for convenience and to show that they recognized how his adopted surnames—Lawrence, Ross, Shaw, whatever they were—did not belong.

The father's self-appointed exile reduced his means to a craftsman's income, which the landowning pride of caste forbade him to increase by labour. As five sons came, one after the other, the family's very necessaries of life were straitened. They existed only by the father's denying himself every amenity, and by the mother's serving her household like a drudge.

Observers noticed a difference in social attitude between the courtly but abrupt and large father, and the laborious mother. The father shot, fished, rode, sailed with the certainty of birth-right experience. He never touched a book or wrote a cheque. The mother kept to herself, and kept her children jealously from meeting or knowing their neighbours. She was a Calvinist and an ascetic, though a wonderful housewife, a woman of character and keen intelligence, with iron decision and charming, when she wished.

The father's family seemed unconscious of his sons, even when after his death recognition of their achievement might have done honour to the name. The five brothers, accordingly, were brought up to be self-sufficient, and were sufficient till the war struck away two and left in their sequence gaps in age that were overwide for sympathy to cross. Then their loneliness seemed to rankle, sometimes. To friends who wondered aloud how he could endure the company of the barrack-room and its bareness T.E. might retort, almost fiercely, that he had gone back to his boyhood class and was at home. "The fellows" were his—but this declaration of birthright seemed to strain the truth.

Once when I remarked this he replied—"not perhaps as much as you feel. I can be on terms with scholars, or writing people, or painters or politicians; but equally I am happy with bus conductors, fitters or plain workmen: anybody with a trade or calling. And all such classes are at home with me, though I fancy none would call me 'one of them.' Perhaps my upbringing and adventures—and way of thinking—have bereft me of class. Only the leisured make me uncomfortable, as I cannot play or pass time."

His first eight years were wandering—Scotland, the Isle of Man, Brittany, the Channel Islands, Hampshire. Eventually, the family's migrations brought them to Oxford, for reasons of education. T.E. arrived there with a child's lip-knowledge of French, and a fund of book learning. He had learnt his letters through hearing his eldest brother taught them, and in his fourth year was reading newspapers and books. Latin at six, through private tuition, and then at eight began his attendance at the City of Oxford School, a day-school small in numbers and low in fees. The fees he made lower for himself from the age of twelve upwards, by winning scholarships in a series that covered his tuition till he had taken his degree at the University.

"School," he said later, "was an irrelevant and time-wasting nuisance, which I hated and contemned." Here he shared the experience of most men of original minds. His career was yet another example of the truth that self-education is the only form of education. Formal lessons were small beer against his private reading, which had already ranged relatively far and wide in the three languages he understood. The discovery of grammars for English, French and Latin was an unpleasant interruption to the enjoyment of their books; just as the long school hours, and the plague of homework cut into the pursuit of archaeology that was already the child's passion. He hunted fragments of Roman or mediæval pottery on every site or in any chance excavation and went off alone on long cycling tours to collect rubbings from country church brasses and to photograph castles. His study of mediæval art was linked with that of armour, and led on to a new interest in the military art.

While still at school, he spent his holidays in tours through France, where he pursued cathedrals and castles with impartiality and equal zest, while travelling as light in luggage as in pocket. During one of these tours, when sixteen, he had his first dose of malaria, probably contracted sleeping out in the marshy delta of the Rhône while study-ing the fortifications of Aigues Mortes. Within the span of a few years he saw every twelfth century castle in France, England and Wales, and became an expert in roof climbing through his practice of going up towers and roofs in order to get new angles of photography for archi-tectural purposes. But the study of military architecture led him on, especially through reading the works of Viollet-le-Duc, to study the siege operations to which castles gave rise, and then to the campaigns of which they formed part.

The theme of the Crusades caught his imagination, although his sympathies were attracted by the opponents of the Crusaders, or "by those Crusaders who settled in Syria and learnt civilized ways, only to be cried out against by the rougher new arrivals." But the idea of a Crusade, the idea underlying it, revolved in his mind, giving rise to a dream Crusade, which implied a leader with whom in a sense he identified himself yet remained as himself a sympathetic observer. Naturally, it would be a Crusade in the modern form—the freeing of a race from bondage. Where, however, was he to find a race in need of release and at the same time of historical appeal? The Arabs seemed the only suitable one left, and they fitted in with the trend of his interests.

Thus, early, did the dream of his mission come, if it took a curiously detached form. It quickened his interest in the military side of history and archaeology, and, unconsciously moving towards its fulfilment, he began to study the history of wars, especially of wars that were

risings. He ranged widely, reading all he could about the Risorgi-·
mento, the wars of the Condottieri, and even translating extracts from
Procopius.

The mischance of being laid up with a broken leg, which abruptly
ended his physical growth, was turned to the profit of his mental
growth. The accident occurred when wrestling with another boy.
That was the sort of physical contest he could relish, because it was a
natural form. For *organized* games, football or cricket, he had no
liking. They were competitions governed by conventions and attaining only a figurative end. While he was more full of physical energy
than most boys, he preferred to expend it not in kicking goals, but in
exploring towards some goal. One aspect of this bent was his love of
tracing the source of streams. Another was his ceaseless search for
fragments of ancient and mediæval pottery, a search in which he acquired not only an uncanny flair but a remarkable knowledge. And
he was always elusive, going off by himself, avoiding observation
while on his wanderings, returning when he chose—the individual
among yet apart from the herd.

But although he loved the sense of freedom, he acquired while still
young the power of being free in a deeper than the physical sense.
In his teens he took a sudden turn for military experience at the urge
of some private difficulty, and served for a while in the ranks. He has
remarked since on the difference between the pre-war and the post-
war Army, especially the hard drinking and the brutality of conduct
and manners in the former as compared with the latter. But this
experience, if its restrictions irked him, rather strengthened than
weakened his essential apartness.

It became more marked in the greater freedom of his next phase,
as an undergraduate. At school they had wanted him to try for a
mathematical scholarship, but a consequent surfeit of the subject
led him to change over suddenly to history just before he was
eighteen. After six months he tried for a history scholarship at St.
John's College, but failed. At the next shot he gained an exhibition
at Jesus College, Oxford, where the fact that he had been born in
Wales gave him official preference. He had rooms in College only
for one term; otherwise he lived at home during the years he was
in statu pupillari. The conditon, laid on his mother, of reporting
that he was "home by twelve" allowed of elastic interpretation. He

was often out again soon after midnight. The still hours of darkness were the time he favoured for working, for his walks abroad or even for visiting his friends. These were few, if rich in variety, as he only seemed to care for company when it offered some fresh and different facet to his intellectual curiosity. But the few with whom he made contact quickly came, then as in later years, under his spell. That much overworked word expresses the effect of his personality as no other word can.

He refused to take part in the ordinary College life, and the other undergraduates would hardly have realized his existence if his imperceptibility had not been pressed so far as ultimately to provoke curiosity. He had then as later the extreme unobtrusiveness which compels notice. If undesired, this may yet have been enjoyed, for he had an impish streak. The curiosity he aroused appealed to his sense of humour, which lay deep beneath the surface, as intangible as himself. His was the sense of humour that is synonymous with a philosophy of life. I suspect that Socrates consoled himself thus.

In his studies Lawrence was equally "free." He had decided to read for the History School, but he paid little attention to the prescribed books, and perfunctory attendance at the prescribed lectures. His reading widened with every opportunity, pursuing many interesting if academically irrelevant avenues, from mediæval poetry to modern strategy. He used to borrow six volumes at a time from the Oxford Union library, in his father's name and his own, and often changed them daily. For he thought nothing of reading all day and half through the night, lying on a rug or mattress, a habit that had the convenience of allowing him to go to sleep where he lay—he has preserved it, slightly adapted, for later life in the cottage where he intends to settle down. He not only read fast but absorbed quickly, for he had a way of "sensing" a subject, as a bee draws in the nectar as it flits from flower to flower. It was always the unexpected, the undiscovered, or the inaccessible sources that he sought —"Originals and sidelights, not compilations."

But this habit of study did not accord with the normal examination course. It was more suited, as he was more suited, to the mediæval conception of university studies. In the circumstances he was for tunate to have chosen Oxford, and not a more modern, mass-production university. It was suggested that to compensate his neglect of the usual course of reading, he should submit a thesis on some special subject. He chose—"The Influence of the Crusades on the Medieval Military Architecture of Europe."

Towards it he had already behind him the knowledge gained from his visits to the castles of France and Britain. He now decided to spend the long vacation before he took "Finals" in seeing the castles of the Crusaders in Syria, and also, characteristically, in tracking down remains of a more remote race, the Hittites, whose remains he had been studying with Dr. Hogarth. Contrary to what has been said, T.E. had known Hogarth some time before he conceived this visit to Syria—"I had attracted his notice by the way I arranged the medieval pottery cabinets in the Ashmolean, which had been neglected." This was the first link in a momentous chain of causation. When he mooted his idea of spending the "Long Vac" in Syria Hogarth warned him that the summer was a bad season for such a journey, and that in any case it would mean considerable outlay on the necessary retinue and camp-equipment. To this T.E. replied that he was going to walk, and going alone. The fact of walking would entitle him to hospitality in the villages he passed through. "It would also," he admitted later, "have led to my immediate arrest by the suspicious Turkish Government—but Lord Curzon obtained for me, from the Turkish Cabinet, an open letter to its governors in Syria, to afford me every assistance! This was a piquant passport for a tramp to carry."

Even so, it was a hazardous adventure, but he carried it through successfully despite a return of malaria and a narrow escape from murder. First he tramped on foot through the country over which Allenby's cavalry would sweep like a flood some ten years after— with himself on their flank. From Beirut he went to Sidon, thence past Lake Huleh (the Waters of Merom) into Trans-Jordan, back by Nazareth and over Carmel to Acre and then up the coast to Antioch, on a varying course that made his route like a spider's web over mountain Syria. After visiting, and photographing in detail, some fifty of the ruined castles in Syria he pushed on northward beyond Aleppo to Aintab, where he collected a number of Hittite seals, and then turned east across the middle reaches of the Euphrates to Urfa and Harran.

He had picked up a smattering of conversational Arabic from a

Syrian Protestant clergyman living in Oxford, the Rev. N. Odeh, and he improved it with practice in the Syrian villages where he lodged at night, usually in the Sheikh's house if there was no khan, or inn. To a man more dependent on comfort the hospitality that he received in these poor quarters would have been a hardship, but to T.E. it was merely an interesting experience. He had no craving for European drink or meat, and none of the usual European's qualms over using his hand in place of spoon and fork. Although he looked a mere boy, more youthful than his actual years, there was something in his manner that commanded the attention of the Arabs, just as it did of the more perceptive among Europeans he met.

It was during the last stage, near the Euphrates, that a covetous Turkman, mistaking his cheap copper watch for gold, followed in his tracks and eventually seized a chance to spring on him and bring him down. The Turkman tried to kill him with his own Webley pistol, only to be foiled because Lawrence pulled out the trigger-guard, so collapsing the pistol, before the Turkman wrested it away. Even so, nothing but the accidental intrusion of a shepherd pre-vented him from smashing T.E.'s head. Thus reprieved, T.E.. with a bad headache, walked to the nearest town and would not rest until he had obtained the help of a body of Turkish police whom he brought back to the village where the robber had taken refuge. After a lengthy argument the man was surrendered and his booty re-stored. "What I was really after were my Hittite seals, not the watch!"

The adventure failed to cure T.E. of his love of solitary wander-ing. Indeed, actual contact with the Bedouin had replaced their idealistic attraction for him with a stronger tie, while loosening the uneasy and already precarious hold of civilized habits. He may have lost his romantic ideas about the Bedouin themselves—at any rate he has none now—but he was drawn to their way of life. The desert, like the malaria, was in his blood.

He had not long to wait for a chance to feel it again. Once back at Oxford, after a four months' tour, he settled down to prepare his thesis. Its general trend was that the Crusaders had brought more military architectural science to Syria than they took away, and that their work owed little to Byzantine influence. The thesis gained him first class honours in the final examination for his degree. Despite the impression it made he refused to print it, on the ground that it was only a preliminary study and not good enough to publish. He now thought of doing a fourth year and taking a B.Litt. on mediæval pottery.

But, better than a "first," he had gained the admiration of Hogarth, who was henceforth his patron and the familiar spirit who presided over his fortunes. "I owe to him every good job I've had except my enlistment in the Air Force."

"Trenchard let me in to the R.A.F. Till then D.G.H. had been a godfather to me: and he remained the best friend I ever had. A great man."

It was Hogarth who now induced Magdalen College to give him a four years' senior demyship, or travelling endowment, and took him on the British Museum expedition to Jerablus on the Upper Euphrates, the presumed site of ancient Carchemish of the Hittites. On this first trip T.E. was a handyman who proved his value best of all by his knack of keeping the native labour-gangs in a good humour. But in addition he did all the pottery, and produced, before the season ended, a complete stratification of types and rims from the surface to thirty feet down; also he did the photography.

When the November rains came and interrupted the work, Hogarth sent T.E. to Egypt in order that he might learn something of scientific methods of digging under Sir Flinders Petrie, whose camp was near the Fayoum. There is a good story that T.E. asked at the station how he could find the Petries, and was told "to walk in the direction of the desert till he saw flies swarming and then make for where the flies were thickest and there he would find Flinders Petrie." The latter, however, if careless, revealed an amusing streak of conventionality. For T.E.'s appearance in the shorts and blazer that he had been accustomed to wear at Carchemish drew from the great Egyptologist the ironical reproof—"Young man, we don't play cricket here." The irony was greater than he imagined, for his apparent haziness as to the difference between the garbs of cricket and football was surpassed by T.E.'s aversion to any game. But although it was not long before Flinders Petrie corrected his first impressions of the new recruit, T.E. himself found that excavation in Egypt soon palled. It had reached a point where it lacked the lure of the unknown that still surrounded the Hittite civilization, and it had become too minutely organized a branch of research for his taste.

He returned to Carchemish again the following year with Hogarth, and subsequently assisted Woolley there right up to the coming of war in 1914. The work offered plenty of variety, for his province embraced the photographs, sculpture, pottery and the copying of inscriptions. Twenty years later he remarked—"It was the best life I ever lived"—better even than the R.A.F. that was the refuge of his maturity. Even in the off-seasons, during the long winter floods and the heat of the summer, he only went home occasionally for short spells, and spent the rest of the time travelling round the Middle and Near East, or staying at the diggings alone. During the digging season he received fifteen shillings a day; during the rest of the year, while travelling, he lived on his demyship of a hundred pounds a year, supplemented by casual earnings of queerly varied kinds. Once, for example, he took on a checker's job in coaling ships at Port Said. In five years he came to know Syria like a book, much of north Mesopotamia, Asia Minor, Egypt and Greece. He was always going up and down, "Wherever going was cheap."

The solitary spells at Carchemish not only saved money but gave him a better opportunity to make contacts among the local Arabs and Kurds, and through close acquaintance to reach an understanding of their ways and thoughts. Although he was not, and never would be, an Arabic scholar—he has always been most frank in refuting this popular belief—he learnt to talk it well enough for conversational purposes, and his limitations were covered up by his fluency, if also by his profound understanding of native ways. This was more than, indeed essentially different from, the acquired knowledge of the outside observer. "Particularly, my poverty let me learn the masses, from whom the wealthy traveller was cut off by his money and attendants." It was an immersion in them, by sympathetic projection. And by this faculty he came to perceive what he expressed later—when it was the secret of his power—in the words—"Among the Arabs there were no distinctions, traditional or natural, except the unconscious power given a famous sheikh by virtue of his accomplishment; and they taught me that no man could be their leader except he ate the ranks' food, wore their clothes, lived level with them, and yet appeared better in himself."

It was by this complete abandonment not only of the conventions but of the resources of civilized life, by what other Europeans would have considered an abasement, that T.E. became a naturalized Arab instead of merely a European visitor to the Arab lands. He was helped by his indifference to the outward deference that other Europeans, and especially Englishmen, demand. And the way was eased by his tramp habits and outlook. From a "street Arab" to a "white Arab" was not a difficult transition.

It was while at Carchemish that he adopted the habit of wearing native dress on occasional and specific wanderings. Short and slight, fair and clean-shaven, he was apparently the last man to carry off such a guise successfully, and his obvious incongruities have provoked scornful comment from various European experts in externals. Yet there is ample evidence that by the Arabs he was accepted, if not mistaken, for one of themselves. According to him that was not difficult in Northern Syria "where the racial admixture has produced many fair natives, and many with only a broken knowledge of Arabic. I could never pass as an Arab—but easily as some other native speaking Arabic." Yet here he passes over the deeper explanation—his ability to get inside an Arab's skin when donning his outer garments. It was the more easy for T.E. to do so because he already shared the Arabs' deep-rooted desire for untrammelled freedom, and had no more desire than they had for the material possessions that offer comfort at the price of circumscription. In the desert he found, like them, the stark simplicity that suited him, and although he never lost the power to adapt himself to, and appreciate, the more subtle pleasures of civilized society, it was in the desert that he found the solitude that satisfied his deepest instinct.

But to imagine him as always brooding would be essentially false. He was no hermit. It would be nearer the truth to say that he was always perceiving. And that reflection on these impressions was a process of swift mental appreciation rather than meditation. Such at least is my own impression, which may be right or wrong, for all those who meet Lawrence see a facet of his personality that largely depends on their own cast of thought, and so is often different. Moreover, the same man at different meetings may see different aspects. It has led some of his friends to christen him the "human chameleon." But this term hardly fits the figure, or conveys the idea, so well as if one says that he is essentially dynamic or, better still, fluid —in the likeness of mercury, divisible into globules yet inherently coalescent. Perhaps his own explanation is better still—"at an O.T.C. field day I was once told to disguise myself as a battalion in close order: and have done, ever since!"

There is a curious duality in T.E.'s appearance. At a casual glance he may easily escape notice, owing to his short stature, his weather-reddened face, and a dull look that often serves as a convenient mask when he wants to merge into the background. But at a closer view one is struck by the size of his head, with its rampant crest of fair hair springing from the high forehead, and the strangely penetrating blue eyes, whose predominant expression is kindly yet remote. The size of the head would be more noticeable if it were not for the way that the intellectual brow is balanced by the strong jaw, which in turn redresses, and seems to be controlling, the sensuous shape of the mouth. The general effect in repose is rather severe, but it disappears when he speaks or smiles—he has a voice of extraordinary charm and an utterly disarming smile.

It is in the mouth that one may perhaps trace an aspect of T.E. that is more misunderstood than any other—an extreme sensuousness that is entirely unsensual, in the accepted meaning. For what most astonishes the public is his disregard of the pleasures that the ordinary man pursues and his relish for what other men would regard as discomforts to be avoided. Thus he speaks of himself as sexless; meaning that he is devoid of sexual appetites. He takes no interest in food, and when by himself is satisfied with one meal a day, of the simplest kind, although he will eat a normal dinner when with friends. Fruit, especially apples, is the only form of food for which he seems to have any real liking. He neither drinks nor smokes. He has occasionally tasted wine, but prefers water as being more varied in flavour. This is not a jest: his senses are very highly developed—but different. He says himself that he hunts *sensation*—in the deeper sense of the word. He is always eager for a new sensation, but he does not repeat it if unpleasant. Pleasure and pain, as he emphasizes, are matters of individual judgment. He finds exhilaration in what other men would shrink from, and pain in what are often their pastimes. "High diving would be pain"—it is a question of difference of tastes, not of a taste for discomfort. And in his judgment "the more elemental you can keep sensations, the better you feel them." A taste for wine mars the more subtle appreciation of water.

This explanation may serve to modify the common assumption that his way of life can be ascribed to an innate asceticism. He declares himself that he is "not an ascetic, but a hedonist." The denial is easier to accept than the affirmation—when one remembers how the brow balances the jaw, and the jaw controls the mouth. His "hedonism," itself different from the normal, is an essential part of him: but it is only a part. It helps us, however, to understand his "Street Arabism."

On his excursions, he has told me—"I travelled always with someone from our Carchemish digging gang, and we thoroughly enjoyed ourselves, taking a few camels on hire-carrying, sailing down the Syrian coast, bathing, harvesting and sight-seeing in the towns." Urfa, in particular, made a lasting impression on him by its bazaars and magnificent Byzantine castle. One of his expeditions in the valley of the upper Euphrates gave him, however, a far less pleasant memory and an awkward adventure—the first of his two enforced "enlistments" in the Turkish Army.

Lured by the report of a statue—of a woman seated on the backs of two lions—that might have been Hittite he set off in native dress accompanied by one of his workmen. The district was too north for Arabs to wander and near Birijik he and his companion were arrested as suspected deserters from the Turkish Army. They were kicked down the stairs of a noisome and verminous dungeon, T.E. being bruised all up one side and his fellow-prisoner suffering a bad sprain. They were left all night in confinement to contemplate the prospect of compulsory military service, but in the morning T.E. managed to bribe their guards to let them go.

At Carchemish the outlets T.E. found were characteristic. His time was not merely divided between the excavations at the great mound and wandering among the natives. He went for bathes daily in the Euphrates, and added zest to them by building a water-chute of clay, down which he used to toboggan into the river. He made frequent trips on it, defying its dangerous currents, in a canoe fitted with a small auxiliary motor of uncertain ways which he brought out at a cost he could ill afford. Water work had come to him naturally, from his childhood in his father's sailing yachts, and he had been an adept in handling a canoe ever since his school-day river explorations at Oxford. He practised shooting, with automatic pistols at matchboxes and other minute targets, until he became an exceptionally fine shot. Indoors, he spent hours in developing the photographs that were his speciality, but he also found time to continue his reading. The hut where he abode, when he did not sleep in the open as he often chose, contained a library that gave the place an air of Oxford-on-the-Euphrates.

With the native workmen, mainly Kurds and Arabs, relations were more than good. If this enviable state owed much to T.E.'s way of conversing with them, the devotion he inspired was even more a tribute to his strength of character and, in particular, his quietly fearless air.

Sir Hubert Young, who was one of his visitors, relates that "by his mere personality he had turned the excavation into a miniature British consulate," and tells a story of "his way of asserting his position as the unofficial Qonsolos, or representative of the great British Government." When out on a trip by canoe they came upon several stalwart-looking Kurds who were dynamiting fish. T.E. walked straight up to the biggest, reminded him that it was against the Turkish law, added that it was "a shameless thing to do," and ordered the man to come with him to the police station. The Kurd looked down contemptuously at him and declined emphatically, whereupon T.E. seized him by the arm and began to march him off. The other Kurds followed, however, throwing stones and drawing their knives. The situation looked ugly, and at Young's urging, T.E. released his prisoner. But, unwilling to be defied, he went straight to the nearest police post, and when he found the inspector showing signs of typical Turkish inertia, stirred him into activity by a threat to have him removed, as his predecessor had been.

Several opportunities of character test were provided by the German engineers then engaged in bridging the Euphrates at Carchemish to carry the famous Baghdad railway, the instrument of such ambitious designs. While T.E. was away in the Lebanon, and Woolley home on leave, the Germans attempted to utilize some mounds of archaeological importance to build up their railway embankment. After vain protest, the Arab overseer left in charge mounted guard over the mounds with a rifle and threatened to shoot anyone who came near. Meantime T.E., who had himself been notified by telegram, telegraphed to Constantinople and collected a high Turkish official, with whom he made a dramatic appearance on the scene to the discomfiture of the Germans, who were compelled to abandon their plans.

Not long after, a German engineer beat one of the Englishmen's house-servants on a flimsy pretext. T.E. went to the German camp and demanded that the offender should offer a public apology to the victim. The chief engineer, a surly, hard-drinking man, retorted that flogging was the only way to deal with natives, and washed his hands of the matter. This did not satisfy T.E. who, in his ominously quiet voice, remarked that in such a case he would have to take the engineer forcibly and make him apologize. The German looked at T.E.—and gave in.

But the Germans themselves were later to have cause to bless that power of his, if they did not appreciate it. Dissatisfaction with the working conditions led to a riot in their camp. T.E. and Woolley went across to find several hundred furious Kurds besieging the handful of Germans. They stopped firing instantly when the two Englishmen appeared, but the besieged foolishly continued, and it was only by the exertions and cool determination of the Englishmen, risking the bullets of the men they were trying to save, that a massacre was averted. Even then, in the sequel, the neighbouring Kurds held up progress of the work until, finally, the Englishmen were called in to adjudicate the dispute; they persuaded the Kurds to accept a payment of blood-money for a man who had been shot. The Turkish authorities wished to confer decorations on the Englishmen for settling the trouble, but their offer was declined. In view of the part that T.E. was to play within a few years there would have been a delicious irony in his acceptance.

But this sense of gratitude was not shared by some of the Germans. They harboured the belief that T.E. was at the root of the troubles they experienced with their native workmen, a belief not unnatural to those who saw the contentment in the other camp and were unable to see the cause. Moreover, conscious of the designs that inspired the Baghdad railway, they were sensitively quick to suspect T.E. of designing to sabotage it, or at the least to spy upon it. And here his own impish side came uppermost. Young relates that "he said gleefully that he did not go out of his way to remove this impression. On the contrary, he took a mischievous delight in rousing the German's suspicions and cutting him out in every possible way. He even told us that he had gone so far one day as to drag some large pipes up to the top of the mound, whereupon the German had reported in a frantic telegram, which somehow fell into his hands, that the mad Englishman was mounting guns to command the railway-bridge over the Euphrates."

Whether the last part be fact or surmise, we may say of the story that it is so good that it ought to be true. And Lawrence, whose impishness sometimes extends to his stories, has the artistic sense to supply the appropriate complement even if it were missing.

Again, one cannot avoid the suspicion that he was influenced by his sense of humour as well as by his sense of gratitude for their help when he took a couple of the Arab head-men back to Oxford with him in the summer of 1913. They took the experience very calmly, and the aspect of Oxford that they most admired was that of the "beautiful glazed bricks" in the public lavatories, while their chief surprise was furnished by the bicycles. T.E. amusingly tells of the delight with which they learnt to ride, on women's bicycles because of their flowing garments, and how they careered in circles round a stupefied policeman in the centre of Carfax.

That winter, after his return to Syria, a more serious mission awaited him. Woolley and he were at Aleppo, resting after a hard spell at Carchemish, when a telegram came from London telling him that they were wanted to take part in an expedition to Sinai. They went south accordingly and were met at Beersheba by Captain Newcombe, a Sapper officer, who was to be their companion. They learnt that their part in the expedition was to be an archaeological camouflage for a military survey, by Newcombe and his assistants, of the country beyond the frontier of Egypt. He on his part had an equal surprise, for he had not unnaturally assumed that the archaeologists would be as venerable as their subject, only to be confronted by two youngsters, one of whom looked barely eighteen.

Newcombe, who had already been surveying the frontier zone, had written home to the War Office to suggest that the survey be extended to cover the region between Beersheba and Aqaba. The War Office thought it wise to arrange a camouflage and, as this purpose coincided with an archaeological desire to fill certain gaps in scientific knowledge, the expedition was carried out under the auspices of the Palestine Exploration Fund, on whose behalf the necessary permit was obtained from the Turks. One may add that Lord Kitchener, then British Agent in Egypt, in approving the scheme had shown anxiety lest Turkish suspicions be aroused.

The party travelled southward from Beersheba to Khalasa, and thence by a zig-zag route, through the wilderness to Ain Kadeis, supposed to be the Kadesh-Barnea of the Israelite wanderings. Instead of the verdant oasis pictured by some imaginative explorers, to the beguilement of modern Biblical geographers, they found it to be merely a small spring in a stony and barren valley. An American traveller, Dr. Trumbull, who visited the spot in 1882, and wrote a rapturous account of it, had told of the delight with which his Arab servants "stripped and plunged into the lower and larger pool for a bathe." Lawrence, in giving the exact measure of its shallowness, ironically remarked, "Our guide also washed his feet in it."

The site of Kadesh-Barnea was but one of many fantastic suppositions, about Biblical traditions and Byzantine antiquities, that Lawrence and Woolley helped to explode. But the expedition had a future as well as a historical value. For, later in his course, T.E. passed by way of Wadi Musa and Jebel Harun (the traditional Mount Hor on which Aaron was buried) to Ma'an on the new strategic Hejaz railway that linked Medina with Damascus. Thus he unknowingly did a preliminary reconnaissance of the scene of his operations in the second half of 1917. T.E.'s historical interest had already led him to spend some of his off-season travels in studying the approaches to Syria from the desert, and this study from Saladin's point of view helped his own strategy later, even though he did not operate at the same places as Saladin and the railway was a fresh addition. "My problem and Saladin's were not far apart." He also remarks—"Saladin's conquest of Syria was an accident, born of lopping off the edges."

More notable still, T.E. on this Sinai "survey" also explored the ground for his first great war exploit at Aqaba, although not in the way that has been recorded. It has been said that when the Turks refused permission for the party to visit this little port on the eastern arm of the Red Sea, Lawrence volunteered to go there on his own and obtain certain bearings that Newcombe needed. The facts are different. The Turks were not asked for permission. Newcombe went there alone to survey this potentially important strategic point while Woolley and Lawrence pursued their exploration in the north. On arrival, despite rebuffs, his persistence won the day and he was finally left at peace to carry out his work. But before long Lawrence left Woolley to follow Newcombe, whom he found in camp about two miles from Aqaba.

Near here, on a little island about a quarter of a mile from the shore, there was a ruined castle which had played its part in Crusading history, alternately in Moslem and Christian hands. Lawrence was eager to examine it for constructions by Renaud of Chatillon or Saladin. An interest in military defences of such remote importance aroused the Turks' suspicions and they posted a guard over the boat he had intended to use. Thereupon Lawrence borrowed camel water-tanks from Newcombe, bound them together into a crude raft, and ferried himself and one of his Carchemish followers over to the island. He reached Jebel Faroun unobserved, and found it interesting, but completely in ruins, with even the cisterns broken. The return journey proved more difficult, as the wind was against him, while the presence of sharks in the water made the raft seem a rather frail protection, so that he felt no small relief when at last he reached land.

During his stay at Aqaba T.E. made an inland excursion of more future significance. For he went several miles up the gorge of the Wadi Ithm, through which ran the direct route to the important station of Ma'an on the Hejaz railway. It was far enough for him to see that it was impregnable against an advance from the coast side —a piece of knowledge that was to bear fruit three years later. He was certainly a dangerous visitor for the Turks to harbour even though they could not foresee the consequence of his curiosity. But his wandering habits sufficed to arouse their suspicions, and on his leaving Newcombe's camp to return north, the Turks sent a police officer with him as escort. Disliking this check on his curiosity, Lawrence gave the policeman the slip and made his way to Petra. Here he found Lady Evelyn Cobbold, who lent him the money for his fare back to Damascus from Ma'an.

This expedition, with its veiled military purpose, gave a reinforcement to thoughts which were already stirring in Lawrence's mind since his sojourn at Carchemish. His basic intention in exploring Syria was always to write a strategic study of the Crusades; but incidentally he saw many other things. From Carchemish he had watched the construction of the Baghdad railway with his own eyes, and thus had the keener perception of its potential menace to the outposts of Britain. The Armenian revolutionaries had come to him for help and advice, and he had dipped far into their councils. The opposition party of the Kurdish reactionaries against the Young Turks had encouraged him to ride in their ranks and seek opportunity in the Balkan crisis. From the Arabs among whom he moved he had heard of their aspirations for freedom from the Turkish yoke. He had even made contact with sections of the secret society which, within and without the Turkish Army, was actively working towards such an end.

The knowledge gave a new meaning to his old dreams, and brought them on to the horizon of reality. The expedition to Sinai was, he could feel, a definite step towards his aim and theirs. Indeed, the title of that famous story of spying on the German coastline, *The Riddle of the Sands,* might have been coined still more aptly to fit his recent activities. Before long he would himself propound a fresh riddle in the desert sands that the Turks would never succeed in solving.

BOOK II

HISTORICAL PROLOGUE

CHAPTER II

"THE SICK MAN"

The curious revolutions of a century in Anglo-Turkish relations—The intrusion of Germany—The outbreak of the World War—The side-steps that took Turkey into the War—The lost opportunity at the Dardanelles

THE century that preceded the World War shows nothing more curious in the diplomatic sphere than the ever-changing yet ever-repeating relationship between Britain and Turkey. It might aptly be entitled "the Near East Knock-about turn."

The beginning of the nineteenth century found us fighting along-side the Turks against Napoleon. Yet in 1807 a British fleet passed through the Dardanelles in an attempt to compel Turkey to give way to Russia, and then sailed for Alexandria to support the Mamelukes in their revolt against the Turkish suzerainty. In 1826 our sympathy with the Greeks in their struggle for independence was expressed by our ships in sinking the Turkish fleet at Navarino, yet in the following year we set our face against Russia and reverted to the policy of preserving at all costs the integrity of the Ottoman Empire. In 1852 British public and political opinion was showing its mistrust of Turkey's sincerity in the path of reform, but in 1854 a British army was fighting in the Crimea to defend Turkey against Russia. In 1867 the Sultan was in London receiving the Order of the Garter at the hands of Queen Victoria, but in 1876 Britain was wrathfully denouncing the Bulgarian Atrocities and execrating the "Unspeakable Turk," who was not only massacring his subject peoples but suspending payment on his debts. However, a year later, the British fleet was again in the Bosphorus, covering Constantinople with its guns against the advancing Russians.

In 1882 the British Army occupied Egypt, to the intense displeasure of the Turks. In 1885 Britain and Turkey had reached an amicable agreement and their respective High Commissioners were working side by side in Egypt. The result was an arrangement that the British occupation would come to an end in 1890. But French and Russian diplomacy intervened to disturb the atmosphere, and

persuade the Sultan not to ratify the convention. So the British remained in occupation, and the Turkish High Commissioner remained as a cipher.

The picture reminds one of a kind of mediæval clock with symbolical figures to represent Concord and Discord, Peace and War,
bobbing in and out alternately. This extraordinary series of re-
versals is largely to be explained by the counter-pull of Britain's
moral impulses and material interests. The behaviour of Turkey
towards her subject peoples repeatedly offended the Englishman's
sense of justice as well as his sentiment. But whenever there was a
threat to our Mediterranean trade routes, or a danger that France,
and, still more, Russia, might profit from the offender's punishment,
the Englishman's moral sense gave way to his political instinct, the
weight of commercial interest reversing the balance. As Napoleon
wrote in 1808—"Who is to have Constantinople? That is always
the crux of the problem." It proved to be so for another century.

In the light of those hundred years of history and their sequel,
the use of our national gift for compromise may not seem altogether
happy. Such delicate adjustment, to be truly effective, requires a
Machiavelli—and the Englishman is not Machiavellian. He can
never rid himself of moral scruples sufficiently to fill the part. Thus
he is always and inevitably handicapped in an amoral competition,
whether in duplicity or blood-and-iron. Realization of this inherent
"weakness" suggests that Britain might find it better to be more
consistently moral. At any rate the experiment has yet to be tried.

On the other hand, there is plenty of experience to show the
dilemmas and dangers into which Britain's maladjustment of morality and materialism has landed her. The most striking example was
provided in that sphere of international relations where Britain had
been most inconsistent. And it came in the opening months of the
World War. Or, rather, it came to a head then. For the scales had
for a number of years been tilting against Britain's influence with
Turkey. The cause, this time, was not an outburst of British moral
indignation but a new trend in Britain's European policy.

This gave a new point to old memories. And the point was directed at us, leading to what the British Prime Minister termed a
"treacherous stab in the back." His feelings surely overcame his historical sense. For in view of the past century's record there was a

MAP I

THE NEAR & MIDDLE EAST

ODESSA

BLACK SEA

CAUCASUS

CASPIAN SEA

GALLIPOLI
Helles
Dardanelles

CONSTANTINOPLE

ERZERUM   SARIKAMISH

SMYRNA

ALEXANDRETTA   URFA   NISIBIN

JERABLUS   MOSUL

ANTIOCH   ALEPPO

MED.ⁿ   SEA   SYRIA   BAGHDAD

PERSIA

KUT

J. DRUSE   Euphrates   Tigris

ALEXANDRIA   JERUSALEM   JERICHO

PALESTINE

Senussi   SUEZ   MA'AN   BASRA

CAIRO   Sinai   AQABA   BUSHIRE

EGYPT   RED   ARABIA

WEJH

MEDINA

N.

JIDDA   MECCA

Pt. SUDAN

SEA

KHARTOUM

Darfur   A - E

SUDAN   ADEN

Scale of miles
100   0   100   200   300

piquant irony in the way writers referred to our "century-old friendship with Turkey," and in the shocked indignation of the public at what was termed Turkey's base ingratitude.

The truth was that Turkey had no assured grounds for relying on our support in her policy, or even in her resistance to Russian policy. She could perceive that our support in the past had only been tendered, reluctantly, when it suited our interests to give a check to Russia. Thus the drawing together of Britain and Russia which followed the Entente with France and was completed by the Anglo-Russian agreement, shook Turkey to the core. It produced a sense of insecurity greater than she had ever known.

That negative effect was accentuated by a positive influence. Germany's growing ambition for eastward expansion, her dream of empire extending to the Persian Gulf, had led her to extend her friendship to Turkey. The strengthening of her influence there meant the loosening of Britain's. Little by little the wedge was inserted, beginning with a German military mission. If its energetic zeal for efficiency was found irksome, the Turk found a redeeming restfulness in his new friend's silence when the treatment of Turkey's subjects was called in question. While the British lion roared with indignation at the reports of atrocities, the German eagle soared above such trifles in quest of its ultimate goal. After the moral lectures he had so often received from Britain, the Turk could not but appreciate the comfort of Germany's indifference to his methods.

The German wedge, moreover, had a man of weight behind it. This was Baron Marschall von Bieberstein, who from 1897 to 1912 was ambassador at Constantinople. To a race who admired strength above all, whose "chivalry" was only extended to the strong, Marschall von Bieberstein's huge frame, scarred face and trampling manner formed a living picture of the growing power of Germany. He had an able successor, whose forceful character was blended with foxiness, in Baron von Wangenheim, nicknamed the "Cuirassier diplomat."

There was one man who might have counteracted the impression with that of Britain's more mature and quieter determination. This was Kitchener, who seems to have had an unrealized desire for the post. Instead, the successive British Ambassadors during these critical years lacked both the necessary prestige and strength of personality.

Moreover, during the critical weeks of late July and early August, 1914, our representative was even absent from his post on leave.

Yet, despite the assiduous way she was wooed by Germany, Turkey once more turned to her old supporter when again in danger, from Italy in 1911, and made an overture for alliance with Britain. The proposal was put aside by the British Government, although not without realization of the consequences. This is shown in a letter that Mr. Winston Churchill wrote from Balmoral to Sir Arthur Nicolson at the Foreign Office—"Will it not if it comes to war or warlike tension throw Turkey into German arms more than ever—thus making the complete causeway: Germany—Austria—Rumania—Turkey? . . . Do you think it possible that Germany has been marking time for this to happen in order to secure an atmosphere more suited to thunderbolts?" Nevertheless, while foreseeing the risks, he himself came to the conclusion—"clearly we must prefer Italy to Turkey on all grounds—moral and unmoral."

Britain's aloofness rankled deeply in the "Young Turks," who had seized control of Turkey only to find themselves beset by external dangers; despoiled of Tripoli by Italy and of Macedonia by the armed alliance of their erstwhile Balkan subjects in 1912. Some of the new leaders of Turkey still clung, almost pathetically, to the hope of renewed ties with Britain, but their feelings—both emotional and diplomatic—were opposed by a certain chilling influence in the British Embassy, where a powerful prejudice against "Young Turk" freemasonry was combined with a lingering support of the powerless Sultan and his palace clique. This prejudice had a concrete base in the discovery that the Grand Orient of Turkey was in close touch with the extreme Nationalists in Egypt. Moreover, there were shrewd observers who became convinced that Turkey's destination was inevitable from the moment Germany appeared "in shining armour" by Austria's side in 1909—that in Turkish measure British sympathy could never balance the scales against German might. But, as it was, the antipathy checked several friendly advances while the Germanophile side of the "Young Turk" movement grew stronger under the contrast of treatment. And although Germany's proffered embrace had its embarrassments it held no such obvious danger as the bear-hug of Russia.

If the fear of rape by Russia supplemented by the hope of loot

—at Russia's expense—was the main factor in bringing Turkey into the war against Britain, the immediate impulse was provided by three ships. They were the new German battle-cruiser *Goeben,* and the British-built battleships *Sultan Osman* and *Reschadieh.* As a shrewd step to enhance German prestige—which had suffered from the defeats of the German-trained Turkish Army in the recent Balkan War—and to weaken the one remaining foothold of British influence—our Naval mission—the *Goeben* was sent out to Constantinople early in 1914 and for long lay anchored near the entrance to the Golden Horn.

Then in the war-charged atmosphere of late July, the ever-present fear of Russian lust for the Dardanelles developed almost to panic pitch. Certain of war between Germany and Russia, uncertain of Britain's participation, and egged on by Enver Pasha, the Germanophile and German-trained leader of the Young Turks, the Turkish Grand Vizier responded to previous German overtures by asking Wangenheim, on July 27th, for a secret alliance against Russia. Next day the proposal was accepted, and on August 2nd the Treaty was signed, unknown to most of the Turkish Cabinet. On the morrow the first mines were laid in the Dardanelles. Enver had already mobilized the Turkish Army on his own initiative.

Nevertheless, the news of Britain's entry into the war against Germany came to Turkey as a shock which nearly burst the new treaty. It caused such a reaction, indeed, that it even produced an astonishing offer to Russia of a Turkish alliance. But this offer did not suit Russia's ambitions, even though it promised her the one chance of a channel through which she could receive munitions from her French and British allies. She preferred isolation to the sacrifices of her dream of annexation, and did not even report the offer to her allies.

Turkey's sudden reversal of attitude was short-lived, and within a few days her new fear of British power had given way to her old fear of Russian ambition. The revival of confidence owed much to an access of annoyance. Smarting under the sting of defeat in the Balkan War, Turkey had been awaiting delivery of her first two modern battleships with an eager pride that was all the more general because the purchase-money had been raised by collections among the people. On August 3rd, however, Turkey was notified that the

British Government was taking over the ships. The news caused an explosion of anger. Everyone who had contributed his mite felt a sense of having been robbed. And the popular outcry was at its height when, on August 10th, the *Goeben* together with the cruiser *Breslau* appeared at the entrance to the Dardanelles. They had slipped past the British Fleet near Sicily.

An officer of the German military mission, Lieut.-Colonel Kress von Kressenstein, brought the news to the War Minister, Enver Pasha, and told him that the forts were asking for instructions. Enver replied—"I can't decide that now. I must first consult the Grand Vizier."

"But we must wire immediately."

There was a moment of turmoil in Enver's mind. Then came the answer—"They are to allow them to enter."

Kress asked a further, and guileful, question: "If the English warships follow the Germans, are they to be fired on if they also attempt an entrance?"

"The matter must be left to the decision of the Cabinet."

"Excellency, we can't leave our subordinates in such a position without issuing immediately clear and definite instructions. Are the English to be fired on or not?"

Another pause. Then—"Yes."

General Kannengiesser, a German witness of this momentous discussion, says, "We heard the clanking of the portcullis descending before the Dardanelles."

International law was evaded, British objections frustrated, Turkish pride satisfied, and Enver's nervous colleagues calmed by arranging the fictitious purchase of the two German warships. Turkey was not yet ready nor agreed upon war, and Britain had every reason to avoid it.

Thus, during the weeks that followed, the Turks were successively enabled and emboldened to advance along the path to war by Britain's characteristic indefiniteness, her passivity in face of growing provocation. The German crews were kept, the German admiral was appointed to command the Turkish Navy, the British Naval mission was removed from control, and then forced to withdraw. British ships were detained and their wireless dismantled, while a stream of German soldiers and sailors filtered into Constantinople.

On September 27th the Straits were definitely closed, on German initiative once again.

Meantime, Turkish Ministers, ever ready with glib assurances, congratulated themselves on this gullibility of the British—whose restraint was, rather, due to their acute sense of vulnerability, as a power with millions of Moslem subjects. Fear of a *Jihad,* the proclamation of a Holy War, overhung British policy like a cloud.

But Britain's continued refusal to take offence was at least worrying to the war-party in Turkey and its German whips. So Enver decided to prick Britain's most sensitive spot, and arranged for several aggressive reconnaissances across the Egyptian frontier into Sinai. The potential threat to our communications through the Suez Canal caused Kitchener, now War Minister at home, considerable anxiety and hastened the measures for sending a large protective force from India. But the Germans in Turkey became still more uneasy when this fresh provocation failed to goad Britain to war.

A more dramatic and decisive effort was staged. On the evening of October 27th the German Admiral, with Enver's connivance, led the Turkish fleet on a raid into the Black Sea against Britain's most sensitive ally. Odessa and other Russian ports were shelled.

The story of this provocation, as related to and recorded by Lord d'Abernon after the War, is illuminating. The official sanction came to the German Embassy in a sealed envelope addressed to the Admiral. An official took the initiative of opening it and the precaution of sending on merely a copy. The first report that reached Constantinople was that the *Goeben* had been sunk. So, assuming that the order had been sunk with her, the Grand Vizier conciliatingly replied to the Russian protests by denying that any such order had been given. Thereupon the German Embassy sent to him saying— "The order of which you deny the existence, because you think it was sunk with the *Goeben,* is in a safe place . . . at the German Embassy. Pray cease to deny that the Turkish Government has given the order to attack Russia."

Thus the war-fearing Grand Vizier was compelled to stand aside helplessly while German craft, in a dual sense, deprived the Entente of any possible excuse for avoiding war with Turkey. On October 30th, the Russian Ambassador demanded his passports, and was followed by the British and French, after a final appeal for the dis missal of the German military and naval missons.

The best chance for both Britain and Russia was now in taking the offensive instantly. The defences of the Dardanelles were obsolete and incomplete. The only two munition factories in Turkey lay on the shore close to Constantinople and open to easy destruction by any warships which penetrated thither. The neglect of the opportunity, and the forfeiture of time that could never be regained, form a tale of almost incredible haphazardness on the part of Britain, of suicidal shortsightedness on the part of Russia. Britain was certainly hampered by lack of available forces, and Russia, still more, by excess of jealousy—lest anyone else should establish a claim to participate in the destiny of the Dardanelles.

But both were fettered, above all, by a narrow doctrine of strategy. The soldiers of Europe had come to accept rigidly the theory of Clausewitz that all efforts and all forces should be concentrated in the main theatre and against the main enemy. As interpreted by his pupils it was a theory without elasticity and without regard to the practical question whether such "concentration at the decisive spot" was likely to produce an effective result at the actual time. The dead hand of Clausewitz on the strategy of his country's opponents may well be counted as his supreme patriotic legacy.

On November 3rd the Franco-British fleet briefly bombarded the outer forts of the Dardanelles. Its only use was to help the German authorities in trying to overcome Turkish inertia over the defences. But the effect of this warning has been overrated, for Turkish lethargy was almost as boundless as British indefiniteness. Not until the end of February did the Turks post more than one division on the Gallipoli peninsula, and not until March did the improvements in the defences approach completion. In part, this state of weakness seems to have been due to a feeling that it was a hopeless waste of energy to prevent a passage. If the experts, German or Turk, doubted their power to stop a purely naval attack, they were still less confident of resisting a combined land and sea offensive. The Turkish Staff History frankly states that "Up to February 25th, it would have been possible to effect a landing successfully at any point on the peninsula, and the capture of the Straits by land troops would have been comparatively easy."

But in England Mr. Winston Churchill was almost alone in showing a definite appreciation of the importance of opening the Dardanelles—and of the time factor. From August onwards he frequently tried to arouse the interest of the War Office, which, for several years had not even made a perfunctory review of the question. Three weeks after Turkey entered the War he raised it again at the first meeting of the new War Council, pointing out that such an attack was the true method of defending Egypt. But other eyes were still focused on the Western Front, and he received no support from Kitchener. It is fair to say that Kitchener mooted the idea of a landing near Alexandretta—at the "corner" between Asia Minor and Syria—to cut the Turks' rail line of communication with their territories in the Middle East, but he was advised that a large force would be necessary for more than a momentary effect. So, the project was shelved, and the conclusion accepted that the passive defence of the Suez Canal was the only possible way of protecting Egypt. It meant that the Turks were granted a fresh lease of repose.

In Germany, on the other hand, Falkenhayn, the new directing military brain, fully realized "the decisive importance of Turkey joining in the struggle." It placed a barrier across the channel of munition supply to Russia, and promised an invaluable distraction to the military strength of Britain and Russia. This lever was now applied, before the Allies attempted any move. Under German dictation, Turkey struck as early as mid-December against the Russians in the Caucasus. Enver, however, overreached himself and his ambitious plan ended in disaster at the battle of Sarikamish—it was the cold rather than the human foe that destroyed the attacking army. The disaster was the more serious because the first-line Caucasus army was the only efficient force Enver possessed.

Turkey was no more fortunate in her next venture—to cut the Suez Canal artery of Britain's power in the East. The Sinai Desert was a natural check on an invasion in strength, and the Turkish force, totalling some 20,000 men, which eventually delivered a fragmentary attack on the Canal, near Tussum and Ismailia, in the first week of February 1915, was easily repulsed, although allowed to make good its retreat.

Nevertheless, if both the Caucasus and Sinai offensives were tactical failures, they were of great strategic value to Germany by pinning down large Russian and British forces. At the time of the attack on the Canal there were 70,000 troops in Egypt, although only part were then fully trained. The force was still kept up to that strength in midsummer, although 28,000 were counted as a reserve for the Gallipoli expedition. After the evacuation of Gallipoli it rose to 100,000. Indeed, Sir John Maxwell, commanding in Egypt, considered that a far larger force was needed to guarantee the safety of Egypt, suggesting twelve infantry divisions on the Canal and three to hold Egypt and the Western Frontier. Even the General Staff at home conceded that eight were necessary on the Canal. In midsummer 1916 the garrison of Egypt exceeded 174,000 men while a further 237,000 were occupying at Salonika what the Germans satirically called their "largest prisoners of War camp."

Such was the most uneconomic sequel to our multiple-mistimed efforts to force the Dardanelles in 1915. A paper written on the eve of that year by Lieut.-Colonel Maurice Hankey, Secretary of the War Council, had diagnosed the deadlock on the Western Front and suggested that in the actual conditions Germany could most effectively be struck through her allies, especially Turkey. He had advocated the use of the first three new army corps for an attack on Constantinople as a means to knock Turkey out of the war, bring the weight of the Balkans into the scale of the allies, and open communication with Russia—abundant in wheat but deficient in munitions.

In the light of history there can hardly be a doubt that such a force, the equivalent of 150,000 men, would have sufficed to achieve success with a margin to spare—if it had been used when the actual landing was made on April 25th. Instead, 75,000 were sent. Even this number, exactly half, might well have sufficed a month or six weeks earlier. By early June, the utter failure of the offensives in France inspired Churchill to urge that we should double the force at the Dardanelles. But a month passed before the Government finally decided to do so; by the end of July they were ready to sanction still larger reinforcements. But the consequence of the belated decision and tardy steps was, first, that the second attempt could not be made until early August; and, second, that the force was once more outweighed by the Turkish reinforcements that had been brought up in the meantime. The effort was too late in the sense of being too small *for the actual time.*

Worse still, the delay had far-reaching repercussions. It allowed a new danger to arise and a new drain of force to be created. The Germans were allowed time to prepare a campaign to open communication with Turkey by knocking out Serbia. And the Dardanelles lack of success, due to loss of time, encouraged Bulgaria to enter the war as Germany's partner. As a result Serbia was overrun, and the sequel to this disaster was the unwilling occupation of Salonika by a Franco-British force, which became another investment too large for the Allies' bank-balance, yet too small to produce a dividend.

As for the Gallipoli expedition, with winter approaching and opportunity waning, a withdrawal was now decided upon and carried out. During the early hours of December 9th, the last lighters quitted the derelict piers of Helles with the last British troops who would set foot on the peninsula until after the war, while behind them the dark sky was suddenly reddened with the glare of blazing dumps and stabbed with Turkish rockets soaring skyward in alarm. In the circumstances evacuation may have been the most reasonable course, but it restored Turkey's freedom of action. It thereby exposed Egypt to danger anew, and our Mesopotamian expedition to a fresh danger.

If the horizon of most strategists in the West was narrowed to the Western Front, Kitchener certainly perceived the menace. All his associations, all his instincts, made him acutely sensitive to any movement towards Egypt. Already, in October, when the evacuation of Gallipoli was in the air, he had urgently demanded from Maxwell a report of the Turkish communications in Asia and Syria. The work of preparing it fell largely on a temporary second-lieutenant in Cairo whose commission bore the name T. E. Lawrence.

CHAPTER III

THE LIFE-LINE

The chains of empire—The construction of the Hejaz and Baghdad railways—The Turkish menace to Egypt and the Suez Canal—Active or passive defence?—Britain's Alexandretta project, and its shelving—The menace looms close—The revolt that brought relief

WHEN the twentieth century opened, the Turkish Empire was still in the eighteenth—as regards its means of imperial communication and control. Virtually roadless and railless. In all the vast territories beyond Asia Minor there were only two short stretches of railway, both narrow-gauge, one connecting Damascus with the sea at Beirut and the other linking Jerusalem with the port of Jaffa.

But in 1900 the Sultan Abdul Hamid set on foot the construction of a far-reaching railway line to connect his Arabian provinces with Damascus. It would not only help to strengthen his control over them but would avoid the unpleasant necessity of passing through the foreign-controlled Suez Canal. And it could be achieved in an economical way that delighted the heart of Abdul Hamid. For, by announcing it as a means of facilitating the pilgrimage to Mecca, its construction was carried out with money subscribed by pious Moslems throughout the world. The term "a pious fraud" might have been coined to fit the Hejaz railway.

Moreover, its construction was carried out by German engineers. Their Government watched their work with a more than benevolent eye. For if the Sultan looked forward to strengthening his authority in the Hejaz, Germany looked forward to controlling, through him, the Western shores of Arabia. It promised a means of exerting pressure on Britain's Suez Canal and Red Sea artery. The railway followed, generally, the pilgrim track and ran through desert that offered few serious difficulties save the scarcity of water. In 1904 the 285 mile stretch from Damascus to Ma'an was opened, and in 1908 the railway reached Medina, 820 miles from Damascus. It was intended to prolong the line to Mecca, 280 miles distant, although delays supervened; and an eventual extension to the Yemen was con-

MAP 2

THE HEJAZ RAILWAY

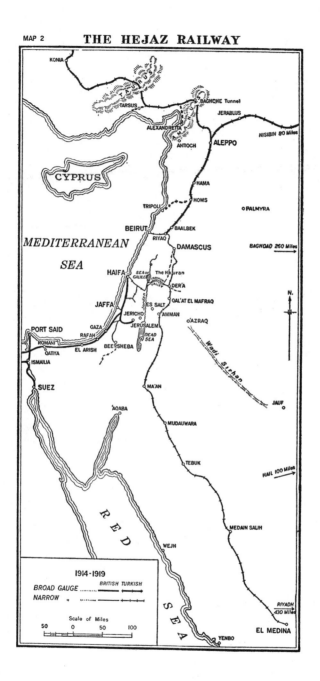

templated by the Germans.

The ulterior purpose of the Hejaz railway was to a large extent masked not only by its pious foundation but by another vast railway scheme, the aim of which became more palpable. This was the Baghdad railway. Back in 1888 a concession to build a railway in Anatolia which would link Angora with Constantinople had been granted to a group of German and British capitalists. The Germans subsequently bought out the British rights. In January, 1902, they were granted a further concession to extend the railway from Konia through the Taurus Mountains, across the Euphrates to Mosul, down the Tigris to Baghdad, and thence on to Basra, thus linking the Bosphorus—and Berlin—with the Persian Gulf. The scheme caused much apprehension in England, because of its potential threat to her sphere of influence. The Germans then offered to let the British participate, but on terms which would have established German control in perpetuity. The proposal collapsed—but the railway carried on, in disjointed sections.

It sprouted both to east and west of Aleppo, the pivotal point where it linked up with the south-running Hejaz railway. The eastern stretch extended to Jerablus on the Euphrates, and as far again beyond. By 1917 this distance was doubled, and it had reached Nisibin; but over a hundred miles still separated it from Mosul, and there was then another hundred down the Tigris before it could join the short shoot that ran out from Baghdad.

This railway system, designed to be the steel cord that should bind the crumbling Ottoman Empire together, plays such a part in the story of the war years that one needs to keep it ever in the mind's eye. It may be pictured as a huge **T** with the upper stroke slanting from the Bosphorus to Baghdad, and the lower stroke running from Aleppo to Medina. The latter alone was complete—with a break of a gauge at Riyak. For in the upper stroke there was not only a wide gap in the eastern half, but there were still, at the outset of the War, two breaks west of Aleppo.

One was in the passage through the Taurus Mountains; troops and supplies coming from Constantinople had to be detrained at Bozanti and moved by a narrow mountain road to Tarsus, twenty miles distant, where they could be entrained again—but only for a short distance. For the other uncompleted stretch was in the Amanus

COLONEL LAWRENCE

Mountains, where the five-mile long Bagche tunnel had still to be pierced. In consequence, on reaching the Amanus break, some forty miles beyond Tarsus, the trains were usually switched down the branch line to Alexandretta, where their occupants detrained again, and went by road to Aleppo, or a station just west of it, before rejoining the railway. The alternative, slower and more difficult, was to march over the Amanus Mountains.

The Alexandretta branch had originally been planned as the main line, but its course ran too close to the Gulf of Iskanderun to be strategically comfortable, and fears of its interruption from the sea had led to a change in the course of the main line.

By October, 1915, there were still twenty tunnels on the Taurus section to be pierced, but the road, from Bozanti to Tarsus, had been improved. And work on the Bagche tunnel had gone ahead so well that it promised to be ready at an early date.[1] Moreover, there had been a more ominous extension in Palestine which unmasked a new aspect of the Hejaz railway scheme.

The branch from the Hejaz railway which ran from Deraa down to the sea at Haifa had thrown out an offshoot down the coastal Plain of Sharon which not only linked up with Jerusalem but extended south to Beersheba. And from Beersheba it would soon extend another twenty odd miles to El Auja on the Egyptian frontier.

Thus the original big **T** had grown a small attached **T** on the western side of the lower stroke. By this, Egypt might now be menaced by forces far stronger than hitherto—if they were available. And the forces, indeed the bulk of the Turkish Army, had now it seemed been set free by the British withdrawal from Gallipoli. Moreover, since the enemy occupation of Serbia, they could be supplied with munitions direct from Germany.

Such was the situation that caused anxiety to Kitchener, and still more to Maxwell, on the eve of 1916. Instead of gripping the Turk by the throat we now merely smelt his tail—a forked tail. It was a delicate position, for tails can be used to inflict painful blows, without serious risk to the animal itself.

[1] Actually the gaps were not covered until early in 1917, and even then only by a light railway link. By the irony of fate the first through trains began running in September, 1918—just in time to greet the final victorious onrush of the British.

Maxwell's thoughts reverted to the idea of averting the danger by striking the Turk in the pit of his stomach, near Alexandretta. He urged that the evacuation of Gallipoli would have disastrous moral and material effects unless such a counterstroke were delivered. Sir Henry McMahon, the High Commissioner in Egypt, concurred. Kitchener, who had come out to the Mediterranean to examine the problem of Gallipoli, listened sympathetically. But the General Staff at home opposed it strongly, both in detail and on the general ground, now such a familiar chorus, that "the scheme offended against a fundamental principle of strategy: to retain the power of concentrating strength for a great offensive in a decisive theatre of war." By this, of course, they meant Flanders, which was the bounds of their horizon.

In face of these objections, Kitchener referred the question to Sir Charles Monro for a detached opinion. In strict truth, his opinion could hardly be termed this—for he had commanded an army in France and had only made a brief visit to the Mediterranean. And while there he had already recommended the abandonment of the Gallipoli venture. But, most surprisingly, his reply went far to endorse the project, and to discount the objections of the General Staff. He agreed that Maxwell's estimate of 100,000 troops would suffice not merely to cut the Turkish communications but to hold a position that would keep them severed indefinitely with security to itself. That reply, one may add, was influenced by the strategic arguments of Second-Lieutenant T. E. Lawrence, injected into the receptive ear of a superior whose voice carried weight.

The scales seemed to have been tilted decisively towards the project. But at this point a new ally came to the aid of the discomfited General Staff. The weight of France was thrown into the scales against the proposed landing in Ayas Bay. And it was impelled by a political rather than a military motive.

For on November 13th, 1915, the French military attaché presented the following note:

"Should the British Government be considering a disembarkation of troops in the Gulf of Alexandretta in order to cut the railway to Palestine, they will have to take into consideration not only the economic interests but also the moral and political position of France in these countries.

"French public opinion could not be indifferent to any operations attempted in a country which it considers as destined to form part of the future Syrian state; and it would require of the French Government not only that no military operations should be undertaken in this particular country without previous agreement between the Allies, but also that, should such action be taken, the greater part of the task should be entrusted to French troops and the French generals commanding them. . . ."

This must surely be one of the most astounding documents ever presented to an Ally when engaged in a life and death struggle. For it imposed what was really a veto on the best opportunity of cutting the common enemy's life-line and of protecting our own. As the French Government did not propose to send troops, their intervention killed the plan. The British General Staff may also be considered as accessories to the crime. It was no less—when we count the large force engaged and losses incurred in the frontal advance into Palestine that had alternatively to be undertaken.

The first attempt, in the spring of 1917, to force the Gaza gateway was made with over 100,000 troops—and failed with a loss of over ten thousand. It was renewed in the autumn with some 200,000 men, and when, after a year of struggle, the advance finally reached Aleppo, the British battle casualties alone had reached nearly fifty thousand, despite the superbly economic conduct of the actual campaign. The veto on the Alexandretta stroke had meant that, once this way of hamstringing the enemy had been foresworn, we had to fall back on the painfully slow method of masticating the Turkish Empire from the tail upward if we were to operate against it in any way.

But more than a year passed after the evacuation of Gallipoli before the British forces took the initiative in any real way. And during that year of inactivity the garrison of Egypt rose at one time (March, 1916) to as high as 275,000 men. The best that can be said for this great concentration of idle force is that it served as an imperial strategic reserve, which could be, and was, drawn on by other theatres of war.

The "campaign" of 1916 might be summed up briefly by saying that throughout most of the year the two sides crouched growling at each other a safe distance apart, the monotony varied only by the occasional Turkish pastime of stretching forward suddenly to pull a few hairs out of the lion's mane, an audacity which the lion repaid with a sharp slap when it was repeated.

A curious stretch of imagination had led the British Command to magnify beyond all reason the size of the Turkish forces which might be assembled for the invasion of Egypt. That magnification might be charitably described as due to a mirage of the desert, did one not know that the inflated estimate sent home was contrary to the facts known on the spot—to the information furnished to the head of the military intelligence by his subordinates, the active intelligence staff officers. The false estimate was persisted in despite their protests. They at least were not subject to the common vice that hierarchy breeds—that of telling a superior what he wishes to hear and what flatters his sense of importance. In such a case the superior is often the more to blame.

At the beginning of 1916 Sir Archibald Murray, previously Chief of the Imperial General Staff, had arrived to take over the command.[1] In February he wrote to his successor at home, Sir William Robertson, that it would be possible for the Turks to bring down a quarter of a million men to Beersheba and push them across the desert. Robertson put the figure at 100,000, and even this was certainly an over-estimate. Half the number of Murray's estimate might conceivably have been brought to Beersheba, but they could hardly have been maintained there, and far less could they have been moved across the Sinai desert.

In the actual event, Turkish lethargy and inefficiency, accentuated by distractions from other enemies than the British, removed any danger. Nothing happened until April. Then a small force of 3,500 moved out along the desert route nearest the Mediterranean shore against the British posts which had been established in the Qatiya Oasis as a shock-absorber in front of the Canal. The Turks overwhelmed the garrisons and then made their retirement. This neat little surprise coup was directed by the Bavarian colonel, Kress von Kressenstein, who was the inspiration and brain of the Turks in Palestine for the first three years of the war. After the Qatiya insult, peace settled on the desert no-man's-land for another three months. Kress on his part was waiting for artillery, machine-guns, mortars

[1] His first appointment was to command the forces on the Suez Canal front, but in March he took over the whole force in Egypt, and Sir John Maxwell went home.

and aircraft from Germany. The British were consolidating their position.

Then in July Kress advanced again with some 16,000 men, and this time pushed beyond Qatiya to Romani. But he tempted fortune by lingering too long near Qatiya, waiting for his heavy artillery, and the delay allowed the British to prepare an encircling embrace when at last, after ten days, his attack developed. It failed, and he had a narrow escape from the trap. Once outside the lion's jaws he succeeded in fending off the disjointed pursuit and even administered a sharp rap to the pursuers. If the British had missed a fine opportunity of netting the whole Turkish force, Kress had suffered a defeat and risked a disaster because his means were not adapted to his end. His force was too small for a sustained advance, while too large and encumbered for a raid.

A few months earlier a fundamentally similar fault had marred another Turco-German move of similar intention on the opposite frontier of Egypt. Here in the Western Desert the tribes belonged to the Moslem sect of the Senussi. With them the Turkish proclamation of a *Jihad* against the infidel, in general a failure, had a measure of success. Nuri Bey, a half-brother of Enver, appeared on the scene and incited the Senussi to harass the British in Egypt. Another Turkish officer, Ja'far Pasha, set to work to drill the Arab levies. Ja'far was a Baghdadi Arab of marked capacity and even greater capaciousness. He spoke eight languages and had been trained in the German Army. But his efforts to discipline the Bedouin and make them into a regular force had merely the effect of making them into a regular target—for the British.

So long as the Senussi's followers stayed drilling in the desert they were a menace. The news created serious unrest in Egypt and grave apprehension, of an internal rising, to the British authorities. It even led the British to evacuate the coast. But when, in December, 1915, the Senussi's troops advanced against our frontier force their progress was checked, although they baffled several British counter moves; and in February they were decisively routed, Ja'far himself being captured.

By contrast with these unsuccessful efforts to harass the British, the Turks themselves would soon receive a lesson at their expense, in the technique of harassing warfare and in the way to convert the roaming Bedouin into an effective agent of war. The teacher would be an Englishman—T. E. Lawrence. And the opportunity was provided by a rising of the Arabs against Turkish rule.

This event, so far-reaching in its effects, took place in the Hejaz. Thereby the birthplace of the Moslem religion, a warrior faith, became the birthplace of the first scientific theory of irregular warfare. The scene, also, of its application.

The revolt opened in June, 1916. Its first long-range effect was on the British. For the news of it inspired them to exchange their hitherto passive defence of Egypt for an offensive move into Turkish territory—to quote the official history of the campaigns in Egypt and Palestine: "Sir A. Murray was now directed by the C.I.G.S. to consider seriously that advance to El Arish which had previously been merely a vague possibility." Moreover, the Hejaz rising set up that much-needed distraction to the Turkish initiative and the Turkish forces which the British, since the evacuation of Gallipoli, had hitherto failed to provide from their own resources. The revolt would spread, in space, scale, and effect until it ultimately became known to the world as the Arab Revolt.

CHAPTER IV

THE UNDERCURRENT

1914–1916

The Arabs' pre-war dreams of independence—Kitchener's assurance to the Sherif of Mecca—The Sherif refuses Turkey's behest to proclaim a Holy War—McMahon pursues negotiations with the Sherif which culminate in Britain's wide, if qualified, pledge of October, 1915, to recognize Arab independence. Meantime another British agent, Sir Mark Sykes, independently makes a different arrangement, negotiating a treaty with the French for the future division of the still unconquered Turkish Empire—The Turks attempt to suppress the Arab movement, and dispatch reinforcements to the Hejaz—The Sherif hastens the long-contemplated revolt—in June, 1916

DURING the years immediately before the War, Kitchener in Cairo, with his Oriental habit of keeping his ear close to the ground, was well aware of subterranean stirrings among the Arab subjects of the Turkish Empire. As he spun his spider's web of information for Britain's imperial interests, many significant clues and secret currents came to his knowledge. Among them were the ambitious dreams of Hussein, Sherif of Mecca, and his sons, of a vast Arab confederacy under the suzerainty of their family. A vision of the past glory of the Abbasid Empire floated before their eyes.

In February, 1914, the Young Turks appointed Vahib Bey, who was known for his violently anti-Arab sentiments, as Vali, or Governor, of the Hejaz. After his arrival in Mecca he ordered the Sherif to hand over a hundred old Mauser rifles with which his guard was armed. The insult provoked a riot. That same month the Emir Abdulla, the Sherif's second son, came to visit Kitchener in Cairo, and told him privately of the Sherif's ambition to achieve independence for the Hejaz. He found a sympathetic listener, who had himself long cherished the idea of founding an independent Arab State in Arabia and Syria.

Then the war came and Kitchener left Cairo for London to supervise schemes of vaster scope and more immediate execution. But amid the cares of creating a New Army of millions he did not forget the possibility of converting the Arabs into a British asset. Moreover, a reminder came to him from the depths of Arabia in the

42

MAP 3

ARABIA, SYRIA & MESOPOTAMIA

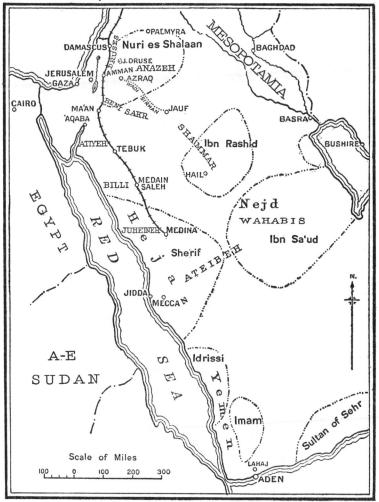

form of a cryptic message sent by a circuitous route—"Following for Lord Kitchener. 'Remember our conversation—The day has come.'" The ominous bearing of Turkey gave emphasis to the matter. If the Turks were to proclaim a *Jihad,* the attitude of the Sherif of Mecca would have an important influence on its scope and its success.

Thus towards the end of September, Kitchener sent a message to the Emir Abdulla to inquire whether the Sherif would be on the side of Britain or against her if Turkey joined in the war. The reply was friendly but guarded. The Sherif's ambition was tempered by his caution, and he was typically Arab—some might say traditionally British—in his care to sit on the fence, with a foot still on either side, until the right moment had arrived and the outlook had cleared. He implied that he would not side with the Turks of his own choice, but evidently wanted an assurance from the British side before he took the risk of defying his overlord in Constantinople. He did not forget that it was the policy of the Turks to keep alternative Sherifs in stock there. He himself and his sons had been held for years as hostages by Abdul Hamid until the revolution of the Young Turks had caused a convenient revolution in his fortunes and put him in Mecca in the place of his cousin.

But there were several factors to check the British from committing themselves hastily. Any definite assurance might precipitate that very conflict with Turkey that Britain, on moral even more than on material grounds, was striving so hard to avoid. The religious problem was a complex one, and Britain, with millions of Moslem subjects, had to consider the issues carefully before supporting a challenge to the Sultan of Turkey, who as holder of the Khalifate was their spiritual head. Hussein, as the Sherif of Mecca and descendant of the Prophet, counted for much, but it was doubtful whether he had the temporal weight to lay claim to the Khalifate.

When Turkey entered the War against Britain, these considerations lost much of their force. The Sherif might not have adequate weight for the Khalifate, but he had enough to be a counterpoise to the *Jihad.* At Kitchener's instigation a fresh message was sent through Abdulla. It gave the Sherif a definite assurance that if he and the Arabs actively aided Britain in the War, she would recognize and support their independence in return.

Another cautious reply came back to Cairo. It was more definite on the subject of neutrality, but intimated that the Sherif's position in Islam made it impossible for him to break with Turkey immediately. His hesitation this time was largely explained by the fact that he was still sounding other Arab leaders; his third son, Feisal, had gone to Syria to gauge the value of the Arab secret society there which had just appealed to him for support in a proposed mutiny.

But in essentials the Sherif had already rendered Britain a service greater than any that could be expected in the material realm. For he had refused, much to the Turks' indignation, to proclaim the *Jihad* from the Holy Cities, and thus had largely drawn its sting.[1] Outside Turkey itself the *Jihad* would have little meaning despite the assiduous efforts of Turkish and German "missionaries." Britain had a war with Turkey on her hands, but to all intents she was saved the back-breaking burden of a Holy War.

In this state of more than benevolent neutrality the relations between Britain and the Sherif remained throughout 1915. It would have been exchanged much earlier for active intervention if the British project of a landing near Alexandretta had been fulfilled. For in this event a mutiny had been arranged among the Arab troops of the Turkish Army in Syria. On the other hand, Arab assistance might also have ceased much earlier, because the Arabs' idea was apparently to make the embarrassed Turks an offer of peace in return for a recognition of their independence, so that they might have a chance of keeping it even if the British failed to win the War. So long as the Alexandretta landing hung fire Feisal advised his father to hang back, until the prospects became clearer. When the British landed, instead, on Gallipoli, he went thither as an officer in the Turkish Army to watch the trend of the struggle. Meantime Sir Henry McMahon, the new High Commissioner in Egypt, seconded by Sir Reginald Wingate, Governor-General of the Sudan, fulfilled the Foreign Office policy of cultivating the friendship with Hussein.

[1] In taking this decision Hussein appears to have been influenced and was undoubtedly strengthened, by the attitude of Ibn Sa'ud, whom he consulted in January, 1915, when pressed by the Turks to proclaim a *Jihad*. Ibn Sa'ud's reply was to the effect that Hussein should evade the Turkish demand by pleading fear of British reprisals against the Hejaz ports. Before sending it, Ibn Sa'ud discussed the issues with Captain Shakespear, a British political officer then at his camp, who stood high in his esteem. Seven days later Shakespear was killed in a tribal battle between Ibn Sa'ud and Ibn Rashid, the pro-Turk Emir of Hail.

In July a promising bud appeared on the Arab side. The British pressure, and the Turkish losses, on Gallipoli, together with Townshend's advance in Mesopotamia, had an influence on this initiative. News travels fast through the desert. A closer influence was exerted by hunger-pressure at home. The Hejaz was being ground between an upper and a nether millstone—on the one hand, the Red Sea blockade which Britain partially enforced, and might tighten, against the Hejaz; on the other, the partial land blockade which the Turks had instituted, through their control of rail traffic, as punishment for the Sherif's refusal to proclaim the *Jihad* against Britain. Writing to McMahon, the Sherif requested that Britain would guarantee the independence of all Arab lands as the reward of a revolt against Turkey. The bud had a long stem, longer than the British cared to contemplate.

For his detailed proposals were that Britain should acknowledge Arab independence within an area that stretched from the Taurus Mountains in the north to the Indian Ocean, excluding merely the Aden Protectorate, and from the Mediterranean to the Persian frontier. He followed up this immense vision of empire with a private letter in which he begged that the annual donation from Egypt to the Holy Cities might be resumed. Without it, the Hejaz faced bankruptcy, for the interruption of the annual pilgrimage to Mecca had deprived this barren land of its chief source of revenue.

The British, in answering, donned Hussein's discarded mantle of caution. Their reply abounded in cordiality, assured the Sherif that Britain would arrange for the transmission of the pious donations if he would guarantee their safety, remarked that the discussion of boundaries was premature, and dropped the question of the Khalifate in discreet silence.

To the Sherif, not unnaturally, the warmth of these expressions of friendship suffered a chill in transmission. He communicated his feelings to McMahon, who began to press upon the Foreign Office the urgency of giving the Arabs an adequate guarantee. The overcast prospects of the Gallipoli expedition gave a deeper emphasis to McMahon's arguments, which were backed by very detailed information as to the political conditions in the Arab lands.

This had been gathered and collated not only by the military intelligence branch in Egypt—of which Lawrence was a nominally

humble, if actually invaluable, and equally obstreperous, member—
but even more by a group of experts that McMahon had gathered
round him. This collection of travellers, archaeologists, and political
officers was transformed a few months later in February, 1916, into
an "Arab Bureau," under the direction of Dr. Hogarth, who, by one
of the war's strange metamorphoses had come to bear the stripes of
a Commander in the Royal Naval Volunteer Reserve.

During the first part of the War the Government of India, in
virtue of its concern with Aden, had been responsible for dealing
with Arab questions on the whole Red Sea Coast. Distance did not
lend enchantment to its view, nor help its information. At the end
of March, 1915, responsibility for Arab affairs down to a point eighty
miles south of Mecca was transferred to the High Commissioner in
Egypt. The change brought not only an increase of efficiency but an
increased value to the Allied cause.

The impression was reinforced both by the general stream of reports as to unrest in the Turkish dominions and by special information concerning the Arab secret societies within the Turkish Empire
and their preparations for a rising. In Mesopotamia there was the
Ahad, a military brotherhood, composed of Arab officers in the
Turkish Army who were bent on gaining military knowledge so
that they might the more effectively destroy their masters when
the moment was ripe. Some of its members were in high positions,
and stayed in them throughout the War, working insidiously rather
than openly. A larger society, predominantly civil, was the Fetah
in Syria. This was so organized, and so assiduous in cultivating adherents at home and possible allies abroad, that its activities were
more difficult to hide. The way that the Turks, so contrary to their
usual habit, were refraining from measures of suppression seemed
a testimony to the wide dimensions of the movement and suggested
that the Turks might find it wiser to bribe it than to break it. If
that course were taken the *Jihad* might become a dangerous reality.

Hence both McMahon and Maxwell urged the British Government at home, and Kitchener in particular, to do something more
definite to encourage the Sherif and towards meeting his proposals.
As a result, McMahon was instructed in October to tell the Sherif
that Britain pledged herself to recognize and support the independence of the Arabs within the boundaries he had proposed,

subject to certain exceptions. These were the districts, not purely Arab, that lay along the Syrian coast from the Taurus Mountains down to the west of Damascus. But the reservations were also made, first, that the assurance was limited to those parts of the Arab territories where Britain was free to act without detriment to the interests of France; and, second, that the districts of Basra and Baghdad would be subjected to a measure of British control.

These terms stretched far, but the elasticity of the contract lay mainly in its power of contraction. The real significance lay in the reservations, which had a vagueness that spelt confusion among those who formulated them as well as among those who heard them. By reason of them Britain was to be involved in an entanglement with Arab policy akin to that in which she had been involved for a hundred years in her effort to adjust herself to Turkish policy. The entanglement might have its origin in the casuistry of policy, in that inability of nations to rise even to the relatively low standards of honest dealing that prevail among individuals. But its embarrassments would be due in large measure to the relatively high standard of honour attained by the individuals who were instruments of that policy. England's policy would once again run on the rocks of the Englishman's conscience, and provide yet another object-lesson of the dangers of following Machiavelli without being thoroughly Machiavellian.

Although McMahon had pressed the Foreign Office to arrange terms of alliance with the Arabs, he was disquieted by the vagueness of those on which he was instructed to negotiate an agreement, and he sent a warning to the Foreign Office in which he emphasized the importance of keeping faith with the Arab leaders as well as the dangers of underrating the possible development of the Arab movement. Further, he urged the need for unity of control over all negotiations.

In the meantime, however, the Foreign Office had been using that eminent but erratic political traveller, Sir Mark Sykes, as another agent on Kitchener's initiative—and his own. After carrying out a secret mission to the Middle East, Sykes was deputed by the Foreign Office to enter into negotiations with M. Georges Picot, representing France, as to the future boundaries of the Arab States and the respective spheres of influence of Britain and France—in the

prospective partitioning of the Turkish Empire among its con-
querors. One wonders whether any of the parties remembered a
previous occasion in Palestine when a condemned man's cloak was
thus divided up before he passed away. A recollection of that undy-
ing story might have prepared them for another resurrection.

The discussions eventually had issue in a map, which remains an
historical curiosity. On it were marked the zones defined in the
Sykes-Picot agreement, which laid the powder-trail of controversy. A
Blue Zone showed where a French administration would be established. It covered all Syria north of Acre and west of Damascus
and Aleppo, and extended well into Asia Minor. A Red Zone
similarly indicated where Britain would establish an administration.
It comprised the valley of the Tigris and the Euphrates from north
of Baghdad to the Persian Gulf. Two further zones, "A" and "B,"
showed respectively the French and British spheres of influence,
where they would support an Arab State or confederation of States.
These zones embraced the desert and its fringes. "A" was a triangular
area of which the base ran from Aleppo to the Sea of Galilee, while
the apex was at Rowanduz near the Persian frontier. This put the
important city of Mosul into the French sphere of influence. "B"
area lay to the south, its western boundary running from the Sea of
Galilee along the Jordan to the Dead Sea, then out to the coast at
Gaza, and along the old Sinai frontier to Aqaba. To the east it went
as far as the boundary of the projected Red Zone in Mesopotamia.

Arrangements had also to be made for Russia to have an adequate
meal off Turkey's carcass. After further negotiations, Notes were
exchanged, in May, 1916, between the three powers, which defined
their respective portions. If we picture them in terms of the natural
simile, France and Britain were to have the wings of the turkey,
Russia to have the breast, the Arabs were allotted the "innards" and
legs, while the head and neck were left.

The trouble that arose over this division was due not merely to
its prematurity but to its obscurity. While Sykes was the hand on
the carving knife in these arrangements with Picot, McMahon was
negotiating with the Arabs. And the left hand of Britain's foreign
policy did not know what the right was doing.

Indeed, the first intimation that McMahon received was when
Sykes returned to Cairo and in conversation, producing a map, re-

marked, "What do you think of my treaty?" Like a high velocity shell, the burst thus coincided with the sound.

McMahon's fingers in the Arab Bureau, Lawrence among them, were still more cut off from the knowledge of the reality. Although they later gained an inkling, the Sykes-Picot agreement only became known to the Arab contestants when it was made known to the world by the Bolshevik Government publishing broadcast the secret treaty which it found in the archives after the Russian Revolution. To lessen the shock Sykes and Picot were sent to the Hejaz early in May, 1917, at the urgent request of the Arab Bureau, so that they might explain to Feisal and Hussein the broad provisions of the treaty and the intentions of the British Government.

But by the time they arrived the collapse of the British offensive against Gaza had made the vista of Syria remote, and hence the two commissioners deemed it best to leave their treaty in a gentle haze when interpreting it to Hussein. In this they were perhaps helped by the difficulty of translation into Arabic.

That, however, was a long way ahead. Early in 1916 the negotiations with the Sherif ended in an agreement to take action as soon as the moment was ripe. If he made objection to various points in the guarantee, it is unlikely that, with his experience of the ways of diplomacy, he was wholly deluded either as to the ambiguity or the complexity of the issues that underlay its broad phrases. That he was sufficiently satisfied at the time is suggested by the fact that McMahon was not forced to offer an additional inducement which he had been authorized to make. This was to abandon the reservation about Basra and Baghdad if that concession was necessary to turn the scales.

The Sherif, it is true, had other more urgent considerations to hasten his decision. The British naval blockade of the Arabian coast was inevitably aggravating the internal distress caused by the lack of pilgrims. The Turkish attitude was foreboding danger both to his own rule and to the chance of a successful rising.

Relieved of the British pressure at the Dardanelles, the Turks deemed the moment opportune to crush the Arab movement within their own ranks and territories. Early in 1916 Jemal Pasha suddenly swooped on the secret society in Syria. Arab units were dispersed to distant parts and suspected rebels were put to death wholesale. Apart from those brought to summary trial and execution, the gendarmerie were turned loose to punish the Arabs and their families in the Turk's too familiar style. These measures were brutally effective not only in quenching the intended rising, but in deterring most of the Syrian Arabs from taking an active part in the later Arab advance. On the other hand, they forfeited such allegiance as the Arabs had hitherto given the Turks and sapped the morale of the Arab troops in the Turkish Army, to its ultimate cost.

Feisal himself was in Syria at the time of these massacres, as an unwilling and unwelcome guest of Jemal. Although he was an object of suspicion, the Turks felt that it was still unwise to strike directly at him and his family. But he was compelled to swallow frequent insults, and, worse still, was taken out by Jemal with malicious pleasure to watch the hanging of his Arab sympathizers and intending supporters.

The turn of the Hejaz Arabs was likely to come next. Indeed, a special Turkish force under Khairi Bey was being formed in Constantinople for dispatch by rail to Medina, whence it was intended to march to Mecca, there to "show the flag" and overawe the Arabs, before moving on to the Yemen. Such an overland march was an innovation, and to make it possible the force was organized as a mobile column 3,500 strong with a light field battery and two machine-gun companies.

The force was accompanied by a German mission of small size but considerable importance under Major von Stotzingen, who bore letters of recommendation one of which, from Countess Schlieffen, was phrased with unconscious humour—"He does not obtrude his personality and has not those characteristics which often make the Germans disliked in foreign parts." His orders were to set up a wireless station on the coast in order to open up communication with German East Africa, as well as back to Turkish General Headquarters. Stotzingen was also to direct anti-British propaganda in Darfur, the Sudan, Abyssinia, and Somaliland. For this purpose the party included a German adventurer, Karl Neufeld, who had been rescued by the British from the Khalifa's grip after the battle of Omdurman in 1898 and had been expelled from the Sudan by them on the outbreak of war in 1914.

The ultimate purpose of the mobile column seems to have been more than merely sedative. For in July, 1915, one of the two Turkish divisions in the Yemen—the other had to watch the Idrissi, the bitterly anti-Turk Emir of Subayyeh—fell on the small British force at Lahaj and drove it back into Aden. An Indian Brigade landed three weeks later and temporarily raised the siege, but after its departure the Turks remained a potential menace to our hold on Aden, being themselves provisioned by the Imam of the Yemen for two years after they had been cut off from home by the rising in the Hejaz. If they had been reinforced by the new mobile column, Aden itself might have been stormed. The interception of this danger, as well as of Stotzingen's mission, was not the least of the services to Britain achieved by the Arab Revolt.

The dispatch of the column was the danger signal which, reversing the usual order, released the train of action. Feisal, who had been advising delay after the frustration in Syria, was himself a witness of the preparations to send these Turkish reinforcements, and he realized that the immediate dangers of delay outweighed the potential advantages.

Nevertheless the revolt opened under serious material handicaps. In fulfilment of the agreement with Hussein, Wingate had begun to send rifles and ammunition, as well as money and food, across the Red Sea from the Sudan. But both McMahon and Wingate had been anxious for the Sherif to hold his hand until he had been more fully equipped. They were still urging delay when the news travelled back that the rising had taken place—on June 5th, 1916.

BOOK III

THE ARAB REVOLT

INTRODUCTION TO BOOK III

For those who prefer to skip the historical prologue in Book II.

THE humour of history is nowhere better illustrated than in the relations between Britain and Turkey during the 19th Century. Supported in arms when her immunity—particularly from a Russian bear-hug—coincided with Britain's interests, Turkey was scolded and chastised between times for her moral lapses. But as the 20th Century dawned, this paternal relationship was altered by the intrusion of a wooer who offered Turkey a strong arm to rest upon without the accompaniment of moral homilies. Turkey proved susceptible to such advances. And when the new friend came to blows with the old guardian, on the outbreak of the World War in August, 1914, fear of Russia combined with faith in Germany's strength to draw Turkey into arms against Britain, at the end of October.

This was a valuable gain for Germany and Austria. It locked the Black Sea door by which Russia's manpower might have been supplied with munitions, helped to cover their own Balkan back door, and promised to divert part of the British and Russian forces. On the other hand, Turkey herself was disquietingly vulnerable. Her head and neck, on the edge of Europe, lay dangerously exposed to a severing cut, while her sprawling body in Asia was predisposed to paralysis.

The Dardanelles guarded the approach to Constantinople, but their defences were out of date and incomplete, while Turkey's only two munition factories lay on the shore beyond, easy of destruction by an enemy who forced the passage. As for the Turkish Empire, its weakness lay, first, in its long drawn out and brittle communications; secondly, in the restlessness of its subject peoples, especially the Arabs. The railway system formed an immense **T**, of which the horizontal line, from Constantinople through Aleppo to Baghdad, was still far from being completed; the thousand mile vertical line ran down through Syria to the Hejaz, on the eastern shores of the Red Sea, having its terminus at Medina.

The course of the struggle would largely depend on how far Turkey's opponents profited by her inherent weaknesses to diminish the damage caused by her entry into the war against them. That issue, in turn, was largely determined by the grip of a century-old German theory on their minds—Clausewitz's doctrine that all efforts and all forces should as far as possible be concentrated in the main theatre against the main enemy. Because of their strict and strait allegiance to a doctrine which had hardened with time into dogma, the Allied strategists neglected the opportunity offered by Turkey's weaknesses, allowing her time to cover these and to develop her own activities. In consequence, with fateful irony, their determination to avoid diverting their strength to secondary ends led them eventually to dissipate their strength more lavishly, for tertiary ends—in safeguarding themselves, especially in Egypt, against danger from the Turks.

The first year witnessed the British attempts to open the Dardanelles with forces that were always too late and too few for the time of their action. When a withdrawal was decided on in the autumn of 1915, an alternative plan of severing the railway T near its joint was conceived. But this Ayas Bay project was still-born, the objections of the General Staff at home being reinforced by a French political veto on British intrusion into Syria.

Early in 1916, after the evacuation of Gallipoli, the British forces in Egypt rose to over a quarter of a million men, a large proportion of whom remained. They were kept there by fear for the safety of the Suez Canal, Britain's Imperial artery to India. They were kept idle by the General Staff's reluctance to embark on fresh "side-shows." Such passivity invited the pin-pricks which came from the Turks on both the eastern and the western frontiers of uneasy Egypt.

The need of providing an outside distraction to the Turks was perceived by the High Commissioner, Sir Henry McMahon. Several months of long-range negotiation with Hussein, the Sherif of Mecca, ended in an agreement that the Arabs in the Hejaz were to rise against the Turks, when the time was ripe, while Britain guaranteed, with certain reservations, the independence of the Arab lands that then formed part of the Turkish Empire.

Meantime, however, another representative of the Foreign Office, Sir Mark Sykes, had been independently engaged with the French in carving up the Turkish Empire, on a different plan. This Sykes-Picot

TURKEY'S LIFE-LINE

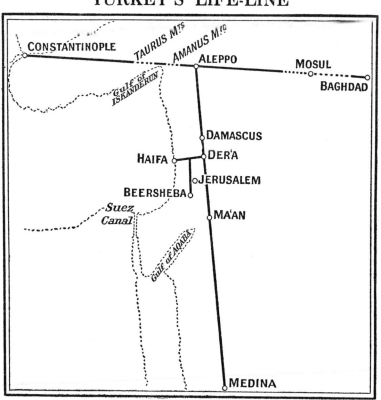

Treaty contained the germ of future trouble with the Arabs.

A fourth party, the Turks, now intervened by sending forces south to forestall trouble to themselves. The news of their dispatch hastened the Arab rising, which began in June, 1916.

CHAPTER V

THE TOCSIN RINGS

June, 1916

The rising suffers from lack of organization—The Arabs seize Mecca and the coast, but the Turks maintain their hold on Medina—Reaction sets in, and depression grows—There is a manifest need for British aid, but this is hindered by internal complications.

Lawrence's career in the opening months of the war—He is sent to Egypt where he is employed on intelligence work and also on certain special missions—Difficulties with his superiors pave the way to a greater opportunity

THE Sherif himself had organized the revolt. The results were less apparent than the evidence of disorganization. Wingate's comment on the Sherif's forces was a fair verdict—"His army is practically a rabble and run on Dervish lines." There were some fifty thousand Arabs available, but with less than ten thousand rifles among them, and of these only a proportion were modern rifles. There were no guns or machine-guns. Worse still, no arrangements had been made by Hussein to keep his forces fed and maintained in the field. Feisal had only slipped away from Damascus in time for the rising, but in any case neither he nor his brothers appear to have been consulted by their father over the details of the plan. They simply received his orders to begin the revolt. If cautiously shrewd, he was a vain and self-willed "autocrat of the breakfast table," jealous of his prerogatives.

But the Turks promised to provide tough fare, hard to bite and large to swallow. The garrison of the Hejaz was mainly provided by the Turkish 22nd Division, whose three regiments had their headquarters at Mecca, Jidda, and Medina—the last being now reinforced by Khairi Bey's mobile column. In addition battalions of the 21st Division, which had its headquarters in Asir, occupied Lith and Qunfideh, along the coast south of Jidda, the port of Mecca. The total force in the Hejaz was probably over 15,000 strong, and it had not only the advantage of fortified positions but the traditional Turkish capacity for defending them.

On June 5th, Ali, the Sherif's eldest son, and Feisal raised the

MAP 4

THE HEJAZ

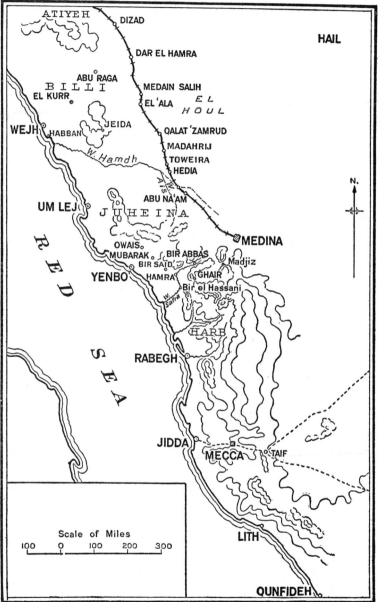

ATIYEH
DIZAD
HAIL
DAR EL HAMRA
ABU RAGA
BILLI
MEDAIN SALIH
EL KURR
EL 'ALA
EL HOUL
JEIDA
WEJH
HABBAN
QALAT 'ZAMRUD
MADAHRIJ
W. Hamdh
TOWEIRA
HEDIA
ABU NA'AM
UM LEJ
JUHEINA
OWAIS
MEDINA
MUBARAK
BIR ABBAS
BIR SAID
Madjiz
YENBO
HAMRA
GHAIR
Bir el Hassani
W. Safra
HARB
RED
RABEGH
SEA
JIDDA
MECCA
TAIF
LITH
Scale of Miles
100   0   100   200   300
QUNFIDEH

crimson banner of revolt on the outskirts of Medina in obedience to their father's orders. Some thirty thousand Arabs had assembled in response to the call. Next day Ali moved north through the mountains to cut the railway near Medain Saleh, 180 miles distant, while Feisal attempted to take the city by storm. Those of the Arabs who gained an entry were soon ejected; they were not the equals of the Turk in close quarter fighting. And at longer range they were exposed to the Turkish artillery whose shells provided a nerve-shattering new experience. In vain Feisal, who knew from Gallipoli experience the comparative innocuousness of such fire, rode about the plain in an effort to calm the tribesmen. The Ageyl and Ateiba tribesmen went to ground and stayed there. The Beni Ali had already tipped the scales by running away. For the next month Feisal had to content himself with establishing a loose blockade, and then even that was broken. Perchance in reflection it did not seem altogether auspicious to have begun the revolt at the place where Mahomet went originally as a fugitive and ultimately to rest in his tomb.

Elsewhere, however, the rising had opened with a string of scintillating successes. From Mecca the bulk of the garrison had moved to their summer station at Taif, seventy miles to the south-east. The skeleton that was left comprised only a thousand men, some of whom were quartered in barracks within the hill-girdled city while the others occupied the forts on the heights outside. The Turkish commander, moreover, despite his uneasiness over the menacing appearance of armed Bedouin, was taken by surprise when the actual attack came on June 9th. It developed by degrees, and with amusing naïvety he telephoned to the Sherif—"The Bedouin have revolted against the Government. Find a way out." Enjoying the joke, Hussein answered with veiled irony—"Of course we shall." He promptly ordered a general attack. The Turks put up a stout defence for three days, but on the 12th the Arabs succeeded in setting fire to the barracks, and thus smoked out their occupants. They followed up this success and by the next evening the whole of the defences had been overcome and the garrisons captured, save those of two small forts outside the city. These defied all efforts, and a month passed before they surrendered. But in their resistance they contributed to the Sherif's wider success by committing the folly of shelling the mosque that contained the Ka'aba. Their shells only missed the supremely sacred Black Stone by a few feet, and they set the Kiswa on fire. The lives of a handful of worshippers was a cheap price for the moral that Hussein was able to draw for the enlightenment of the Moslem world in a proclamation which Lawrence took and turned into majestic English.

Meantime, in ignorance of these dramatic events, Hogarth and other members of the Arab Bureau had come across the Red Sea to meet the Sherif's representative. Expecting to discuss the future revolt, they found it in being. When they landed at a point near Jidda on June 6th, they were met, to their surprise, by the Sherif's youngest son, Zeid, instead of by Abdulla. Zeid explained that his elder brothers were engaged in more active business. But what the British officers could glean as to the situation did not impress them with the Sherif's capacity to sustain a prolonged effort. Hogarth carried back to Egypt the Sherif's urgent appeal for another ten thousand rifles at least, and above all for some mountain artillery— which must be manned by Moslem crews. This rooted objection to any infidels coming near the Holy Cities, even in their protection, was for a time to be no small handicap to the Arab cause.

Wingate grasped the situation and rose to the emergency at once. He realized the risk of using Egyptian troops to aid Arabs in driving out Turks, but he was a man of vision as well as of decision—and an Arab confederacy had long been his pet vision. He saw that the politico-strategic issues outweighed the politico-tactical risks. Two mountain-batteries under their own Moslem officers, together with a battery of four machine-guns were embarked at Port Sudan under a senior Egyptian officer. Three ships, carrying this "fire-brigade" as well as three thousand rifles, and a large supply of food and ammunition, sailed on June 27th and arrived next day at Jidda.

This port had just been opened through British leverage. It had originally been attacked by the Sheikh of the Harb tribe with four thousand of his followers on the same day that Hussein struck at Mecca. But here once again, as at Medina, shell and machine-gun fire proved too much for the Arabs. Nevertheless, by cutting off the water supply they made the garrison's position hopeless. Two days later the cruisers *Fox* and *Hardinge,* the latter belonging to the Indian Marine, shelled the Turkish positions north of the town.

As at Gallipoli, naval gunnery had little effect on entrenched Turks, whose positions could not be accurately observed. But on the evening of the 15th the British sea-plane carrier *Ben-my-Chree* appeared on the scene, and her only three available aircraft flew over the port dropping bombs on various targets. The bombardment was about to be resumed next morning when, at dawn, the white flag went up and the garrison of 1,400 men surrendered to the Arabs. As the *Fox* signalled to the *Ben-my-Chree*, "probably the sea-planes decided the matter."

This important success was soon followed by others—that gave an ironical tinge to the German wireless *communiqué* of June 27th: "We are in a position to deny absolutely that there has been any rebellion in the Hejaz at all." Rabegh, a hundred miles north of Jidda, was lightly held and easily taken. On July 27th, Yanbo, a hundred miles beyond Rabegh, also surrendered. Of the ports along the Hejaz coast, only Wejh in the extreme north remained in Turkish hands. Inland, the hill-station of Taif, five thousand feet above sea-level, was still untaken. Abdulla, with a force of some five thousand tribesmen, had invested it, but avoided any such rashness as an assault. With its well-entrenched garrison of three thousand Turks and ten Krupp field-guns, Taif was a hard nut to crack. Abdulla waited until the nut-crackers arrived.

They comprised an Egyptian mountain-battery of four guns that had been brought from the Sudan, and a howitzer captured from the Turks—a fact which lent irony to its present use and influence. For, opening fire on July 16th, this artillery speedily dominated the Turkish field-guns, moving gradually closer in. The Arabs watched with exultation, delighted with the noise even more than the effect, but they preferred to remain admiring spectators, risking no assault. Their leader, Abdulla, already somewhat fat for his thirty-five years, had too much shrewdness and perhaps a too keen sense of humour to indulge in audacious ventures, especially when time was so palpably on his side and the tables were so amusingly turned on the Turks. His discretion was justified when the garrison of 2,000 men finally surrendered unconditionally on September 22nd, after the Governor, Ghalib Pasha, had been badly frightened by several shells falling upon his residence. This capture brought the Sherif's bag of prisoners to over five thousand Turkish soldiers. Many of the Arabs and Syrians among them volunteered to enter his service, and later formed the nucleus of a regular force.

But if the sun shone at Taif, it had become still more clouded in the northern area. The railway service from Damascus had been restored after momentary interruption, and trains were running about twice a week into Medina, taking four days on the journey. The command at Medina had now been taken over by Fakhri Pasha, who had risen to fame as organizer of the Adana massacres in 1909; an expert in such forms of reprisal and intimidation, he was not long in sustaining his reputation. Disheartened by the original failure, part of the Beni Ali had tried to make terms with the Turks. The subsequent negotiations gave Fakhri an opportunity which he exploited in a way that had a reminiscent flavour of the trick brought off by the Romans and their Numidian allies against the Carthaginian camps near Utica in 203 B.C. He made a sudden sortie on June 27th, drove off Feisal and surrounded the suburb which Feisal had occupied. After their successful assault his men sacked and burnt the place, massacring the inhabitants, men, women and children, with few exceptions. After rape, the females were thrown into the flames as a variant to death by mutilation.

This experience of the Turkish mode of war made the more impression because of its breach of the Arab code of war, which rules not only that women and children should be spared, but also material property, if it cannot be removed as loot. The Arab's chivalry is guided by a sound business morality. He kills for cash and not for charity. If this relative immunity from the blood-lust that sweeps over more animal races is testimony to his good sense, it does not make him good material for a "Crusade"—which demands a fanatical enthusiasm. As it in part explains his past subjection to the Turk, so it also helps us to understand the difficulties that were to be met by those who cherished the dream of inspiring him to a supreme and selfless effort for freedom and empire. A Cavalcade was more in his line than a Crusade.

But battles have often been won by bluff, and wars more often by movement than by slow murder. There was a military value inherent even in a cavalcade for those who knew how to use it. This only awaited the martial genius who could understand the strength of weakness and turn the limitations of the Arab into assets. By strange contrast, this dynamic realist was to reveal himself in the man to whom the Arabs had been a romantic ideal.

In midsummer, 1916, there was still a hard road to travel before the right way was reached. Honour might urge the Arabs to avenge the massacre of their people but their lucidity of mind dissuaded them from throwing their bodies against machine-guns. They fell back out of range. Ali also withdrew from the railway and linked up with Feisal. The Arab forces now contented themselves with guarding the tracks that ran through the hills to Mecca.

Even here they were not long left in peace. On August 3rd the Turks took the offensive again, and drove Ali twenty miles south of Medina after a running fight that lasted for a day and a night. The rocky hills, so helpful to solitary snipers, were the main check on a continued advance. But at this moment of Arab depression the newly arrived mobile column might well have pushed through to Mecca. The Turks' lack of a time-sense came to the relief of the Arabs. The Turkish commander chose to wait until fresh reinforcements reached him at Medina and permitted him to undertake a thorough subjugation of the Hejaz. Eight battalions were being sent, as well as a new Sherif, Ali Haidar, ready to make a triumphal entry into Mecca, with the Turkish holy carpet. The flavour of such a vengeance was too good to lose by hurry. Thus the Turks forfeited the best chance of nipping the revolt in the bud.

Time was allowed for the Arabs to gain the prestige of successful revolt as the news spread in widening ripples over the sands of the desert, gathering a volume greater than the reality in its passage.

Time was also allowed for the Arabs to repair their preparatory omissions and to improve their defective organization. But they took little advantage of the respite. Organization did not come naturally to the town-Arab or peasant-Arab, still less to the Bedouin. Nor did it fit their family basis. If they came together in force, that force became as shifting as the sands. It frequently happened that each member of a family would serve in turn for a few days, using the family rifle, and then be replaced by a brother. Those who were married were accustomed to divide their time between war and their wives. And the fluctuations of the family system prevailed a stage higher in the tribal. An entire contingent of a clan would sometimes go home for a spell. These disorganizing influences were accentuated by the sensitiveness and suspicion of the Arabs, and their inter-tribal feuds. The tie of a common enemy was often insufficient to bear for long the strain of a mutual dislike. Lines of division, indeed, were innumerable. The absence of horizontal distinctions which has appealed to so many foreign observers, Lawrence among them, was offset by a superabundance of vertical intersections.

The chief military asset of the Arabs lay in their power of strategic mobility—their ability to move long distances at short notice without the encumbrances that clog an orthodox force. But this power had more limitations than are usually realized. Only a small proportion of the Arabs—barely a tenth of Feisal's original force—were camel-men. The fact that the bulk moved on foot aggravated their problem of feeding themselves if they moved far from home. Thus food was a factor only second to family in tethering them to their own tribal area. It meant that if operations were transferred to a new area the strategist had largely to depend on raising new forces from the tribes there. This "localization" of the Arab armies has an interesting analogy with the cramping effect of the English county militias of the seventeenth and eighteenth centuries or the state militias during the American Civil War—the Georgia militia, for example, were only brought to the battlefield of Grahamville by the amusing ruse of switching their train on to a branch line that took them over the South Carolina border in the dark, so that they fought next day in blissful ignorance of the fact that they were defending the soil of another state.

When the first enthusiasm waned, the maintenance of the Arab rising depended on the Sherif's power to feed his followers and also to compensate them for the loot they were now failing to secure from the Turks. Here Britain's help was the decisive factor. The supply-ships that came into Jidda and Rabegh were the backbone of the revolt. Through them, and them alone, the Sherif was able to feed his forces and their families. With British money he was able to pay two pounds a month for a man and four for a camel. As Lawrence has remarked—"Nothing else would have performed the miracle of keeping a tribal army in the field for five months on end."

Less happily, those who were nearest the ships and so farthest from the fighting front tended to fare best. Thus in an accentuated form the familiar tendency of civilized armies was witnessed here. And as these tribal armies had no discipline to check them, the natural consequence was a reflux towards the base that drained the fighting forces.

Ali and Feisal found that only a trickle of supplies was reaching them. And no money. To maintain the martial ardour of his men Feisal hit on the ruse of filling a chest with clinking stones, "had it locked and corded carefully, guarded on each daily march by his own slaves, and introduced meticulously into his tent each night."

But these devices could not suffice for long. So Ali, exercising an elder brother's privilege, went down to Rabegh to find out why the British were not fulfilling their promises. He found that the local chief had preferred to take the chance of a quick profit in the expectation that the Turks would settle the Sherif's account, and leave his clear of debt. Sending for Zeid, who brought reinforcements from Jidda, Ali made a show of force. The conscience-stricken chief took to the hills, while Ali took possession of Rabegh, where he discovered a fine hoard of British supplies. The brothers decided to take a prolonged rest at Rabegh.

Thus Feisal was left to play a lone hand in the hills near Medina, striving to hold together his force, which was now melting as well as shifting. The sheikhs told him: "You promise arms and food and none come"; tired of waiting they slipped away. And while the war languished the Turks were not only gathering weight at Medina, and strengthening their grip on the railway northward, but were collecting transport and supplies from their particular desert ally, the Emir of Hail, as well as from the north. The Arab rising might soon be extinguished unless Britain contributed something more than the sinews of war.

Such was the view of the men, with one notable exception, who came in close touch with the situation. But there was a multiplicity of factors and a complexity of direction that hindered their views from having effect.

The external control of Arab affairs was a tangled skein, even before French threads were woven into it. The political side was directed by the High Commissioner in Egypt, Sir Henry McMahon, whose appreciation of the value of the Arab movement was matched by his courage in espousing it. At his elbow was Mr. Ronald Storrs, whose versatility matched his variety of interests. Storrs had been Oriental Secretary to the British Agency at Cairo since 1909, and reinforced his chief with a knowledge of the people on the other side of the Red Sea, and a knack of smoothing out difficulties nearer home. But the High Commissioner's sphere of influence was limited because the Government of India still kept responsibility for the affairs of Arabia south of the Hejaz. And his powers of action were limited because he depended for the means of action upon the Commander of the forces in Egypt, now Sir Archibald Murray, who was not only saturated in the conventional doctrine of concentration but had the soldier's traditional sensitiveness to the appearance of political interference. Murray in turn was governed by the General Staff in London, while McMahon was under the Foreign Office.

But the actual control of any military moves across the Red Sea was vested in a third person, the Governor-General of the Sudan, Sir Reginald Wingate. He had been appointed to "the command of operations in the Hejaz," which meant that he was responsible for advising the Sherif as to the Arab operations and for the employment of any British forces that might be sent. His sympathy with the Arab rising was equalled by his eagerness to exploit the opportunity, but he was a general without an army, for his own forces in the Sudan were scanty, and still occupied in quenching the embers of revolt in Darfur. The problem of giving long-distance advice to the Sherif was hardly less difficult, and was exceeded by the difficulty of securing its acceptance.

To ease this, Wingate sent Lieut.-Colonel C. E. Wilson, Governor of the Red Sea Province of the Sudan, across to Jidda as his representative. It was a high responsibility, but a happy choice. For a time Wilson had to work unaided at the task of comforting, counselling and reconciling the various Arab leaders, but in the end he acquired an ascendency over them that was only less remarkable than the confidence he inspired in the suspicious Sherif. This was due not to diplomatic cleverness, but to the fact that he was so open and honourable that the Arabs, who do not lack penetration, came to place a trust in him that they would never have given to a subtler counsellor. But they perhaps forgot, to their own detriment later, that he was the man on the spot, and not the man at the top.

Another fortunate chance lay in the fact that the command of the sea was exercised by a sailor so free from red-tape and so ready in co-operation as Vice-Admiral Sir Rosslyn Wemyss, commanding the East Indies Station. He truly fulfilled the role of godfather to the Revolt, in the military sphere, until the infant was able to take care of itself.

There was a human link between these several authorities in Gilbert Clayton, a brigadier-general at forty-one, who combined in his person the triple office of Sudan Agent, head of the Military Intelligence in Egypt, and head of the Political Intelligence. He was also in liaison with the staff of the Naval Commander-in-Chief and supervised the Arab Bureau. He not only played many parts but possessed the gifts to develop them. Although seemingly casual, and even lazy, he had a knack of keeping touch with all relevant matters, together with a capacity to smile at troubles that often helped to allay them. His sense of humour was of no less value in dealing with his variegated subordinates than in composing the differences between superiors, and it was especially called on to protect one of the former from the frequent wrath of senior officers whose sense of dignity had quenched their sense of humour. Without the support and understanding of Clayton, as well as of Hogarth, the seeds of Lawrence's genius might have withered in a stony soil.

When the War came, in August, 1914, Lawrence had been back at Oxford, working on his part of a record of the Sinai trip which he had made with Woolley. Undisturbed by the general upset of life in England Lawrence continued work on this book, which was published in 1915 by the Palestine Exploration Fund under the title of *The Wilderness of Zin.*

Lawrence's action may suggest that he was more interested in finishing the book than in a war which most young men thought was likely to be over before they had a chance to fight. But although he was to be the Drake of the desert, and later to be a familiar sight on Plymouth Hoe, he did not continue his book in August, 1914, from the same reason that Drake had continued his bowls. The real cause lay in Kitchener's anxiety to avoid offence to Turkey so long as a chance remained of keeping her out of the war. "Turkey was sore about the Sinai survey, which it felt had been a military game. K. (the only begetter of the survey) insisted on the Palestine

Exploration Fund's bringing out its record of our archaeological researches, p.d.q., as whitewash. Woolley and I had instructions to get it done instanter."

The task did not take long to complete, and Lawrence promptly took the initiative in finding a place in the military system where his particular knowledge could be of real service. It has been said that he tried to enlist and was rejected on the ground of poor physique; this has the piquant irony that makes a good story, but here happens to be untrue. But there is still a delicate flavour in the actual fact that owing to the glut of recruits the height standard was raised to a level beyond Lawrence's stature—five feet five inches. Napoleon, also, would have been rejected by the British Army in August, 1914.

What happened next is best told in Lawrence's own words to me—"Woolley and I wrote to Newcombe, when the book was finished, and asked his advice about a war job. They were difficult to get. Newcombe told Cox, of the Intelligence, about us, and got our names on the waiting list." Woolley grew tired of waiting and obtained a commission in the artillery. "I asked Hogarth (prominent in the R.G.S.) if he could expedite me something." Hogarth suggested that the Geographical Section of the General Staff was the right place, and apparently spoke about Lawrence through some intermediary channel. Anyhow, Lawrence received word from Hogarth to call on Colonel Hedley at the War Office.

Sir Coote Hedley has told me that he has no recollection of being approached on Lawrence's behalf and that he was surprised when one day in September a War Office messenger ushered into his room a young man, hatless and in grey flannels, who "looked about eighteen." His name, however, dispelled any doubts, as Hedley was well aware of his work in Sinai and had heard some good stories about him from Newcombe. Thus he readily took Lawrence into his office. Lawrence had appeared at an opportune moment, as all save one of the officers in the Geographical Section, Newcombe among them, had been called away to active service on the outbreak of war. And the only one left, Captain Walter Nugent, was within a week of departing to France. "Nugent hurriedly instructed me in my G.S.G.S. duties and Hedley and I were left alone in the office." Among other important work left unfinished was that on the 1/250,000 maps of the Sinai Peninsula, which were to connect the maps of Palestine, surveyed and published by the Palestine Exploration Fund, with those of the Sinai Peninsula, prepared by the Geographical Section, which started from the Egyptian end.

Lawrence began work while still a civilian, and his change into uniform was precipitated through the shock his appearance gave to Sir Henry Rawlinson, who had just been appointed to command the new expedition to the relief of the Belgian Army. Lawrence went to show the newly printed maps of Belgium to Rawlinson who "nearly had a fit when he saw me," and exclaimed, "I want to talk to an officer." Hedley then said to Lawrence, "We must get you a commission"; this was arranged without the formality of any medical examination—which was obviously superfluous after the practical tests of endurance he had already passed triumphantly in Syria and Sinai. It was more important than he should be in uniform, so he went off to the Army and Navy Stores and fitted himself out with a second-lieutenant's uniform without waiting until his appointment was gazetted.

Hedley found his new assistant more efficient even than he had hoped. Indeed, there is a story that some weeks later Hogarth asked Hedley how his new apprentice was doing, and received the answer, not unmixed with humour—"He's running my entire department for me now." With a public-spirited generosity that is not too common in the departmental machine, Hedley told Callwell, the Director of Military Operations and Intelligence, that he had in his office "the ideal officer" for Egyptian intelligence work. Meantime, realizing that he would soon lose Lawrence's help, he tried to get the Sinai maps finished as soon as possible. Lawrence needed no prompting. If he had not been restrained he "would have worked all through the night," for "he hardly noticed what time it was."

In December, after Turkey had entered the War, it was decided to strengthen the Intelligence Service in Cairo. Newcombe was called back from France, and told that he was to go out to Egypt as assistant to Clayton. Among the officers he was to take with him were George Lloyd, Aubrey Herbert, Leonard Woolley, and Lawrence—they became known in Egypt as "the five musketeers." Newcombe and Lawrence left London on December 9th ahead of the others and travelled by rail to Marseilles, where they embarked on a French liner for Egypt, thereby enjoying a jest at the expense of the others, who followed in discomfort on a troopship.

In Cairo the fountainhead for information about the Turkish Army was another civilian, still uncommissioned. This was Philip Graves, who had been *Times* Correspondent in Constantinople before the war. Foreseeing the coming conflict, he had turned himself into a military expert, keeping watch on the progress of the Turkish Army reorganization that followed the Balkan War, and studying both measures and men with a closeness that the British official intelligence failed to approach. Thus when Turkey aligned herself with the enemy in 1914 the War Office handbook was as out of date as Graves's knowledge, from superior sources, was up to date. The contrast gives rise to the reflection that there is a type of official mind which would rather die—or let others die—through ignorance than conquer through unofficial information.

On going to Cairo, however, after Turkey's entry into the war, Graves found in Clayton a man who was ready to profit by his unique knowledge of the opposing army. It was the more valuable because it embraced not merely the personnel but the personalities of the opposing commanders, their virtues and vices. Thus he was able to furnish illuminating appreciations that sometimes ran like this—"A rather oily young Turk . . . Is quite unreliable, fairly unscrupulous, but not inefficient. Supposed to have made a good deal of money out of brothel-keepers, though his friends say that this was for the benefit of party funds. Frequented Diplomatic Society, especially French circles. Reputed to live pretty fast."

The knowledge that Lawrence possessed of the lower social strata in the Turkish Empire, and also of the Arab secret societies, made him an apt complement to Graves. Hence his services were utilized not only in preparing maps but in helping Philip Graves to compile the enemy's "Order of Battle"—the disposition of the various Turkish divisions and detachments, as pieced together from the reports of our agents and from the examination of prisoners. In this task he was helped by past exercise of his habit of gathering odd trifles of information and his extraordinary perceptiveness of details which other men missed. If Conan Doyle had been born a generation later he would have found in Lawrence an apt model from which to create Sherlock Holmes.

This flair led to a further extension of Lawrence's duties, that of examining suspects who were brought in. He frequently confounded them, and dumbfounded the Watsons, by his deductions from points of dress, manner and speech. To his fellows Lawrence's success in eliciting information seemed uncanny. His own explanation is "I always knew their districts, and asked about my friends in them. Then they told me everything." After seeing the man and listening to his first few words, Lawrence was usually able to "put him within twenty miles of his home," and would then remark— "Oh, you come from Aleppo. How is ——?"

In Egypt, as formerly at Carchemish, Lawrence's many-sidedness made him a general handyman. In conjunction with Graves he produced successive fresh editions of the Turkish Army handbook, and supervised the printing of them himself. He was employed in gathering information about the seditious movement in Egypt, wherein the readiness of the conspirators to betray each other gave a relieving touch of humour to a sordid business. He was sent on a mission to the Western Desert. He was sent on a mission to Greece, to get in touch with the British secret agents there. This was appreciated by him still more as a chance to feel the magic of that "landscape of extraordinary purity of line," to feed his eyes once more on the shape and colours of the Greek hills—"conscious works of art." It was like a cleansing shower between one cesspool and another.

In the spring of 1916 he had a long-range hand in a more important matter, the "capture" of Erzerum by the Russian Caucasus Army after a curiously half-hearted defence—readers of John Buchan's subsequent novel, *Greenmantle,* may find it worth while to remember that fiction has often a basis of fact.

The immediate effect of this success in the Caucasus was that it stimulated the War Office to attempt a repetition in essentially different conditions, and in consequence Lawrence was sent on a secret mission to Mesopotamia. Ostensibly he went there on behalf of the Intelligence in Cairo as a step towards improving the preparation and printing of maps for the Mesopotamian Expeditionary Force, and, in particular, to give advice on the compilation of maps from air photographs, a new art in which he had become expert while it was still a mystery to the Indian authorities. But although most of his fellows knew only that this task had been given him, he had received confidential instructions direct from the War Office that he was to accompany Captain Aubrey Herbert, M.P., on an embassy to Khalil Pasha, in command of the Turkish Army then besieging Townshend's force in Kut.

The object was to open negotiations with Khalil Pasha in the hope that he might allow the garrison to go free in return for a generous bribe. Lawrence also had a third aim, in his own mind, which was to explore the possibilities of creating a revolt among the Arab tribes on the Turkish lines of communication, so that the besiegers of Kut might themselves be cut off from supplies and reinforcements.

But on arrival at Basra he found the atmosphere unfavourable alike to his official mission and his private purpose. The last-minute idea of buying off the Turks had been conceived by Townshend, adopted by Kitchener, and accepted by Lake, the Commander-in-Chief in Mesopotamia. But it went against the grain of many of the British generals. Although they had been baffled in their efforts to relieve Townshend's starving force, their defeats in open fight did not make them respond to, far less relish, what seemed to them the idea of gaining their object by underhand methods. Hence they looked coldly on a mission which affronted their soldierly code of honour. On the more practical ground that the attempt would have a worse effect on our prestige even than a military defeat, Sir Percy Cox, the Chief Political Officer, refused to associate himself with the negotiations. It should be added that Lawrence himself was also against it, because he considered that Khalil, as Enver's nephew, was too assured of money from home and too certain of military success to be thus bought off.

The result justified these expectations. The garrison of Kut was at the last gasp when the negotiations were attempted, and the Turks spurned the offer of a million pounds to let them go free on parole. In vain, the Cabinet at home doubled their offer, and thereby provided the world outside Britain with a piquant jest at the "nation of shop-keepers." The censorship might keep it from our own people, but the Turks took care to broadcast to other peoples. The actual parleys were a humiliating experience for the envoys. Under a white flag, Herbert, accompanied by Colonel Beach and Lawrence, crossed no-man's-land; on entering the Turkish lines, they were blindfolded before being taken back to Khalil's headquarters. All that they succeeded in extracting from him was the release of some of the sick and wounded in exchange for unwounded Turkish prisoners.

Khalil would not accept Arab prisoners, saying that most of them were no better than deserters; they would only be court-martialled and shot if they were returned. When the British officers asked him not to punish the Arab inhabitants of Kut, whose share in the siege was involuntary, he showed amusement at their concern for such carrion, but assured them that he had no intention of being vindictive. He hanged only nine at the outset, which in view of his past record was perhaps a proof of his mercy.

Lawrence's personal project proved equally abortive. The time had passed for saving Kut and most British officers were too scornful of the Mesopotamian Arabs to visualize them as potential allies, especially at the price of encouraging their pretensions. Lawrence here was opposed not only by military short-sight but, in certain quarters, by a vision as far-ranging as his own, if different from it— a vision of British rule extending its borders, to the benefit of administrative order if not to the satisfaction of native ambitions. Lawrence's unconcealed contempt of the military mismanagement of the campaign in Mesopotamia did not make his views on the Arab question any more palatable to the senior officers he met, and, during his brief visit, he attained a remarkable degree of unpopularity which was to have wider effects in the years to follow.

On embarking at Basra for the return trip to Egypt he found that his solitary fellow-passenger was a general, Webb-Gillman, who had been sent out by the War Office on a mission of investigation. At first Webb-Gillman seemed inclined to resent the intrusion of this unconventional subaltern upon his meditation, but his sense of humour was tickled by Lawrence's suggested division of the deck for their respective perambulations, and he took full advantage of their companionship. Hearing that Lawrence had compiled a report on conditions in the Mesopotamian Force he asked to see it, and discussed every page with Lawrence at length before starting to write his own submissions.

This knowledge consoled Lawrence for the editing he suffered when, on arrival in Egypt, he handed in his report on what he had observed of interest to the staff in Egypt. He had fulfilled the demand with a generosity that caused the recipients acute indigestion. To quote Colonel Stirling—"He criticized the quality of the stones used for lithographing, the system of berthing barges alongside the quays, the inefficiency of the cranes for handling stores, the lack of system in shunting and entraining on the railways, the want of adequate medical stores, the blindness of the medical authorities and their want of imagination as to their probable requirements. And, horror of horrors, he criticized the Higher Command and the conduct of the campaign in general!"

Sir Archibald Murray, who knew of his visit to Mesopotamia, asked to see the report. "There was consternation that night in the General Staff, for we were convinced that, if he were to read it, apoplexy would be the result and we should lose our C-in-C. Hurriedly, therefore, we sat down and bowdlerized the report until we considered it fit to be put before his professional eye; Lawrence, however, was abundantly right in most of his criticisms—particularly on the medical question—as was proved by the tragic muddle which occurred when the wounded first started coming down."

But although this "devastating" criticism was to be abundantly justified by history it was vigorously resented at the time. Those professional soldiers who were in his immediate circle, men who recognized his value, who had a sense of humour, learnt to tolerate his jests at their profession and even enjoyed the smarting sting of truth. Although their instincts rallied in defence of their profession, the defence was undermined by a deep-down feeling of agreement. But to those who were solidly buttressed by dignity and orthodoxy, the idea of a temporary second-lieutenant indulging in military criticisms and sitting in judgment on generals was revolting. The pill was not even coated with the sugar of superficial and sartorial correctness. He was often curt with seniors, and free in correcting their ignorance. He offended their eyes, as well as their ears, by the colour of his collar, the pattern of his tie, and his habit of going about without a Sam Browne belt.

To those brought up in the military convention that infallibility is the privilege of seniority, there was continual irritation in the complete assurance, almost dogmatic, with which Lawrence used to utter verdicts on any matter that came within his own range of knowledge. And because that range was astonishingly wide, it widened all the more the gulf between him and his official seniors. Yet if they tried to "put him in his place," they were left with a sense of having been ineffectual, and were apt to be checked by something they could not define, so they sought to apply corrective pressure through his immediate superiors.

Newcombe had gone back to France before 1915 was out, and Lawrence had been absorbed into Murray's swollen staff organization where his chief, Holdich, was a man who could not tolerate Lawrence's "cheek" or his superior knowledge. While they were both serving on Maxwell's staff, they had been on good terms, but in the way that is too often characteristic of the servants of authority Holdich seems to have changed with the change of command and to have taken on the colour of his new superiors. For the causes of his divergence from Lawrence, as well as from others of his own subordinates, were more than personal. Lawrence's estimates of enemy strengths were given to the nearest hundred; Holdich suppressed them and put forward his own which seemed to his subordinates "to be only in the furthest ten-thousands." Lawrence himself has remarked—"Holdich was excellent in Operations and fatal in Intelligence." The history of the Palestine campaign from 1915 to 1917 certainly endorses the second half of this judgment. The only way that the junior members of the Intelligence Staff could get the true figures through was under the cloak of publishing fresh editions of the Turkish Army Handbook!

Lawrence's excessive enthusiasm for the Arab Revolt was an additional offence in the eyes of several members of the General Staff, whose prejudice against the Revolt on principle was accentuated by their personal prejudices against McMahon and Clayton. Lawrence seemed a traitor in the General Staff camp. On his part, he now began to repay their dislike by multiplying his aggravations, correcting their prose style, on paper, and their ignorance, over the telephone. Here he was deliberately provoking the power of a military bureaucracy to deposit its inconveniences on some out-of-the-way shelf. But he slipped through their fingers by slipping into the Arab Bureau, where a corner was found for him by the good offices of

Clayton. And the Arab Revolt was now about to open up a better opportunity for him. In October, while his transfer was being privily arranged through London, he took ten days leave and used it to make his first trip to the Hejaz, accompanying Ronald Storrs.

CHAPTER VI

MEN OR A MAN

July–December, 1916

The danger of the Turks recapturing Mecca leads the British Government to contemplate the dispatch of troops to Rabegh—General Staff opposition—France takes a hand in the game—Lawrence's first visit to the Hejaz—He finds in Feisal the necessary prophet-leader—On his return he advises against the dispatch of troops—Meantime the reluctant General Staff is on the point of being driven to send them—A decision is put off, but the Arab situation grows worse—Relief comes suddenly

THE midsummer dream had changed into an autumn spectre. The news that filtered across the Red Sea was depressing to the British representatives in Egypt and the Sudan who had hailed with delight the outbreak of the Arab Revolt as the fulfilment of long-cherished hopes and an invaluable relief to the pressure on Egypt. By the Indian Government the rising had been viewed with marked distaste, so that its threatened collapse was taken lightly. In England, although the public at that time but dimly perceived the significance of the rising, in governmental circles its echoes carried far—arousing a controversy that gave the obscure port of Rabegh a ringing fame which lasted until, late in the year, it was drowned in the clatter of Mr. Asquith's fall.

The problem of giving practical support to the rising had come before the War Committee of the Cabinet on July 6th.[1]

It made a number of recommendations. The chief was that the British force in Egypt should push forward to El Arish and also occupy Aqaba, so as to threaten the Turkish communications with the Hejaz.

But the advance to El Arish was slow to mature while the Sherif

---

[1] Sir Mark Sykes was called into consultation. He had embodied his proposals in a formula that—"Towards all Arabs . . . whether independent allies, as Ibn Sa'ud or the Sherif, inhabitants of protectorates, spheres of influence, vassal states, we should show ourselves as pro-Arabs, and that wherever we are on Arab soil we are going to back the Arab language and Arab race, and that we shall protect or support Arabs against external oppression by force as much as we are able, and from alien exploitation." The significance of his formula lies in its illumination of his own view when drawing up the Sykes-Picot agreement.

had showed a reluctance towards the idea of British troops landing at Aqaba. Thus the British higher command, reluctant to spare troops, were only too glad of an excuse to profit by his uncertainty and avoid the necessity.

The dangerous situation in the autumn, however, brought a call to send him direct help. The prospect of a Turkish advance from Medina on Mecca loomed menacingly close. It was most likely that the Turks would move by way of Rabegh, the route which offered less difficulties and more water. Moreover, it was stacked with the supplies that the British had accumulated for the Sherif's use, and thus offered a tempting prize.

Faced with this danger both McMahon and Wingate urged that a British brigade should be dispatched to Rabegh. Murray strongly resisted the proposal. He seemed to have little faith in the success of the rising or insight into its possible value, and was thus the more unwilling to spare troops from his own immediate zone of operations. It was easy to conjure up arguments. The appearance of British troops so near the Holy Cities might antagonize the Moslem world and even the Arabs it was intended to succour. More account was to be taken of the Sherif's past hesitation than of his present desire for such help. If troops were sent, they might serve no useful purpose, because the Turks might choose to go by the inland route.

McMahon had a conference with Murray at Ismailia on September 13th, in an effort to overcome these objections. Unable to reach agreement they referred the matter to the authorities at home. A stream of telegrams passed to and fro between the High Commissioner, the Sirdar, the Foreign Office, the Commander-in-Chief in Egypt, and the Chief of the Imperial General Staff at home. The Foreign Office submitted the issue to the War Committee, which referred it to the General Staff for an opinion.

Murray found strong support for his objections from his successor at home. Sir William Robertson had taken up office with a fixed determination to cut down all distant distractions in order to concentrate every possible man on the Western Front. Freed of the Gallipoli "side-show," to his delight, but entangled at Salonika, to his disgust, he had no intention of being drawn into a fresh commitment.

In a memorandum of September 20th, 1916, Robertson set forth his views, with a definite recommendation that no troops should be sent. Any direct help should be limited to "such as the Navy could give."

Several Ministers, in particular Lord Curzon and Mr. Austen Chamberlain, did not agree with Robertson's recommendation. They suggested that the men on the spot, McMahon and Wingate, were more likely to know what was needed and what the Arabs' feelings would be, than the General Staff in London. Finally it was arranged that the views of the Viceroy of India and of the Commanders-in-Chief in Egypt and Mesopotamia should be obtained.

The Viceroy's answer reflected the consistently deprecatory attitude of Indian officials towards the Arab rising, which had been a "displeasing surprise" to them, while the bombardment of Jidda had been deplored. The Viceroy now set forth various objections to the dispatch of troops to Rabegh and ended by declaring that the collapse of the revolt would be far less prejudicial to us in India, and also in Afghanistan, than would military intervention in support of the revolt. General Maude's answer from Mesopotamia seemed to reflect a similar attitude. He suggested that the tribes in his sphere were not sufficiently interested in the revolt to care whether it succeeded or failed. Murray took an optimistic line, suggesting that no troops were needed at present.

These answers did not satisfy the Ministers who were calling for prompt measures. But Robertson declared he had nothing to add to his original memorandum, and in face of his uncompromising opposition, the Ministers yielded. His satisfaction, however, was short-lived, and his resistance was soon tested again by the turn of events, which brought not only renewed pressure from the Foreign Office but a new pressure from France.

When the news of the Arab Revolt had reached France, its bearing on the ideas that on their part underlay the Sykes-Picot treaty was quickly perceived. It inspired the French to take a hand in stirring the broth that had already so many cooks.

Their view was expressed in a Ministry of War document of August 5th:—

"The Arab rising against Ottoman domination was favourable in a measure to French interests; from the political point of view, it might spread among the people of Palestine, Syria, and Little Armenia, free those provinces momentarily from Turkish persecution and pave the way for a French intervention; from the military point of view it might immobilize the Turkish forces in proportion to its extension; from the Islamic point of view, it might lead the majority of our Moslem peoples to regard the Turks as the assailants of the Holy Places and, in consequence, increase their loyalty towards France, who was fighting the allies of the Ottomans."

The French Prime Minister laid stress on the importance of reopening the pilgrimage and sending "some religious notables of assured loyalty who might carry to the Emir [of Mecca] presents and subsidies, with the felicitations of our Moslem subjects." To this political deputation should be added a French military mission, composed exclusively of Moslems but under the direction of a French officer.

These measures were at once put into effect. Lieut.-Colonel Brémond, who had served for years in North Africa and was an accomplished Arabic scholar, was appointed head of the mission. He was to establish his headquarters in Egypt while the Arab part, under a Moslem artillery officer, Major Cadi, went to the Hejaz.

The mission reached Alexandria on September 1st, and a fortnight later sailed for the Hejaz accompanied by the political deputation. On landing at Jidda it received a ceremonial reception, marked on the Arab side by flowers of speech and on the French side by the delivery of a million and a quarter gold francs. The French-African pilgrims followed a few days later. Religious enthusiasm and financial joy overflowed as the cavalcade set forth for Mecca. But after the return from Mecca, Si Kaddour Ben Ghabrit, the head of the deputation, reported that the Sherif had shown no eagerness to accept the offer of French military support, suggesting that it might harm his cause.

Ben Ghabrit, however, warned the French Foreign Office that unless such help was at hand when real danger arose, the Arabs were likely to make terms with the Turks. He added a significant hint—"our installation in Syria will probably be a source of difficulties with the Sherif of Mecca, if we do not profit by his present weakness to make an agreement with him that will limit his ambitions while recognizing such of his desires as are reconcilable with our interests."

These difficulties, and possibilities, had not escaped the attention of the British Foreign Office. But the intervention of the French mission could not be avoided; hence it might as well be accompanied by military participation of more practical utility. The day after the mission landed at Alexandria the British Government asked the French to send a detachment. The War Office suggested a field battery and as many specialists as possible, so long as they were Moslem soldiers. But this wish could not be fulfilled immediately because the French had no natives trained as artillery men and few as specialists. In November a detachment which included machine-gunners and engineers as well as two batteries, and totalled a thousand men, was assembled at Suez, there to complete its training. It would be of service later, but it had no effect on the immediate emergency.

To compensate their own unreadiness the French now added their voice to the chorus that was urging the dispatch of a brigade to Rabegh.

Fakhri Pasha had not yet moved against Mecca, but, inevitably, with every week that passed the menace of a move became more imminent. Although none of the British officers could predict the duration of Turkish inertia, there must surely, they felt, be a limit.

Despite their early losses the Turks' strength in the Hejaz was almost as high as at the outset. It comprised some 10,000 troops based on Medina, 2,500 along the railway to the north, and 1,200 garrisoning Wejh.

The Arab forces were now distributed in three groups, one of about 5,000 men under Ali, based on Rabegh; another of about 4,000 under Abdulla, near Mecca; and the third of about 7,000 under Feisal which was now based on Yanbo, with the idea of operating against the railway. But although they kept guard on the hills, they kept at a distance from Medina. Moreover, Ali and Abdulla seem to have left most of the strain to be borne by Feisal, and his men even could not stand much.

On October 19th he fell back from Bir Abbas to Hamra in face of a Turkish advance, which was subsequently reported as consisting of a reconnoitring party of eighty Turkish camel-men.

Three days previously Storrs and Lawrence had landed at Jidda, where Abdulla met them. Lawrence, who was on the look-out for an inspired prophet and leader, a new Mahomet, soon formed the opinion that Abdulla did not fill the part. His character was portrayed in his short stout build, round smooth face, full lips and twinkling eyes. In Arab opinion he was both an astute politician and a far-sighted statesman. In Lawrence's view he suggested the former rather than the latter. He was more full of complaints than of inspiration, if he relieved them by a cheerful cynicism. And although he suggested that nothing might remain save to die fighting before the Holy City, it was his father that he cast for this heroic end. The Sherif, who now came through on the telephone from Mecca, confirmed this decision, whereupon Abdulla, "smiling a little," asked that a brigade of British troops, Moslems if possible, should be kept ready at Suez to avert such a disaster, should the Turks begin an advance from Medina.

Lawrence suggested, in answer, that he would like to visit Feisal and see the situation for himself. Storrs, on the telephone, persuaded the Sherif into giving a reluctant permission. The telephone, incidentally, was a new toy whose fascinations had not faded; that evening the Englishmen were called to the telephone to hear another new toy, the Sherif's brass band, newly captured from the Turks, playing in Mecca. And when Storrs expressed his appreciation, the Sherif said he would send it down by forced marches next day, so that he himself in turn might have the pleasure of hearing it from Jidda.

On the second morning, after this treat had been given, Lawrence sailed for Rabegh, where he met Ali. He likewise could be dismissed from the quest. Worn and tired at thirty-seven, with drooping mouth and delicate hands, his physical frailty had its accompaniment in a character more well-meaning than well-balanced. For Lawrence's onward journey Ali provided him with a camel and a couple of guides. To hide the fact that an infidel was going into the interior of the holy province, Ali delayed Lawrence's start until after dark, and in addition made him wear an Arab cloak and headcloth. As they rode through the night Lawrence's thoughts were "how this was the Pilgrim Road, down which, for uncounted generations, the people of the north had come to visit the Holy City, bearing with them gifts of faith for the shrine; and it seemed that the Arab Revolt might be in a sense a return pilgrimage, to take back to the north, to Syria, an ideal for an ideal, a belief in liberty for their past belief in a revelation." It reveals the romantic faith of the man who would inspire the inverted Crusade.

After pausing for a meal and resting a few hours at a hamlet sixty miles out, Lawrence reached Hamra late on the second day and found Feisal awaiting him.

"I felt at first glance that this was the man I had come to Arabia to seek—the leader who would bring the Arab Revolt to full glory. Feisal looked very tall and pillar-like, very slender, in his long white silk robes and his brown headcloth bound with a brilliant scarlet and gold cord. His eyelids were dropped; and his black beard and colourless face were like a mask against the strange, still watchfulness of his body." He reminded Lawrence of the monument of Richard Cœur de Lion at Fontevraud. The likeness went deeper than the surface.

After a greeting Feisal politely inquired—"And do you like our place here in Wadi Safra?"

"Well; but it is far from Damascus."

It was a thrust that drew blood and yet formed a binding tie, as when two men opened their veins and mingled their blood in the ancient rite.

But even Feisal's spirits were low. Although they had risen when he was reinforced by the Egyptian battery, they had been damped by the discovery that the Turkish artillery easily outranged these antiquated pieces. It spelt an end to the dream that they might reduce Medina as Taif had been reduced. Feisal candidly admitted that he had fallen back for a rest. His insistent demand was for artillery, modern artillery.

Lawrence had a similar but even more vehement appeal from Maulud, a real fighting soldier and the first regular soldier to join Feisal. As a Turkish officer Maulud had been such a firebrand of Arab nationalism that he had been twice degraded and had spent two years of exile as secretary to Ibn Rashid in Nejd. Then, commanding a Turkish cavalry regiment in Mesopotamia he had been taken prisoner by the British at Shaiba, but as soon as he heard of the Arab rising he had volunteered to join Feisal's forces. Galled by the consciousness of their impotence he cried out to Lawrence— "Don't write a history of us. The needful thing is to fight and fight and kill them. Give me a battery of Schneider mountain-guns, and machine-guns, and I'll finish this off for you. We talk and talk and do nothing."

A discussion after supper gave Lawrence a significant glimpse of the Arab point of view. He had expressed sympathy with the Arab leaders who had suffered at Jemal's hands in Syria, when, to his surprise, he was met with the retort that they had paid, if indirectly, a just penalty for their readiness to accept French or British suzerainty as the price of assistance. And although Feisal did not join in the condemnatory chorus, he took care to impress its meaning on Lawrence, pointing out that Britain's established reputation for swallowing the territories she came to protect was bound to cause uneasiness among infant allies.

Next day, Lawrence took the opportunity of studying the Arab forces at close quarters. "They usually took me for a Turk, and were profuse in good humoured suggestions for my disposal." He made a note—"They are a tough-looking crowd, all very dark-coloured, and some negroid: as thin as possible, wearing only a thin shirt, short drawers and a headcloth which serves for every purpose." Lawrence leaves to the imagination the state of the hair beneath, but there is an Arab proverb that a deserted head shows an ungenerous mind. Feisal's new army was lavish in at least one respect— "They go about bristling with cartridge belts, and fire off their rifles when they can. They are learning by practice to use the sights. As for their physical condition, I doubt whether men were ever harder."

It seemed to him that their unity was still an uneasy bond, and might be too easily frayed by adversity; that the shock of one serious defeat in the field, with heavy loss, would break their will to continue the war. But he found new comfort in the sight of the country, so rough and precipitous. The only practicable routes were through valleys that would more justly be called gorges. Hence he felt that even these Arab irregulars should be capable of holding up any Turkish advance so long as they were provided with light machine-guns to sweep the defiles. "The average range possible is from 200 to 300 yards," he noted in his report, "and at point blank ranges the Arabs shoot quite well. The hill-belt is a very paradise for snipers, and a hundred or two of determined men (especially with light machine-guns, capable of being carried by hand up-hill), should be able to hold up each road."

Having sized up the situation, Lawrence obtained an escort as far as Yanbo, where he waited until a British warship put in, and gave him a passage to Jidda, which he reached on November 1st. Here he found Admiral Wemyss, with whom he crossed the Red Sea to Port Sudan, where they met two British officers, Joyce and Davenport, who were on their way to Rabegh. Lawrence travelled on with Wemyss to Khartoum, where he gave his impressions to Wingate before going down the Nile to Cairo.

Lawrence himself considered the situation "full of promise" so long as some skilled British officers were attached to the Arab leaders as technical advisers. He was opposed to the idea of sending British units into the Hejaz, having formed the opinion that such a landing would turn the tribes against the Sherif. In both these views, however, he found himself in a minority—at this moment and place.

This was natural, for pessimism, proverbially, is always greater at the base than in the front line, and Lawrence alone of the European officers had been near the front. The others inevitably felt the depression that prevailed at Rabegh, and inclined to the opinion that a landing in force there was the only sure way to prevent the Turks from regaining Mecca. A natural tendency to measure a military situation by regular standards impelled them to the conclusion that the Arab Army was incapable of offering any serious resistance to the Turks. It was a just conclusion so long as the Arabs tried to practise regular methods.

As a result of his conference with Wemyss, Wingate telegraphed home on November 7th that, in order to hold Rabegh against a strong attack, and after making allowance for naval assistance, at least one brigade of regular troops with artillery was required. As an alternative, if this was refused, he suggested a trained Arab force of 5,000 men, also with artillery. Realizing the likelihood of further opposition and delay at home, and its dangers, he added that he proposed to dispatch the guns and machine-guns and a flight of four aircraft, already sanctioned, and to begin organizing a force of Arabs.

Wingate's telegram was hailed by the General Staff at home as proof of their contention that any intervention would become an unlimited liability. Robertson seized on and emphasized the "at least." He had had another battle with the War Committee on November 2nd, when Ministers had referred to "what was then happening to Rumania and had happened a year before to Serbia"; they had drawn "a gloomy picture of the figure we would cut in the eyes of the world if another ally was allowed to perish for want of help."

With a touch of pathos, Robertson subsequently complained that such arguments "were not easy to meet on the spur of the moment." For lack of counter-arguments he felt that "the only safe course was rigidly to adhere to the conclusions previously reached . . ." [1] A year later, to England's cost and his own undoing, he was to adopt the same attitude over the Passchendaele offensive, where he insisted on giving a blank cheque to Haig despite his own doubts, and wrote the terrible confession—"I confess I stick to it . . . because my instinct prompts me to stick to it than because of any good argument by which I can support it." A strategy that was prompted by animal instinct instead of by reasoned calculation, and that could not be justified by reasoned argument, carried its own condemnation even before bitter experience confirmed this. In his attitude to the Arab campaign he was saved from a similar condemnation by history because a strategist appeared, from the ranks of amateur soldiers, who was capable of evolving from reason a strategy suited to realities.

As he still stood fast the War Committee tried to shift the inconvenience by shifting the decision to a sub-committee, composed of Sir Edward Grey, Lord Curzon and Mr. Austen Chamberlain. Here, Grey was dominated by his habitual reluctance to override official military advice, but the qualms of the other two ministers were subdued by their sense of the danger in Arabia and its possible repercussions. After a prolonged discussion, that he found "rather unpleasant," Robertson was asked to report what force was necessary

[1] See Note 1 at end of chapter.

to hold Rabegh against the potential attack. He grudgingly agreed to do this, although he added the warning—"I could never bring myself to issue an order for British troops to be employed in the manner contemplated." It was an unmistakable threat of resignation if policy were to override his idea of strategy, and it had the more effect at a stage of the war when statesmen, in all countries, had become thoroughly subservient to soldiers through their fear of popular clamour.

Robertson drew up a report in which he emphasized that we ought to be "strong enough to meet the maximum, and not the minimum, numbers which the enemy could employ," and on this basis estimated the requirement as two infantry brigades, two artillery brigades, and two camel corps companies, with auxiliary services, "a total strength of about 16,000 men." As there were not more than 15,000 Turks altogether in the Hejaz even on Robertson's calculation, this was certainly a generous estimate for a force that would be standing on the defensive, covered by the guns of the Navy. But the higher it was put, obviously, the less likely it was to be sent.[1]

The report when presented, or the threat that preceded it, sufficed to satisfy the Prime Minister; and the attention of other ministers was distracted by the political moves which preceded the fall of Mr. Asquith's Government. Rabegh was buried in its ruins and returned to the age-long obscurity from which it had so surprisingly emerged. When the new War Cabinet was formed under Mr. Lloyd George its members naturally had no desire to precipitate an immediate conflict with their chief military adviser on such a minor issue. And although there were subterranean rumblings, any danger of revived controversy and of Robertson's renewed embarrassment was allayed by a solution that was suggested from the Arabian shore. It was not without reason, and for more than a military reason, that Robertson in later years paid tribute to "the inspiration of Colonel Lawrence" in achieving a change in the situation.

At the time he prepared his report it is clear that, despite his assurance, he was by no means sure of its acceptance. Murray, indeed, took the precaution of concentrating two brigades at Suez, ready to embark for Rabegh if definite orders came from England. There the force remained until, late in January, Murray was ordered to

[1] See Note 2 at end of chapter.

send a whole division back to France and told at the same time that he need no longer hold troops in readiness to go to Rabegh. These measures cast a somewhat ironical reflection on the vehement assertions of inability to spare troops.

Meantime alarms and excursions continued on the Red Sea coast. The Turkish printing presses in Medina poured out propaganda sheets in which their new nominee as Sherif, Ali Haidar, announced his intention of "bringing back the Arabs into the right path" and the imminent arrival of Turkish divisions from Europe to assist the task. These sheets, circulating wide, had an ominous effect. Then on December 1st Feisal sent word to Jidda that Fakhri Pasha had left Medina and was advancing down the Wadi Safra. Feisal called for reinforcements but the growing tension between the brothers, and the inattention of Ali and Abdulla to active operations, made his prospect a barren one. British ships had brought to Rabegh nearly four thousand Arab prisoners of war from India, but only a fraction of them proved willing to join the Sherifian forces. And all of them wanted to be officers. As for the small contingent of Egyptian troops which had been sent as a guard for the aircraft, they were occupied at first in guarding themselves. It was touch and go for some days whether the Arabs might not attack them, although less from hostility than from greed of loot. It was lucky that a man of Joyce's character was present to steady the Egyptians.

Down in the south a new gain was lost. Sherif Nasir had occupied Qunfideh in October, under the guns of a British warship, but when this left on December 5th the Turks, with Bedouin help, chased out Nasir's men.

Early in December also, three Turkish battalions with 600 camelry and three guns attacked Feisal, and drove him back on Yanbo. His men fled after trifling loss. Desertions multiplied, while the Turks now commanded the route between Yanbo and Rabegh, and had cut off Feisal from Ali, save by sea. Lawrence landed at Yanbo during the crisis.

On December 10th the Sherif came down to Jidda from Mecca for a meeting with Wilson and Brémond. He handed Wilson a letter asking for the dispatch of six battalions to Rabegh, and saying that although he would prefer Moslems, in view of the circumstances he would accept Christians. Wilson telegraphed accordingly to the

Sirdar. But by next morning the Sherif had changed his mind and withdrew his request.[1]

Talk, talk, talk—so it went on. Some of the Arab leaders at the base urged that troops should be sent; others hinted at peace negotiations with the Turks. The rifles that had been poured into the country in thousands had largely disappeared, many of them sold, some to the Turks. Part of the food supplies had also, it was suspected, gone the same way. On Christmas Eve, Wilson and Brémond with several local officers held a conference to consider the evacuation of Rabegh, but decided to hold on as long as possible. The approaching Turkish force was reported as about 5,000 strong.

On December 29th Wingate took over the office of High Commissioner in Egypt, from which McMahon had been ousted by hostile forces. As the only way to settle the issue of whether troops were desired, Wingate sent a telegram, through Colonel Pearson, that was virtually an ultimatum to the Sherif that he should make up his mind one way or the other. The Sherif replied with one that by its very vagueness led Pearson to read it as an acceptance of the aid of British troops. Pearson telegraphed accordingly to Cairo, and Wingate thereupon asked Murray to dispatch Mudge's brigade which was standing ready.

It was arranged that the French detachment would go with it. Mudge's orders were that on landing at Rabegh he would cover the base and occupy an oasis on the approaches.

The embarkation was fixed for January 9th. The long awaited step was at last decided upon. It was never taken. The orders were cancelled—and finally.

On January 6th, Wilson had reached Jidda on his return from a quick visit to Egypt. On his way he had stopped at Yanbo, where he had seen not only Feisal but Lawrence. Although Wilson had hitherto been strongly in favour of sending British troops to Rabegh, he came back with a changed opinion. He was more optimistic as to the situation and more apprehensive of the reaction that might follow the landing of British troops.

On arrival at Jidda Wilson saw the Sherif's last telegram, and deemed it unsatisfactory. He wrote to Wingate to suggest that no troops should be sent unless the Sherif would actually demand them

[1] See Note 3 at end of chapter.

in writing and hold himself responsible for the consequences of their appearance in the Hejaz.

On January 9th Wingate sent a telegram to the Sherif in these terms. Although many of his entourage were in favour of acceptance, the Sherif hesitated to accept the responsibility. He remained undecided for two days. On the 11th he replied that he had no need of British troops for the moment, although he wished to retain the possibility of calling on them later if circumstances changed.

But Feisal, with Lawrence at his side, had already set out from Yanbo on a two hundred mile flank march up the Red Sea Coast, to Wejh. This was captured on the 23rd by an advance party of Arabs landed from ships. Two days later the British brigade in waiting at Suez was handed back to Murray.

"In War," said Napoleon, "it is not men, but the *man* who counts." It is still more true of irregular war.

One hundred and twenty-one years earlier, in January, 1796, a young man of twenty-six had subtly persuaded the Directory to adopt an audacious plan which likewise began with a flank march along the coast—of the Riviera. Lawrence, now on the threshold of his first Arabian campaign, was exactly two years older than Napoleon Bonaparte in his first Italian campaign—for both were born on the same day of the year, August 15th. Lovers of coincidence may find an extraordinary chain. On October 16th, the day that Lawrence landed in Arabia, Napoleon was made General of Division in reward for his services in the Vendémiaire rising, the crisis that formed his opportunity. On March 27th Napoleon assumed command of the Army of Italy, and Lawrence carried out his first independent attack against the Hejaz railway. On May 10th, the anniversary of the "Bridge of Lodi," from which Napoleon dated his vision of "superhuman" achievement, Lawrence would definitely cut loose from the British mission, to embark, alone with the Arabs, on the expedition that raised the Arab campaign onto a new plane and set him on a pinnacle apart.

But the parallel should not be pressed too far. Napoleon never attained wisdom nor learnt the folly of phantom ambition. Shrinking from truth, he stumbled into the abyss.

NOTE 1

At the meeting on November 2nd the War Committee bowed before Robertson's rigid obduracy, but they did not share his easy view that "the possible occupation of Rabegh by the Turks had never been a matter of much importance." Instructions were sent to Wemyss "to give all the naval protection to Rabegh which he could," and to land a naval detachment if necessary. The Sirdar was to send whatever military aid he could spare from the Sudan. The French Government was asked to dispatch any troops they had available near the scene. After Wingate's telegram of November 7th there was a fresh impulse to develop these vague provisions into definite measures, an impulse which gained impetus from a fresh move by the French. Brémond had added his voice to the appeal for a brigade, and at the same time had expressed unwillingness to allow his detachment of artillery and machine-guns to leave Suez unless they were assured of proper infantry support at Rabegh. The French Government backed him and suggested to the Foreign Office that Murray could easily spare a brigade from the Sinai front in view of the Turks' relatively low strength there. It also offered to lend Murray a couple of Senegalese battalions in order to facilitate the withdrawal of one of his British brigades.

This French intervention was none the more palatable to Robertson because of its implied reflection on his strategical dispositions.

NOTE 2

Robertson's report further stated that troops could not be taken from any other theatre, and that if they were taken from Murray's force in Sinai he would have to suspend the advance to El Arish which the War Committee had ordered. (In view of this declaration, it is interesting to note that there were in Sinai only two weak Turkish divisions, totalling some 13,000 rifles, opposed to the British, who had more than treble their strength.) On the other hand, if this advance was made it would relieve the menace to Mecca far more effectively than any landing at Rabegh "by threatening the enemy's communications with the Hejaz." "It was, moreover, improbable that the reported advance from Medina on Rabegh and Mecca was being attempted, and, if attempted, that it would succeed." "The difficulties to be overcome would be enormous, even for the Turks who were accustomed to desert warfare." For all these reasons, he submitted in conclusion "the expedition ought not to be sent."

The report, certainly, is proof that a General Staff appreciation may have more resemblance to counsel's address to the jury on behalf of his client than to a judicial summing up. The idea that an eventual advance to El Arish on the Mediterranean coast six weeks hence might have an immediate effect on the situation near Mecca, and be an effective threat to the Hejaz railway, 120 miles distant across the Dead Sea and desert, is peculiarly amusing. It certainly surpasses any of those amateur calculations of Lloyd George's which Robertson was so fond of denouncing. The humour of this confident assurance becomes still more apparent in retrospect when we remember that the British advance was held up a few miles beyond El Arish, and there remained until the following autumn.

NOTE 3

Dissatisfied both with the situation and Hussein's attitude, Brémond, who was an ardent advocate of armed intervention, crossed the Red Sea to visit the Sirdar, accompanied by Captain (later Lord) Lloyd. He declared to Wingate that nothing could stop the Turks, and that money alone was keeping the Arabs in the field. Hence, to avert the fall of Mecca, he urged that the British should at once land at Aqaba or advance by Gaza to cut the Hejaz railway, that they should occupy Rabegh in strength, that they should occupy Wejh as another base of action against the railway, and leave Medina alone for the time being. When Wingate pointed out that he had no troops available, and could barely scrape together fifteen hundred to deal with the local menace in Darfur, Brémond remarked that Uganda had furnished no men to Britain, whereas French West Africa had raised tens of thousands.

CHAPTER VII

THE WEDGE

December, 1916–January, 1917

Lawrence's advice against sending British troops to the Hejaz wins him favour—He is sent himself, instead—He arrives to find Feisal driven back and Yanbo in danger—A searchlight display restores the balance—A new move turns the scales—Feisal's army sets out on a march up the coast—The capture of Wejh turns the flank of the Turkish menace to Mecca

ON LAWRENCE's return to Cairo after his first visit to Feisal, he had written a report for Clayton which was similar to but rather stronger than the views he had expressed at Khartoum. It was "a short and very pungent note, opposing the dispatch of a brigade, root and branch." He considered that the Arabs were capable of maintaining themselves in the hill-belt, which crossed the routes to Mecca, so long as they were supplied with plenty of light automatics, with adequate artillery to offset the Turkish guns, and with technical advice. But from his own experience he was definitely against the dispatch of British troops; in his opinion their arrival would create so much suspicion and prejudice among the Arabs that it would destroy such unity as now existed. Moreover, he regarded British infantry as too cumbersome for operations in such barren and rugged country, and thought that the Turks were quite capable of evading a static force at Rabegh.

He pitched his argument the more strongly because of the preparations he found in progress to send a force. Soon afterwards he had cause to reinforce his objections because of his discovery that Brémond, in pressing for its dispatch, was influenced by political motives—Lawrence's suspicions were aroused by a conversation in which Brémond hinted that, if the Arabs resented the landing of Allied troops, their resentment would be directed against the Sherif, who would in consequence become more dependent on Allied support—and more subservient.

On Lawrence's part, also, one may surmise that his objection to a military expedition was not purely military. Brémond, later, hinted that Lawrence's objection was due to personal ambition, as "the arrival of a British general and a brigade would have relegated him to a subordinate position." This suspicion does not accord with the fact that Lawrence first raised his voice against the proposal at a time when there was no thought of sending him to the Hejaz and when he had no desire to go.

There was a far more natural reason, in Lawrence's long-standing desire to see the Arabs achieve their freedom and keep it independent of foreign tutelage. If he did not wish to see them "protected" by the British, still less did he wish to see them absorbed by the French, and turned into good Frenchmen. The improvement in their civic virtues would not, for him, compensate the loss of what he regarded as the essential spirit of liberty. And the French were not only a more extensive threat to his idea, but a more active threat. They would be the cuckoo in his nest.

Lawrence's report earned him new respect in a quarter where he had formerly been regarded as a disrespectful and eccentric young civilian in uniform. He was suddenly translated in the eyes of General Headquarters from amateur to expert status. This, however, is the usual fortune of critics when their criticism happens to suit their professional audience. Lawrence's observations and arguments against sending a brigade to Rabegh were most welcome to those who did not wish to spare it. "Murray and his staff turned round and said I was a broth of a boy. They telegraphed my note *in extenso* to Robertson, who sent me a message of thankfulness."

So excellent an expert must be utilized further and sent where he could continue to uphold such sound views. As this newly formed opinion in high quarters coincided with that already held by the man who knew his work best, Lawrence was told by Clayton to return to Yanbo, where he would act as liaison officer with, and adviser to, Feisal. His reaction to this new commission, which was to be of such far-reaching consequence, may be related in his own words:

"This being much against my grain I urged my complete unfitness for the job: said I hated responsibility—obviously the position of a conscientious adviser would be responsible—and that in all my life objects had been gladder to me than persons, and ideas than objects. So the duty of succeeding with men, of disposing them to any purpose, would be doubly hard for me. I was unlike a soldier: hated soldiering: whereas the Sirdar had telegraphed to London for certain regular officers competent to direct the Arab War.

"Clayton replied that they might be months arriving, and meanwhile Feisal must be linked to us . . . So I had to go; leaving to others the Arab Bulletin I had founded, the maps I wished to draw, and the file of the war-changes of the Turkish Army, all fascinating activities in which my training helped me; to take up a role for which I had no inclination. As our revolt succeeded, onlookers have praised its leadership: but behind the scenes lay all the vices of amateur control, experimental councils, divisions, whimsicality."

If there is a flick of irony in these last words, there is, I am sure, none of that false modesty which the foreigner terms English hypocrisy, and with which the Englishman struggles to hide his thoughts from himself, succeeding in proportion to his individual lack of humour. Lawrence's words are rather those of a man who realizes the limitations of other men all the better for being conscious of his own, and whose low opinion of himself springs from an acute perception of the lowliness of all humanity. To me at least, his words are the natural product of his strange, because uncommonly successful, power of detachment.

It was early December when Lawrence landed again at Yanbo, where the British had now established a base for Feisal and were accumulating supplies. There also was the nucleus of a regular Arab force in process of formation, and a British instructor, Captain Garland of the Egyptian Army, who was a connoisseur in the art of demolition by dynamite. Lawrence was to be one of his most apt pupils. Down south at Rabegh several more British officers, headed by Joyce and Davenport, had arrived with three hundred Egyptian troops and a flight of the Royal Flying Corps. These officers were also helping to train several hundred assorted Arabs who formed another instalment of the new Sherifian Regular Army. How many they were no one exactly knew, for their Turk-trained officers had retained the modern Turkish, or 18th century British, habit of drawing rations for a generously estimated number.

Lawrence rode inland to Mubarak, where he came unexpectedly in sight of hundreds of camp-fires, and heard "the roaring of thousands of excited camels" as well as other sounds of confusion and alarm. He found that it was Feisal's force, just arrived, and Feisal himself explained the cause. A Turkish detachment had slipped round his outposts in the Wadi Safra and cut them off; then descended on Bir Said where they took Zeid's main contingent by surprise, and dispersed it in wild flight. Feisal himself, who had left Zeid on guard while he tried to raise another tribal area, had heard of the disaster and rushed back with his five thousand to bar the road to Yanbo.

There was such an air of panic in the encampment during the night that it was fortunate the Turks did not follow up their success. Before dawn Feisal decided to move to another position, as much to distract his men's minds as on tactical grounds. Lawrence spent the next two days with Feisal, and during them obtained an insight into Feisal's methods of command which intensified his admiration for the leader who was holding together so shifting and shiftless a force.

"Feisal, fighting to make up their lost spirits, did it most surely by lending of his own to everyone within reach. He was accessible to all who stood outside his tent . . . and he never cut short petitions, even when men came in chorus with their grief in a song of many verses, and sang them around us in the dark . . . His extreme patience was a further lesson to me of what native headship in Arabia meant. His self-control seemed equally great."

When Lawrence saw the arrival of the sheikhs of the Harb and Ageyl whose carelessness had been mainly responsible for the disaster, he feared a scene, and thought of the meaning of Feisal's name —"the sword flashing downward in the stroke." But, instead, Feisal rallied them "gently, chaffing them for having done this or that." "I never saw an Arab leave him dissatisfied or hurt—a tribute to his tact and to his memory; for he seemed never to halt for loss of a fact; nor to stumble over a relationship."

Lawrence also paints a picture of camp routine. Just before daybreak the army Imam uttered the call to prayer, in a strident voice. As soon as he ended, Feisal's Imam "cried gently and musically from just outside the tent"—an ordinary bell-tent with a camp-bed, and rug, and an old Baluch prayer carpet. An hour or so later, the flap of Feisal's tent was thrown back, as a sign that he was open to callers from the household. "After the morning's news a tray of breakfast would be carried in." It consisted of dates, with occasionally some odd biscuits or cereals. Then Feisal dictated his correspondence to his two secretaries, the task being liquidated with sips of bitter coffee and sweet tea alternately. At about eight o'clock Feisal would buckle on his ceremonial dagger and walk across to the reception tent, sitting down at the end facing the open side, with his entourage in a semi-circle behind, and the suppliants waiting outside for their turn.

The audience was usually finished by noon, when the household and guests reassembled in the living-tent to await the luncheon-tray, laden with many dishes. But Feisal himself was a very light eater—he smoked incessantly—and was apt to wave the tray away too soon for the satisfaction of those who loved their food. After lunch came talk, over coffee and syrupy green tea, and then after perhaps an hour's retirement to his tent, the reception was renewed. A walk followed, if there was time. Soon after six the supper tray appeared, followed by talk, the recital of Arabic verses, and an occasional game of chess, with cups of tea at intervals until, very late, Feisal retired to sleep.

Feisal asked Lawrence if he would wear Arab clothes while in camp, as khaki was associated by the Arabs with Turkish officers, whereas Arab dress would not only attract less notice but also help his acceptance by the tribesmen as one of their accredited leaders. On Lawrence agreeing, he was fitted out "in splendid white silk and gold embroidered wedding garments which had been sent to Feisal lately (was it a hint?) by his great-aunt in Mecca."

It was after this visit that Lawrence made a report on the Arab forces which foreshadows his future strategy—"As a mass they are not formidable, since they have no corporate spirit or discipline, or mutual confidence. Man by man they are good: I would suggest that the smaller the unit that is acting, the better will be its performance. A thousand of them in a mob would be ineffective against one-fourth their number of trained troops: but three or four of them in their own valleys or hills, would account for a dozen Turkish soldiers. When they sit still they get nervous, and anxious to return home. Feisal himself goes rather to pieces in the same conditions. When, however, they have plenty to do, and are riding about in small parties tapping the Turks here and there, retiring always when the

Turks advance, to appear in another direction immediately after, then they are in their element, and must cause the enemy not only anxiety but bewilderment."

Lawrence's stay in camp was brief. It was more urgent to see if the defences of Yanbo were progressing. But Feisal followed close on his heels. The Turks had attacked again soon after Lawrence's departure and after a long-range exchange which offered the illusion of success, the men of the Juheina tribe on Feisal's left wing had suddenly careered off the battlefield. Their subsequent excuse was that, being tired and thirsty, they had dashed back to camp to make themselves a cup of coffee. An Arab battle had certainly a flavour of comic opera, but the humour of this could best be appreciated in retrospect. The disappearance of the Juheina had led Feisal to fall back hurriedly on Yanbo. Lawrence had telegraphed to Captain Boyle for Naval aid, but the question was whether it could arrive in time. "Our war seemed entering its last act." He did not miss the opportunity of taking "a fine photograph," from the parapet of the Medina gate, of the fugitive army as Feisal led it into Yanbo.

This was a good place to defend if only the weapons were available. Built on a coral reef, some twenty feet above the water, the little town was half-encircled by the sea while the land approaches ran across a flat expanse of sand that could be raked by machine-guns from the walls and also by ships' guns from the sea. These arrived with reassuring promptness. Boyle concentrated five ships within twenty-four hours, sending one of them, the shallow-draught monitor M31, up to the end of the south-eastern creek of the harbour, where she lay across the Turks' probable line of approach, dominating it with her six-inch guns. As darkness fell her searchlight rays crossed with those of the *Dufferin* on the plain outside the town, flood-lighting the approach.

The air was tense that night. About eleven there was an alarm when a Turkish reconnoitring patrol encountered the outposts, and Garland called out the garrison to man the defences, which had been hastily wired and buttressed with earth. All the ships' searchlights were turned on to traverse the plain with their beams. But nothing more happened. When Lawrence himself woke, after a good eight hours' sleep on board the *Suva*, the plain was deserted. "Afterwards, we heard the Turks' hearts had failed them at the silence and the blaze of lighted ships from end to end of the harbour, with the eerie beams of the searchlights revealing the bleakness of the glacis they would have to cross. So they turned back: and that night, I believe they lost their war."

So it may well have seemed to those at Yanbo at that critical moment. Yet, with a longer horizon, the idea of a single dramatic turning point seems questionable. It does not accord with the nature of the Arab war, diffuse in time and space. In such a war, ideas that gradually evolved into a changed *state* had a more decisive significance than any particular act. If the change that was now about to develop might be dated from the passive pyrotechnic display at Yanbo, a discussion which took place on New Year's Day, 1917, has a greater claim, because it gave birth to the idea that made an old project practicable.

Back in October Feisal had proposed an advance along the coast to occupy Wejh, 180 miles north of Yanbo, and form a new base there from which to operate against the Hejaz railway, threatening the life-line of the Medina Garrison. But the project was postponed and its prospects undermined by the Arab reverses in December. The Sherifian forces had been thrust back on the defensive, and were clinging precariously to Yanbo and Rabegh. It was only Feisal's personal hold over the tribes that was keeping them together. If he were to move away, his departure might easily spell the fall of both Yanbo and Rabegh, for neither Ali nor Zeid had the same power of personality and their performances hitherto had diminished such prestige as they had enjoyed. Yet if Feisal remained the end was almost as probable. The immobilization of the Arabs, if it continued, would soon mean the demobilization of their forces.

Wilson came up to Yanbo, on his way to Egypt, and urged on Feisal the necessity of the move to Wejh, as well as its value. He promised that the Fleet would support the advance and also safeguard Rabegh until Wejh had been occupied. Feisal was fully alive to the advantages, but still dubious about the risks. The cloud was dispersed by the light of a new idea, which promised to distract the attention of the Turks from the coast in the south while Feisal was moving north. It originated with Lawrence, although completed by Feisal's local knowledge in the choice of the best sites.

This vital suggestion was that Abdulla, who had advanced from

Mecca in December to the neighbourhood of Medina with four or five thousand irregulars, should move to the Wadi Ais some fifty miles north of Medina. From this well-watered valley amid the hills he could not only be an immediate menace to the railway but could intercept the caravans that were bringing supplies to Medina from Hail in Central Arabia. The Turks were making slow progress towards Rabegh, hampered by the raids of the Harb tribe in their rear, and they would hardly fail to react to this greater menace to their life-line.

Once adopted, the plan was put into operation with remarkable promptness. On January 2nd Lawrence carried out a preliminary move to gain experience in raiding and help cloak the departure from Yanbo. With a party of thirty-five Arab camel-men he rode south-east to a valley near the Turkish lines of communication, climbed over the precipitous ridge, and opened fire on the tents of a Turkish post. Satisfied with the panic they had caused, Lawrence's party crawled back over the ridge, regained their camels, and rode back to Yanbo, bringing in two stray Turks whom they had run across.

The same morning, January 3rd, the Arab army made a preliminary bound to Owais, a group of wells fifteen miles inland from Yanbo, and about ten miles north of Mubarak. Here they could still cover Yanbo and yet have taken a stride on their way to Wejh, while awaiting a reply from Abdulla. For simplicity of organization Feisal made up the mass of his expedition from the Juheina tribe, in whose territory he was now operating, although he added a sprinkling of the Harb, the Ateiba, and the Billi—in whose territory Wejh lay— to give it "a many-tribed character." He also took his Ageyl bodyguard, twelve hundred dashing camel-men, who had been originally raised by the Sheikh of Russ from the peasants of the Central Arabian oases for service in the Turkish Army, and had come over to Feisal complete when the Revolt took place.

Lawrence accompanied Feisal on the march out to Owais, a colourful procession. When the starting signal was given Feisal and his bodyguard mounted, while the other contingents, standing beside their couched camels, lined the road waiting to follow in his wake. As he passed each in turn they gave a silent salute, to which he responded with a "Peace upon you." Once the column was on the

way the drums struck up and the whole broke into a song in honour
of Feisal and his family. Lawrence rode on his left and Sharraf on
his right, while immediately behind came three banners of faded
crimson silk with gilt spikes. "It looked like a river of camels, for
we filled up the Wadi to the tops of its banks, and poured along in
a quarter of a mile long stream."

Lawrence himself rode back from Owais to Yanbo to settle details
of the naval co-operation in the advance on Wejh. As a precaution
against any sudden Turkish spring on Yanbo, he took the opportunity of moving the accumulated stores aboard the *Hardinge*. The
problem of loading them quickly without civilized port facilities was
solved by a happy expedient. The *Hardinge* had large square ports
on her lowest troop-deck along the water-level; these were opened
and a thousand tons of rifles, ammunition, food and other supplies
were pushed straight in "like posting letters in a box." And when
Boyle arrived in the *Suva*, he generously promised to allow the
Hardinge to be used as a floating base throughout the northward
march. Thus of old had the Persian host been victualled in their
invasion of Greece.

Meantime Ali, under pressure from Wilson and the Sherif, advanced some forty miles out from Rabegh, while the British aircraft
bombed the Turkish encampments. This drew Fakhri's attention
effectively and led Ali to push raids almost to Medina. Indeed, he
became so emboldened that he telegraphed back to say he was about
"to take up dispositions for the siege of Medina!" He had actually
moved a few miles nearer, when a Turkish air-raid on his own camp
caused a fresh recoil. But by that time Feisal was in Wejh.

Abdulla for his part had continued his march north as planned. It
had led the Bedouin to rally to his cause; they surprised and destroyed a Turkish battalion posted south of Medina. On January
13th Abdulla himself attacked and captured a Turkish convoy bound
for Medina and laden with gold—nearly half the Bedouin then disappeared with their loot. On January 19th Abdulla established himself safely in the Wadi Ais.

As soon as Feisal had received news that Abdulla was moving, he
had begun to slip by stages behind the coastal hills to Bir el Waheidi,
where he was nearly half way to Wejh and only four miles from the
coast, at Umlej. Lawrence went thither by sea, with Boyle, to await

him. They were joined on the 16th, the day after their arrival, by Major Vickery, of the Royal Artillery, who was the forerunner of the newly-formed British Military Mission under Newcombe.

Vickery, from long service in the Sudan, was a first-rate Arab linguist as well as a most capable soldier. Among other Regulars he was strongly unconventional, both in appearance and outlook, but like others of this stimulating type he was apt to remember his caste and don a conventional mask in face of unprofessional soldiers. His own informal way was affronted by Lawrence's, and especially by what seemed airy talk of the Arab army "tapping at the gates of Damascus within a year." Lawrence's exultant burst of enthusiasm grated on Vickery, who had not felt the depression now magically lifting as Yanbo was left. Vickery, on the other hand, jarred Lawrence by a remark that service in Arabia was professional suicide, and also offended his sense of fitness by wearing a British helmet under his Arab headcloth. An old Arab guide, who saw Vickery riding in front of him, suddenly cried "Mashallah, the head of an ox!" astonished at the spread of his headcloth—and this so tickled Lawrence's sense of humour that his laughter stung. Thus a needless friction was generated between two men, both exceptional in their own ways. Vickery disappeared from the scene too early to share in the ultimate triumph, or to discover in Lawrence those qualities which made other Regulars such surprising admirers and so surprisingly ready to be guided by the man who was nominally their junior.

Vickery, on arrival, went with Boyle and Lawrence to Bir el Waheidi to confer with Feisal as to the arrangements for the advance on Wejh. The force totalled over ten thousand, of whom 5,100 were camelry, and 5,300 were on foot. Fifty, whom Maulud proudly called cavalry, were mounted on mules and had already proved so useful that Lawrence had telegraphed to Egypt for another fifty mules, which were now landed—they stampeded as soon as they were ashore and caused a hilariously exciting disturbance before they were recaptured and saddled. For its fire-support the force had ten machine-guns and a battery of four Krupp mountain-guns, now manned by Arab crews. It had been found that as long as they were handled by Egyptians, the Arabs, as at Mubarak, were apt to leave the guns to maintain the battle while they took a rest. Another advantage of the transfer was that, instead of the battery having a complement of 360

THE KAABA, MECCA

Photo. T. E. Lawrence

DAWN IN NAKHL MUBARAK (FEISAL'S ENCAMPMENT). DECEMBER, 1916

camels, in the hands of the Arabs this was reduced to eighty, although the same amount of ammunition was carried.

Indeed, the whole baggage of Feisal's force was carried by 380 camels, and although so great a reduction was only possible through the aid of the Navy as a floating-base, it threw into vivid relief the Arabs' relative independence of transport in comparison with any regular force. In moving light lay the key to success, for the stretch of country that the force had now to cross was so barren and waterless that hunger and thirst were serious risks, especially as Feisal was taking along so many militarily superfluous foot for the sake of creating a moral impression of Sherifian power and Arab unity.

The last water before reaching Wejh was at Abu Zereibat in Hamdh, nearly fifty miles short of their goal. It was decided that the army should be split up into sections, leaving Bir el Waheidi on the 18th and moving independently to Abu Zareibat, where they would concentrate on the 20th. And to ease the further problem of the final lap, Boyle agreed to land twenty tons of water two days later at Habban, where there was supposed to be a possible harbour.

The actual attack would be supported by the Navy with six ships, and sea-planes to direct their fire. The *Hardinge* also took on board a party of five hundred Arabs who were to be landed, with a naval detachment, on the unguarded northern flank of Wejh, at dawn on the 23rd, by which time it was reckoned that the camelry would have closed all the enemy's bolt-holes into the interior. Vickery took charge of this landing party.

At noon on the 18th all was complete. Like Sherman's army at Atlanta in 1864, also famous for its economy of baggage, Feisal's was about to plunge into the depths of the unknown, but depths known to be more barren, from which they could only hope to emerge if and when they clasped hands with the Fleet at their distant goal. As with Sherman's army, the telegraph, here a wireless telegraph, brought them as a final comfort good news from the theatre they were quitting—that Yanbo and Rabegh were still secure and Abdulla close to the Wadi Ais.

"After lunch the tent was struck. We went to our camels, where they were couched in a circle, saddled and loaded, each held short by the slave standing on its double fore-leg. The kettle-drummer, waiting beside Ibn Dakhil, who commanded the bodyguard, rolled his drum seven or eight times, and everything became still. We watched Feisal. He got up from his rug . . . caught the saddle-pommels in his hands, put his knee on the side and said aloud, 'Make God your agent.' The slave released the camel, which sprang up. When it was on its feet Feisal passed his other leg across its back, swept his skirts and his cloak under him by a wave of the arm, and settled himself in the saddle. As his camel moved we had jumped for ours, and the whole mob rose together."

The Ageyl, on an order, moved out to right and left as wings. A patter of drums, and the poet of the right wing burst into a song, of Feisal and the delights he would afford them in Wejh. The right wing took up the refrain. A few moments later the poet of the left wing retorted with a similar extempore verse, and then the whole bodyguard burst into their marching song.

The march had not gone far, when two solitary horsemen appeared. They proved to be the Emir of the Juheina and Colonel Newcombe, who had just landed at Umlej, heard the news and galloped to catch the column. He was brimming over with joy at being in time for the adventure, and he brought to it an outlook that accorded with that of both Feisal and Lawrence.

His coming, which might so easily have caused discord, because of his seniority, made for harmony as well as activity. "Skinface" Newcombe was one of those exceptional men who, themselves standing out above the mass, recognize unhesitatingly the superior gifts of another, because they are free from the jealousy which commonly enfolds like a cloud the peaks of mankind's range. Long sojourn in the desert may have aided Newcombe's clear sight. He judged men by their worth, not by their rank, and having convinced himself of Lawrence's qualities his sole idea was to give them full scope. Like a cricketer who comes in to bat late in the innings when his side's best batsman is master of the bowling, Newcombe sought nothing better than to back up the man who was making the runs. When he joined the expedition he asked Lawrence, "What do you want me to do?" —saying that "seniority didn't matter a damn."

One of the first points on which he took Lawrence's advice was on the question of wearing Arab dress. Lawrence remarked that "if a few Arabs were to go to Wigan in Arab dress, the children would probably throw stones at them." Newcombe saw the point and from that time on dressed as an Arab as long as he was with Feisal's army.

The second day's march was delayed by heavy rain until the afternoon; towards evening progress quickened when the force reached the Egyptian pilgrim road, a broad, well-beaten track that ran beside the shore. More delays were caused by lack of water on the route, and lack of time-sense among the Arabs. The primitive Juheina had no unit of time smaller than the day, or of distance longer than the span or shorter than the stage—itself a variable, according to the rider's inclination and his camel. And they could not realize a number larger than the digits. Such conditions were a complication to staff work!

The force was two days behind time-table when at last it reached the Wadi Hamdh, a trough fifteen miles wide which was the mouth of a dry river longer than the Tigris. Here was the flood-water pool of Abu Zareibat, where they camped, and were joined by Sherif Nasir of Medina, young and audacious, who had been harassing the Turks at Wejh for weeks past. Many also of the Billi tribes came to swell the advancing host, and to consume more time in talk. Newcombe decided to ride ahead on a fast camel to meet Boyle at Habban, arrange that the *Hardinge* should return there again with water, and secure if possible a postponement of the naval part of the attack on Wejh. But on reaching Habban, himself delayed by the Arabs' leisureliness, he found that the *Hardinge* had left an hour before. So he could do nothing, beyond waiting until she returned—a trying experience for so energetic a leader.

Lawrence, following next day with the army, heard distant firing that suggested the Navy had grown tired of waiting for the Arabs.

When they at least reached Habban on the afternoon of the 24th, they found that the *Hardinge* had returned and her boats were landing water-tanks in a hazardous sea. They heard also that Wejh had already been attacked, although the *Hardinge* had come away before the end. After making a heroic speech to the garrison on the importance of fighting to the last man when he heard that Feisal had reached Abu Zareibat, the Governor had slipped off in the night with his few camelry, heading for the Hejaz railway. The two hundred Turkish infantry had stayed to fight, but were subdued by the naval gun-fire, so that the landing party captured the place without much difficulty. Only about a third of the garrison escaped.

The news, and the prospect of loot that might soon be gone, now so quickened the time-sense of the Arabs that they began trickling northward during the night. Only a small proportion had been able to get a drink from the water-tanks at Habban, for the animals had come first. The men, indeed, covered the last fifty miles on half a gallon of water and no food. But no physical pangs could check them now. When dawn broke, Feisal and his assistants rallied the contingents ready for the final advance, and attack if necessary, for it was uncertain whether the garrison was still holding out. Fragments of it were soon met, trying to escape, but only one put up a show of resistance.

No further shot greeted the Arabs as they crested the last ridge, and they found the little town in the possession of the Arab landing party, which had lost a score of men killed. By European standards it was a cheaply won victory, but Lawrence had become so imbued with Arab standards that the news made him rather uneasy because of the way its ripples would be likely to spread through all the families bereaved. Bloodless victories were the kind that the Arabs appreciated, as an inspiration to further ones, and Lawrence's understanding of this need marked a stage in the evolution of his theory of irregular warfare.

Nevertheless, the capture of Wejh proved a turning point for good in the evolution of the Arab Revolt. From that moment the danger of Mecca waned, and a new danger to the Turkish garrison of Medina loomed on the horizon. For the moment it was only a potential danger, as Wejh was one hundred and fifty miles from the railway life-line, but it had the practical effect of an actual stroke without the cost of it. The initiative passed definitely to the Arabs. British aircraft and Arab spies reported a general reflux of the Turkish troops towards Medina. Zeid was emboldened to advance, and found the defiles of Medjiz and El Ghair abandoned.

A large part of the Turkish Hejaz force was drawn off bit by bit to guard the railway. A detachment of about five thousand, known as the 2nd Composite Force, was formed at Tebuk, an important station three hundred miles north of Medina. Another, called the 1st Composite Force, was formed at Ma'an from battalions of the Turkish 7th Division brought down from Syria—another entry to the credit account of the Wejh move. This force, originally about three thousand strong, later rose to seven thousand. Every unit of force drawn north brought compound interest to the Arab cause, augmenting the adherents of the Sherif as the Turk's power of retaliation diminished. Moreover, these Turkish forces could no longer be concentrated. They had to be parcelled out among the many stations on the line, posted in wire-surrounded block houses. Instead, merely, of division of one into three, it meant multiple subdivision.

Such were the results that flowed from this driving of a wedge into the flank of the railway zone on which the Turks depended. Hitherto the Arabs had knocked at the pointed end of the railway, and hurt themselves in the effort. Now they had exposed its vulnerable length. The almost bloodless move to Wejh had pierced no vital organ, won no decisive battle, but it had changed the Turks at Medina into a beleaguered garrison although they suffered no actual siege.

* * * * *

INTERLUDE

The Art of Handling Arabs—and Others

The domestic sequel to Wejh was less happy than the strategic. Relations between the Arabs and the British military mission passed through a difficult phase, during which the issue balanced on a knife-edge—not merely proverbial. That improvement came and prospect widened was due to Feisal's example of tact, to the proof given by several of the British Officers that they were capable of holding their own in Arab tests of endurance, and to Lawrence's subtly extending influence—especially with Feisal.

The weeks that followed the capture of Wejh had given rise to many awkward incidents, and an ominous atmosphere. The Arab chiefs were so quick to suspect interference that they were ever ready to resent the presence of infidels. Many of them behaved as if the British officers were their servants, and set an example of rudeness that was imitated by their followers, as well as by their slaves. When a remonstrance was made to Nasir he replied, "Don't forget that until a month ago we never had a European in this country; if we had, we should have shot him. You must give us time to get used to it."

On another occasion, when Newcombe asked questions of an envoy from Jauf, the Arab contemptuously remarked that he had not come to meet a Kafir, but to see Feisal.

When this and other instances of contemptuous behaviour came to Feisal's ears he assembled his followers and spoke to them straightly, telling them not to forget when dealing with a British officer that he had come far to help them, deserved respect, and should be treated as one of themselves. Better still, Feisal set the example himself. Thus, gradually, the British officers came to be tolerated and even, in varying degree, appreciated.

Nevertheless, there was a long way to go between this equality and the ascendency which one among them later attained. At this time Lawrence still kept in the background—in the conference tent as well as outside. Although he was already in Feisal's confidence he paraded it so little that many of the Arabs who came to Feisal's camp ignored his presence or treated him with scant respect. To some of his own countrymen, bred in the tradition of British superiority and commissioned dignity, his indifference to slights that made their blood boil was a source of perplexity. Astonished at his unruffled manner when slaves brushed past him or spat in his presence,[1] they were inclined to ascribe his capacity "to eat humble pie" to his upbringing, to his own "Street Arab" past. But on the memory of some of the more discerning was engraved a picture of Lawrence "sitting mute, giving no orders but using his influence, watching everything that passed and weaving his schemes."

When the campaign moved north, his method would change—and he would come out more into the open. Not only because his own prestige had grown, but because none of the Sherifs, save Feisal, carried the weight in the north that they did in the Hejaz. Lawrence's journey north in May, which culminated in the capture of Aqaba two months later, would mark the transition.

But from his earlier experience he evolved a theory of the art of

[1] Lawrence has enlarged upon this point for my education, remarking that the officers' astonishment showed that they "knew more about the manners of Egypt than of Arabia. The slave was only behaving before me as in his master's presence. Arab grandees habitually play with their slaves. I was *glad* to be accepted as natural.

"Arabian slaves are privileged persons, and rank next to children. A slave, for instance, can eat with his master, and usually does. A servant, never. A slave can sleep with his master—a servant must sleep outside the door. A slave can call his master by name—a servant, not."

handling Arabs which he wrote out in the form of "Twenty Seven Articles"—as a confidential guide to newcomers from the British Army who might wish to profit by that experience. It is so illuminating, not least on his own mind, as to be worth reproducing in extract:

The "Twenty Seven Articles"

Handling Hejaz Arabs is an art, not a science, with exceptions and no obvious rules. . . .

1. A bad start is difficult to atone for, and the Arabs form their judgments on externals that we ignore. When you have reached the inner circle in a tribe, you can do as you please with yourself and them.

2. Learn all you can about your Ashraf [1] and Bedu. Get to know their families, clans and tribes, friends and enemies, wells, hills and roads. Do all this by listening and by indirect inquiry. Do not ask questions. Get to speak their dialect of Arabic, not yours. Until you can understand their allusions avoid getting deep into conversation, or you will drop bricks. . . .

3. In matters of business deal only with the commander of the army, column, or party in which you serve. Never give orders to anyone at all, and reserve your directness and advice for the C.O., however great the temptation (for efficiency's sake) of dealing direct with his underlings. . . .

4. Win and keep the confidence of your leader. Strengthen his prestige at your expense before others if you can. Never refuse or quash schemes he may put forward; but ensure that they are put forward in the first instance privately to you. Always approve them, and after praise modify them insensibly, causing the suggestions to come from him, until they are in accord with your own opinion. When you attain this point, hold him to it, keep a tight grip of his ideas, and push him forward as firmly as possible, but secretly, so that no one but himself (and he not too clearly) is aware of your pressure.

5. Remain in touch with your leader as constantly and unobtrusively as you can. Live with him, that at mealtimes and at audience you may be naturally with him in his tent. Formal visits to give

[1] The Arab plural of "Sherif."

advice are not so good as the constant dropping of ideas in casual talk. When stranger sheikhs come in for the first time to swear allegiance and offer service, clear out of the tent. If their first impression is of foreigners in the confidence of the Sherif, it will do the Arab cause much harm.

6. Be shy of too close relations with subordinates. Continual intercourse with them will make it impossible for you to avoid going behind or beyond the instructions that the Arab C.O. has given them on your advice, and in so disclosing the weakness of his position you altogether destroy your own.

7. Treat the sub-chiefs of your force quite easily and lightly. In this way you hold yourself above their level. Treat the leader, if a Sherif, with respect. He will return your manner and you and he will then be alike, and above the rest. Precedence is a serious matter among the Arabs and you must attain it.

8. Your ideal position is when you are present and not noticed. Do not be too intimate, too prominent or too earnest. Avoid being identified too long or too often with any tribal sheikh. To do your work you must be above jealousies, and you lose prestige if you are associated with a tribe or class, and its inevitable feuds. . . .

9. Magnify and develop the growing conception of the Sherifs as the natural aristocracy of the Arabs. Inter-tribal jealousies make it impossible for any sheikh to obtain a commanding position, and the only hope of union in nomad Arabia is that the Ashraf be universally acknowledged as the ruling class. The Arab reverence for pedigree and the Prophet give hope for the ultimate success of the Ashraf.

10. Call your Sherif "Sidi" in public and private. Call other people by their ordinary names, without title.

11. The foreigner and Christian is not a popular person in Arabic . . . Wave a Sherif in front of you like a banner and hide your own mind and person. If you succeed, you will have hundreds of miles of country and thousands of men under your control, and for this it is worth bartering the outward show.

12. Cling tight to your sense of humour. You will need it every day. A dry irony is the most useful type, and repartee of a personal and not too broad character will double your influence with the chiefs . . . Do not cause a laugh at a Sherif except amongst Sherifs.

13. Never lay hands on an Arab; you degrade yourself. You may think the resultant obvious increase of outward respect a gain to you; but what you have really done is to build a wall between you and their inner selves. It is difficult to keep quiet when everything is being done wrong, but the less you lose your temper the greater your advantage. Also then you will not go mad yourself.

14. While very difficult to drive, the Bedu are easy to lead, if you have the patience to bear with them. The less apparent your interference the more your influence. They are willing to follow your advice . . . but they do not mean you or anyone else to be aware of that. It is only after the end of all annoyances that you find at bottom their real fund of goodwill.

15. Do not try to do too much with your own hands. Better the Arabs do it tolerably than that you do it perfectly. It is their war, and you are to help them, not to win it for them. Actually also, under the very odd conditions of Arabia, your practical work will not be as good as, perhaps, you think it is.

16. If you can, without being too lavish, forestall presents to yourself. A well-placed gift is often most effective in winning over a suspicious sheikh. Never receive a present without giving a liberal return. . . . Do not let them ask you for things since their greed will then make them look upon you only as a cow to milk.

17. Wear an Arab headcloth when with a tribe. Bedu have a malignant prejudice against the hat, and believe that our persistence in wearing it . . . is founded on some immoral or irreligious principle . . . if you wear a hat your new Arab friends will be ashamed of you in public.

18. Disguise is not advisable . . . At the same time if you can wear Arab kit when with the tribes you will acquire their trust and intimacy to a degree impossible in uniform. It is, however, dangerous and difficult. They make no special allowances for you when you dress like them. You will be like an actor in a foreign theatre, playing a part day and night for months, without rest, and for an anxious stake. Complete success, which is when the Arabs forget your strangeness and speak naturally before you, counting you as one of themselves, is perhaps only attainable in character: while half success (all that most of us will strive for; the other costs too much) is easier to win in British things, and you yourself will last

longer, physically and mentally, in the comfort that they mean. Also then the Turk will not hang you, when you are caught.

19. If you wear Arab things, wear the best. Clothes are significant among the tribes and you must wear the appropriate, and appear at ease in them. Dress like a Sherif, if they agree to it.

20. If you wear Arab things at all, go the whole way. Leave your English friends and customs on the coast and fall back on Arab habits entirely. It is possible, starting thus level with them, for the European to beat the Arabs at their own game for we have stronger motives for our action, and put more heart into it than they. If you can surpass them you have taken an immense stride towards complete success, but the strain of living and thinking in a foreign and half understood language, the savage food, strange clothes, and stranger ways, with the complete loss of privacy and quiet, and the impossibility of ever relaxing your watchful imitation of others for months on end, provide such an added stress to the ordinary difficulties of dealing with the Bedu, the climate, and the Turk that this road should not be chosen without serious thought.

21. Religious discussions will be frequent. Say what you like about your own side and avoid criticism of theirs, unless you know that the point is external, when you may score heavily by proving it so. With the Bedu, Islam is so all-pervading an element that there is little religiosity, little fervour, and no regard for externals. Do not think from their conduct that they are careless. Their conviction of the truth of their faith, and its share in every act and thought and principle of their daily life is so intimate and intense as to be unconscious, unless roused by opposition. Their religion is as much a part of nature to them as is sleep or food.

22. Do not try to trade on what you know of fighting. The Hejaz confounds ordinary tactics. Learn the Bedu principles of war as thoroughly and as quickly as you can, for till you know them your advice will be no good to the Sherif. Unnumbered generations of tribal raids have taught them more about some parts of the business than we shall ever know. In familiar conditions they fight well, but strange events cause panics. Keep your unit small. . . . The more unorthodox your proceedings, the more likely you are to have the Turks cold, for they lack initiative and expect you to. Don't play for safety.

23. The open reason that Bedu give you for action or inaction

may be true, but always there will be better reasons left for you to divine. You must find these inner reasons . . . before shaping your arguments for one course or another. Allusion is more effective than logical exposition: they dislike concise expression. Their minds work just as ours do, but on different premises. There is nothing unreasonable, incomprehensible, or inscrutable in the Arabs. Experience of them and knowledge of their prejudices will enable you to foresee their attitude and possible course of action in nearly every case.

24. Do not mix Bedu and Syrians, or trained men and tribesmen . . . Arab townsmen and Arab tribesmen regard each other mutually as poor relations, and poor relations are much more objectionable than poor strangers.

25. In spite of Arab example, avoid too free talk about women. It is as difficult a subject as religion, and their standards are so unlike our own that a remark, harmless in English, may appear as unrestrained to them, as some of their statements would look to us, if translated literally.

26. Be as careful of your servants as yourself. . . .

27. The beginning and ending of the secret of handling Arabs is unremitting study of them. Keep always on your guard; never say an unnecessary thing: Watch yourself, and your companions all the time: Hear all that passes, search out what is going on beneath the surface, read their characters, discover their tastes and weaknesses and keep everything you find out to yourself . . . Your success will be proportioned to the amount of mental effort you devote to it.

CHAPTER VIII

SPREADING RIPPLES

February–March, 1917

Feisal's success brings in fresh allies—Operations against the railway are begun—Political friction and French ambitions—Lloyd George urges an advance into Palestine—Despite weak opposition, the advance is slow to mature—"they turn the desert into a workshop and call it war"—The delay brings a threat of Turkish withdrawal from Medina to reinforce Palestine—A call to Lawrence—And a chance for reflection

THE capture of Wejh opened a new horizon in both the political and military spheres. The former received attention first, largely owing to Lawrence's sage advice, pressed with emphasis, that it would be best to enlarge their political base of action before beginning military action—so that the subsequent operations could be of wider range and yet more secure.

The political effects of the wedge became manifest almost immediately, and continued to augment, giving a larger meaning to an old Chief's remark during the advance from Yanbo—"It is not an army, it is a world which is moving on Wejh."

The Billi tribe, for the most part, did not delay to offer their services to the man who had so successfully established himself in their territory. This accession, although an uncertain one, enabled Feisal to release the Juheina to assist Abdulla in the Wadi Ais area.

North of the Billi territory lay the Beni Atiyeh, who likewise promised allegiance and free movement through their country. North of them again, lay the southern-most tribes of that vast area ruled by Nuri Shaalan, the Emir of the Ruwalla, and head of the great confederation of the Anazeh. Although his military support against the Turks could hardly be expected yet, because of his dependence on the markets of Damascus and Baghdad, his benevolent neutrality was essential to an extension of operations. For he controlled the Wadi Sirhan, a two hundred mile chain of water-holes which stretched from Jauf, his capital, to Azrak near the Syrian border. The free use of this communication cord was needed by Feisal if he were to secure the active help of Auda, the great fighting chief of the eastern

Howeitat. And upon Auda's help depended the possibility of extending the tide of revolt to Aqaba and Ma'an.

These desires received promise of fulfilment soon after the occupation of Wejh. First arrived a welcome present of baggage camels from the Ruwalla. Then came emissaries from the eastern Howeitat, while an ever-increasing stream of sheikhs and volunteers from lesser tribes came in to offer allegiance. Them, Feisal made take the oath on the Koran—"to wait while he waited, march when he marched, to yield obedience to no Turk, to deal kindly with all who spoke Arabic, and to put independence above life, family and goods." But oaths notwithstanding, it was mainly Feisal's personality, his tact and his patient impartiality, which stilled their hereditary feuds and kept the peace among them. British gold, dipped out in handfuls, also acted as an ointment.

Another important individual accession was that of Ja'far Pasha, who had last been in action on the far side of Egypt leading the forces of the Senussi against the British. After his capture he had tried to escape from the Citadel at Cairo, but the blanket-rope had, not unexpectedly, failed to bear his weight, and, crippled by his fall, he had been re-taken—and fined the value of the blankets! When he heard of Jemal Pasha's execution of his Arab friends in Syria he volunteered to assist the Sherif and was now given command of the new Arab regular force that was being formed.

Finally, after weeks had passed, Auda himself appeared, gauntly majestic, the very figure of a warrior.

In thirty years of incessant warfare he was said to have slain seventy-five men with his own hand, excluding Turks whom he did not trouble to count. He had been wounded thirteen times, and married twenty-eight times. A slumbering volcano, he was a charming companion until he ceased to smile save that he loved to tell appalling stories about the private character of everyone, himself included. That day of his coming was a day to be remembered. It meant so much to their cause. But he relieved the solemnity by giving them a lighter incident to remember, when he suddenly dashed out of the tent and pounded his false teeth in pieces, explaining—"I had forgotten. Jemal Pasha gave me these. I was eating my lord's bread with Turkish teeth."

By the time Auda joined them, the military sequel to the capture of Wejh was in active development. It took the form of a concerted series of raids on the Hejaz railway, with the aim of interrupting supplies and loosening the Turks' hold on Medina. Now that British officers, of bold initiative and trained judgment, were available, as well as ample explosives, these raids became a far more serious interruption than in the past, when the Arabs had simply pulled up a few rails—usually re-laid by the Turks within a few hours. No longer would trains run into Medina every alternate day with unruffled regularity.

The five hundred mile stretch of railway between Ma'an and Medina was divided into three almost equal sections—Ma'an to Tebuk, Tebuk to Medain Saleh, Medain Saleh to Medina. From Medain Saleh, a caravan route ran eastwards to Hail in central Arabia. Just south of it was El Ala, whence a caravan route ran to the Red Sea coast at Wejh, one hundred and thirty miles distant. But these two important stations, like Tebuk, were strongly garrisoned. Hence the opening raids were aimed above and below them.

The first heavy stroke was delivered by Garland. Setting out from Wejh on February 12th, with a party of fifty Bedouin, and moving south-east he reached the railway at Toweira after an eight days' camel ride. Relying on Arab reports that trains now ran only during the daytime, he judged that he had time to make an extensive break carried out at leisure under cover of the night. He therefore sent a party to lay explosive charges under a bridge south of the station, while he himself mined a section farther down the line. Then to his dismay, he heard the sound of a train coming from the north. It made a brief stop at the station, and then steamed on its way. With only a few minutes in hand he had just time to complete the laying of a reduced charge and to run back from the line—when the train was barely a couple of hundred yards away. The explosion came when he had gone only fifty yards. The engine left the rails, and toppled down the embankment. The crash aroused the Turkish post at the station, and the garrison hurried out of their blockhouses. It was a testimony to the coolness of the Arab entrusted with the other demolition that he paused to fire his charge and blow up the bridge before they reached him.

The raids multiplied in scale and frequency, and Newcombe proved his raiding talents. On the night of March 3rd, he attacked

Dar el Hamra, north of Medain Saleh, with a party of Arabs. The station was stormed, fifteen prisoners were taken, and a stretch of the line was wrecked. More might have been wrecked if the Arabs had been as thorough as in their search for loot.

Hornby became another famous raider. Both he and Newcombe revelled in playing lone hands, and took to Arab dress completely. Later Joyce and Davenport joined in the game, after their arrival from Rabegh.

For Wingate, as well as the officers on the spot, quickly appreciated the advantage of operating against the enemy's tenuous and sensitive flank, instead of against his short hill-barred front below Medina. This led to a progressively northward concentration of force and effort. On March 8th, Wingate gave orders to Wilson to evacuate Rabegh and bring the Egyptian detachments, as well as the Arab regulars, up to Wejh. There also was now installed the flight of aircraft under Major Ross, the Egyptian detachment continuing to act mainly as the guard over its landing ground. The French detachment, however, was only moved as far as Yanbo, where it formed a new base, and continued to assist the forces of Ali and Abdulla. It was now at last reinforced by a mountain battery, for which Brémond had long appealed.

This separation of the French and British also helped to diminish the chances of friction, which, even though personal relations were often good, was so apt to arise from differing political interests and still more, from suspicion of each other's motives. Differences were accentuated, first, by the tendency of Hussein and Abdulla to play off one ally against the others in order to keep them both from interference, and, second, by each ally's fear of arousing Arab suspicions if they appeared to be co-operating too closely. Abdulla, in particular, was ever ready to sow the seeds of distrust. In October, when urging the dispatch of a force to save Rabegh, he had complained to the French—"What the British fear is not Moslem opinion, but that you will come in their train." The capture of Baghdad by the British in March caused a fresh access of mistrust, and Abdulla accused the British of breaking faith with the Sherif. But the Arabs were even more mistrustful of the French efforts to establish a political and commercial footing in the Hejaz, and showed an amusing aptitude in frustrating them.

A fresh source of trouble for both had arisen through Hussein's action at the end of October, 1916, in proclaiming himself—"King of the Arab Nation." Both British and French were taken completely by surprise, and both found it equally unpalatable. For the French it was an obvious challenge to their future intentions in Syria. To the British it was not merely distasteful from the point of view of ultimate policy but had the immediate practical disadvantage of offering offence to the other great Arab Chiefs, especially Ibn Sa'ud, and so being likely to turn them against both Hussein and the British. The High Commissioner in Egypt had promptly telegraphed Hussein to express disapproval. The French and British Governments in accord followed this up by delivering similar notes. They were willing to recognize him as king of the Hejaz and as "chief of the Arab population in revolt against the Turks."

But to find a suitable form of address proved a worse difficulty, because of the various senses attached to the word "Djelala." The French pointed out that it had the meaning of "Majesty" and was employed by them in addressing the Sultan of Morocco. As the British had refused this to the Sultan of Egypt they did not like to cause trouble by granting it to Hussein, and their attitude was interpreted by the French as meaning that they regarded the Hejaz as a British dependency. Eventually, after weeks of agitated correspondence the British officers were instructed to address him as "your Lordship." It mattered little because there was no exact relationship between Arabic and European words, and commonsense soon led both British and French representatives on the spot to modify their instructions accordingly.

There were cross-currents also in the military sphere—and undercurrents. Stimulated by the capture of Wejh and anxious to use his large detachment still in waiting at Suez, Brémond sought to win support both in Cairo and on the Arab coast for his project of occupying Aqaba. He found general agreement as to the idea but polite differences of view when it came to the question of execution. The General Staff in Egypt had no more desire to send a force to Aqaba than formerly to Rabegh. Feisal, whom he visited at Wejh on January 31st, had no desire to see a Franco-British force at Aqaba. When Brémond spoke of the place being lightly held, Feisal neatly turned the argument into a reinforcement for his own reply, that

FEISAL'S ARMY COMING BACK INTO YANBO. DECEMBER, 1916

THE TRIUMPHAL ENTRY INTO AQABA. JULY 1917

he could and would undertake the capture of Aqaba without European aid.

Brémond had already seen Lawrence in Cairo and had tried to enlist his support. He had only succeeded in arousing Lawrence's suspicion of his ulterior motive. A Franco-British force at Aqaba might be as great a barrier as a hostile Sirhan to his aim of spreading the Arab Revolt into Syria. Hiding his deeper objection he told Brémond that Aqaba must be taken from the rear as otherwise the mountain-barrier behind it would bottle up any advance from it towards Ma'an. Failing to deter the Frenchman by this sound strategic argument, Lawrence hastened back to Wejh to warn Feisal before Brémond arrived. He had the pleasure of listening to Feisal's answers to Brémond, and enhanced Brémond's displeasure by his aggravating smile.

Baulked in his Aqaba design, Brémond was henceforth reduced to fostering the operations against Medina. Doubts of his zeal in this direction had apparently been aroused in France, for Joffre, the Commander-in-Chief, had recently sent him a telegram saying— "From your telegrams, you seem to fear the taking of Medina by the Arabs, by reason of the encouragement that it will give to their aims in Syria. This attitude, already known to the English and to the Sherif, is likely to give rise to the belief that we are trying to go back on our agreements, and may have serious consequences for the development of our action in the Levant. It is essential therefore that your attitude should not lend itself to such an interpretation."

By one of the sublime ironies of human affairs this reluctance to achieve the capture of Medina was now to be shared by the man most opposite to Brémond—although for very different reasons. Lawrence's new attitude was due partly to a fear that the Turks, ejected from Medina, would be able to strengthen their hold on Syria, and thus check the spread of revolt there. It was due also to the growth of a new theory of war in his mind, which rejected and reversed the theory of the French, and also the British, official school of war.

Its growth coincided with a change in the military situation.

Under the impulsion of Britain's new Prime Minister, the initiative against Turkey was at last to be regained. Immediately he came into office in early December Mr. Lloyd George pressed for an offensive campaign in the East with a view to some striking success, economically won, that would enhearten the allied peoples, wearied by the drab slaughter of the Somme. Sir William Robertson did his utmost to resist this demand, an affront to his sacred principle of "concentration at the decisive spot," and his resistance stiffened when Murray, asked what force he would need to press his advance beyond El Arish over the frontier, suggested that he would like two additional divisions, if they could be lent to him temporarily.

Robertson replied to Murray on December 12th, that "the Prime Minister wishes you to make the maximum possible effort during the winter," but added himself that no further troops could be sent until the winter was over. A telegram from Murray next day showed that he had reckoned on using three of the possible divisions for passive defence of his communications. On December 15th Robertson instructed him—"to be as aggressive as possible with the troops at your disposal subject to your main mission of defending Egypt," and added that he did "not quite understand why," when Murray had occupied El Arish and cleared the enemy from Sinai, it should be necessary to keep so large a proportion on the lines of communication. The question seems pertinent when we compare this estimate with the far smaller force that the Turks allotted to guard their far longer lines of communication against an omnipresent threat.

When this new impulse came from home Murray's preparations to occupy El Arish were almost completed. They had certainly been long in maturing. In his truly excellent history of the Palestine Campaign, General Wavell, himself an eminent professional soldier, remarks—"The lines of communication organized for the advance across Sinai were a typically British piece of work—slow, very expensive, immensely solid. The famous epigram of Tacitus on the Romans—'they make a desert and call it peace'—might aptly be inverted for this British advance—'they turn the desert into a workshop and call it war.'"

It is claimed that "it was Sir Archibald Murray's foresight in basing the advance from the first on so broad a foundation as the standard-gauge railway and 12-inch pipeline, which made possible the subsequent drive of the army up to and beyond the gates of Aleppo." But this drive did not take place until twenty months later, thus allowing a somewhat long interval in which any defects of a more rapid preparation in 1916 could have been remedied. And in the original advance, which at last began at the end of 1916, solidity did not suffice to prevent a check.

"Elaborate water arrangements" delayed the pounce on El Arish until December 20th. "Then, just when all was ready, the enemy withdrew." An empty town was occupied on the morning of the 21st. The garrison of this Turkish outpost, 1,600 strong, had fallen back on the fortified posts of Magdhaba and Rafah. The former, which lay inland, and was thus a threat to the flank of any further advance, was captured by Chauvel's mounted force on the 23rd, after the garrison had put up a fight so stout that Chauvel, fearing lest he might be held there without water, had actually issued orders for a withdrawal just as the defenders began to give way.

The railway was pushed forward across the twenty miles to El Arish by January 4th—a contrast to the previous rate of progress. On the evening of the 8th, Chetwode advanced against Rafah with Chauvel's force and an additional brigade. He surrounded the Turkish position soon after dawn, but the curious course of the Magdhaba fight was here repeated. In the afternoon orders for a withdrawal had been issued when, suddenly, before the order could reach them, the men of the New Zealand Mounted Brigade stormed the key of the position.

But it was Turkish folly, and the false pride of keeping their foot on Egyptian territory, which had provided the British the chance of bringing off these two coups. Kress von Kressenstein had vainly urged the withdrawal of these outlying garrisons to the main Gaza-Beersheba line of defence. And the loss of over three thousand men seriously diminished the already weak garrison of this position.

To meet the advance of three British infantry divisions, and two mounted divisions, the Turks had only one weak division and the remains of a second. And they suffered a continual drain from Arab desertions, an effect which may justly be counted an indirect credit to the revolt in the Hejaz. A third weak division was brought down by the Turks in February, during the lull of nearly three months that followed the British advance to Rafah. But even so they could oppose only some 13,000 fighting men (rifles and sabres) necessarily scattered, to the 40,000 of the British.

Thus there was the prospect of the "big success" that the British

Government desired. It was important, however, that no large reinforcements should reach the Turks. Three weak divisions were holding down the restless Arabs in Syria, and at the most one of these might be spared.

But in Arabia there was a Turkish force almost as strong as that which faced the British in Palestine. Far stronger indeed, if we count the three divisions south of the Hejaz. At present that force was being pinned down at no expense of man-power to the British save a handful of officers. Such a distraction of the enemy's force from the "decisive spot" in Palestine should surely have gladdened the heart of the most doctrinaire upholders of the text-book principle of concentration. But if Medina were abandoned and the Turkish forces withdrawn northward, the scales in Palestine would be decisively changed.

Early in March a telegram from Jemal Pasha was intercepted by wireless in Cairo. Only part of it could be deciphered. That part, however, seemed to convey an order for the evacuation of Medina, and for the Turkish forces to retire north up the railway in mass. "It suggested an order of march, with baggage and headquarters on an accompanying train."

The obvious danger to the British plans in Palestine led to an urgent appeal from Cairo to Feisal, to take Medina if possible or otherwise intercept the garrison on its retreat up the railway. A messenger was sent down to Wejh by a special ship to tell the British mission of the intercepted telegram and urge prompt action. Newcombe was up country, operating against the railway, so Lawrence took the responsibility of urging instant action. To meet the appeal Feisal hastened to move forward detachments to a chain of four advanced bases near the railway, against which the raids were now multiplied. And Lawrence himself decided to set out for the Wadi Ais, to spur Abdulla to attack Medina as the General Staff desired. He was ill with dysentery at the time the message came from Clayton, but he refused to let his weakness baulk him, and he set out with a small escort of mixed tribesmen on the long camel-ride through the hills. But the effort taxed his strength so hardly that he could scarcely keep his seat, and twice suffered from fainting-fits. In this pitiable state his mind was haunted by the ever-present thought that he might collapse completely on the way, and be handed

Photo. T. E. Lawrence

FEISAL'S AGEYL BODYGUARD. JANUARY, 1917

over to the worse than unmedical care of the desert tribesmen, his mission unfulfilled.

To add to these physical and mental trials, at the first evening's halt a quarrel occurred among the party in which one of them, a Moor, murdered an Ageyli. It was settled with primitive justice by an informal court-martial on the murderer. The other Ageyli demanded the desert law of blood for blood, and Lawrence in vain tried to dissuade them. Finally, seeing that if baulked they would take vengeance privately, which would start a new blood feud, Lawrence forced himself to carry out the summary execution of the murderer, shooting him with his own hand.

Somehow, he scarcely knew how, Lawrence succeeded in holding out against his weakness until Abdulla's camp was reached on March 13th. There he delivered his message and then staggered to a tent, where he lay ten days recovering his strength. As his head cleared, while still too weak to be on his legs, he had time to think. More time than he had ever had since the Revolt began, and with experience behind him on which he could reason. His thoughts went back to the many books of military theory he had read in pre-war days. They worked forward from these to the actual conditions of the campaign in which he was engaged. The contrast between that theory and present reality were so great that, gradually, startling new ideas took form in his mind—ideas that would be revolutionary in effect.

CHAPTER IX

MARTIAL REVERIES

March, 1917

IN 1757 Marshal Saxe's *Reveries on the Art of War* was published posthumously. The book became a military classic of the 18th century; it was translated into English in the very year of it publication. Its immediate success may have owed something to Saxe's fame as a commander, the man who had beaten the English in Flanders. But it owed more to the originality of Saxe's military ideas, which had already made their mark in the actual practice of war. Now, more developed in his book, and generating a greater force, they came like a shattering blast to the encrusted conventions of his time.

In an age of regularity he introduced irregularity as a lever. In an age of immobility he coiled the spring of a new mobility. In an age of professional pedantry he showed more freedom from custom— and more of the scientific spirit of inquiry—than any of the generals of the French Revolution, who were able to operate in much freer conditions.

He was, perhaps, fortunate to be not only Maurice of Saxony but the most successful of all the Marshals of the century. He certainly showed discretion in withholding publication of his *Reveries* until after his death. For his manner of criticism was no less devastating than his proposals. He prefaced them by the remark—"War is a science so obscure and imperfect" that "custom and prejudice confirmed by ignorance are its sole foundation and support." He described the prevailing theory of War and its sacrosanct dogmas as no better than "maxims blindly adopted, without any examination of the principles on which they were founded . . . our present practice is nothing more than a passive compliance with received customs to the grounds of which we are absolute strangers."

In seeking to rescue his successors from the bondage of convention which had reduced 18th century warfare to a draught-board formality, he saw that the conditions which produced immobility and rigidity must first be remedied. And he saw most of the ways in which to remedy them, though not all of his ideas were applied even in the Wars of the Revolution. Some waited for the 20th century.

In his dictum that the "whole secret of the art of war rests in the legs and not in the arms," he anticipated Napoleon's well-known saying that his victories were won by the legs of his soldiers. Saxe also saw like Sherman in Georgia, and in contrast to Napoleon and his 19th century disciples, that there is a limit, determined by mobility, to what one may call the "economic size" of any particular army. And that the effective strength of an army may cease to increase when its numbers cause a decline in mobility, unless it is engaged in passive defence or is within fortified lines.

Saxe declared that "a general of parts" with an army of such economic size would be able to dominate an enemy double the size —"for multitudes serve only to perplex and embarrass."

The army of his dream took its inspiration from the Roman Legion, that remarkable blend of strength with flexibility, but he did more than merely adapt this to the 18th century conditions, suggesting innumerable improvements in armament, equipment, and tactics all tending to develop the power of manœuvre and apply fire in manœuvre, especially through releasing the independent action of the individual. In particular, he proposed to cut down transport and rid himself of the encumbrances of magazines. But the significance of Saxe's legionary organization was greater as a whole than in its parts. For here in embryo was the "divisional system"—the organization of an army in separate divisions capable of moving and acting independently. It meant that an army, hitherto a limbless trunk, grew arms with which it could grip the enemy at different points while it struck him at others. Through this, above all, strategy was to be revolutionized in the Wars of the Revolution.

Saxe was no less creative when he passed on from these "branches" of an army to what he styled the "sublime branches of the art of war." Here his teaching is distinguished by its variety yet continuity of ideas on the art of playing upon the enemy commander's mind, upsetting his balance and dislocating his dispositions. In his imaginary cases one can trace Napoleonic combinations in embryo mingled with a Hannibalic guile—every plan hides a trap.

Saxe's fame was obscured, and his influence thereby diminished, by the spectacular successes that Frederick the Great achieved so soon after his death—victories that for all their brilliance brought Frederick to the verge of ruin and cast the shadow of bankruptcy over a strategy which, in its pursuit of decisive battle, lost sight of the goal of war. As a creative military mind Frederick's cannot compare with Saxe's. It is an irony of history—and also a tragedy—that his reputation should have overshadowed Saxe's. But in France, at least, and by his criticism no less than his construction, Saxe paved the way for that renaissance of military thought which in turn, through the more developed ideas of men like Bourcet and Guibert, gave birth to what is erroneously termed the Napoleonic method. Napoleon certainly applied it, within the limits of his understanding. He did not create it.

In the glare of his triumphs, however, the source of his system was lost to sight. Nor was that all. The very system itself that was the source of his success became obscured, first, by his gradual distortion of it. The difference between the system to which he was the fortunate heir, and the theory which became his legacy, might be expressed by drawing a distinction between Bonaparte and Napoleon. General Bonaparte applied a theory that created an empire for him. The Emperor Napoleon developed a practice which wrecked his empire. It wrecked other empires a century later.

From 1806 onwards the superiority of numbers which Napoleon enjoyed, from the vast resources of imperial power, had a growing influence on his conduct of war. If he still exploited mobility, he unconsciously pinned his faith to mass, and subordinated his art to his weight. In his campaigns after Jena he was too apt to rush at his opponents, confident that his machine would crush them if he could only bring them to battle. His victories were won less by surprise than by sheer offensive power, expressed in his new artillery tactics of a massed concentration of guns to blast a selected spot. At Eylau he suffered a check, and at Aspern his first defeat.

His victories, moreover, were purchased at a cost which caused an increasing drain on his military bank-balance of man-power. The intoxication of success had upset his balance of mind. In 1813 his bankruptcy was declared and in 1815 an undischarged bankrupt, in debt again, went to serve his sentence at St. Helena—a world debtor's prison.

He paid the penalty of violating the law of economy of force, which depends on mobility and surprise. The new mobility—as conceived by Saxe, Bourcet and Guibert—had the purpose of concentrating superior strength against the enemy's weak points, of concentrating it unexpectedly at vital points that the enemy had been deceived into weakening. It was abused when employed merely to form a superior mass—to multiply numbers at unweakened points. The true virtue of the new power of mobile concentration lay in its variability, not in its density. It meant the power to shuffle a hand so deftly that a trump could always be produced at the critical point: not merely a quickened power to assemble a hand.

But Napoleon had tended increasingly to forget his early sleight of hand, and to rely on the hand that fortune dealt him, trusting in the mere strength of his cards. Thus he lost points and finally the rubber.

The lesson was lost on the generations that followed, blinded by the glamour of his colossal gamble. The original Napoleonic system was obscured by the Napoleonic legend. In this darkening of military thought there developed a swing of the pendulum back to immobility—due to the new theory of mass, on which fresh weights were piled by Napoleon's disciples, beginning with Clausewitz and culminating with Foch. Gathering momentum the pendulum continued with fatal force until it crashed on the hard realities of 1914 and buried itself in the immovable trenches of the Western Front, from which it was only extracted after four years of effort that left Europe exhausted.

Only in the East, especially the Middle East, was mobility given opportunity, and the opportunity taken. But there, more significantly, arose a new and extreme theory of mobility, which was applied with dramatic success and had a far-reaching effect in irregular warfare. But it has, also, a message for regular warfare, of still greater potential range.

That theory evolved from the reveries of Lawrence as he lay on his sick-bed in Abdulla's camp.

His thoughts travelled back to the military books he had read while at Oxford. They were an astonishingly wide collection for a man whose main interests were mediæval architecture and pottery, a far wider course of study than almost any regular soldier had undertaken, certainly in England. He began when about fifteen or sixteen, on what he calls—"the usual school-boy stuff," Creasy's *Fifteen Decisive Battles of the World,* Napier's *History of the War in the Peninsula,* Coxe's *Marlborough,* Mahan's *Influence of Sea-Power on History,* Henderson's *Stonewall Jackson.* Tough matter for a school-boy's digestion—and Henderson was the bounds of many a Staff College student's horizon. Mixed with these Lawrence read many technical treatises on castle-building and sieges—old ones such as Procopius, Vegetius, and about Demetrius Poliorcetes.

A little later he came to Clausewitz and his school, to Caemerrer and Moltke, Goltz and some of the post-1870 French military writers. These seemed to him "very partial books," even Clausewitz, and so, being dissatisfied, he worked back to Napoleon himself. On the way he had a look at Jomini and Willisen, and in the latter at least struck a definition of strategy that made a deep impression—"the study of communication." Then he was drawn, through reading a French study of Napoleon's Italian campaign, to "browse" in Napoleon's correspondence—a series of thirty-two volumes!

This had inspired Lawrence with a desire to study the text-books that Napoleon himself had studied. Thus he came to Guibert and, going a step further back, to Bourcet and Saxe. So far as I have discovered there is only one copy in England of Bourcet's treatise, and that lies in the War Office library. This, like other rare books, Lawrence tracked down through the advice of Reginald Lane Poole—"my most unpontifical official tutor at Oxford, who had read every book, and remembered the best ones."

These writers pleased Lawrence because he found "broader principles" in them. Saxe stayed in his mind, yet at the back of his mind. Later Lawrence would regard Saxe as "the greatest master of his kind of War," but that was after Lawrence himself had made war, and gained practical experience. At the time he felt that "Clausewitz was intellectually so much the master of them all that unwillingly I had come to believe in him."

Apart from this intellectual interest in the theory of war, Lawrence had studied quite a number of battlefields—mainly for the interest of re-creating them on maps. Beginning with sieges, directly related to his pursuit of castles, he had "tried to get an idea of the bigger movements." He had "visited Rocroi, Crécy, Agincourt, Malplaquet, Sedan," and one or two other battlefields of 1870. He also "saw Valmy and its neighbourhood and tried to re-fight the whole of Marlborough's wars." Then, when he went to Syria, he followed step by step the campaigns of the Crusaders.

But these excursions were not undertaken with any conscious purpose of fitting himself for future command. Nor was his reading. "My interests were only in pure theory, I looked everywhere for the metaphysical side, the philosophy of war, about which I thought a little for some years." Now in an unforeseen way he had been drawn into action and found himself "unfortunately as much in charge of the campaign as I pleased."

In such circumstances the clear-thinking man is often more handicapped than the purely instinctive man, or at least more conscious of his handicap when suddenly called on to practise what he has casually thought about as a pastime. The strangeness of direct contact with an activity familiar at second-hand makes him acutely aware of his own deficiencies of training. He is apt to exaggerate the proficiency of fellow-workers whose air of naturalness in the little things they are used to doing effectively conceals from him, for a time, their limitations in that sphere outside the familiar routine that they fulfil without reflection. But if he continues, and has leisure to reflect, his greater capacity for thought may provide an impulse to clear the ground of accumulated débris, and achieve a new construction on his wider foundations of study, which he can now check by personal experience of actual conditions.

Plunged suddenly into action at Yanbo, Lawrence's immersion had been too complete hitherto for him to rise to the surface and get his head above water. Now, however, enforced inactivity served him as a life-buoy. It is true that after his first visit in October he had written a reasoned appreciation of the situation which showed a masterly treatment of the immediate problem, but there had been no time until now to ponder the course of future action or develop a theory on which to act.

His thought retraced the course of the campaign in the Hejaz, from the time that Rabegh had seemed in imminent peril. The professional soldiers had put their fingers on Rabegh as "the key of Mecca," and had urged the importance of holding it. None of them, British or French, had regarded the Bedouin as of any value in defending it or any other fixed position. The course of events had justified their view.

Yet he himself, with no professional reputation to lose, had reported that "the tribesmen (if strengthened by light machine-guns and regular officers as advisers) should be able to hold up the Turks indefinitely, while the Arab regular force was being created." The issue paradoxically, had justified his view also. Although the Arabs had given way whenever attacked, Rabegh was still intact.

This might be sheer luck. Indeed, the Turks had given his appreciation a rude shock by breaking through the belt of hills that he had deemed impregnable. Yet their advance, with its worst obstacles passed, had petered out. True, it might certainly have been renewed, and have reached Rabegh, if Feisal had not suddenly moved to Wejh, and produced a threat to the Turks' communications that had sent them scurrying back. Perhaps it had been the mere prospect of this threat that had made them hesitate so long in their advance on Mecca. Even so, it looked as if this failure to reach Rabegh, when they began advancing, might be largely explained by the distance they had had to travel—by the one hundred and forty miles that separated Rabegh from Medina. So long as the Arabs had space to fall back, their delaying power might be equivalent to defensive power. And they could have the advantage of unlimited space so long as they had no vital point to cover. That advantage was possible with a nomadic people—hence a further argument for transferring operations northwards. "The virtue of irregulars lay in depth, not in force."

But merely to delay the enemy, and prevent them from winning, was not enough—according to the text books. Field Service Regulations said that "the defensive attitude must be assumed only in order to obtain or create a favourable opportunity for *decisive offensive action*." This meant that the Arab tribal forces could be only a strategic stop-gap until the Arab regular force was ready for action. "Irregulars would not attack positions and so they seemed to be incapable of forcing a decision."

"As was almost inevitable in view of the general course of military thinking since Napoleon, we all looked only to the regulars to win the War. We were obsessed by the dictum of Foch that the ethic of modern war is to seek for the enemy's army, his centre of power, and destroy it in battle.'

That was the purpose which Lawrence had come all the way from Wejh to persuade Abdulla to attempt. The Medina garrison must be destroyed. But how was it to be done? Spurred on by the urgent appeal from Cairo he had set out from Wejh to carry the message, without pausing to think out its implications. But now in his tent, with the fever subsiding, he could cogitate the problem at leisure, as far as the flies permitted. His mission began to seem rather unreal, if it had a spice of humour.

Lawrence sought to find, and it was not easy to find, "an immediate equation between my book-reading and our present movements.

"However, the books gave me the aim of war quite pat, 'the destruction of the organized forces of the enemy' by 'the one process, battle.' Victory could only be purchased by blood. This was a hard saying for us, as the Arabs had no organized forces, and so a Turkish Foch would have no aim: and the Arabs would not endure casualties, so that an Arab Clausewitz could not buy his victory. These wise men must be talking metaphors, for we were indubitably winning our war—and as I thought about it, it dawned on me that we had won the Hejaz war. We were in occupation of 99 per cent of the Hejaz. The Turks were welcome to the other fraction till peace or doomsday showed them the futility of clinging to our windowpane."

It was a satisfying thought, and a surprising one, yet the more he turned it over in his mind the clearer it shone. But then what about Medina? And the answer flashed out from reflection—"why bother about Medina?" Even if it could be captured, which was clearly impossible with present means, what would be the good of capturing it? Indeed—here was a further thought—would it not be harmful to do so?

"It was no base to us, like Rabegh, no threat to the Turks, like Wejh: just a blind alley for both. The Turks sat in it on the defensive, immobile, eating for food the transport animals which were to have moved them to Mecca, but for which there was no pasture in their now restricted lines. They were harmless sitting there; if we took them prisoners they would cost us food and guards in Egypt: if we drove them northward into Syria, they would join the main army blocking us in Sinai. On all counts they were best where they were, and they valued Medina and wanted to keep it. Let them!

"This seemed unlike the ritual of war of which Foch had been priest, and so I began to hope that there was a difference of kind between him and us. He called his modern war 'absolute.' In it two nations professing incompatible philosophies set out to try them in the light of force. A struggle of two immaterial philosophies could only end when the supporters of one had no more means of resistance. An opinion can be argued with: a conviction is best shot. The logical end of a war of creeds is the final destruction of one, and Salammbo the classical text-book instance." Foch seemed to have gone back to the old wars of religion. His philosophy might apply to the struggle between France and Germany, but not to the British attitude, "for all efforts to make our men hate the enemy, just made them hate war . . ." Moreover, any war that stopped short of the extermination of the enemy people, as even the World War would, obviously fell short of "the Foch ideal." Thus although Foch and his fellows of the 19th century school of military thought talked as if "absolute" war was the only kind, Lawrence now began to realize that it was "only a variety of war: and I could then see other sorts, as Clausewitz had numbered them, personal wars for dynastic reasons, expulsive wars for party reasons, commercial wars for trading reasons.

"Then I thought of the Arab aim, and saw that it was geographical, to occupy all Arabic-speaking lands in Asia. In the doing of it we might kill Turks: we disliked them very much. Yet 'killing Turks' would never be an excuse or aim. If they would go quietly, our war would end. If not, we would try to drive them out: in the last resort we would be compelled to the desperate course of blood, on the maxim of 'murder' war, but as cheaply as possible for ourselves, since the Arabs were fighting for freedom, a pleasure only to be tasted by a man alive."

This new realization of the narrow horizon of the accepted teachers of the 19th century, the men who had formulated the doctrines which the armies of Europe were now trying to carry out, with rather poor result, led Lawrence's thought back to those 18th century teachers, whose "broader principles" had long ago impressed him.

It gave him a new appreciation of Saxe in particular, and of those *Reveries* which Carlyle, the devotee of Frederick, had scornfully dismissed as a "strange military farrago, dictated as I should think, under opium." If Lawrence had ever had any inclination to accept such a verdict he lost it now. Through experience he now saw Saxe, not as a dreamer, but as a supreme realist.

It was Saxe, he remembered, who had written—"I am not in favour of giving battle, especially at the outset of a war. I am even convinced that an able general can wage war his whole life without being compelled to do so." Foch had held Saxe up to ridicule for that remark, contrasting it with Napoleon's remark in 1806—"There is nothing I desire so much as a great battle." In scornful comment Foch had added, "The one wants to avoid battle his whole life, the other demands it at the first opportunity."

Lawrence, freed by contact with experience from the metaphysical spell of Clausewitz, could now appreciate Saxe's practical point of view. He saw that Saxe had kept his mind on the ultimate aim of war, to which battle is only a means. Saxe himself had fought several battles, all victories. But he did not fight battles for battle's sake, like Napoleon and his heirs were inclined to do. Lawrence began to wonder whether, having been compelled to cut adrift from Foch's theory, he could not instead apply Saxe's. Where Foch's had, obviously, no relation to the actual conditions, Saxe's might be adapted.

It was Saxe who had remarked—"there is more address in making bad dispositions than is commonly imagined, provided that they are intentional, and so formed as to admit of being instantaneously converted into good ones: nothing can more confound an enemy, who has been anticipating a victory, than a stratagem of this kind . . ." The remark might have been coined to fit the Hejaz campaign. So long as the Arabs had been concentrated in face of the Turks the scales had turned against them. Once they began to stretch out it had turned the other way. And the more they had become separated the worse had become their enemy's plight.

Lawrence now turned to study his future problem in this new light. "My personal duty was command, and I began to unravel command and analyse it, both from the point of view of strategy, the aim of war, the synoptic regard which sees everything by the standard of the whole; and from the point of view called tactics, the means towards the strategic end, the steps of its staircase." "In each I found the same elements, one algebraical, one biological, a third psychological. The first seemed a pure science, subject to the laws of mathematics, without humanity. It dealt with known invariables, fixed conditions, space and time, inorganic things like hills, and climate, and railways, with mankind in type-masses, too great for individual variety, with all artificial aids, and the extensions given our faculties by mechanical invention. It was essentially formulable."

"In the Arab case the algebraic factor would take first account of the area we wished to conquer, and I began idly to calculate how many square miles . . . perhaps a hundred and forty thousand . . . and how would the Turks defend all that . . . no doubt by a trench line across the bottom, if we were an army attacking with banners displayed . . . but suppose we were an influence (as we might be), an idea, a thing invulnerable, intangible, without front or back, drifting about like gas? Armies were like plants, immobile as a whole, firm rooted, nourished through long stems to the head. We might be a vapour, blowing where we listed. Our kingdoms lay in each man's mind, and as we wanted nothing material to live on, so perhaps we offered nothing material to the killing. It seemed a regular soldier might be helpless without a target. He would own the ground he sat on, and what he could poke his rifle at.

"Then I estimated how many posts they would need to contain this attack in depth, sedition putting up her head in every unoccupied one of these hundred thousand square miles. I knew the Turkish Army inside and out, and allowing for its recent extension of faculty by guns and aeroplanes and armoured trains, still it seemed it would have need of a fortified post every four square miles, and a post could not be less than twenty men. The Turks would need six hundred thousand men to meet the combined illwills of all the local Arab people. They had one hundred thousand men available. It seemed the assets in this part of command were ours, and climate, railways, deserts, technical weapons could also be attached to our interests, if we realized our raw materials and were apt with them. The Turk was stupid and would believe that rebellion was absolute, like war, and deal with it on the analogy of absolute warfare. Anal-

CAPTAIN LAWRENCE, EARLY IN 1917

ogy is fudge, anyhow, and to make war upon rebellion is messy and slow, like eating soup with a knife.

"So much for the mathematical element, which I annoyed the others by calling hecastics. The second factor was biological, the breaking-point, life and death, or better, wear and tear. Bionomics seemed a good name for it. The war-philosophers had properly made it an art, and had elevated one item in it, 'effusion of blood,' to the height of a principle. It became humanity in battle, an art touching every side of our corporal being, and very warm. There was a line of variability (man) running through all its estimates. Its components were sensitive and illogical, and generals guarded themselves by the device of a reserve, the significant medium of their art. Goltz had said that when you know the enemy's strength, and he is fully deployed, then you know enough to dispense with a reserve. But this is never. There is always the possibility of accident, of some flaw in materials, present in the general's mind: and the reserve is unconsciously held to meet it. There is a 'felt' element in troops, not expressible in figures, guessed at by the equivalent of δόξα in Plato, and the greatest commander is he whose intuitions most nearly happen. Nine-tenths of tactics are certain, and taught in books: but the irrational tenth is like the kingfisher flashing across the pool, and that is the test of generals. It can only be ensued by instinct, sharpened by thought practising the stroke so often that at the crisis it is as natural as a reflex.

"Yet to limit the art to humanity seemed to me an undue narrowing down. It must apply to materials as much as to organisms. In the Turkish Army materials were scarce and precious, men more plentiful than equipment. Consequently our cue should be to destroy not the Army but the materials. The death of a Turkish bridge or rail, machine or gun, or high explosive was more profitable to us than the death of a Turk. The Arab Army just now was equally chary of men and materials: of men because they being irregulars were not units, but individuals, and an individual casualty is like a pebble dropped in water: each may make only a brief hole, but rings of sorrow widen out from them. We could not afford casualties. Materials were easier to deal with and put straight. It was our obvious duty to make ourselves superior in some one branch, gun-cotton or machine guns, or whatever could be made most decisive. Foch had laid down the maxim, applying it to men, of being superior at the critical point and moment of attack. We might apply it to materials, and be superior in equipment in one dominant moment or respect.

"For both men and things we might try to give Foch's doctrine a negative twisted side, for cheapness' sake, and be weaker than the enemy everywhere except in one point or matter. Most wars are wars of contact, both forces striving to keep in touch to avoid tactical surprise. Our war should be a war of detachment: we were to contain the enemy by the silent threat of a vast unknown desert, not disclosing ourselves till the moment of attack. This attack need be only nominal, directed not against his men, but against his materials: so it should not seek for his main strength or his weaknesses, but for his most accessible material. In railway cutting this would be usually an empty stretch of rail. That was a tactical success. We might turn the average into a rule (not a law—war is antinomian, said Colin), and at length we developed an unconscious habit of never engaging the enemy at all. This chimed with the numerical plea of never giving the enemy's soldier a target. Many Turks on our front had no chance all the war to fire a shot at us, and correspondingly we were never on the defensive, except by a rare accident. The corollary of such a rule was perfect 'intelligence,' so that we could plan in complete certainty. The chief agent had to be the general's head (de Feuquières said this first), and his knowledge had to be faultless, leaving no room for chance. We took more pains in this service than any other staff I saw.

"The third factor in command seemed to be the psychological, that science (Xenophon called it diathetic) of which our propaganda is a stained and ignoble part. Some of it concerns the crowd, the adjustment of spirit to the point where it becomes fit to exploit in action, the pre-arrangement of a changing opinion to a certain end. Some of it deals with individuals, and then it becomes a rare art of human kindness, transcending, by purposeful emotion, the gradual logical sequence of our minds. It considers the capacity for mood of our men, their complexities and mutability, and the cultivation of what in them profits the intention. We had to arrange their minds in order to battle, just as carefully and as formally as other officers arranged their bodies: and not only our own men's minds, though them first: the minds of the enemy, so far as we could reach them:

and thirdly, the mind of the nation supporting us behind the firing-line, and the mind of the hostile nation waiting the verdict, and the neutrals looking on.

"It was the ethical in war, and the process on which we mainly depended for victory on the Arab front. The printing press is the greatest weapon in the armoury of the modern commander, and we, being amateurs in the art of command, began our war in the atmosphere of the twentieth century, and thought of our weapons without prejudice, not distinguishing one from another socially. The regular officer has the tradition of forty generations of serving soldiers behind him, and to him the old weapons are the most honoured. We had seldom to concern ourselves with what our men did, but much with what they thought, and to us the diathetic was more than half command. In Europe it was set a little aside and entrusted to men outside the General Staff. In Asia we were so weak physically that we could not let the metaphysical weapon rust unused. We had won a province when we had taught the civilians in it to die for our ideal of freedom: the presence or absence of the enemy was a secondary matter.

"These reasonings showed me that the idea of assaulting Medina, or even of starving it quickly into surrender was not in accord with our best strategy. We wanted the enemy to stay in Medina, and in every other harmless place, in the largest numbers. The factor of food would eventually confine him to the railways, but he was welcome to the Hejaz railway, and the Trans-Jordan railway, and the Palestine and Damascus and Aleppo railways for the duration of the war, so long as he gave us the other nine hundred and ninety-nine thousandths of the Arab world. If he showed a disposition to evacuate too soon, as a step to concentrating in the small area which his numbers could dominate effectively, then we would have to try and restore his confidence, not harshly, but by reducing our enterprises against him. Our ideal was to keep his railways just working, but only just, with the maximum of loss and discomfort to him. . . .

"The Arab war was geographical, and the Turkish Army for us an accident, not a target. Our aim was to seek its weakest link, and bear only on that till time made the mass of it fall. Our largest available resources were the tribesmen, men quite unused to formal warfare, whose assets were movement, endurance, individual intelligence, knowledge of the country, courage. We must impose the longest possible passive defence on the Turks (this being the most materially expensive form of war) by extending our own front to its maximum. Tactically we must develop a highly mobile, highly equipped type of army, of the smallest size, and use it successively at distributed points of the Turkish line, to make the Turks reinforce their occupying posts beyond the economic minimum of twenty men. The power of this striking force of ours would not be reckoned merely by its strength. The ratio between number and area determined the character of the war, and by having five times the mobility of the Turks we could be on terms with them with one-fifth their number.

"Our success was certain, to be proved by paper and pencil as soon as the proportion of space and number had been learned. The contest was not physical, but mineral, and so battles were a mistake. All we won in a battle was the ammunition the enemy fired off. Our victory lay not in battles, but in occupying square miles of country. Napoleon had said it was rare to find generals willing to fight battles. The curse of this war was that so few could do anything else. Napoleon had spoken in angry reaction against the excessive finesse of the eighteenth century, when men almost forgot that war gave licence to murder. We had been swinging out on his dictum for a hundred years, and it was time to go back a bit again. Battles are impositions on the side which believes itself weaker, made unavoidable either by lack of land-room, or by the need to defend a material property dearer than the lives of soldiers. We had nothing material to lose, so we were to defend nothing and to shoot nothing. The precious element of our forces were the Bedouin irregulars, and not the regulars whose role would only be to occupy places to which the irregulars had already given access. Our cards were speed and time, not hitting power, and these gave us strategical rather than tactical strength. Range is more to strategy than force. The invention of bully-beef has modified land-war more profoundly than the invention of gunpowder." [1]

Here set out in his own words we have the new theory of irregular warfare as it took form in Lawrence's mind. To paraphrase would

[1] Anyone who is interested in the pre-war sources of Lawrence's military ideas will find a fuller study of them in my book, *The Ghost of Napoleon* (published in 1933).

be an impertinence, and also an injury to knowledge. For even though one may have come, by a different road, through larger fields of war, to a view of war wherein Saxe developed and Lawrence adapted would fit the picture of regular warfare, no similarity of view would justify the attempt to gild the lily—to interpret, with less command of words, what is so lucent as to repel the loan of a lens. No one could dare to "improve" Lawrence's exposition of the theory that took form, if not perhaps final form, during his reveries in the Wadi Ais. It is, however, in the light of that exposition that we should interpret Lawrence's initiative in the events that followed.

CHAPTER X

SPREADING THE INFECTION

April–June, 1917

Lawrence raids the railway from Abdulla's camp—He returns to Feisal's camp to find a plan in development for a narrowly concentrated attack on the railway—Disliking this plan, he privately concerts a long-range alternative—He sets off with a few Arab chiefs on a ride to the Syrian desert—While a force is being raised in the Sirhan, Lawrence makes a still more daring ride through Syria itself past Baalbek and Damascus

As soon as Lawrence was well enough he began to discuss future action with Abdulla. Instead of suggesting an attack on the Medina garrison, still safely there, he proposed a series of raids on the railway, and offered to show the way himself. The kind he had in mind would be "enough to annoy the enemy without making him fear its final destruction." But he found that he had no need to dissuade Abdulla from more severe measures.

Abdulla's theory of war seemed to be that the tongue is mightier than the sword, and although he revealed a fluidity of thought that should have pleased Lawrence, it never crystallized into positive action. He was certainly full of projects. In a conversation on March 20th with Lawrence and Captain Raho, an officer from French Africa, he spoke of moving into the Yemen, to free it from the Turkish yoke, but apparently it was only another of his verbal smoke-screens to hide his real intention—of sitting still. He was, however, definite in rejecting French demands for a bombardment of Medina, saying that he would reduce it by famine. From Lawrence's new point of view Abdulla's evasions were most reassuring; they were, also, a practical confirmation that his new theory was in accord with reality.

There was, however, among Abdulla's assistants a more energetic warrior in Sherif Shakir, "a very centaur on horseback," who, despite great wealth, affected a nomadic simplicity of life to match his reckless disposition. Shakir needed little prompting to make a raid against the railway; and promised to bring eight or nine hundred of

MAP 5

THE NORTHERN THEATRE

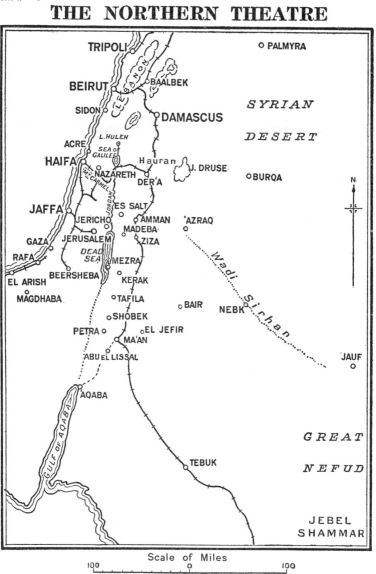

TRIPOLI

o PALMYRA

BEIRUT

BAALBEK

SIDON o

SYRIAN

DAMASCUS

DESERT

L. HULEH

ACRE

SEA OF GALILEE

HAIFA

Hauran

J. DRUSE

NAZARETH

MT. CARMEL

DER'A

o BURQA

JAFFA

ES SALT

N

JERICHO

AMMAN

'AZRAQ

MADEBA

GAZA

JERUSALEM

ZIZA

RAFA

DEAD SEA

EL ARISH

BEERSHEBA

MEZRA

MAGDHABA

KERAK

TAFILA

o BAIR

NEBK

SHOBEK

Wadi Sirhan

PETRA o

EL JEFIR

MA'AN

ABU EL LISSAL

JAUF

AQABA

GREAT

GULF OF AQABA

NEFUD

TEBUK

JEBEL
SHAMMAR

Scale of Miles

100   0   100

the Ateiba and a mountain-gun. Lawrence, although still unfit, went ahead on March 26th with a small advance party, including Raho, to look for a suitable target. He found it at Aba el Naam, a station garrisoned by some four hundred Turks—"and twenty-five goats." But when Shakir arrived, he brought only three hundred men, too few to storm the station. So Lawrence decided to occupy the attention of the garrison by a direct bombardment, while he aimed to blow up the railway to north and south, and thus trap a train which had halted there. This gave Lawrence the opportunity of laying his first mine—"the Martini lock to fire it was a device used by the Boers in South Africa against us!" Then he went back to rejoin the force and wait for morning. The action opened by a bombardment of the station; a shell hit the train and caused the engine to uncouple and steam off towards Lawrence's mine. But the charge exploded late, and the crew were allowed the chance of repairing the slight damage to the engine owing to the sudden disappearance of the machine-gunners who had been posted to open fire on it. Meantime Shakir's men, covered by smoke from the burning trucks, had captured two of the enemy's outlying posts. But they hesitated to assault the station, and retired content, taking some thirty prisoners, and leaving a battered station.

Lawrence lost no time in making a fresh effort. He set out again two days later from Abdulla's camp with a party of Juheina tribesmen and buried a Garland mine near Madahrij station to catch a train coming north from Medina. This time the train passed over the mine without exploding it—owing apparently to a slight ground subsidence, caused by a heavy storm, that prevented contact between rail and trigger mechanism. But the failure this time was a relief, not a disappointment, to Lawrence; for, when seemingly too late, he had seen that the train was full of women and children who were being evacuated from Medina. Later, when electric mines became the rule, Lawrence, according to other officers, took extreme precautions to avoid wrecking any refugee train, and, if in any doubt as to whether a train contained women and children, gave it the benefit of the doubt.

But he also took care to turn this lucky failure to profit. After dark he went out to reset the mine. Searching for the hair-trigger buried in the ballast was hazardous work, and he had visions of blowing up his own party instead. In his report he remarked—"Laying a Garland mine is shaky work, but scrabbling along a line for 100 yards in the ballast looking for a trigger that is connected with two powerful charges must be a quite uninsurable occupation." But at last after an hour, he found the trigger and fixed it afresh. Then he blew up a small bridge and cut the rails at numerous points as a bait for the Turkish breakdown-train from Hedia which duly hurried to the scene and was caught by the mine.

Having done something to develop the pin-prick strategy, and growing tired of Abdulla's evasions, Lawrence returned to Feisal's camp early in April to preach his new gospel there. Since the move to the advanced bases, the British officers together with Sharraf, Maulud, and a large force of Billi had been amplifying the attacks on the railway. They were becoming too serious for Lawrence's taste, and looked like becoming more so since more machine-guns, and even two armoured cars, had arrived. Newcombe was planning to move Feisal's whole force astride the railway near Medain Saleh, and thus cut off Medina definitely. Lawrence, in contrast, now deemed it wiser to restore the Turk's confidence by reducing the enterprises against him, so as to "keep him in his present absurd position—all flanks and no front."

"In detail I criticized the ruling scheme. To hold a middle point of the railway would be expensive, for the holding force might be threatened from each side. The mixture of Egyptian troops with tribesmen was a moral weakness. If there were professional soldiers present, the Bedouin would stand aside and watch them work . . . Jealousy, super-added to inefficiency, would be the outcome. Further, the Billi country was very dry, and the maintenance of a large force up by the line was technically difficult."

"Neither my general reasoning, however, nor my particular objections had much weight. The plans were made, and the preparations advanced. Everyone was too busy with his own work to give me specific authority to launch out on mine. All I gained was a hearing and a qualified admission that my counter-offensive might be a useful diversion."

What he had in mind was far more than an alternative offensive— I presume "counter-offensive" is a slip of the pen—to the one aimed at Medain Saleh. In fulfilment of his theory his idea was to spread

OUTSIDE FEISAL'S TENT AT WEJH

Photo, l. E. Lawrence

the infection of revolt over as wide a space as possible. That meant spreading it northward. And for this a more northerly base was needed. His aim thus coincided with the long-cherished project of occupying Aqaba—but with the vital difference that in his design it was to be taken by the Arabs from the interior instead of by a Franco-British force from the sea.

The venture was in the true Elizabethan tradition—a privateer's expedition. When it succeeded, authority would hail it with delight and reap its fruits. Later still, official narratives would even refer, disingenuously, to the "mission entrusted to Captain Lawrence." But, in truth, it was a purely private venture, undertaken without orders and even without assistance from any British source. Feisal provided the money, camels, stores and explosives for the scheme.

For its execution Lawrence had found not merely an ally but a blood-brother in Auda, an inverted Crusading baron who seemed to have marched straight out of Lawrence's former mediæval dream-world to greet him. With Auda, he concerted a plan. Accompanied by Sherif Nasir, as Feisal's deputy, they would set out to find the eastern Howeitat in their spring pastures of the Syrian desert, raise a mobile camel-force among them, and bring this down south for an attempt to seize Aqaba by surprise from the east—a pounce on its back. "The eastern was the unguarded side, the line of least resistance, the easiest for us. Our march would be an extreme example of a turning movement, since it involved a desert journey of six hundred miles to capture a trench within gunfire of our ships; but there was no practicable alternative." Lawrence was convinced that the longest way round would prove the shortest way there—his mind was ever on the mountain wall that towered behind Aqaba and could be so easily used by the Turks to block any advance from a landing. But he also looked beyond, to the issue. He had pledged himself to fight for Arab independence, not for the enlargement of the British Empire.

The venture was launched on May 9th. It was a small party that Nasir led forth that afternoon. Besides Lawrence and Auda, it included Nesib, who was to be Feisal's envoy to the Syrian peasants, Zeki, a Syrian officer, and an escort of some two score camelry. Baggage was light—each man carried a 45 lb. bag of flour as his rations for six weeks; there were six camel-loads of explosive for demolition work en route, and twenty thousand pounds in gold to encourage recruiting.

The first stage was a short one, to the little fort of Sebeil, on the old pilgrim route from Egypt. They started again after dark, travelling more comfortably in the comparative coolness of the night than, after a bare two hours' rest before dawn, they did during the following day. This was a foretaste of ordeals in store. The white sand reflected a cruel glare from the summer sun and the bare rocks on either side of the path threw off waves of heat that made heads ache and swim. They could have crossed this torrid zone more rapidly but for the baggage camels, which grazed all day as they went along. Auda, anxious about their poor condition, would not allow them to be hurried. The hours lingered interminably but relief came at last when towards evening they reached the oasis of El Kurr, where they met Maulud and others. From these they learnt that Sharraf, whom they wanted to meet at their next stopping place, was away on a raid.

The news caused them to rest in the shade of the palmtrees for a couple of nights, a welcome excuse for some. "To townsmen this garden was a memory of the world before we went mad with war and drove ourselves into the desert: to Auda there was an indecency of exhibition in the plant-richness, and he longed for an empty view. So we cut short our second night in paradise, and at two in the morning went on up the valley." On the second morning out from El Kurr the narrowing valley converged to precipitous cliffs up which they had to climb by a mere goat-track, so steep and treacherous that only by dint of pulling and pushing were the camels enabled to reach the top. Even so, they lost two camels in the pass. Lawrence himself was suffering from a fresh access of fever, made worse by boils, and was thankful when, dipping down into the sun-sheltered Wadi Jizil gorge, they came in sight of Sharraf's encampment. He was still away, so that they enjoyed three more days' rest.

During it Lawrence unwillingly acquired two devoted servants. Lying in a day-dream, he was suddenly disturbed by an Ageyli youth named Daud who had come to intercede with him for a beloved friend who was in trouble with the captain of Sharraf's Ageyl, and had been sentenced to a beating for his mischief. Lawrence made inquiries, but found the captain of the Ageyl adamant and only secured the offer that Daud might take a share of his friend Farraj's punishment if he liked. This concession Daud joyfully accepted. Next day two youthful figures, bent with pain, hobbled up to Lawrence and declared themselves his servants. He promptly rejected the offer, whereupon Farraj, not to be spurned, went down on his knees to Nasir in almost girlish appeal that he would soften Lawrence's heart. And in the end Lawrence accepted Nasir's advice to take them.

Sharraf at last arrived, with news of a fresh rail-breaking success and, better still, of new pools of rain-water near the railway. "This would shorten our waterless march to Fejr by fifty miles." Next day they left Abu Raga, and had only gone a short way when they sighted five or six camel-riders coming from the direction of the railway. Were they friend or foe? Auda and Lawrence, who were ahead, moved so as to be ready to fire. The doubt was soon quenched and at the head of the approaching party Lawrence saw a "fair-haired, shaggy-bearded Englishman in tattered uniform." It was Hornby, returning from another of the lone-hand expeditions in which he shared the honours with Newcombe. After a greeting, and a brief exchange of news, the march was continued. Mile after mile of it lay over a lava-field that was trying for the soft feet of the camels and meant a tediously slow gait for their riders, scorched by the sun overhead but afraid to go faster lest their mounts should go lame. To add anxiety the camels were all sick with mange, picked up in the infected ground of Wejh. If they were to break down in the forced march that lay ahead the party would be stranded in the desert. The services of Daud and Farraj now proved a boon by their assiduous care of Lawrence's mount, whose itching face they soothed with butter as an ointment.

On the eleventh day out from Wejh they at last reached the railway near Dizad, some fifty miles south of Tebuk. A few of the party crawled up a sand-peak to reconnoitre it unobserved. To their relief, it looked quiet and deserted, with no sign of the Turkish patrols of which they had been warned. Under Lawrence's guidance the Ageyl fixed gun-cotton and gelatine charges to the rails and lighted the fuses, while Auda was inspired to poetic improvisation by the thunderous proof of the dynamic power of dynamite. As a parting gesture they cut three telegraph wires, fastened the ends to half a dozen camels, and drove them forward, to drag a growing tangle of wire and broken poles behind them, until the accumulated weight brought the camels to a halt. Then "we cut them loose and rode in the falling dusk laughing after the caravan."

Now they had come to a vast desert plain, sloping downward to the east, that was called El Houl, "the desolate," because it was so utterly void of the least trace of life. On the twelfth day they rode in the teeth of a desert wind of such intensely dry heat that their shrivelled lips cracked open and the skin of their faces chapped. For three days after Lawrence's throat was so dry that eating was painful. But they pushed on relentlessly, driven by the thought of the next water ahead, and the thought of their fate if they failed. By sunset they had covered fifty miles and, starting again before dawn, at noon reached "the well of our desire." For danger of raiding parties they had to retire to a hidden spot half a mile from the well, putting out sentries.

A fourteenth day's ride over the interminable plain brought them to another pool. On the fifteenth they sighted a corner of the Great Nefudh, the famous belts of sand-dunes which cut off Jebel Shammar from the Syrian Desert. "Palgrave, the Blunts and Gertrude Bell amongst the storied travellers had crossed it, and I begged Auda to bear off a little and let us enter it, and their company: but he growled that men went to the Nefudh only of necessity, when raiding, and that the son of his father did not raid on a tottering, mangy camel. Our business was to reach Arfaja alive."

So they marched on over monotonous sun-reflecting sand and the still worse stretches of polished mud, stabbed in the eyelids and stabbed in the back of the head till they nearly swooned from an eddying pain that only relaxed as if to let them "store new capacity for suffering."

That night Auda became anxious lest another hot headwind might delay them a third day in the desert, for they had no water left. So they started again earlier than ever, and when morning came the Ageyl dismounted and led their camels on foot to eke out the poor beasts' remaining strength. Lawrence suddenly noticed that one of his men, Gasim, was missing. The loaded camel, riderless, was being led by one of Auda's Howeitat. No one seemed to care much what had happened to Gasim who, besides being surly, was a stranger from

Ma'an. The man's own road-fellow was a Syrian peasant who knew nothing of the desert and had a foundered camel.

Lawrence felt that he must take the duty of rescue on himself if he was to establish his claim to be a leader of the Arabs, not merely an attached foreigner. So he rode back alone in the emptiness. "My temper was very unheroic, for I was furious with my other servants, with my own play-acting as a Bedouin, and most of all with Gasim . . . It seemed absurd that I should peril my weight in the Arab adventure for such a worthless fellow." Lawrence had ridden for about an hour and a half when at last through the shifting mirage he saw an object that might be a man or might be a bush. He turned off the track, and moving nearer, saw that it was Gasim, a pitiable figure stumbling painfully along. Lawrence hauled him pillion-wise on to the camel's rump, stirred her up and turned about. Gasim's moaning wails spurred the camel on, so that Lawrence was afraid she might founder. As Gasim would not stop, Lawrence ferociously threatened to throw him off—the threat seemed so genuine that it quieted him.

After nearly four miles a jumping black bubble in the mirage ahead split into three, and became palpable as Auda and two other men. "I yelled jests and scoffs at them for abandoning a friend in the desert. Auda pulled at his beard and grumbled that had he been present I would never have gone back." When, however, they had rejoined the caravan and Nesib showed vexation at the way Lawrence had risked his own life and Auda's "for a whim," Auda promptly turned on him, "glad to rub into a townsman the paradox of tribe and city; the collective responsibility and group-brotherhood of the desert, contrasted with the isolation and competitive living of the crowded districts."

The excitement followed by the argument helped to distract their thoughts from the pain of the journey until a few hours later they saw sand-hills fringed sparsely with tamarisk. It was the promised land, the Sirhan—and safety.

Even so they had to sleep that night on the prospect of water, not on the fact. Not until eight o'clock next morning did they reach the wells of Arfaja. Here they spent a day's rest in, relatively, luxurious ease. Yet that night they had a brusque reminder that the desert was not the only danger, nor the only barrier to Arab unity. For when drinking coffee round the camp-fire, a hail of bullets suddenly broke up their "coffee-housing." One man lay mortally wounded. Others might have followed but for the instant action of Auda's cousin in kicking sand over the fire. The sheltering darkness gave them a chance to find their rifles and beat off the raiders.

From this long desert journey Lawrence acquired the Arab habit of drinking—to drink to overflowing point when the chance came, and go sparingly on a few sips for several days on end between wells. He also gained further insight into the mind of the Syrian Arab. As they rode along the Sirhan from oasis to oasis, Nesib and Zeki entertained the party with pictures of how they would plant and reclaim all this country when they had established the Arab Government of their dreams. "Such vaulting imagination was typical of Syrians, who easily persuaded themselves of possibilities, and as quickly reached forward to lay their present responsibilities on others." Lawrence's reflection gained point from the fact that when he pointed out that Zeki's camel was full of mange, Zeki launched forth into a long discourse on the "Veterinary Department of State," minutely organized and scientifically equipped, that would be established when Syria was freed. He and Nesib became so absorbed in planning its organization during the next few days that they ignored all reminders about dressing the camel's itching skin—until, at last, it died.

Lawrence also lifts a corner of the veil over his own mind when he tells of his reply to their complaint that he had the English fault of snatching at the merely opportune, whereas their nature was to be content with nothing short of perfection. "O Nesib, and O Zeki, will not perfection, even in the least of things, entail the ending of this world? Are we ripe for that? When I am angry I pray God to swing our globe into the fiery sun, and to prevent the sorrows of the not-yet-born: but when I am content, I want to lie for ever in the shade, till I become a shade myself."

It was their nineteenth day since leaving Wejh when they reached one of the encampments of the Howeitat. After feasting that evening, a solemn council of action followed in the morning. The first resolve was to send a present of six bags of gold, a thousand pounds in each, to the Emir Nuri Shaalan. This it was hoped would encourage him to turn a blind eye to their mustering of force, and a kind eye to the families and herds while the fighting men were away. Auda was to be the envoy.

The rest of the party, and Lawrence with them, were meantime made the guests of the Howeitat, and feasted twice daily. Each morning they went in solemn procession, on led horses, to a different family's tent.

Each time, without variation, a similar pyramid of mutton in an encircling wall of rice was borne into their midst in the same huge tribal food-bowl. The centre-pieces were the boiled sheep's heads, "propped on their several stumps of necks, so that the ears, brown like old leaves, flapped out on the rice surface." Then, over all, cauldrons of boiling fat were poured over the pyramid. Then the guests would be called to eat, would feign a polite preliminary deafness, each urging the other forward, would finally kneel around the bowl, and, after turning back their sleeves, would all dip their hands simultaneously into the fiery mass. Urged on by their standing host, they would eat at a speed increased by the silence that was a conventional tribute to the excellence of the fare. When the greediest eater was finally satiated, a discreet signal to rise would come from Nasir, the chief guest.

The imp in Lawrence could not be wholly restrained from relieving the solemnity of the feast by passing "some hideous, impossible lump of guts" in place of the choice tit-bit which custom demanded that guests should occasionally hand to each other. But he adapted himself better to the strain than Nesib and Zeki, who broke down internally under this round of hospitality.

On May 30th it was happily ended through the tribe moving on to fresh pastures, accompanied by their guests. This chance of sharing in a Bedouin trek was an interesting experience, and would have been restful but for the plague of deadly snakes which infested the Sirhan that summer.

Walking about at night in bare feet was perilous, but resting was hardly less so, for the snakes were keen to share the warmth of blankets with their owners. Seven of Lawrence's party were bitten. "The Howeitat treatment was to bind up the bite with snake-skin plaster and read chapters of the Koran to the patient until he died." Four of the seven, however, recovered under this treatment. But to Lawrence, who had an acute horror of all reptiles, these days were a strain, as they were to most others except the mischievous pair, Farraj and Daud, who delighted in alarming their seniors by the cry of

"Snake!" This playful habit had a sequel akin to the nursery-tale cry of "Wolf!" For one day Lawrence sharply ordered them not to cry it again; an hour or so later he noticed them smiling and nudging each other, and following their glance saw a brown snake coiled under a nearby bush ready to strike at him. He instantly heaved himself out of the way while one of his men leapt in to kill the snake with his riding-cane. "I told him to give the two boys a swinging half-dozen each, to teach them not again to be literal at my expense." Lawrence's order was taken up in chorus by other long-suffering men, each claiming his six of revenge, until the tally was so large that the punishment was exchanged for a sentence of drawing water under the women's orders, more humiliating if less physically painful.

A few days later they met Auda, returning with an escort of Ruwalla horsemen that was an instantly visible sign of the success of his mission. These now took the oath of allegiance to Nasir, as Feisal's representative. "Besides their formal presents, each new party deposited on our carpet their privy, accidental gift of lice; and long before sunset Nasir and I were in a fever with relay after relay of irritation." Lawrence's sense of humour is, also, rather like the lice in the carpet, deposited wherever he goes and taking others unawares. He even dared to parody Auda's epic style in telling lurid stories, to the huge delight of Auda himself.

Since their arrival in the Sirhan they had been gradually moving along it north-westwards towards Azrak. And at Nebk, about midway between Arfaja and Azrak, they decided to make their preparations for the swoop on Aqaba, which lay almost due westward, and about two hundred miles distant by the route through Bair.

While Nasir and Auda were discussing plans, Nesib formed a new, and entirely different, picture of a triumphal march on Damascus, in which the Howeitat would be joined by the Druse and the Syrian Arabs. Lawrence alone seems to have grasped the dangers of this premature step, this imaginary conquest of Syria which would in reality have been a rush into the Turk's jaws while the adventurers were isolated both from Feisal and from the British forces. It was all the more rash because of the fact, which they knew before leaving Wejh, that the British advance had been held up in front of Gaza, after two costly assaults.

In Lawrence's view Aqaba was essential to prop open the door to

Syria; if they tried to go straight through to Damascus the door would slam back on its hinges, and would be difficult to open again. Nor was that all. So long as the Turks held Aqaba they might use it to threaten the rear of the British advance into Palestine. Lawrence was not forgetful of the duty of helping the British Army, nor did he overlook the fact that if the Arabs performed this service, they were likely to receive more help, in material, from the British. As the mobile right wing of Murray's force they would be valued more highly than as a remote distraction. And at the same time they would be fulfilling Lawrence's tactical principle of extension of depth.

The possibility of Nesib's plan being accepted instead led Lawrence to take a devious way of frustrating it, by playing on the latent jealousies among the Arab leaders, suggesting to Auda that Nesib wanted to supplant him in the leading role, and to Nasir that a man of his pedigree should not suffer himself to be dominated by an inferior. There is a certain irony in the way that Lawrence, the prophet of Arab unity, practised the ancient Roman maxim—"Di vide and rule."

To the possibilities of such personal hegemony he now seems, consciously or unconsciously, to have awakened. Perhaps to it may be traced the astonishing episode that followed, his four hundred mile ride through Syria and back to Nebk.

Although their airy design of an immediate advance on Damascus, to the neglect of the concrete Aqaba plan, had been frustrated, Nesib and Zeki proceeded with a more limited mission of sowing the seeds for a future rising in Syria. To this end they now went north to the Jebel Druse to open propagandist operations.

Lawrence decided to go north also, to explore the strategic possibilities of his intended post-Aqaba step and to take soundings among the Syrian tribes, feeling that he was likely to gauge the depth of their assurance with more realism than Nesib. Moreover, his appearance among them would be an encouraging sign of Britain's prospective power to intervene, while by his own intervention he might help to allay their mistrust of Britain's ultimate intentions. Yet he himself was by no means happy as to these. He had just gained an inkling of the Sykes-Picot agreement which left him profoundly uneasy, although when confronted by Arab suspicions he blandly dismissed them.

He undertook the ride through Syria in a mood of recklessness, seeking to drown in a deep draught of danger the memory of the way he had pledged himself to the Arabs as surety for Britain's good faith. Disgust at his own countrymen's double-dealing was heightened by the exasperation aroused in listening day after day to the endless scheming of Nesib and Zeki. "To hell with them all," seems to have been his inward comment, "they're going to make an awful mess of it, but at any rate I'll go up and test them myself."

He left Nebk on June 3rd and returned on the 16th. Even in the *Seven Pillars of Wisdom* he tells nothing of his experiences. Legend has woven a fanciful pattern round them, and it may have amused him to leave this untouched. Another reason for reticence was that during this journey he kept no notes, both because he rode so far and fast, and because of the risk of their falling into the Turks' hands. But on his return to Egypt after the capture of Aqaba he wrote a report of the journey for Clayton.

When a friend asked to see this report a few weeks later, he wrote back:

"I handed it to Clayton whose eyebrows went high (some of it was comic, some scurrilous, some betrayed horrible secrets) and who sat on it. I don't think anyone in the Savoy ever saw it, whole. It certainly never went to H.C. or W.O. or F.O., and I am too tender-hearted to ask after it now. It was an MS. document of three pages, and compressed two months' march into it: rather dull, except to one who knew Syrian politics. . . . It's all ancient history now."

Here is the partial outline of this amazing ride. He was unaccompanied by any of his party, and escorted instead by successive local guides, among them an old sheikh whom he had known before the war. He passed by Burga, which lies in the desert east of the Jebel Druse, and subsequently turned north-west to a spring which lies between Tadmor, ancient Palmyra, and Damascus. Eventually he reached the Aleppo-Damascus railway near Ras Baalbek. Here he blew up a small bridge—as reported in an enemy signal which was intercepted by our forces at the time. Then he bore south, travelling under the auspices of the Syrian revolutionaries; he visited many of their leaders and discussed with them plans for a rising when the moment was ripe—he took care to dissuade them from a premature move.

Out of this purpose arose the most amusing incident of his trip. One of his hosts sent a message to Ali Riza Pasha, the Turkish Base Commandant at Damascus who, like so many of his fellows, was privy to these underground movements. Ali Riza came out to see Lawrence on the outskirts of Damascus and in their interview Lawrence asked him to keep Damascus quiet, telling him that Aqaba was for the time their real objective.

He did not actually enter Damascus, nor did he see, as alleged, posters that put a price on his head and displayed a portrait of him. On his way back to Nebk, however, he stopped at Ziza to see the Sheikh of the Beni Sakhr. And there while he was sleeping a relative of the Sheikh crept into the tent and whispered, "They've sent to the Turks to say you are here." Lawrence deemed it wise not to give the Sheikh the benefit of the doubt. Crawling out through the back of the tent, he mounted and rode away.

The most important incident of the whole trip was a meeting with Nuri Shaalan, whom Lawrence saw in his tent near Azrak while on his own way towards Nebk. For the time, Lawrence desired of Nuri Shaalan no more than his benevolent neutrality. Nuri Shaalan, however, was perceptibly nervous lest his relations with the Turks might be compromised by the presence of Nasir's gathering force in the Sirhan. To his surprise, Lawrence suggested to him to "Send in to the Turks and say we are here." This astonishing candour veiled a strategic subtlety—calculated to serve a double purpose. For in easing Nuri Shaalan's position it might smooth the Arabs' path to their goal. Knowing that the expedition was now ready to move, Lawrence wanted the Turks to think it was an imminent menace to Damascus while it would be actually moving south to capture Aqaba.

CHAPTER XI

STRATEGY FULFILLED

June–July, 1917

From the Sirhan Lawrence moves down on Aqaba—approaching from the rear—As a preliminary distraction, he cuts the railway in the north, near Deraa—On July 1, 1917, the Arabs cross the line south of Ma'an—A Turkish force accidentally forestalls them at Abu el Lissal—After a day-long fight the Turks are routed by a sudden charge at dusk—The path thus cleared, Lawrence descends the Wadi Ithm, frontally impregnable, reaching Aqaba and the Red Sea on July 6—This almost bloodless success has far-reaching strategic effects

WHEN Lawrence arrived back at Nebk, he found that Auda had been quarrelling with Nasir. But the trouble was easily smoothed out and just before noon on June 19th the expedition set out on the march to Aqaba that was to change, for a second time, the face of the Arab war. The size of the expeditionary force, only five hundred strong, gave it an air of Gideon that was both symbolically and geographically apt in the circumstances. The first bound was westwards to Bair, a group of wells and historic ruins some sixty miles distant, and about forty miles short of the Hejaz railway.

On the second day, as they approached Bair, Auda asked Lawrence to ride ahead with him. His son, slain in a blood feud, had been buried there, and Auda, intending to pay the tribute of a lament over the grave, was paying Lawrence the tribute of companionship in his grief. But when they drew near Bair, they saw smoke rising from the wells and found that three had been dynamited. Luckily they discovered that the smallest was intact and, managing to repair one of the others, staved off the peril of being without water. The discovery, however, aroused uneasiness lest the Turks might have destroyed the wells at El Jefer, their intended next bound, just east of Ma'an. So they decided to pause a week at Bair while they sent a reconnaissance to El Jefer, and also took soundings among the local tribes whose support they needed.

The plan they had formed was to debouch suddenly from El Jefer, cross the railway south of Ma'an and capture Abu el Lissal, a large

MAP 6 **'AQABA-MA'AN ZONE**

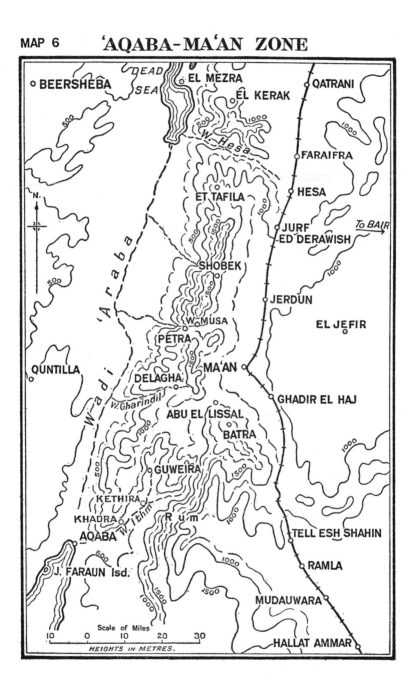

BEERSHEBA

DEAD SEA

EL MEZRA

EL KERAK

QATRANI

W. Hesa

FARAIFRA

ET TAFILA

HESA

To BAIR

JURF ED DERAWISH

'Araba

SHOBEK

JERDUN

EL JEFIR

W. MUSA

PETRA

QUNTILLA

DELAGHA

MA'AN

W. Gharindil

GHADIR EL HAJ

ABU EL LISSAL

BATRA

GUWEIRA

W. Ithm

KETHIRA

Rum

KHADRA

AQABA

TELL ESH SHAHIN

J. FARAUN Isd.

RAMLA

MUDAUWARA

Scale of Miles

10   0   10   20   30

HEIGHTS IN METRES.

HALLAT AMMAR

spring at the head of the pass that ran down from the Ma'an plateau towards Aqaba. The capture of Abu el Lissal was thus the key to the gate; it would enable them to shut off from Ma'an the Turkish posts on the Aqaba road, which would then be likely to collapse from hunger even if they were not overthrown by a tribal rising.

In preparation for the coup it was necessary to lull the Turks' suspicions. This seemed difficult, not only because the desert was a place of echoes and every unfriendly Arab a potential Turkish informer, but because Aqaba was such an obvious objective. Lawrence pinned his faith to the Turks' long-proved stupidity, and planned to play on their fumbling suspicions by measures of distraction. He certainly wove a fine web.

When himself in the Jebel Druse he had dropped hints of a move towards Damascus. Nuri Shaalan had helped by passing a warning to the Turks, and Lawrence counted on Nesib's incautious and unconscious aid towards the same end. Newcombe had also unintentionally let papers fall into the enemy's hands which outlined the scheme of a far-flung move by Tadmor against Aleppo.

Lawrence crowned the edifice of deception by a northward raid with a hundred Arabs against the railway between Amman and Deraa. It meant a long and hard ride if they were to be back in time, for the spot chosen was over a hundred miles north of Bair. On the second evening they approached the Dhuleil bridge, but found it unexpectedly well guarded and repairs in progress. So they decided to go a little farther north in search of a good spot for laying a mine. To catch a train would be even more effective than to blow up a bridge, for Lawrence wanted to give the Turks the idea that the Arabs' main force was in the neighbourhood. They found a site of excellent promise and took up a waiting position in a rocky amphitheatre high on the rear face of a nearby hill.

During the morning there was an alarm, when they sighted a body of Turks mounted on mules, heading towards them. But they slipped out of a position that might have become a trap without the Turks seeing them, and moved to another hill at Minifir. From here when darkness descended Lawrence went down to the line and buried a large automatic mine in a drainage culvert below the track. The next day was spent in tedious waiting for the expected train to come, but the afternoon was enlivened by the reappearance of the

Turkish detachment. Although the enemy were twice their strength, the Arabs were eager to attack them, trusting in surprise and the superior weight of a camel-charge against mules for the advantage. The Arabs claimed that in a mounted fight they could always beat the Turks, and estimated that their own loss was not likely to be more than half a dozen men. But Lawrence refused to sanction the attempt, counting this too large a price to pay for a success that was superfluous to their mission of pure distraction.

Even Marshal Saxe might have questioned Lawrence's extreme standard of economy, yet Marshal Foch would surely have approved his paramount aim of conserving every possible man to expend, if necessary, at Aqaba. Lawrence, however, had further motives. He did not want to burden himself with two hundred prisoners, and he feared that a bag of two hundred mules would be so rich a meal that it might spoil the Arabs' appetite for Aqaba. Although his restraint was not appreciated by the Arabs he gained his way, through the forceful aid of their leader, Zaal.

No train, however, appeared to compensate the forfeit, and for lack of water the party could wait no longer. So after dark they went down to the line and blew up rails, choosing the most curved ones as the most difficult to replace. They left the mine to catch the repair-train. Then they rode south, moving across the chord of the great Amman bend in the railway, until they came near Atwi station. Here the sight of a Turkish soldier driving a flock of sheep proved too strong for the hungry Arabs to resist. Zaal with a small party stalked a cluster of officers and officials who were drinking coffee outside the booking-office. Zaal's shot that killed the fattest of them was the signal for a rush to plunder the station yard, and under cover of the turmoil the sheep were driven off to the hills. The Turks defended themselves successfully in a part of the station, but the Arabs set fire to the other part and also cut rails and telegraph wires over a long stretch of line, without losing any men. Then, retiring a few miles, they settled down to kill and cook the sheep, and afterwards marched through the night to Bair.

Here they had good news. Nasir had obtained a week's supply of flour, which would secure them freedom of manoeuvre, and also promises of support from the clans on the route to Abu el Lissal. A messenger also arrived from Nuri Shaalan to say that four hundred

Turkish cavalry had been sent down the Sirhan in search of them, but were being guided by the most time-wasting route.

It was, clearly, important to profit by the grace thus provided. So on June 28th the Arab expedition left Bair for El Jefer. They found the wells demolished but were able to open up the shaft of one, and thus enjoyed not only the water but the humour of picturing the Turks' false sense of security. The attack was planned to take place two days before the Turks' weekly caravan of supplies set out from Ma'an to revictual the posts on the Aqaba route. Meantime the blockhouse that covered the approach to Abu el Lissal was stormed by the local Dhumaniyeh tribesmen as arranged.

The moment that this news came, on July 1st, the expedition moved out from El Jefer and headed for the railway, sending a party to hinder the Ma'an garrison by stampeding its camels. On reaching the railway they blew up the bridges on a long stretch of the line, with the particular idea that the Ma'an garrison would move south down the line instead of south-west to Abu el Lissal. This hope, however, was dissipated by the discomfiting report that a Turkish column had already appeared at Abu el Lissal, forcing the Dhumaniyeh to abandon the blockhouse.

The Turks' arrival was sheer accident; a Turkish relief battalion had just arrived at Ma'an and was forming up in the station yard ready to march into barracks when the news of the attack on the blockhouse reached them. A mountain-gun was added and the battalion marched off to the rescue—before the news of the attack on the railway could arrive. Finding the blockhouse a shambles, the commander encamped at the spring of Abu el Lissal.

This ill-stroke of fortune was a lesson to Lawrence in the accidents of war that may wreck the best-laid plan unless it has variants. And here a variant was difficult.[1] But a sense of time and an instinct

---

[1] Is is noteworthy, however, that Lawrence had conceived one—a fresh testimony to the way he had absorbed the strategic wisdom of the ages. "My alternative plan—for I hardly expected to crush the battalion at Aba el Lissan—was to hold them there on the defensive, and force them to fight their communications open again to Ma'an. This would take all their reserve and transport. While so occupied they would not be able to look towards Aqaba: but half our force would have gone down via Batra towards Rumm, and fallen upon Guweira, and then marched down the [Wadi] Itm to Aqaba, which we would have taken while the [Turkish] force at Lissan was being contained. It was a feasible plan: but it was inferior to what we did, as the destruction of the Ma'an garrison at Lissan gave us leisure, at Aqaba, to organize it as a base and for defence." (Cont. p. 158.)

for surprise may change the balance of fortune. And here both were shown. The moment that the ill-news came, Nasir's men threw their baggage on the camels and were on the march instantly. They rode all night and at dawn reached the hills near Abu el Lissal, where they were met by the rather dejected Dhumaniyeh. No waiting strategy could now avail, and action was promptly planned.

The Arabs extended, moving along the encircling hills until they had surrounded the still-sleeping encampment, while Zaal rode off with the fifty horsemen to cut the telegraph and telephone wires to Ma'an. Then they began to snipe the Turks, hoping to goad them into an uphill charge. The Arabs kept continually in movement, disappearing and reappearing at ever fresh points, so that the Turkish riflemen had no targets and their mountain-gun expended its shells fruitlessly. The heat of the day was so great that such activity became a strain and ultimately a torture, to skin and throat. But if the Turks were able to sit still in their hill-cupped camp, they were sitting in a furnace, and were less fit to withstand the fiery test. Thus as the day prolonged the stratagem that won many an ancient battle was here repeated, whether consciously or not. The Turks were being ripened for the sickle.

The sickle fell under the impulsion of an insult. Lawrence, exhausted with the heat and depressed with the prospect, had crept into a hollow where there was a trickle of muddy water from which he could moisten his lips. There Nasir joined him. After a time Auda appeared, and smiled rather scornfully at their frailty, retaliating for some of Lawrence's past criticisms by the question what he thought of the Howeitat now. But instead of amends Lawrence angrily offered a new insult—"By God, indeed they shoot a lot and hit a little."

Auda tore off his headcloth, threw it on the ground, and rushed back up the hill like a madman, calling to his men, who assembled round him and then scattered downhill. Lawrence, now disturbed as to what he had done, hurried after Auda whom he found alone on the hill top. But the only thing that Auda would say was, "Get your camel if you want to see the old man's work." By the time Nasir and Lawrence had reached the lower "step," where the camelry had

Inferior, probably, in effect, but from the point of view of military art history is the poorer by its too successful avoidance.

now assembled, Auda and his fifty horsemen had disappeared. Lawrence rode forward to the edge and saw them charging down the last slope into the valley at full gallop, firing from the saddle at the Turkish infantry, who had just formed up to force their way back to Ma'an. The charge came in their rear; they swayed at the sight, and then suddenly broke.

Nasir screamed to Lawrence, "Come on!" The four hundred camelry poured down the slope. The Turks' attention was all on Auda, "so we also took them by surprise and in flank; and a charge of ridden camels going nearly thirty miles an hour was irresistible."

As Lawrence himself was on a racing camel, he outstripped the others and was alone when he charged into the Turks' ranks. The camel suddenly fell and he was shot out of the saddle like a rocket, travelling far before he hit the ground. Luckily, however, the body of his camel behind served as a boulder, dividing into two streams the charging mass that would otherwise have surged over his own body, stamping it flat.

By the time he recovered the fight was over. It only lasted a few minutes, and like most mounted successes was more truly a massacre achieved by surprise and velocity. Three hundred of the Turks had been slaughtered before the Arabs' lust for vengeance was sated, and a further hundred and sixty, mostly wounded, were then taken prisoner. The Arabs had only two men killed. Auda was intoxicated with the rapture of battle and came up crying, "Work, work, where are words, work, bullets, Abu Tayi"—he had shown Lawrence what his tribe of the Howeitat could achieve. His clothes, his holster, his scabbard, and his field-glasses had all been riddled, but he was unscathed—a miracle which he ascribed to an eighteenpenny Glasgow reproduction of the Koran, for which he had been gulled into paying a hundred and twenty pounds many years earlier.

From prisoners they learnt that Ma'an at the moment was occupied by only two companies, not enough to hold its defensive perimeter. The news was a temptation to turn aside and take it. Such a chance would not come again, for the Turks were sure to send early reinforcements. The Howeitat clamoured to seize the opportunity, and Auda himself inclined towards the idea.

But Lawrence here proved in practice, as already in theory, that the strategist in him was master of the tactician. He refused to be drawn away from his strategic end by a tactical success, following the precept of Foch instead of anticipating the practice of Ludendorff. But unlike Foch he sought a strategic end that was tactically attainable, and to that extent was more in accord with Ludendorff's intention, if happier in its application.

A base was necessary for the successful continuation of his strategic design, and only by taking Aqaba could he obtain it. If the Arabs went to Ma'an now, they would soon be thrown out, and then be stranded without supplies or support. The Arabs were, in fact, thrown out of Abu el Lissal soon afterwards.

While it was Lawrence's strategic reasoning that checked them from turning back against Ma'an, it was Auda's tactical instinct, coupled with his superstitious fear of lying among the dead, that got the Arabs on the move again the same night. Lawrence was feeling "the physical shame of success, a reaction of victory, when it became clear that nothing was worth doing, and that nothing worthy had been done." In search of some covering for the wounded prisoners he went back to the battlefield to take some of the dead men's clothes, only to find they had all been stripped. An impulse moved him to straighten out the heap of corpses, laying them side by side as if in a sleep that gave him a longing to share their company rather than that of the triumphal plundering mob.

But once back with the force the strategist revived within him. While the force rested in a hollow, letters were dictated to the sheikhs of the coast tribes, telling them the news of victory and inviting them to keep the Turkish garrisons engaged until the force arrived. There was grand strategy, not merely strategy, in the further series of letters to the commanders of the three Turkish posts, Guweira, Kethira, and Khadra, on the way to Aqaba, telling them that "if our blood was not hot we took prisoners, and that prompt surrender would ensure their good treatment and safe delivery to Egypt." Lawrence was treading in the path of Scipio and Saxe in smoothing the enemy's path to surrender.

Close on the heels of the messengers followed the army. It looked like a Turkish army, for the Arabs, following the habit of primitive victors, had donned the tunics of their dead foes. After a five mile ride from Abu el Lissal across the plateau they came to the edge and saw the Guweira plain far below them, as a man looks down from the gallery of a vast amphitheatre. As the column wound down the precipitous corkscrew descent of the Negab Pass they could appreciate the hopelessness of any advance from the sea, even if, by a miracle, the road from Aqaba to Guweira had been opened.

Hampered by the fatigue of victory and their prisoners, the march was slow. Only fifteen miles had been covered when the force halted for the night short of Guweira. But here they were met by the local sheikh, Ibn Jad, with the news that the garrison of Guweira, a hundred and twenty strong, had surrendered. This removed one of the most serious obstacles in their path, for Guweira was the northern gateway to the gorge of the Wadi Ithm.

Resuming the march next day, July 4th, they came to Kethira, eighteen miles on. Here to their disappointment they found that the commander of this cliff-top post, commanding the valley, was bent on resistance. They suggested that their new ally, Ibn Jad, might prove his worth by attacking it, after dark. Misliking the prospect, he argued that the full moon would mar the attempt. But Lawrence had noticed in his diary that an eclipse was due, and so "cut hardly into this excuse; promising that to-night for awhile there should be no moon." The eclipse came, and while the superstitious Turkish soldiery were firing rifles and clanging copper pots "to rescue their threatened satellite," the Arabs climbed into the post and took the place by surprise. Seventy infantry and fifty mounted men were taken prisoner.

Next day the Arab force descended the Wadi Ithm gorge, so narrow that in places the bottom was only a few yards wide. There were many places where, as Sir Hubert Young has remarked—"one company with two or three machine-guns could have stopped an army corps." To meet the oncoming menace, the Aqaba garrison, three hundred strong, had hastily marched inland to reinforce the post at Khadra. But all their entrenchments faced seawards, so that they were laid bare by the unexpected approach from the rear. And the local tribesmen, eager for a share of the plunder, had already risen and were surrounding the Turks.

Twice, a summons was sent to them to surrender, and repelled by bullets. Many of the Bedouin clamoured for an assault. Lawrence's reasoned preference for relying on hunger-pressure was affected by the shortness of food in his own force. However, a third attempt was made with moral suasion. This time it produced a promise of surrender in two days, if help did not come from Ma'an. It was pointed out to a Turkish officer that the Arabs could not be restrained so long. Delay would mean massacre. The Turk yielded, promising to surrender at daylight.

But during the night fresh tribesmen swarmed to the scene, like flies to the jampot, and, not knowing the arrangement, opened fire on the Turks as soon as it was light on the 6th. Nasir, however, intervened, and his march down the valley with the Ageyl checked both sides. Firing ceased, and the Turks at once surrendered.

While the post was being looted, Lawrence raced on to Aqaba, only four miles farther, and splashed into the cooling sea. Historical aptness should have called to his lips the cry of the Ten Thousand—"Thalassa, Thalassa." But, in fact, his thoughts were entirely "on his feet" at this moment of triumph.

Two months had passed all but three days since the little expedition had left the sea-coast at Wejh. Since then it had covered a vast elliptic curve through the depths of Arabia before returning like a boomerang, and with snowball increase of force, to strike the neighbour-port of Wejh in the back. But the longest way round had proved the easiest way there.

The capture of Aqaba was like a sudden break in the clouds that overhung the Egyptian front in the spring and summer of 1917. From the point of view of moral effect it was the one definite achievement that could be set off against the double British failure before Gaza. Strategically, it removed all danger of a Turkish raid through Sinai against the Suez Canal or the communications of the British army in Palestine. It also opened up a new line of operation by which the Arabs could give positive assistance to a renewed British advance.

Tactically, the Aqaba operation had inflicted a permanent loss of some 1,200 men, prisoners and killed, on the Turks—at a cost of two men killed in the conquering force. There is, indeed, a slightly ironical flavour in the fact that Lawrence, in his first trial of the new bloodless strategy, had levied a blood-tax on the enemy at the highest rate that modern "murder war" can perhaps show. By the strictest canons of orthodox strategy, by the World War standards of "killing Germans" or "killing Turks," it was an unrivalled achieve-

ment. The British forces in trying unsuccessfully to capture Gaza in March and April had only succeeded in killing or capturing 1,700 Turks at a permanent cost to themselves of 3,000 men. In other words, they had sacrificed roughly two men to "kill" one Turk, the same number that the Arabs had sacrificed to "kill" twelve hundred Turks!

As an object-lesson in the abstract principle of economy of force the Aqaba operation was remarkable. For all this had been achieved by the use of less than fifty men from the Arab forces in the Hejaz. As practical economy of British force it was more notable still. For it was attained by the detachment of merely one unwanted officer from the forces in Egypt.

Greater still were the ultimate effects of Aqaba. For its capture ensured that the "Arab ulcer" would continue to spread in the Turks' flank, draining their strength and playing on their nerves. Unlike their relation to the "Spanish ulcer" the British as an army had hitherto done little to assist the spread of this infection. They lacked a Wellington. But the sun that shone on Aqaba lit up a better prospect in Egypt. For on June 27th, nine days previous to the capture of Aqaba, a new commander arrived in Egypt, Sir Edmund Allenby. It was a prophetic significance that his arrival should thus coincide with Lawrence's vindicatory triumph.

CHAPTER XII

A NEW HORIZON

July, 1917

The capture of Aqaba was unknown to the British—To preserve his prize, Lawrence after making original dispositions for defence, rides across the Sinai desert to fetch succour and supplies—His achievement coincides with the arrival in Egypt of a new British commander—Allenby's promise of support inspires Lawrence to put forward a new plan—The Drake of the desert, he would carry the war into the "Turkish Main," and wage it on privateering methods

IT WAS over three years since Lawrence had seen Aqaba. He had come back to it under strangely different conditions, that lent piquancy to familiar landmarks. The Gulf of Aqaba may be pictured as a croquet hoop laid flat. At the right-hand corner was the little town, now tumbled in abject ruins by repeated naval bombardments. At the left-hand corner was a clump of red rocks that caught the eye from the sea, and, by so doing, had earlier saved the life of a French air pilot who had staggered down to the shore after a crash in the interior. A short way down the left-hand edge was Jebel Faroun, the little island which long-dead Crusaders had garrisoned. The gulf itself was prolonged by a great dry trough, the Wadi Araba, that ran between high cliffs towards the Dead Sea. From it on the right-hand side, a few miles behind Aqaba, diverged the gorge of the Wadi Ithm, which led to Ma'an.

After his first splash of exultation, Lawrence suffered the sudden disillusionment of a goal attained. The life that he had not expected to keep lost the savour that it had borne while being risked. The very drabness of the scene accentuated the barrenness of his satisfaction.

Hunger called him out of this trance, back to the barrenness of the cupboard. There were five hundred of his men, seven hundred prisoners, a couple of thousand new allies to feed, and no supplies, save for the green dates that the palms offered, and the meat that the camels might afford at the price of mobility. He had proved his generalship, but now he had to be a quartermaster-general. Partly

MAP 7 # 'AMMAN-DER'A ZONE

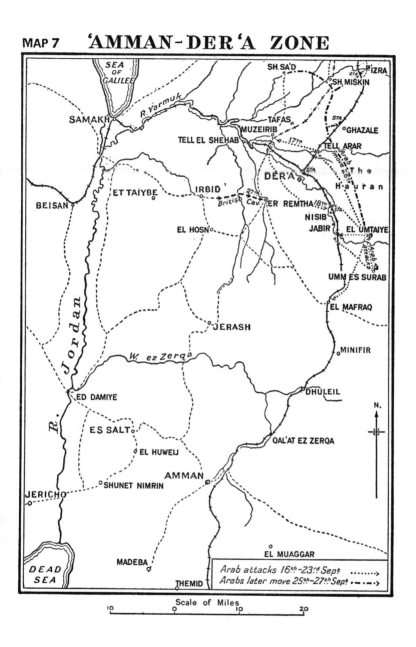

Arab attacks 16th-23rd Sept. ....→
Arabs later move 25th-27th Sept. ·—·—·→

Scale of Miles

because of his irregular leave-taking he had set out from Wejh without the same thorough arrangements for Naval co-operation as in the earlier move to Wejh. He had, indeed, been promised by Boyle that a ship would sail up the Gulf of Aqaba as often as possible, but the problem of keeping watch for the Arabs' arrival was complicated by the uncertainty of this arrival as well as by the Turkish mines in the sea-approaches to Aqaba. Actually, when Lawrence reached Aqaba he heard that a British ship had appeared, and disappeared, about an hour earlier. It meant that he could hardly hope for another visit before a week had elapsed.

Thus two military problems now confronted him; or, rather, two sides to one problem—that of keeping the prize he had gained. How was it to be held against the Turks? How was it to be held on an empty stomach?

The solution of the first was in accord with Lawrence's new and original theory of war. It was arranged to cover all the possible approaches to Aqaba, not by a series of interdependent posts, but by four independent ones, sited in places as nearly impregnable by nature as possible and each menacing the enemy's rear if he tried to advance by the others, so that while not one could be easily taken, none could be neglected. It seemed a good way to paralyse an assailant's initiative.

There was to be a post at Guweira where Auda himself went, a post at Batra on the flank of Abu el Lissal, another in the rocks at Nabathean Petra, and a fourth at Delagha, on the intermediate Wadi Gharandil route to the great Wadi Araba trough. The last provided a backstairs communication between the first and third and would also serve to keep the doubtful Sinai and Beersheba Arabs from joining hands with the Turks from Ma'an. To site posts of this kind successfully in a hurry a soldier needs to be not merely a tactician but a high-speed geographer. Lawrence's map studies with Hedley and the survey of Egypt were of great value to his plans here, as always.

In the solution of the second and more urgent part of the problem Lawrence was also characteristically individual. He decided to go himself across the Sinai desert to Suez and obtain the dispatch of a food-ship. It was a hazardous venture. There were a hundred and fifty miles of the Sinai desert to cross, and only one well on the route. If any rider fell out he was doomed, yet both camels and men were tired when they started. Lawrence himself had been averaging fifty miles a day for a month past.

Picking out eight of the best riders and camels he set off on the night of his arrival at Aqaba. As they rode round the bay they discussed the choice between going gently, and risking collapse from hunger, or going fast, and risking collapse from exhaustion. Finally, they decided to keep at a walk but ride almost continuously. This meant transferring the worst strain to the rider instead of the camel.

The first test came early, in climbing the steep path, one in three and a half, up the Sinai scarp. Men and camels were trembling with fatigue when they reached the top, and one, obviously unfit, was sent back while there was still time.

Near midnight they reached Themed, and paused for a drink at its wells. No more water would be met until they reached Suez. A few minutes' pause at dawn; again at midday when roughly midway, near the ruins of Nekhl; an hour's halt at sunset before crossing the Mitla Hills, another hour at the second day's coming—that was all the rest they allowed themselves. Their failing strength eked out by the cooling breezes that greeted them from the Gulf of Suez, they were among the sand-dunes by noon on the 8th, and at three o'clock rode, weary but relieved, into Shatt, the post on the Canal opposite Suez.

But the manner of their welcome was a fresh trial, hardly bearable. They found the post deserted, with no one to tell them that the troops had moved out to a camp in the desert because of an outbreak of plague. Lawrence found a telephone in the empty offices and rang through to headquarters at Suez, only to be told that he must apply to the Inland Water Transport for a passage across the canal. This he did, only to be told that there was no boat available. Adding that one would be sent in the morning, to take him to quarantine, the Inland Water Board rang off.

"I refused to spend a single superfluous night with my familiar vermin. I wanted a bath, and something with ice in it to drink: to change these clothes, all sticking to my saddle sores in filthiness: to eat something more tractable than green date and camel sinew. I got through again to the Inland Water Transport and talked like Chrysostom. It had no effect, so I became vivid. Then, once more, they cut me off. I was growing very vivid, when friendly northern accents from the military exchange floated down the line: 'It's no b—— good, sir, talking to them f—— water b——.' "

The operator took the initiative of putting Lawrence through to Major Lyttleton at the Embarkation Office. He at once promised to send his own launch, asking Lawrence not to give away the fact of the breach of red-tape. Within half an hour the launch appeared and carried Lawrence across to Suez where, after overcoming the distrustful manner of the Sinai Hotel staff, he had six cold drinks and a hot bath, followed by dinner and bed after he had arranged for the care of his Arab companions.

Next day, armed with ticket and pass he boarded the train for Ismailia and Cairo. On the way he had a fresh encounter with officialdom and was sufficiently refreshed to indulge his leg-pulling propensity. The military police looked suspiciously at this Englishman in bare feet and white silk robes. Instead of showing his pass he curtly said "Sherif of Mecca—Staff." "What army, sir?" "Mecca." "Never heard of it: don't know the uniform." Lawrence retorted, "Would you recognize a Montenegrin dragoon?"

As allied troops were allowed to travel without passes, the police were driven to wire up the line for a special intelligence officer. When he boarded the train, perspiring, Lawrence produced his pass. The would-be spy-catcher did not appreciate the joke.

The train was just running into Ismailia, and here on the platform Lawrence saw Admiral Wemyss, deep in talk with an unknown general. Lawrence seized the chance to speak to Captain Burmester, Wemyss' chief of staff. For a moment Burmester failed to recognize Lawrence, so burned with the sun and so fine-drawn through prolonged strain—his weight had fallen from about nine stone to six stone ten pounds. But there was no barrier of red-tape from the moment of recognition. Stirred by the news of Aqaba's capture, Burmester gave instant orders for the *Dufferin* to load up with all available food at Suez and steam for Aqaba.

From Burmester Lawrence learnt that the unknown general was Allenby, sent out to replace Murray after the second failure at Gaza —of this also Lawrence now heard for the first time. He "fell to wondering whether this heavy rubicund man was like ordinary generals, and if we should have trouble for six months teaching him.

Murray and Belinda had begun so tiresomely that our thought those first days had been, not to defeat the enemy, but to make our own chiefs let us live."

Lawrence had an early chance to gauge Allenby's attitude. On arrival in Cairo he made his report to Clayton, and arranged with him for sixteen thousand pounds in gold to be sent at once to Aqaba, so that Nasir might be able to redeem at once the "notes" that Lawrence had issued. They were pencilled promises, on army telegraph forms, to pay so much to bearer in Aqaba. "It was a great system, but no one had dared issue notes before in Arabia," so early redemption was essential if Arab prejudice was to be overcome for the future. Then, before Lawrence had been able to get new uniforms made, there came a summons from Allenby.

"In my report, thinking of Saladin and Abu Obeida, I had stressed the strategic importance of the eastern tribes of Syria, and their proper use as a threat to the communications of Jerusalem. This jumped with his ambitions, and he wanted to weigh me."

For almost three years in France, Allenby had been the target of criticism. "The Bull," as he was universally known, had fitted his nickname both in action against the enemy and attitude to his subordinates. An ardent cavalryman, trench-warfare had irked his spirit and several times goaded him into launching attacks that were not justified by the openings nor guided by knowledge of the real situation. At other times, showing more research for surprise than was the custom, he had been frustrated by the high priests of the artillery cult, with their ritual bombardments, and by his own inability to counter their technical arguments. He had been irked, too, by subordination to Haig, a man of equal determination but more orthodox thought, whom he had outshone as a column leader in South Africa only to fall behind on the ladder of promotion. The strain between them was not merely due to personal differences. Allenby was a man cast by nature for an independent role, better and bigger in carrying out his own plans than in executing another's. Here he had an essential likeness to Lawrence, in other ways so different.

His transfer to Egypt was a turning point in his career, as it became a fresh turning point in Lawrence's. The steel harness of Western warfare had sat uneasily on Allenby's shoulders, and in this new theatre, itself more open and occupied by a foe less mechanically endowed, he found the right field for his gifts and his instincts. He needed little persuasion to place his trust in mobility rather than in hard pounding.

Even so, Lawrence felt that "he was hardly prepared for anything so odd as myself—a little bare-footed silk-skirted man offering to hobble the enemy by his preaching if given stores and arms and a fund of two hundred thousand sovereigns to convince and control his converts." "Allenby could not make out how much was genuine performer and how much charlatan. The problem was working behind his eyes, and I left him unhelped to solve it."

Lawrence did most of the talking and expounded his ideas of Eastern Syria, its people, and the policy to be adopted. At the end Allenby briefly said, "Well, I will do for you what I can." And Lawrence gradually found that "what General Allenby could do was enough for his very greediest servant." The £200,000 was later increased to £500,000, of which Lawrence had a balance of £10,000 to return when Damascus was reached.

If Lawrence had already perceived a new horizon, Allenby's words brought it closer. The assurance encouraged him to draw up a program and submit it to Clayton. In the discussion that now took place we can see the change that seven months had wrought in Lawrence —the passage he had made between Yanbo and Aqaba. Before going to Yanbo he had tried to evade the responsibility of being adviser. Now he sought the far greater responsibility of being director. But he did not mind whether he had, or who had, the trappings of authority so long as he had the reality.

To be "King without the crown" had been his desire. He did not ask for command but that his policy and strategy should be adopted in the Arab theatre of war—that his new "northern" plan should become the official one. By making this point clear he turned the flank of Clayton's objection that even irregular war did not reverse regular methods so far that the most junior officer should take command. Lawrence was more than willing to accept the practical alternative that Joyce should be sent as commanding officer at Aqaba. For with Joyce, as with Newcombe, he would be assured not only of a free hand but of solid backing. Joyce would make a strong shaft for Lawrence's spear-head, and all the stronger because Joyce had the capacity for that necessary organization which Lawrence was anxious to escape—needed to escape if he was to direct.

Lawrence has an astonishing grasp of detail—to read some of his intelligence reports is a revelation of the rare combination of wide views with minute observation. And I have often been amused, as well as impressed, by his super-methodical organization of some quite petty job—although the method is usually unconventional. But he long ago learnt the truth that the man who tries to do everything himself will never achieve anything big. Experience had shown him that he had to be the spear-head of any big drive that his plan required. The others had courage and the team-spirit, but he alone could supply the decisive ingenuity. To quote his own words, which others have endorsed, "I knew my ground, my material and my allies. If I met fifty checks, I could yet see a fifty-first way to my object. But if I had to be the spear-point I dared not weary myself over ship-loads of rice and flour." Distribution of effort is the beginning of military wisdom.

As for the program itself, the deliverance of Syria now succeeded the deliverance of the Hejaz, which, virtually accomplished, dropped into the background. Now the essential difference between the land that had been delivered and the land that he sought to deliver was that whilst the former was almost entirely desert, the latter was predominantly cultivated. It was easier to lift the yoke from floating globules than from a settled body. The new problem required a new treatment. Lawrence realized that the Arab peoples in the north could only be freed through the aid of the British Army, whose northward advance was the necessary lever to overturn the Turkish dominion that the Arabs could undermine. Each was necessary to the other, and each might help the other's progress. The co-operation need not be close; in fact it would be all the better, strategically and politically, if British and Arabs were long-range collaborators rather than direct associates. Such was Lawrence's idea, and in Allenby he found a ready response to it, "We agreed to keep the Dead Sea and Jordan between us—except when he gave me notice he was going to Amman, and I gave him notice I was recruiting in Sinai." In strategic policy it meant adaptation—to settled instead of nomadic conditions. In principle it should be easier to develop a sense of unity and a creed of nationality, among a people who were tied to their fields. But in actuality, unity was likely to break apart on the many divisions and subdivisions of the people.

The mountain range that runs north and south divides the settled part into a coastal strip and an inland plain, so different in climate as to create utterly different conditions of life. And beyond the cultivated interior lies the vast desert stretch. Moreover the river-valleys running down to the Mediterranean create a series of lateral intersections. Varieties of religion introduce subdivisions within subdivisions. And Turkish policy had craftily deepened the mixture. Moreover, the chain of cities—Jerusalem, Damascus, Homs, Hama, Aleppo, and that exotic plant, Beirut—produced an urban class essentially apart from the peasant population, although differing between cities.

Syria was thus a patchwork quilt of many colours sewn together, under the hand of the Ottoman Government, by the thread of a common language—Arabic. If the colours were mixed, most of them were vivid owing to the general tendency of the Syrian mind to indulge in fanciful day-dreams.

Lawrence's boyhood dream of a united Arabia had shrivelled in contact with Arab realities, especially among the Syrians.[1] But in their dreams he saw a means, the only means, of stirring them as a whole into revolt against the Turks. The fusion would be temporary, but it might suffice to shatter the Turkish Empire—and to secure the victory. To detonate the explosion he must strike their imagination. The fuse must be sufficiently novel to be kept apart from their damping jealousies; it must not be of European manufacture lest it scratch their conceit. Feisal should be the fuse, as a personification and projection of the past glories of the Ommayad or Ayubid dynasties.

In strategic direction the new campaign would be aimed at the Hauran; once the Hauran rose the object of the campaign, Lawrence calculated, would be achieved. Deraa and the Yarmuk Valley would provide the leverage on which to bear in loosening the enemy's hold on the Hauran. To reach them it would be necessary to set up and

[1] A remark that T.E. made to me is worth quotation here:
"I have always been a realist and opportunist in tactics: and Arab unity is a madman's notion—for this century or next, probably. English-speaking unity is a fair parallel. I never dreamed of uniting even Hejaz and Syria. My conception was of a number of states."

mount a fresh ladder of tribes, similar to that from Wejh to Aqaba. It would again be a curved ladder carrying them out through the desert before it turned in. The steps of the ladder would be formed of the Howeitat, Beni Sakhr, Sherarat, Ruwalla and Serahin, "to raise us three hundred miles to Azrak," the oasis which offered an advanced base for operations against the Hauran.

In strategic execution the new campaign would be a repetition of the old, but improved through the experience already gained. Not without reason had the camel been called the ship of the desert. Lawrence's thought travelled back to Francis Bacon's dictum, "He who commands the sea is at great liberty, and may take as much or as little of the war as he will." His own war was more Elizabethan than Fochian—and the Arabs had command of the desert. Desert operations should be like such wars at sea "in their mobility, their ubiquity, their independence of bases and communications, their lack of ground features, of strategic areas, of fixed directions, of fixed points."

"Camel-raiding parties, self-contained as ships, could cruise without danger along any part of the enemy's land-frontier, just out of sight of his posts along the edge of cultivation, and tap or raid into his lines where it seemed fittest or easiest and most profitable, with a sure retreat always behind them into an element which the Turks could not enter." The Arabs' freedom of movement was fortified by an intimate knowledge of the desert-front of Syria. Lawrence himself had traversed much of it on foot before the war, tracing the movements of Saladin. "As our war-experience deepened we became adepts at that form of geographical intuition, described by Bourcet as wedding unknown land to known in a mental map."

The tactics, Lawrence conceived, should always be "tip and run: not pushes, but strokes." The Arabs should never try "to maintain or improve an advantage." They ought "to move off and strike again somewhere else." As he wrote later—"We used the smallest force in the quickest time at the farthest place. If the action had continued till the enemy had changed his dispositions to resist it, we would have been breaking the spirit of our fundamental rule of denying him targets." This was a far subtler and also more profound principle than the familiar "concentration at the decisive spot." More practical too in application. And with slight adaptation it would fit regular warfare, for the use of mobile forces.

The necessary speed and range for this "distant war" could be attained through the frugality of the Arabs, and their efficiency in handling that "intricate animal," the camel, which, like a tank, has a remarkable performance in skilled hands and easily breaks down in unskilled. The Arabs were free from the encumbrance of an elaborate supply system—this has cramped the strategic mobility of modern armies as the machine-gun has crippled their tactical mobility. Each man was self-contained, carrying on the saddle six weeks' food for himself—a half-bag of flour, of forty-five pounds weight, which he baked for himself. "This gave us a range of over a thousand miles out and home, and that . . . was more than ever we needed, even in so large a country as Arabia." And the camels themselves served as an emergency ration, if so tough a one as to deserve the title of "iron ration." The camels lived on grazing as they marched. Thus after their six weeks on the road they would be worn thin and would need to be sent to pasture for a long rest, which meant the replacement either of the camels or of the raiding tribe by another.

The new strategy was well adapted to tribal conditions. "It was impossible to mix or combine tribes, since they disliked or distrusted one another. Likewise we could not use the men of one tribe in the territory of another." For concentration of force this would have been a ruinous handicap. But it suited the principle of the widest distribution of force, enabling the Arab command to have the greatest possible number of raids in course at the same time. And "by using one district on Monday, another on Tuesday, a third on Wednesday," fluidity could be added to mobility.

CHAPTER XIII

SECURING THE BASE

August–September, 1917

Lawrence's persuasion secures the transfer of Feisal's forces to Aqaba, for operations in the north as Allenby's mobile wing—Liquid funds—The Turkish threat to Aqaba is paralysed by pricks—Lawrence begins to operate against the railway

LAWRENCE's first definite proposal towards the new campaign was that Wejh should be abandoned, and Feisal's whole force transferred to Aqaba. When the authorities in Cairo hesitated before this bold suggestion, Lawrence increased its boldness, urging the withdrawal from the Yanbo-Medina area of all the stores and money that were being used to sustain the operations of Ali and Abdulla. While Feisal was at Aqaba far up the flank of the Hejaz railway, and Allenby was before Gaza threatening an advance into Palestine, the Turks were not likely to strengthen the garrison of Medina. The important thing was to prevent them weakening it, and trying to withdraw their forces northward. A little encouragement, through a further slackening of effort in the south, might aid this purpose without involving any serious danger to the Arabs in the Hejaz.

Here, however, Lawrence was donning the mantle of Robertson and pressing a military theory beyond the limits of political expediency. But the stiffening of opposition to this further suggestion brought with it a relaxation of caution towards his first. Thus Lawrence's political instinct was justified, and he promptly exploited the weakening.

Aqaba was only 130 miles from the British position at the Wadi Ghazze, whereas it was 700 miles from Mecca. He suggested that, as a logical consequence, Feisal's force should be transferred from Hussein's sphere of control to Allenby's and become an autonomous army with Feisal its commander, under Allenby's supreme command. Their future lines of operation ran in the same direction.

Before this proposal could be adopted, three potential human obstacles had to be overcome—Feisal, Wingate, and Hussein. Law rence was able to give the assurance that Feisal would accept—they had talked this matter over in Wejh months before. Would Wingate hand over to another the care of the now sturdy infant he had done so much to nurse? Clayton sounded him; he found him willing to see the larger issue and relinquish Feisal's force for Allenby's use. Thus of the possible obstacles, only Hussein remained. Lawrence offered to go down and persuade him.

The *Dufferin* had just returned from Aqaba, and she was ordered to carry Lawrence to Jidda. On the way she called at Wejh; here he disembarked and travelled by aeroplane to Jeida, a hundred miles distant, the advanced base to which Feisal's army had moved early in July in order to operate more effectively against the railway. The air way of travel was a pleasantly quick contrast to his last inland ride in this region, and on arrival at Jeida it was a joy to meet again his old comrades, themselves now crowned with the laurels of many successful railway raids. From him they heard fragments of his experiences in the north, and from them he gathered news of what had happened in the past three months.

On the debit side was the detachment of the Billi from the Sherifian cause. Early in May their Sheikh had joined the Turks at El Ala with four hundred of his men, and although he evaded their invitation to attack Feisal, he induced his brother to leave Feisal's army, bringing away his men and the arms with which they had been supplied. Another accession to the Turkish side, more notable than really influential, was Ibn Rashid, the Emir of Hail. His arrival, indeed, was the sequel to a disaster; for in April, when conveying a large convoy of supplies to the Turks in Medina, he had been trapped and routed by Zeid near Hanakiye, eighty miles northeast of Medina. Zeid had captured three thousand richly laden camels, a similar number of sheep, four mountain guns, and two hundred and fifty prisoners, mostly Turks. This was one of the most important coups of the Hejaz war, and the gain far outweighed the fact that Ibn Rashid himself with about a thousand followers had then joined the Turks at Medain Saleh. His chief effect was to impose an extra strain on their limited supplies.

In the raids on the railway that hampered its working the handful of British officers had continued to play the foremost part. The Arabs, indeed, regarded them as exhausting allies and complained—

"Newcombe is like fire; he burns friend and enemy." And Lawrence, who had strategic reasons for wishing that Newcombe would not press too hard on the railway, remarks that he did four times as much as any other Englishman would have done and ten times as much as the Arabs thought necessary! Their passive resistance had played a part in baulking the original British intention of severing the railway completely, although the Turks had also taken a shrewd step to frustrate a strong concentration of effort—by filling in the wells within reach of their main stations. In the middle of May Newcombe had made several breaks around Muadhdham, between Medain Saleh and Tebuk, slipping away before the forces from these stations could close upon him. He reported that the repairs were being made with old rails, which showed how the Turks were being hit in their weak side—the material side. In July Newcombe and Davenport made a large scale raid, with marked success, on a long section of the line near Qal'at Zamrud, 140 miles north of Medina, while the Arabs captured the station immediately above it. Joyce carried out a series of raids further south around Toweira with a mixed force of Egyptian, French Algerian, and Arab troops, destroying thousands of rails and several large culverts.

Feisal, however, had moved to Jeida without enthusiasm, under pressure from Wilson and Abdulla. His thoughts wandered ever to the north, to Aqaba and to Syria. Thus he welcomed with delight both the news and the message that Lawrence brought. He accepted the new plan instantly, ordered his camelry to march to Aqaba, and made arrangements that the Arab regulars, now numbering about 1,800 men, should be shipped there as early as possible together with all the stores from Wejh. He also gave Lawrence a letter for Hussein.

Next morning at dawn Lawrence flew back to Wejh, and re-embarked in the *Dufferin* for Jidda, where he received Wilson's unstinted promise of moral and material support. Hussein came down from Mecca, and, under Wilson's influence, agreed to Feisal's transfer. Lawrence was struck by the similarity between the two men in the narrow orbit of their thought, their loyalty to a cause, and their intense honesty of purpose, which in Hussein's case led him, perhaps not without cause, to view everyone else, save Wilson, as potential "crooks."

Yet Lawrence himself was hardly less disturbed when a telegram from Cairo reported that the Howeitat were in treacherous correspondence with the Turks at Ma'an, and a second telegram suggested that Auda was in the plot. As he held the keys to Aqaba, the menace was obvious. Lawrence boarded the *Hardinge* and sailed at once for Aqaba, which he reached on the afternoon of August 5th.

On landing he did not tell Nasir of the report, but simply asked for a swift camel and a guide. He also told Nasir that Hussein had granted him a month's leave to visit Mecca, a long sought privilege which so delighted Nasir that he sold Lawrence Ghazala, peerless among camels. Riding through the night up the Wadi Ithm Lawrence reached Guweira and found Auda talking with other leaders in a tent. They showed signs of confusion, but he greeted them gaily, and chatted about trivialities until he had a chance of speaking to Auda and his cousin Mohammed el Dheilan alone.

When he mentioned the subject of their correspondence with the Turks they told an elaborate story of a ruse played on the Turks. It was too elaborate to be convincing. Lawrence pretended to enter into the joke, but he perceived that "there was more behind. They were angry that no guns or troops had yet come to their support; and that no rewards had been given them for taking Aqaba. They were anxious to know how I had learnt of their secret dealings, and how much more I knew. We were on a slippery ledge." So was Lawrence, as an individual, although he does not emphasize the point. He played on their fears by carelessly quoting, as if they were his own words, actual phrases from the letters they had exchanged with the Turks. And he told them incidentally that Feisal's whole army was coming up, and also of the munitions and money that Allenby was sending. Finally he suggested that Auda might like an advance instalment of Feisal's bounty.

"Auda saw that the immediate moment would not be unprofitable: that Feisal would be highly profitable: and that the Turks would be always with him if other resources failed. So he agreed, in a very good temper, to accept my advance; and with it to keep the Howeitat well-fed and cheerful."

Easier in mind, Lawrence set out back to Aqaba after dark. Riding all night, he had a talk with Nasir on arrival and paddled out in a derelict canoe to the *Hardinge* just as the dawn was coming. He had been gone only thirty-six hours, and had not been expected back for a week. But while he went below to sleep, the ship made full steam for Suez. Thence he telephoned a reassuring report to Cairo, in which he said that the reports of treachery were unfounded.

"This may hardly have been true: but since Egypt kept us alive by stinting herself, we must reduce impolitic truth to keep her confident and ourselves a legend. The crowd wanted book-heroes, and would not understand how more human old Auda was because, after battle and murder, his heart yearned towards the defeated enemy now subject, at his free choice, to be spared or killed: and therefore never so lovely."

Lawrence here, in half-humorous fancy, throws a veil of romance over Auda which enhances his picturesqueness by unjustly obscuring his business capacity. The Arabs had undoubtedly come to look upon the British treasury as an inexhaustible gold-shower worked by a hand-pressure tap—the more they pressed the more constant the flow. From the highest to the lowest this belief pervaded them, so that they not only expected presents of money but did not even expect to pay for the goods that money could buy. They were continually asking the British officers for presents, and had no false dignity over their scale. One day, for example, hearing that one of the senior officers of the mission was going to Egypt, Nasir asked him to bring back a pair of boots and made it clear that he expected them without payment. The officer, rather astonished, replied that "it wasn't done" among "people of our station," adding that he would certainly procure the boots if Nasir liked to pay for them. But Nasir took no pains to hide his annoyance and sense of grievance, saying bitterly: "Lawrence gets me all I ask for." It is such experiences as these that have given rise to natural, if unjust reflections on the source of Lawrence's authority among those who have heard of them at second-hand. Without doubt, Lawrence, who had no care for his own money, was prodigal of public money in his efforts to forward the cause. For the military purpose that prodigality showed a far greater wisdom in adaptation of methods to conditions, than any attempt to adhere to financial regulations or English conventions. And it was worth far more than its weight in gold from the military point of view, now and later.

Lawrence, happily, had never been broken in to the departmental harness that placed so tragic a restraint on the development of our resources, and of munition supply in particular. Instead, he acted in accord with Britain's historic tradition and, free from blinkers, saw that it was a choice between money and men's lives. Nevertheless, he personally laid out less than half a million pounds up to the end of the war, and the whole of the British payments to support the Arab Revolt amounted only to four million pounds in gold, of which about half came back in purchases of food and clothing.

The tactful tip of a mere thousand pounds to Auda helped to secure the outer defences of Aqaba against a Turkish advance during the critical weeks, while Feisal's forces were being conveyed to Aqaba. On August 7th Joyce embarked at Wejh with four hundred Arab regulars and a French machine-gun section. Another thousand under Ja'far followed ten days later, and finally on the 23rd Feisal himself arrived with another four hundred and the Egyptian detachment. Armoured cars were also sent, but the aircraft were not available for the moment as they had to be taken back to Egypt because of the strain of the summer heat on men and machines alike. While these forces were arriving, Wemyss' flagship, the *Euryalus,* had kept a godfatherly watch over Aqaba—the moral effect of her four funnels carried much farther inland than her guns could hope to reach. Her crew, moreover, had built a pier which soon proved of invaluable service when a supply officer arrived in the person of Goslett, who had brought business system into the chaos of Wejh.

These measures of security were a race with time, for the Turks for once had acted with unwonted promptness. By the beginning of September they had concentrated 6,000 men at Ma'an, with sixteen guns—all from the north. And later in the month they were reinforced by a cavalry regiment taken away from the Palestine front—leaving only two there. A detachment of two thousand men had been pushed out to Abu el Lissal (55 miles N. E. of Aqaba), which it had fortified.

"Little enough could have been done to stop the enemy had he come forward with determination, but so harassed was he that he never could muster nerve for the attempt." This is the verdict of the British official history of the Palestine Campaign. In this paralysis by pricking, Lawrence's tactical theory had a new fulfilment. Three means were utilized—distraction from a flank, disturbance from the air, and demolitions of the railway.

As the Turks were, obviously, intending a direct advance on Aqaba, Lawrence concerted an indirect threat against their western flank, with the idea of drawing off their attention, and provoking them into an attack up the Wadi Musa (60 miles N. of Aqaba), "where the natural obstacles were so tremendous that the human defending factor might behave as badly as it liked, and yet hold the place against attack." This is a noteworthy contribution to defensive doctrine. He had Wellington's use of the Lines of Torres Vedras in his mind, while intending a characteristic adaptation and development.

"To bait the hook," the Arabs at Delagha began to worry the Turks and soon drew them into a counterstroke from which they recoiled and left booty in the Arabs' hands. Lawrence did not fail to impress the financial lesson on the peasants of the Wadi Musa. And, to give them moral support, Maulud went up with his mule-cavalry and posted himself among the ruins of Petra. This encouraged the local tribesmen to give free play to their animal and rifle-stealing proclivities, to the Turks' increasing irritation.

The air co-operation was arranged with Major-General Geoffrey Salmond, commanding the British Air Forces in the Middle East, and was carried out by a flight from El Arish under Captain Stent. An advanced landing-ground was reconnoitred at Quntilla, in Eastern Sinai, forty miles north-west of Aqaba—Lawrence spent two days' hard work in choosing and marking this landing-ground, and taking up stores for the flight. On August 28th it arrived over Ma'an, flying low, and dropped thirty-two bombs. Eight direct hits were scored on the engine-shed, with serious damage, and two on the barracks caused nearly a hundred casualties. The flight spent the afternoon in patching the machines, which had been caught by several shrapnel bursts. Early next morning three of them took off and headed for Abu el Lissal, where they bombed the camp, scattering both the Turks and their horses. They flew so low that they suffered many punctures, but none of the machines were brought down. As a farewell before returning to El Arish, Stent and his pilots went out again during the midday heat, when the Turks were somnolent, and bombed the battery that had annoyed them.

Lawrence then himself took charge of the railway operations. To increase their effect he had decided to experiment with the direct firing of a charge by electricity at the moment the locomotive of a train passed over the chosen spot. He intended also to capture the train thus stopped. For this purpose, in addition to the Howeitat, he obtained two Sergeant-Instructors from the Army school at Zeitun, one of whom, an Englishman, trained a squad of Arabs to handle Stokes mortars, while the other, an Australian, trained a squad of Lewis-gunners. They became known as "Stokes" and "Lewis" after their beloved tools. Although it was not their duty, and neither could speak Arabic, they volunteered to accompany the raiders. Lawrence was delighted to have this help, and his sense of humour was titillated by their reactions to the strange conditions, "Stokes" becoming more English and punctiliously correct, while "Lewis," treating the Arabs with a free-going familiarity, became rather annoyed when they returned it.

Lawrence chose for his first target Mudauwara station, seventy miles south of Ma'an, with the idea that if he could destroy its well, the only water in the dry sector below Ma'an, "the train-service across the gap would become uneconomic in load."

The detachment reached Guweira on September 9th, and found two sources of disturbance. One was the morning aeroplane from Ma'an which bombed it with time-table regularity. The other, more serious, was the incessant money-wrangle which had now come to a head, between Auda and the other clans of the Howeitat. Some of those in the south towards Mudauwara were threatening to break away, and their threat imperilled Lawrence's purpose. Auda was obstinate, not to be moved even by Lawrence's beguiling chaff, although he retorted by calling Lawrence the "world's imp"—truly a flash of inspiration.

To await events, Lawrence moved off with his party up the valley of Rumm, a journey which ever after remained in his mind. For the valley converged until it became a two-mile wide avenue, between tremendous walls of rock, carved by the weather so that they gave to this "processional way greater than imagination" the likeness of a roofless cathedral in the Byzantine style. Arrived at the springs of Rumm, Lawrence was met by the heads of the discontented clans. Unable to overcome their dissensions, or secure the necessary baggage-camels, he set off alone with one follower and rode back through the mountains to Aqaba by an unexplored short cut, thus traversing the third side of a triangle. Here he explained the situation to Feisal, and obtained the services of a mediator, Sherif Abdulla el Feir, as well as twenty baggage-camels to carry his stock of explosives. On their return to Rumm negotiations succeeded so far as to procure him a hundred men of the Howeitat, but this number was only a third of what he had desired.

The party set forth on September 16th, the various sections glowering at each other. None save his own men would obey Zaal, whom they regarded as Auda's henchman. Thus Lawrence had to assume direct leadership—of a band who seemed to him ominously untrustworthy. Next day they reached a well in a valley a few miles from Mudauwara station, and found the water fouled with the carcasses of camels.

At dusk Lawrence and Zaal, with the sergeants, reconnoitred the station. It looked so solidly stone-built as to be proof against Stokes-mortar shells, and the garrison appeared to be about double their own strength. Lawrence decided to abandon his project of storming it and to devote his efforts to the destruction of a train. So the party moved south next morning to a point where Zaal had told them of a curve in the line and of hill-spurs that would enable them to set an ambush with a good field of fire.

Lawrence found a drainage culvert which suited his purpose; its collapse would be sure to derail the train even if the explosion failed to wreck the engine. Here, between the ends of two steel sleepers, he dug a bed to hold fifty pounds of gelatine, fixed the explosive plugs, and covered up the traces of his work. It took nearly two hours. Then he unrolled the detonator wires, burying them in the sand as he went, towards the ridge, two hundred yards away, whence he intended to fire the mine. Another three hours passed before all was ready. Meantime a site was chosen for the Stokes mortars and Lewis guns on a high ledge that overhung the line and offered a safe path of retreat. Leaving a man on watch they withdrew to a concealed camp in a nearby valley.

The problem now was to keep the Bedouin hidden until a train appeared; and its difficulties soon became manifest. The strain of waiting irked them and they moved about restlessly despite all instructions. About nine o'clock next morning a fighting patrol of about forty Turkish soldiers was seen approaching from Hallat

RAILWAY RAIDING PARTY. NEWCOMBE ON LEFT; HORNBY ON RIGHT

LAWRENCE AMID THE RESULTS OF A RAID

Ammar station in the south. This menace was frustrated by sending a party to meet them and draw them aside by a simulated flank retreat into the hills. The bait was swallowed. But another alarm came about noon when one of the small permanent patrols came up the line. To Lawrence's relief they walked past the hidden mine and his hiding place without any sign of notice. However, about noon he saw, through his strong glasses, a party of Turks about a hundred strong emerge from Mudauwara station and trudge south. It seemed that the only course was to slip away before they reached the spot, and the Arabs began to pack up.

Suddenly the watchman called out that a cloud of smoke was rising from Hallat Ammar. Lawrence and Zaal dashed up the hill in time to see a train coming. In a wild scramble the Arabs took post, the riflemen extending in a long line so that they might rake the coaches at close range. As the train approached, drawn by two engines, a random fire was opened from it. Behind the engines were ten box-wagons packed with troops.

As the second engine was over the culvert, Lawrence raised his hand as a signal to the hidden mine-firer. With a terrific roar the mine exploded, throwing up a column of dust and smoke from which lumps of iron, and even a whole wheel, came flying out. A deathly silence followed. Lawrence ran south to join the sergeants, while a hail of bullets smote the train, from which the surviving Turks tumbled out to seek the sheltering embankment on the far side. Here, however, the Stokes shells caught them, and as they bolted from the shambles the Lewis guns mowed them down. The Arabs rushed in to loot the wrecked train.

The same overriding call brought the detached party hurrying back from the south, oblivious of their duty of holding off the Turks from Hallat Ammar. Lawrence realized that before long he might be caught between these Turks and those from Mudauwara. But it was hopeless to call off the Arabs until they had had their fill of looting, so he used these few minutes of grace to blow up the leading engine as best he could. The Arabs had gone raving mad with the lust of plunder, and in their frenzy fought among themselves over the spoil. They burst open the trucks and dragged the contents on to the side of the line, where carpets and blankets, clothes and clocks, foodstuffs and arms were littered in wild confusion. Meantime a cluster of shrieking women rushed at Lawrence, imploring his protection until pushed aside by their even more abjectly terrified husbands. "A Turk so broken down was a nasty spectacle." A more dignified appeal came from a group of Austrian artillerymen, but when Lawrence turned away, after reassuring them, a dispute broke out in which the frenzied Arabs slew most of them.

Besides about seventy dead, ninety prisoners were taken and, by Lawrence's orders, marched off quickly to the rallying place. The Arabs had only one killed, but they were soon all "missing," having dispersed with their spoil. Thus the three British soldiers were left alone by the wrecked train. Happily, when they were about to abandon the guns and run for it, Zaal and another Arab came back with camels and helped them to load the mortars and Lewis guns. The ammunition had to be left, so they made a pile and set light to it, slipping away themselves on foot under cover of the explosions, which halted the advance Turks.

When they caught up the main body, however, they found that Salem, the negro who had fired the mine, was missing. Lawrence asked for volunteers to go back to find him. After a pause Zaal offered, and then twelve of the Nowasera. With them Lawrence rode back, but found a swarm of Turks around the wrecked train who, sighting them, gave chase. The pursuit was looking dangerous when "Lewis" appeared with his gun, coming back alone to their relief. Even so, the danger was not over when they rejoined the main body. The encumbrances of victory had turned it into "a stumbling baggage caravan," instead of a fluid military force, and they had to water at the well near Mudauwara, uncomfortably close to the Turks, before they could push on to Rumm and safety. They reached it, however, without interference.

"Two days later we were at Aqaba; entering in glory, laden with precious things and boasting that the trains were at our mercy." The sergeants found that Cairo had been clamouring for their return, and so from brief adventure returned to dull routine. "They had won a battle single-handed; had had dysentery; lived on camel-milk; and learned to ride a camel fifty miles a day without pain. Also Allenby gave them a medal each."

The exhilaration that Lawrence found in this type of warfare, *at this time,* is shown in a letter which he wrote to a friend:

"The last stunt was the hold-up of a train. It had two locomotives, and we gutted one with an electric mine. This rather jumbled up the trucks, which were full of Turks shooting at us. We had a Lewis, and flung bullets through the sides. So they hopped out and took cover behind the embankment and shot at us between the wheels, at 50 yds. Then we tried a Stokes gun, and two beautiful shots dropped right in the middle of them. They couldn't stand that (12 died on the spot) and bolted away to the East across a 100 yd. belt of open sand into some scrub. Unfortunately for them the Lewis covered the open stretch. The whole job took 10 minutes, and they lost 70 killed, 30 wounded, 80 prisoners, and about 25 got away. Of my hundred Howeitat and two British N.C.O.'s there were one (Arab) killed, and four (Arabs) wounded.

"The Turks then nearly cut us off as we looted the train, and I lost some baggage, and nearly myself. My loot was a superfine red Baluch prayer-rug.

"I hope this sounds the fun it is. The only pity is the sweat to work them up, and the wild scramble while it lasts. It's the most amateurish, Buffalo-Billy sort of performance, and the only people who do it well are the Bedouin. Only you will think it heaven, because there aren't any returns, or orders, or superiors, or inferiors; no doctors, no accounts, no meals, and no drinks.

P.S. "Give my salaams to Holdich, and tell him to sprint, or we'll be in Damascus first."

Lawrence soon rode out on a fresh venture, this time to train disciples in the art of demolition, taking a French officer, Captain Pisani, together with 150 Arabs. He also took the precaution of starting out with a large caravan of empty pack-camels. "For variety," Lawrence chose to operate in the north near Ma'an and, finding a suitable spot on the railway, an embankment pierced by bridges, he buried a new type of automatic mine and set his fire-ambush. They waited all day and the next night, and when the train at last appeared it passed over the mine without an explosion. But the Arabs were pleased—when they saw that it was merely a water-train.

Lawrence then went down to the line to lay an electric mine over the lyddite. Patrols passed up and down, with no suspicion of its presence. On the second morning, September 6th, a patrol appeared in sight and a train in the distance behind it. Lawrence calculated that the train might arrive first by a few hundred yards. So it proved. As the engine was exactly over the bridge-arch, he gave the signal. Another column of dust and smoke soared skyward, while the Lewis guns poured their bullets into the wreck. A Turk appeared on the buffers of a truck near the tail and, uncoupling, allowed the last four trucks of twelve to slip back down the gradient. And a Turkish officer, from the window, took a shot at Lawrence, grazing his hip. Meantime the Arabs, led by Pisani, had stormed the rest of the train, in which they captured seventy tons of food destined for Medain Saleh. Some twenty Turks had been killed and a number more taken prisoner.

The attackers suffered no loss, although they nearly lost their leader a second time. For in their eagerness to carry away their plunder they left Lawrence to roll up the heavy electric cables single-handed, and when two of them came back to look for him Turkish relief parties were converging from both sides, the nearest only a quarter of a mile distant. But he slipped away just in time.

After the raiding party had returned to Aqaba safely, on September 8th, Lawrence wrote a report which contains an illuminating passage—"A feature of the Howeitat is that every fourth or fifth man is a sheikh. In consequence the head sheikh has no authority whatever, and as in the previous raid, I had to be O.C. of the whole expedition. This is not a job which should be undertaken by foreigners, since we have not so intimate a knowledge of Arab families as to be able to divide common plunder equitably. On this occasion, however, the Bedouin behaved exceedingly well, and everything was done exactly as I wished; but during the six days' trip I had to adjudicate in twelve cases of assault with weapons, four camel-thefts, one marriage-settlement, fourteen feuds, two evil eyes, and a bewitchment. These affairs take up all one's spare time."

From now on the railway raids from Aqaba were multiplied, dislocating the traffic and demoralizing the travellers. During the next four months seventeen engines were destroyed and scores of trucks. "Traffic was disorganized up to Aleppo, for we posted notices in Damascus, warning 'our friends' not to travel by the northern railways, as our threat was about to be extended thither. The Turks had rail-guards up to Aleppo, soon!" As the rolling stock was drawn from a common pool for Palestine and the Hejaz, the success of this strategy of "killing engines" not only diminished the prospect of the Turks being able to evacuate Medina but constricted the artery on which depended the Turkish army that faced Allenby. And at a time when they needed all their strength to oppose the menace of Allenby's advance. For on this the curtain was now about to rise.

CHAPTER XIV

LEVERAGE ON PALESTINE

October–December, 1917

Allenby renews the attack on the gates of Palestine—The bolts are drawn beforehand by resourceful ruses—Meinertzhagen's comedy of craft—Lawrence considers the possibility of raising the Arabs in the Turks' rear, but because of a doubt, decides against this course—He prefers, instead, to risk himself, and accordingly sets out on a raid against the Turkish Army's rail communications

Allenby captures Beersheba, but a delay imperils his main stroke—Newcombe's "mirage" distracts the Turks' attention and opens the way for Allenby's break-through—After further delays, Jerusalem is gained

Lawrence, meantime, attempts to blow up a vital bridge in the Yarmuk valley only to be foiled by a stroke of ill-luck—He falls into the Turks' hands but escapes

GAZA, on the coast, and Beersheba, 35 miles inland, form the two natural gateways into Palestine from the south. Between them lie a series of ridges which form a natural rampart easy of defence. The Turkish field defences stretched eastward for thirty miles from the sea at Gaza, leaving a gap between them and the separate defences of Beersheba—which covered the flank of the main position. The British Army, after dragging its weary length across the Sinai desert, had twice tried in vain to force the strongly fortified Gaza gate. Beersheba, less artificially strong, was protected by the difficulty of transport and water supply for an attacking force.

In an appreciation drawn up by Sir Philip Chetwode and his Chief of Staff, Brig.-General Guy Dawnay, before Allenby's arrival, it was pointed out that to attack Gaza again was to attack the enemy's strongest point. Success could be gained only by sheer weight of artillery, and would be only local success, as the Turks were prepared to swing back from Gaza to a second position in rear, pivoting on their left near Tell esh Sheria. Virtually inaccessible to direct attack, this "nerve centre and pivot" might be exposed by an approach from the south-east. In order to have room to operate, and water for the attacking force, it would be necessary to pinch off Beersheba before the attack on the flank of the enemy's main position was developed.

This plan was not appreciated by some of the other generals who, preferring heavy security to hazardous mobility, clung to the dogma that to overcome the enemy at his strongest point was the way to cause the collapse of the whole. They were not shaken in this belief even though such an attempt had courted twice-repeated failure, and ascribed this to an indubitable mismanagement rather than to a misguided principle.

If Allenby himself was still under the influence of the mass methods of the west when he landed in Egypt, he was susceptible by cavalry instinct to the appeal of mobile manœuvre, and he was not long in adopting the plan foreshadowed in Chetwode's appreciation. In its development he was guided by Dawnay who now joined his Staff and, like Bartholomew the next year, was the brain behind the titular chief of staff.

In a plan where concentration of numbers was more difficult than near the sea, success must depend on distraction, so that a concentrated effect, relatively greater, might be attained by a smaller mass against a point of weakness. For this the enemy must be deceived, and maintained in his delusion. Secrecy was the first condition. Preparations were concealed as far as possible, and the bulk of the troops were kept on the Gaza flank until the last possible hour. The Royal Flying Corps, just reinforced and re-equipped with faster machines, played a greater part in concealing the preparations. But secrecy alone was negative—and in fact the veil was penetrated by the enemy's intelligence.

A positive deception was needed, especially in view of the enemy's preparations to reinforce the Palestine front. It was supplied from the ingenious brain of a British intelligence officer, Richard Meinertzhagen, who drafted the mock agenda for a Staff conference in which a main attack on Gaza was to be preceded by a feint against Beersheba, and instructions for these operations. To give the fake a more persuasive air of reality, he concocted several intimate letters from home to himself, also a private letter of biting criticism on the pseudo-plan from an imaginary friend on the staff, and included twenty pounds in notes. All these he placed in a haversack which he stained with fresh blood from his horse. Then, on October 10th, he rode out into no-man's-land as if on reconnaissance, drew the fire of a Turkish cavalry patrol, drew it after him in pursuit, pretended to be hit, rolled in the saddle, and eventually dropped his haversack as well as his field-glasses and other articles. A few days later a notice was inserted in corps orders saying that a note-book had been lost, and a copy of this order, wrapped round some sandwiches, was also dropped in no-man's-land.

The Turkish N.C.O. who found the haversack was rewarded, and his Corps Commander published an order warning his officers against carrying papers when out on reconnaissance. More important from the British point of view, the Turks now concentrated their efforts on strengthening the defences near Gaza, to the neglect of those on the other flank. Kress von Kressenstein also kept his only reserve division behind the Gaza flank, despite the suggestion of his distant superior, Falkenhayn, that it should be placed at or behind Beersheba. And when the attack on Beersheba actually came, on October 31st, Kress refused the appeal to send reinforcements. To Meinertzhagen's subtle web of ruse were mainly due the faulty dispositions of the enemy, if a share of the credit must go to Murray's successive failures at Gaza, which had apparently persuaded the Turks that British stupidity was limitless.

Distraction was certainly more necessary than ever. Since Allenby's coming the British had been reinforced not only with troops but with heavy artillery, owing to his own demands and Lloyd George's vigorous pressure at home; the army in Palestine had now been raised to seven infantry and three mounted divisions, totalling some 75,000 rifles and 17,000 sabres. But the Turkish strength had also grown, if even more on paper than in reality. Its eight weak divisions and two cavalry regiments mustered some 30,000 rifles and 1,400 sabres.

Moreover, like a looming cloud behind them there was the new *Yilderim* ("Thunderbolt") Army Group which had been formed under Falkenhayn's command to turn the scales in the Middle East. It included seven Turkish divisions now assembling at Aleppo and had a steel core in the new German "Asia Corps" made up predominantly of artillery, machine-guns and other mechanical specialists. Originally intended by the Turks to recapture Baghdad, Falkenhayn had decided to divert it to an offensive on the Palestine front. This was barely forestalled by the British attack.

In considering his means of distraction, Allenby had bethought himself of his Arab allies. A telegram was sent to Lawrence which caught him on his return from the Ma'an raid. An aeroplane carried him across the desert to General Headquarters, where he gave an account of the existing situation around Ma'an, and pointed out the value of partial pressure on the Hejaz artery, rather than complete strangulation, so that the Turks might be induced to cling on to Medina while incapable of serious mischief.

As regards more direct action in aid of Allenby's coming offensive, Lawrence's decision hung between two courses, suspended by a doubt.

"We knew, better than Allenby, the enemy hollowness, and the magnitude of the British resources"—that superior knowledge was the natural consequence of being *behind* the Turkish front. Given fine weather, Allenby should be able to take not only Jerusalem but Haifa also within a month, "sweeping the Turks in ruin through the hills."

"Such would be our moment, and we needed to be ready for it in the spot where our weight and tactics would be least expected and most damaging. For my eyes, the centre of attraction was Deraa, the junction of the Jerusalem-Haifa-Damascus-Medina railways, the navel of the Turkish Armies in Syria, the common point of all their fronts; and, by chance, an area in which lay great untouched reserves of Arab fighting men, educated and armed by Feisal."

The Arabs alone, by their superior mobility and pervasive fluidity, had the chance of striking this solar plexus of the Turkish body. Lawrence "pondered for a while whether we should not call up all these adherents and tackle the Turkish communications in force. We were certain, with any management, of twelve thousand men: enough to rush Deraa, to smash all the railway lines, even to take Damascus by surprise. Any of these things would make the position of the Beersheba army critical: and my temptation to stake our capital instantly on the issue was very sore."

Lawrence's restraint was due to a doubt of the British Army's capability, and a perception of the consequences of failure to the ultimate aim. Although the Arabs around Deraa were ready enough to rise, Lawrence felt that the risk was "not one that Feisal could scrupulously afford unless he had a fair hope of then establishing himself there." A withdrawal "would have involved the massacre, or the ruin, of all the splendid peasantry of the district." "They could only rise once, and their effort on that occasion must be decisive. To call them out now was to risk the best asset Feisal held for eventual success, on the speculation that Allenby's first attack would sweep the enemy before it, and that the month of November would be rainless, favourable to a rapid advance."

"I weighed the English army in my mind, and could not honestly assure myself of them. The men were often gallant fighters, but their generals as often gave away in stupidity what they had gained in ignorance. Allenby was quite untried, and his troops had broken down in and been broken by the Murray period. Of course, we were fighting for an Allied victory, and since the English were leading partners the Arabs would have, in the last resort, to be sacrificed for them. But was it the last resort? The war generally was going neither well nor very ill, and it seemed as though there might be time for another try next year. So I decided to postpone the hazard for the Arabs' sake."

The underlying doubt which held Lawrence back was here a wiser counsellor than his reasoned calculations. For, as he admits, he underestimated "the crippling effect of Allenby's too plentiful artillery, and the cumbrous intricacy of his infantry and cavalry, which moved only with rheumatic slowness."

But although his sense of duty to the Arabs stopped him from risking their future, his sense of duty to Allenby compelled him in compensation to risk himself in a stroke against the communications of the Turks who were facing Allenby. To it he was also impelled by his sense of the importance of proving to Allenby that the Arab wing of his army was a profitable asset.

The site he chose for his stroke was the Yarmuk valley, the narrow and precipitous gorge up which the railway from Palestine climbed to Deraa junction. This section of the railway formed the right-hand half of the cross-stroke of the small "T," attached to the large "T" thus:— ⊤⊢. The line, winding upwards, crossed and recrossed the stream by numerous bridges. The bridge farthest west and the bridge farthest east would be the most difficult to replace. "To cut either of these bridges would isolate the Turkish army in Palestine, for one fortnight, from its base in Damascus, and destroy its power of escaping from Allenby's advance."

For practicability, this plan had the advantage that the Turks deemed danger to the bridges so remote that they guarded them lightly—they were 420 miles from Aqaba by way of Azrak. For potentiality, it had the further advantage that if the Turkish army collapsed under the double pressure from in front and behind, the raiding expedition to Yarmuk could be converted into a general uprising of the Arabs which would carry them like a wave into Damascus, with Allenby following.

Allenby accepted the suggestion and asked that the stroke should be attempted on November 5th, or one of the three following days. His own attack on Beersheba was timed for October 31st, and he hoped to follow it with the main stroke against the Turks' inner flank at Sheria a few days later.

Lawrence then returned to Aqaba to prepare for the expedition. As Nasir was still away, he arranged with Feisal for the services of Ali ibn el Hussein, a young and dashing Sherifian leader who had "out-Newcombed Newcombe" in railway raids around El Ala and had the prestige necessary to carry weight with the tribes near Azrak. Through Ali he could count on the Beni Sakhr, and might obtain the aid of the Serahin. The Ruwalla, unfortunately, had moved away to their winter pastures. The Arab sympathizers in Damascus were also warned to be ready, in particular Ali Riza Pasha, the Turkish Base Commandant and the Sherif's unsuspected ally. And in view of the difficulty of blowing up the great steel bridge which was their target, and the risk of becoming a casualty, Lawrence took an understudy in Wood, the base engineer at Aqaba. For the purpose of holding enemy reinforcements at bay while the demolition was being done, Lawrence arranged to take a party of Indian machine-gunners who had already been operating in the raids from Wejh.

At the last moment they were joined by the Emir Abd el Kader, grandson of the man who had resisted the French in Algeria during the 'forties, and himself head of the colony of Algerian exiles who lived on the north bank of the Yarmuk. He was on his way back from a visit to Mecca, and his offer to help was welcomed because it offered a chance of controlling the middle section of the Yarmuk valley through his men, without the risk of raising the countryside as a whole. After coming to this decision they were disturbed by a telegram from Brémond warning them that Abd el Kader was in the pay of the Turks. It was not easy to tell whether this suspicion of Abd el Kader had more substance than his anti-French views, and Lawrence's view of Brémond inclined him to give Abd el Kader the benefit of the doubt. Feisal remarked—"I know he is mad. I think he is honest. Guard your heads and use him." Lawrence decided to take the risk "showing him our complete confidence, on the principle that a crook would not credit our honesty, and that an honest man was made a crook soonest by suspicion." But Abd el Kader was to prove the grit in the wheels, if less from knavery than from stupidity. Fanaticism and injured dignity were his particular aspects of foolishness.

The expedition left Aqaba on October 24th, riding by way of Rumm to Jefer, where Auda was encamped. Lloyd accompanied them thus far, before going, regretfully, back to Egypt on his way to join the Inter-Allied Staff at Versailles. Lawrence had the more reason to regret his going because of the friction already developing between Ali and Abd el Kader. Auda, too, they found still quarrelling with the lesser chiefs over money, while Zaal, upon whose raiding experience Lawrence had especially counted, showed no relish to share in the venture. Glut of success had changed the "hard-riding gallant of spring into a prudent man, whose new wealth made life precious to him."

As they sat round the fire the night before launching out from Jefer they "felt a creeping reverberation, a cadence of blows too dull, too wide, too slow easily to find response in our ears. It was like the mutter of a distant, very lowly thunderstorm." It was the bombardment of the Gaza defences by the British guns in preparation for Allenby's attack.

Two divisions of Chauvel's Desert Mounted Corps and the four infantry divisions of Chetwode's XX Corps were already sidestepping eastward by nightly stages for the decisive stroke. Sixty thousand rifles and sabres were thus assembled close to Beersheba, held by less than five thousand Turks. Pinned by the British infantry attack on the morning of October 31st, their eastern flank was encircled by the Australian and New Zealand horsemen. Shortly before dusk the town was captured. The left flank, at Sheria, of the main Turkish position now lay exposed.

Water was the main limiting condition. Before the second act could open the water supplies at Beersheba had to be developed. The mass of the mounted force was the brake on its mobility. Fortunately the wells had been captured almost intact, so that Allenby was encouraged to count on being ready to attack the Sheria position on November 3rd, or early on the 4th. It was preceded by a fixing attack on the night of November 1st which bit into a segment of the Gaza defences.

But the water problem at Beersheba belied optimistic hopes, and jammed the machinery of the offensive. Partly this was due to faults in the human factor. Allenby's men and horses had not the same endurance capacity as Arabs and camels. A hot *Khamsin* blew, and in raising clouds of dust produced a thirst that drained the water supplies beyond calculation. And the hope of finding sufficient water north of Beersheba to eke out the supply was also disappointed.

Thus the second act had to be postponed until November 6th. The delay allowed the Turks an ominously long interval in which to reinforce the threatened spot. That they did not do so was due largely to the initiative and self-sacrifice of another member of the British mission to the Arabs. And it offered one more proof that, in distraction especially, the resourceful man counts far more than any number of herd-men.

Newcombe had been shipped back sick to Egypt in July, paying the price of his rail-raiding exertions. While in Cairo he suggested to Allenby that he should move with a small party into the desert east of Beersheba and raise the Bedouin against the Turks at the moment of Allenby's offensive, blocking the road north to Hebron and Jerusalem after Beersheba had been captured. Allenby accepted the proposal, and Newcombe chose seventy British camelry with a few Arab scouts to form his party. It was very strong in fire-power for its size, having ten machine-guns besides a number of Lewis guns and explosives.

Newcombe's detachment moved out from Asluj on October 30th and made a wide circuit to Es Semua, twenty miles north-east of Beersheba. On the evening of the 31st he moved down to the Beersheba-Hebron road and cut the telegraph to Jerusalem. Hearing that night from friendly Bedouin of Beersheba's capture, he determined to bar the Hebron road so as to cut the enemy's northward line of retreat. In thus staking his tiny force Newcombe hoped for the speedy advance of the British cavalry to his relief, a hope which proved vain. But his distraction opened a path through the centre for the British Army.

For it spread such alarm behind the Turkish front that it created a strategic mirage. In it the enemy's imagination saw the bulk of the British Army advancing north up the Hebron road straight for Jerusalem. So strong was the delusion that they forgot that a British Army marches on a weak stomach, which needs constant care. Having at the outset kept their main strength too close to Gaza, they now went to the other extreme. Not only did they dispatch their one division in general reserve to the Hebron flank, but also drew off the reserves from the Sheria sector, where Allenby's blow was about to fall. Thus they "locked up nearly half their force in the Judean Hills, where it took no part in the fighting for a week after the capture of Sheria."

A share of the credit is certainly due to the British cavalry patrols which pushed north after the fall of Beersheba. But from German and Turkish evidence it seems clear that Newcombe earned the lion's share. His own hopes of the hill-Arabs joining him had been disappointed—unlike the Turks they preferred to wait on realities rather than clutch at promises. But the fear of an Arab rising had almost as much effect on the Turks as the reality, for a time.

On November 1st Newcombe's party were attacked by about a hundred Turks whom they repulsed with loss. But next morning, after he had blocked all communication for forty hours, the petty obstruction was cleared away by converging forces from Hebron and Dhahriye. After twenty of his men had been killed, and most of his machine-guns disabled, he surrendered when the German-commanded Turks reached positions from which they could have shot down the survivors. The self-immolation, which came from a self-immobilization, was a sacrifice of doubtful value. It was magnificent but it was not irregular war. The fact that he had appeared from the east seems to have contributed far more than his actual obstruction to the impression he made, for it apparently conjured up a picture of a wide encircling move by British mounted forces heading for Jerusalem.

A graphic description of the effect is given by Obergeneralarzt Steuber, who arrived in Hebron just after Newcombe's capture—

"The place was like a disturbed ants' nest; the staff of Army head-quarters was standing beside its horses saddled for hasty retreat . . . Mounted Turkish gendarmes dashed through the excited populace. The main body of the English was said to be only a few kilometres off. As in all panics of this sort, rumour had grossly exaggerated the facts. A whimsical touch was given to the affair by an old Arab procuress, who in the midst of the universal terror was calmly pre-paring to meet the enemy with a band of scantily clad dancing-girls wearing coloured transparent veils."

By that same evening two Turkish divisions and two cavalry regi-ments were stretched out in the hills near the Hebron road, with a third division on the way. There they remained, rubbing against the edge of the British Army's flank in a series of ineffective actions until on November 6th Chetwode's real blow crashed, like a fist through a paper screen, into the Sheria defences, where two Turkish regiments only were now stretched out to hold six miles of front.

Unfortunately, the great cavalry wave that was to sweep like a torrent through the gap dwindled to a thin trickle, through shortage of water and the excessive effect of machine-guns in checking horse-men. The Turkish army escaped the disaster that had seemed im-minent and the British had to resign themselves to a more deliberate advance up the coastal plain. Not until November 14th did they succeed in capturing Junction Station, thus securing control of the branch railway running up to Jerusalem, and forcing the Turks anew into divergent lines of retreat, one part falling back north while the other withdrew east to cover Jerusalem. Then Allenby swung in, fighting his way eastward through the Judean Hills until, after a further check, Jerusalem was at last gained on December 9th— the keys of the city being vainly offered by the Mayor to a couple of mess cooks, who had lost themselves while looking for water, and then to a couple of sergeants on outpost duty, before he at last found a British soldier willing to accept the prize that countless Crusaders through the centuries had striven for in vain.

The British capture of Jerusalem was a heavy blow to Turkey's prestige, all the more damaging because it followed the loss of Baghdad. But as a moral tonic to the Western Allies its effect was far wider and greater. For it helped to soften the sting of a series of disheartening failures and disasters. The year had seen the collapse of Russia, the extinction of Rumania, the bankruptcy of the Franco-British offensive in the West, the grave mutinies in the French Army, the engulfing of the British in the mud of Passchendaele, the disastrous breakdown of the Italians at Caporetto. Even as December arrived a German counterstroke had turned the hasty joy-bells of "Cambrai" into a mockery. Then, as a timely Christmas present, came the redemption of the place to which the thoughts of Christendom turned at Christmastide. At such a time of the year and the war the gaining of "Jerusalem" delivered a new message of hope.

What of Lawrence meantime? He had been less fortunate than Newcombe in his mission if more lucky in his escape from a danger worse than capture. The omens were inauspicious. As he was setting out from Jefer, on October 31st, Auda whispered in his ear—"Beware of Abd el Kader." Next day there was another disquieting incident when a band of Beni Sakhr appeared from several quarters and closed round them menacingly, firing over their heads. When the hostile tribesmen found Lawrence's party well-posted for defence their manner changed, and they pretended that the lapse was due to ignorance, saying that it was a Beni Sakhr custom to shoot over strangers. Changed suddenly from prospective prey into honoured guests, the party were received at Bair by a parading swarm of horsemen, who hailed Ali with the shout: "God give victory to our Sherif," and cried to Lawrence—"Welcome, Aurans, harbinger of action." Abd el Kader, feeling the need to emphasize his presence, mounted his horse and "began to prance delicately in slow curves, crying out 'Houp, Houp' in his throaty voice, and firing a pistol unsteadily in the air." His seat and his aim were so obviously uncertain that his solo performance went unappreciated. At the feast which followed he again tried to assert his dignity by rising before the others had finished and then grumbling that the meat was tough.

Reinforced by the chief, Mifleh, and sixteen of his followers, the party moved on northward next day, fortified by the distant drumming of the British guns whose echoes floated across the Dead Sea hollow. But the Arabs' reaction was mixed. Lawrence heard them whispering—"They are nearer; the English are advancing; God deliver the men under that rain." Their own dislike of artillery fire gave them a throb of sympathy for the Turks. But it was not only that. "They were thinking compassionately of the passing Turks, so long their weak oppressors; whom, for their weakness, though oppressors, they loved more than the strong foreigner with his blind indiscriminate justice." Lawrence himself was qualified to interpret that feeling.

When still a little short of Azrak they met a band of the Serahin who were just starting out to swear allegiance to Feisal. But when invited to share in an operation nearer home their enthusiasm cooled. They declared that to attack the western bridge was out of the question, as the Turks had just filled the district with hundreds of military wood-cutters. They also showed deep suspicion of Abd el Kader, and so were unwilling to trust themselves in his section of the Yarmuk Valley. Yet without their aid the venture was hopeless, and in an effort to overcome their hesitations Lawrence addressed them round the camp-fire, seeking "to combat in words this crude prudence of the Serahin, which seemed all the more shameful to us after our long sojourn in the clarifying wilderness."

Like the orations which Livy and other classical writers put in the mouths of generals before battle, that address, as remembered, may not be of verbatim accuracy but it has the value of retrospective judgment. It deserves quotation, not so much for its direct historical relation to the issue, but for its light on Lawrence's philosophy.

"We put it to them, not abstractedly, but concretely, for their case, how life in mass was sensual only, to be lived and loved in its extremity. There could be no rest-houses for revolt, no dividend of joy paid out. Its spirit was accretive, to endure as far as the senses would endure, and to use each such advance as base for further adventure, deeper privation, sharper pain."

"To be of the desert was . . . a doom to wage unending battle with an enemy who was not of the world, nor life, nor anything, but hope itself; and failure seemed God's freedom to mankind." Life could only be mastered by holding it cheap. In order to bring forth spiritually creative things, men must avoid being hampered by physical ties and wants. With most men the soul aged long before the body. "There could be no honour in a sure success, but much might be wrested from a sure defeat. Omnipotence and the Infinite were our two worthiest foemen, indeed the only ones for a full man to meet, they being monsters of his own spirit's making; and the stoutest enemies were always of the household. In fighting Omnipotence, honour was proudly to throw away the poor resources that we had, and dare him empty-handed; to be beaten, not merely by more mind, but by its advantage of better tools." To those who attained clear-sight, failure was the only goal. By believing utterly that there was no victory, and by inviting blows one might alone conquer Omnipotence.

"This was a halting, half-coherent speech, struck out desperately, moment by moment, in our extreme need, upon the anvil of those white minds round the dying fire; and hardly its sense remained with me afterwards: for once my picture-making memory forgot its trade and only felt the slow humbling of the Serahin, the night-quiet in which their worldliness faded, and at last their flashing eagerness to ride with us whatever the bourne."

The rare man who attains wisdom is, by the very clearness of his sight, a better guide in solving practical problems than those, more commonly the leaders of men, whose eyes are misted and minds warped by ambition for success. But to give such guidance he must for the moment cease straining after the Infinite and become, in a relative sense, short-sighted. Lawrence seems hitherto to have made this adjustment. But now, one feels, he had for some months so strained himself, in conquest of his physical being, that his power of practical guidance may have been affected. Here, to some degree, if still more in the adverse conditions of the problem, may lie the explanation of what followed. At the same time, it is only fair to quote Lawrence's own comment: "We were only a cat's whisker off success—and it was the boldest thing we ever tried."

Next day, November 4th, they reached Azrak, a magic place, peopled by the ghosts of poets, kings and Roman legionaries. But the inclination to dream was dispersed by the news that Abd el Kader had disappeared, heading for the Jebel Druse. It meant a limitation of their target as well as a threat of betrayal. "Of our three alternatives, Um Keis had been abandoned: without Abd el Kader, Wadi Khalid was impossible: this meant that we must necessarily attempt the bridge at Tell el Shehab."

Lack of alternatives, as Bourcet had been the first to point out clearly, meant a greatly increased chance of the enemy blocking or accident stopping the single path. The very fact that their now inevitable target was the nearest bridge made discovery more likely, especially as to reach it they would have to cross the open country between Remthe and Deraa. Abd el Kader had probably gone over to the enemy and "the Turks, if they took the most reasonable precautions, would trap us at the bridge."

Nevertheless, after taking counsel, they decided to gamble on the incompetence of the Turks. On the night of the 6th they slipped across the Hejaz railway a little below Deraa at a stony place where their passage would leave no signs. And there did not seem to be any unusual activity among the Turkish railway patrols, which was somewhat reassuring as to Abd el Kader's action. A short way beyond they found a pit where they lay up in hiding. It would serve as the jumping-off point for their actual raid across the open, which would have to be made under cover of darkness.

To reach Tell el Shehab on the Palestine branch, blow up the bridge, and get back into safety east of the Hejaz line between dusk and daybreak meant a ride of 80 miles in thirteen hours. Lawrence regretfully decided that this was beyond the capacity of most of the Indian soldiers—"the discipline of their cavalry training had tired out them and the animals in our easy stages." He picked out six of the best under Jemadar Hassan Shah so that he could have one machine-gun available. Apart from his own small bodyguard the party was made up of twenty of the Beni Sakhr as the storming party and forty of the Serahin, less dependable as fighters, to guard the camels and carry the explosives.

As the party crossed the white furrows of the pilgrim road in the dark Lawrence had a momentary thrill as he remembered that it was the same track he had seen a year ago nearly eight hundred miles farther south on his first ride inland from Rabegh. Those miles were the measure of accomplishment, and Damascus but a little way off. Yet the slight distance might suffice for the proverbial slip betwixt the cup and lip. In Lawrence's present mood the feeling overcame him that the Arab Revolt was doomed to be one more of those caravans which set out for a cloud-goal and perished in the wilderness "without the tarnish of achievement."

His reverie was broken by sudden shots from some shepherd frightened by the stealthy approach of the caravan. There was another momentary alarm when a gipsy woman rushed shrieking out of a bush beside the track. Away to the north the station flares of Deraa gleamed like a lighthouse at sea. At last they began to go downhill, then heard "a faint sighing, like wind among the trees far away, but continuous and slowly increasing." It told them they were near the great waterfall below Tell el Shehab, and so, near their goal. They drew rein on a grassy ledge. "Before us from a lip of darkness rose very loudly the rushing of the river which had long been dinning our ears. It was the edge of the Yarmuk Gorge, and the bridge lay just under us to the right."

The explosives were silently distributed among the carriers, while the Beni Sakhr reconnoitred ahead. "A little further; and at last, below our feet, we saw a something blacker in the precipitous blackness of the valley, and at its other end a speck of flickering light." It was the bridge, and the guard-tent on the far bank. Wood posted the Indian machine-gunners ready to spray the guard-tent with bullets, while the rest of the party pushed on to the abutment of the bridge. The solitary sentry, to Lawrence's annoyance, stayed at the opposite end.

Suddenly there was the clatter of a falling rifle. The sentry jumped; his yell brought the guard tumbling out. The Indians were too late to catch them before they took cover. The Beni Sakhr exchanged volleys with them ineffectively, while the Serahin porters dropped their loads into the ravine and bolted, fearing to be blown up if a bullet hit the blasting gelatine.

With the means of demolition lost, the raid had lost its purpose. The only thing was to get away while there was time. The clamour aroused the villages for miles around, but after a tense ride the party reached the railway at dawn, cutting the telegraph wires where they crossed in petty compensation for the prize they had missed. The bitterness of the contrast was gall to Lawrence.

"We were fools, all of us equal fools, and so our rage was aimless. Ahmed and Awad had another fight; young Mustafa refused to cook rice; Farraj and Daud knocked him about until he cried; Ali had two of his servants beaten: and none of us or of them cared a little bit. Our minds were sick with failure, and our bodies tired after nearly a hundred strained miles over bad country in bad conditions, between sunset and sunset, without halt or food."

None of the Arabs cared to return to Azrak empty-handed, so

there was a general shout of approval when Ali suddenly said—"Let's blow up a train." They all looked to Lawrence, the expert. He did not share their delight. "Blowing up trains was an exact science when done deliberately, by a sufficient party, with machine-guns in position. If scrambled at it might become dangerous." He felt that the Indians, who were the machine-gunners, had suffered enough from cold and hunger. His stand on their behalf was accepted by the Arabs, but as they still were eager for a chance at a train Lawrence yielded to their desire.

At dawn, on the 9th, Wood led the Indians back to Azrak while Lawrence took the sixty Arabs back to the railway, near his old site at Minifir, and laid an electric mine beneath the rebuilt culvert. But he had only sixty yards of cable which left the firing point perilously close to the line. A tiny bush about a foot high served to conceal the wires, but not the firer. One train passed before they were ready, and another in the morning, owing to the mist and rainstorms hiding its approach from the man on watch. Everything seemed to be going wrong. However, the bad weather offered Lawrence the consolation that Allenby was unlikely to finish the war before the Arabs were ready for a better effort.

On the 10th the rain still swept the landscape. About noon a train was signalled, and Lawrence hurried over to the embankment to fire the mine. When the train eventually came along, panting up the gradient, he saw that it was packed with troops. It seemed too late to change his plan, so when the engine reached him he pushed down the handle of the exploder. Nothing happened. And then he realized that he was kneeling in the open in full sight of the troop train as it crawled past fifty yards away. "The bush, which had seemed a foot high, shrank smaller than a figleaf." His only chance was that the Turks might take him to be a casual Bedouin, not worth shooting. The miracle happened. Mud and rain had fortunately dimmed the splendour of his white and gold dress. As soon as the train had passed he pushed the wires quickly but deftly under the earth and bolted like a rabbit for cover. A few hundred yards on, the train stuck, and while it was raising steam an officers' patrol came back to have a look at the ground—but failed to discover the wires.

Then followed another cheerless day for the party, hungry and sodden, yet not too sodden to quench their exasperation. And when a new morning came, the luck had changed, as Ali had predicted. A two-engined train with a dozen passenger coaches appeared and Lawrence touched off the mine under the leading engine. So close was he to the explosion that he was hurled backwards, with clothes torn, arms scratched and a toe broken. As, half stunned, he staggered away from the wrecked train, the Arabs on the slope and the Turks on the line blazed at each other over him. Seven of the Arabs were hit in a rush to bring him in. The train was carrying the new commander destined to take over the defence of Jerusalem, and his escort, several hundred strong, checked any hope of rushing the train once the first shock of surprise passed off. The Arabs had now cause to regret their lack of machine-guns. They barely held off the Turkish pursuit until they reached the hill-top and, each man jumping on the nearest camel, fled into the desert where they rallied. The only booty to compensate them for the loss of several lives consisted of some sixty odd rifles seized in the first rush, but these counted for much. "Next day we moved into Azrak, having a great welcome and boasting—God forgive us—that we were the victors."

They decided to hold on to Azrak during the winter, using it as a base of propaganda and centre of intelligence. It would also drive in a new wedge, separating Nuri Shaalan from the Turks. They established their winter quarters in the old fort, which they repaired and made watertight. A caravan was sent to the Jebel Druse to collect provisions, and a stream of desert visitors poured in to exchange presents and hear tales of Aqaba, its forces and its riches. Ali's mixture of reckless bravado and stately charm made him a potent representative of Feisal. He also had something of Lawrence's uncanny detachment.

In the company of Ali and the atmosphere of Azrak, Lawrence could have rested content, living in imagination. It was with an effort that he pried himself apart in order to explore the country round. As Deraa was his future target he felt that he ought to examine it with his own eyes; so he put on bedraggled Haurani clothes, and walked through the defences, accompanied only by an old peasant follower.

For a time no notice was taken of him, but after passing the aerodrome a sergeant suddenly seized him by the arm saying that the Bey wanted him. Protest was vain, and Lawrence was marched off to an office where in reply to questions he "admitted" he was a

Circassian. That might explain his white skin, but it drew him deeper into the mire. For the second time in his life he found himself forcibly incorporated in the Turkish Army, and this time for a purpose for which Turkish officers have notoriously been apt to use their recruits. That night the ordeal came and when Lawrence resisted he was handed over to the tender mercies of the guard to be brought to a suitable frame of mind. After various unpleasant forms of coercion had failed, he was thrashed into senselessness. But his gory state at least saved him from further attentions, and during the night he managed to escape from the hospital to which he had been carried. As he hobbled down the road a tribesman took pity on him, and, mounting him on a camel, carried him to Nisibin, where he found the rest of his party. By a grim irony, it was during this escape that he chanced on the concealed route of approach to Deraa which he had set out to discover.

Once back at Azrak the reaction came and the long strain on his nerves, followed by this last shock, made the place and the company unbearable. Propaganda palled on him—"conscious all the time of my strangeness, and of the incongruity of an alien's advocating national liberty. The war for me held a struggle to side-track thought, to get into the people's attitude of accepting the revolt naturally and trustfully. I had to persuade myself that the British Government could really keep the spirit of its promises." Physical suffering had so accentuated the clearness of his sight that he could not induce the mild watering necessary for practical affairs. And the flattering obsequiousness of the Syrian townsmen seemed to coat him with slime. He decided to break away and go south in search of action.

He left late on November 23rd with only one companion, and despite his physical weakness rode hard—the harder, indeed, because of the sheer detachment of spirit from flesh that through suffering he had attained. He passed Bair on the second night and would not tarry. "I had a heavy bout of fever on me which made me angry, so that I paid no attention to Rahail's appeals for rest. That young man had maddened all of us for months by his abundant vigour, and by laughing at our weaknesses; so this time I was determined to ride him out, showing no mercy. Before dawn he was blubbering with self-pity; but softly, lest I hear him." At noon they reached Auda's camp, but only paused for a greeting and to eat a few dates. Rahail was now past protest and rode as if grimly determined to outstay Lawrence. "Even had we started fair, he had the advantage anyhow over me in strength, and now I was nearly finished." "I seemed at last approaching the insensibility which had always been beyond my reach: but a delectable land for one born so sluggish that nothing this side fainting would let his spirit free. Now I found myself dividing into parts. There was one which went on riding wisely, sharing or helping every pace of the wearied camel. Another hovering above and to the right bent down curiously, and asked what the flesh was doing. The flesh gave no answer, for, indeed, it was conscious only of a ruling impulse to keep on and on; but a third garrulous one talked and wondered, critical of the body's self-inflicted labour, and contemptuous of the reason for effort.

"The night passed in these mutual conversations. My unseeing eyes saw the dawn-goal ahead . . . and my parts debated that the struggle might be worthy, but the end foolishness and the re-birth of trouble."

Those who saw Lawrence when at last, on the 26th, he rode into Aqaba say that he seemed like a wraith, so white and remote. He said but the briefest word, just a mention of the bridge failure in the Yarmuk Valley, and then crept away to a tent.

A few days later he received a summons to go up to Palestine. He went by air to Suez and when he reached Allenby's headquarters he found the air within so full of the noise of victorious battle that it drowned the echoes of his ride to the Yarmuk Valley, a tale on which he himself had no wish to enlarge. Not that his work had been unappreciated. For Aqaba he had been promoted major in order to be made Companion of the Bath, a decoration he never wore. He was also recommended for the Victoria Cross by Wingate, but the circumstances did not fit the customary conditions. A reward that he appreciated more was the chance to be present at the official entry into Jerusalem on December 11th. Hastily rigged out by friends on the staff in the borrowed glory of a British "brass-hat," he took part in the ceremony at the Jaffa Gate—"which for me was the supreme moment of the war." At the lunch after it he heard with delight Allenby's rebuke to M. Picot's suggestion of setting up a civil government in Jerusalem. And immediately after lunch he seized the moment to discuss new military projects with Allenby.

Allenby's idea was, first, to secure his gains by obtaining more elbow-room north of Jerusalem and restoring the railway thither; then, with a push of his right elbow eastward to drive the Turks from Jericho and clear the Jordan Valley north of the Dead Sea. He suggested that Feisal should now move north from Aqaba towards Tafila, near the southern end of the Dead Sea. Thus he could link up with the British on the other side, and help them by cutting off the food supplies which the Turks were drawing from the corn belt between the Dead Sea and the Hejaz railway. The grain-ships which came up the Dead Sea were a buttress to the Turks' power of resistance which it was important to destroy.

Lawrence not only responded to this idea but added a second proposition—that when Jericho was captured, Feisal's base might be transferred there from Aqaba, and his fifty tons a day of supplies and ammunition delivered there. Allenby expressed his agreement, "if and when transport surplusses permitted," and Lawrence went back to Aqaba to prepare for this forward move by stages.

One of his steps was the formation of a bodyguard. The reward offered by the Turks for his capture or killing, hugely raised since he had blown up Jemal Pasha's train, was sufficient reason, if not the only reason. "Of course, the offer was rhetorical; with no certainty whether in gold or paper, or that the money would be paid at all. Still, perhaps it might justify some care." He had taken Farraj and Daud as his personal followers during the expedition that ended with the capture of Aqaba, and had added three Haurani peasants soon afterwards. But all these save Rahail had now been left behind at Azrak, so that he had to find fresh followers—which his reputation made easy.

The beginning had promise. As he was reading in his tent one afternoon a lithe Ageyli stole in, dropped a superb saddle-bag on the floor, and went away; he came again next day and left "a camel-saddle of equal beauty"; on the third day he came empty-handed and asked to be taken into Lawrence's service. His name was Abdulla el Nahabi (Abdulla "the Robber") and he bore a recommendation from Ibn Dakhil, the old captain of Feisal's bodyguard, to the effect that he was "the most experienced Ageyli, having served every Arabian prince and having been dismissed each employment, after stripes and prison, for offences of too great individuality. Ibn Dakhil said that the Nahabi rode second only to himself, was a master-judge of camels, and as brave as any son of Adam; easily, since he was too blind-eyed to see danger. In fact, he was the perfect retainer and I engaged him instantly."

"He examined the applicants for my service, and, thanks to him and to the Zaagi, . . . my other commander, a wonderful gang of experts grew about me. The British at Akaba called them cutthroats, but they cut throats only to my order." "I needed hard riders and hard livers; men proud of themselves and without family."

Lawrence paid them six pounds a month, the normal wage for a man who provided his own camel, and mounted them on his own picked beasts. Thus they were able to spend their money on adorning their own persons. "They dressed like a bed of tulips, in every colour but white, for that was my constant wear, and they did not wish to seem to presume."

This bodyguard served him not merely as a personal protection but as the core of the force with which he made his mobile thrusts —here was the other reason for its creation. It numbered some ninety men in all, though Lawrence was rarely accompanied by more than thirty, both for the sake of mobility and because of casualties— "in my service nearly sixty of them died." But their offensive power was much higher than their nominal strength, because of their armament as well as of their morale. For Lawrence regarded two men to one Lewis or Hotchkiss gun as a reasonable proportion of man-power to weapon-power.

He exploited the mobile possibilities of the light machine-gun to a greater extent than any other leader, or in any other army. In his next campaign he introduced the probing attack by light automatic "fingers"—two months before the Germans pierced the British front in France with the aid of similar but less economic "infiltration" tactics. In his way of using machine-guns with crews of only two men and mounted on camels—they were even fired from the saddle occasionally—he foreshadowed that post-war development, the mechanized machine-gun carrier. Fifteen years later, so stoutly does custom resist commonsense, regular armies would still be debating whether these two-man vehicles should not drag around a trailer with several superfluous men exposed to the enemy's bullets.

Lawrence himself carried an "air-Lewis"—stripped of its clumsy radiator, casing and stock—in a bucket on his camel. It fired such "a wonderfully dispersed pattern" besides being so handy, that he adopted it in preference to the rifle he had earlier used. This rifle had a history: it was a normal British "Short Lee-Enfield" which had been captured by the Turks at the Dardanelles and then, with a gold-engraved inscription, had been presented by Enver to Feisal. Lawrence in turn had obtained it from Feisal. After the war he offered to restore it to the Essex Regiment, its original owner, but received no reply. Instead, King George took an opportunity of adding it to the collection in his private War Museum at Windsor. It has a sinister series of notches cut in it; they were made by Lawrence whenever he brought down a Turk—until he lost zest in keeping such records.

The rest of his personal armament consisted of a pistol and a curving gold-handled dagger, exquisitely carved, such as was carried by Sherifs, although not exclusively. That dagger gave rise to the legend that Lawrence was invested with the rank of Sherif, or, more picturesquely, "Prince of Mecca." A Sherif acquired his title by birth, and by birth only, as a descendant of the Prophet; there could not be such a thing as an "honorary Sherif." The nearest approach to a justification for the story was that one day the Arabs were indulging in the pastime of giving themselves fancy titles. Lawrence was asked, "What title will you choose?" He replied—"Emir Dynamite." This was so apt that it stuck, and for a time became his nickname among the Arabs.

CHAPTER XV

A "REGULAR" CAMPAIGN

January–February, 1918

To aid Allenby, the Arabs operate against the corn-belt east of the Dead Sea which feeds the Turkish Armies—The Turks reacting, fall into Lawrence's Wadi Musa trap; he meantime experiments in mechanized warfare—Following up the Turkish recoil the Arabs press deeper into the corn-belt, and occupy Tafila—The Turks' second reaction gives Lawrence the opportunity of fighting the one pitched battle of his career—according to the best historical models—He follows up this "classical" victory by a highly original coup, capturing a grain-fleet with cavalry—But the Arabs dissipate the money provided to finance a further advance, and Lawrence quits them in disgust, intending to offer Allenby his resignation—Instead, he finds a fresh mission awaiting him

In the campaign of 1918 Feisal's Arab forces had not merely an indirect influence on Allenby's situation but became a co-operating part of his forces. This brought a change in the form of their own operations which assumed a more regular pattern. Their very title, newly coined, of the "Arab Northern Army" seemed to induce a crystallization of their movements and objectives. This had its drawbacks, and brought its disappointments in the first half of the year. Yet, during that period they appear, on the whole, to have created more opportunity for Allenby's forces than these created for them. And the campaign provided Lawrence himself with an opportunity to show his capacity in regular operations that he, half humorously, despised.

Along the corn-belt, which lay parallel to the railway, was a row of four small market-towns, widely spaced, which formed hooks on to which a controlling force could fasten. The southernmost was Shobek, twenty miles north-west of Ma'an. Then came Tafila, almost level with the south end of the Dead Sea. Beyond it lay Kerak, and, at the northern end of the Dead Sea, Madeba.

Early in October the Arabs had encroached on this belt by occupying Shobek for a few days and tearing up the lines of the light railway which the Turks used for collecting wood-fuel for the Hejaz railway. This threat stung the Turks into action at last, drawing them into the trap which Lawrence had baited for them in the Wadi Musa. They launched their effort on October 27th, just as Lawrence himself was setting out on his ride to the Yarmuk Valley. An expedition of four battalions and a cavalry regiment, with ten guns, moved out from Ma'an against Maulud's position near Petra, which was held by two Arab camel companies and two mule companies, totalling barely three hundred and fifty men, together with less than two hundred Bedouin irregulars. After shelling the position for an hour, and also dropping bombs on it, the Turks advanced to the attack. The poorly trained camel men gave way, recoiling on Maulud's mule-mounted infantry, who, buttressed by the steep cliffs, brought the Turks to a halt. Then the Bedouin lapped round both their flanks, harassing them until at evening they retreated, badly bruised. Thus Lawrence's anticipations had been fulfilled, thanks to nature and to Maulud's skilful adaptation of the Cannæ model to Arab conditions, on a Torres Vedras foundation.

A continuation of the raids on the railway together with the harassing of supply caravans caused the Turks first to draw off troops from Abu el Lissal, and then to abandon it, when they no longer had enough to hold the wide position. Thus by January 7th they had been forced back close to Ma'an itself, and by contracting their zone they inevitably relaxed their hold on the countryside. This opened the way for the Arabs to move north into the corn belt.

While Maulud, helped by the intense cold, was thus shepherding the Turks back into Ma'an, Lawrence was engaged in a new experiment—a development of mechanized force. The fact that he had exploited camel-mobility to a pitch undreamt of by regular standards did not, as with so many animal-loving regular soldiers, hide from him the possibilities of mechanization. Now, with a few days breathing space, his mind harked back to the mud-flats he had seen on his Mudauwara raid in September. A motor-road had been made through the Wadi Ithm gorge up to Guweira, and the Rolls-Royce armoured cars and tenders had been brought up there. Lawrence and Joyce arranged to make a reconnaissance with the tenders towards Mudauwara. The surface more than fulfilled expectations, and the cars touched over sixty miles an hour as they raced over the polished mud, while standing up without any fractures to the rough patches between the flats.

The trial was so promising that, after running almost to Mudau-wara, they decided to attempt an immediate operation, and for this purpose went back to fetch the armoured cars, which they rein-forced with a section of ten-pounder mountain-guns mounted on Talbot cars. They came within sight of the railway on New Year's Eve and reconnoitred a Turkish post which offered a suitable target. Next morning Joyce directed the action from a crest overlooking the post, while Lawrence enjoyed the double delight of being the com-fortable spectator of a fight in which no lives were gambled. For the Turkish fire at the armoured cars seemed to him like peppering a rhinoceros with bird-shot. On the other hand, the cars lacked the obstacle-crossing capacity of tanks and so could not eject the Turks from their burrow. But when they came back from their pleasure-cruise they had at least given Lawrence a fresh extension of ideas.

From the point of view of the orthodox strategist armoured cars could be only an auxiliary, because of their lack of assaulting-power upon entrenchments. But to Lawrence, whose chief desire was to see the enemy sitting in entrenchments, they offered a primary weapon. Not only was the railway brought within a day's run from Guweira, but all movement on the Turks' part might henceforth be menaced by an agent that they could not meet in the open. Thus the British had only to develop this new weapon to be within reach of the real aim of strategy—the paralysis of the opponent.

Unfortunately, Lawrence was at least a generation ahead of the military world in perceiving the strategic implications of mechanized warfare. He had no power to obtain the provision of vehicles ade-quate in form and number for their new strategy. Moreover, he could not even secure acceptance of the strategic theory. The British command still hankered after the capture of Medina. Their minds moved along direct channels and they wanted to wipe the Turkish force in the Hejaz off the balance-sheet, instead of encouraging the Turks to sink more capital in this bad investment.

As in the Peninsula a century before, their victories threatened danger to their own purpose. Wellington's early battles had been profitable because they drew the French towards him in Portugal and thereby gave the Spanish guerrillas a chance to tighten their grip in other parts. But when in 1812 he began to press deeper into Spain, his victories caused the French to contract their zone; this concentration in the north revived their power of resistance, and the struggle was thereby prolonged. The French were saved from the sudden and complete collapse which would, in all probability, have come if they had continued to cling on to the whole country.

In Arabia early in 1918 it looked as if the example of 1812 might be repeated. That it was not repeated would seem to have been due to three factors. First, the Turks were more stupid than the French, and refused to heed their German advisers' plea to withdraw their forces from the Hejaz. Second, the British were less effective in their early operations than their forebears under Wellington had been, so that their later operations had the chance of more effect. In fairness it should be recognized that they were fully aware of the dangers of a Turkish withdrawal and that their desire to sever the Hejaz railway permanently was dictated by the idea of preventing such a withdrawal. But they lacked Lawrence's subtle perception of the fact that as long as the railway was not severed, the Turks would continue to send down it food and materials that would have been of more service in bolstering up the Turkish forces in Palestine.

Lawrence showed his subtlety not merely in theory. For as he grew in understanding of his own theory he took pains to ensure that the Arab operations should never sever the railway, by adopting what one may call a Fabian internal strategy. It seemed to him, he has remarked, less bother than setting up a kindergarten of the imagination for the benefit of the British Staff. And his sense of humour was tickled by their readiness to excuse the Arabs' ineffectiveness because of the way it flattered their own sense of professional superiority.

The moves against Tafila were now unfolded. The plan was for a three-fold convergence from east, south and west. As the opening move, Nasir swung out eastward to the plain of Jefer with the idea of swinging in to attack Jurf ed Derawish, the nearest station, thirty miles above Ma'an. His force comprised a band of the Beni Sakhr, a detachment of 300 Arab Regulars under Nuri Said, and one mountain-gun. Nasir's advance was directed towards a ridge which overlooked the station. With characteristic precaution Lawrence had gone there a few days before and reconnoitred a gun-position. The ridge was occupied under cover of darkness, and the line cut above and below the station. At dawn the mountain-gun opened fire and with a lucky hit silenced the Turkish gun on a lower knoll. The Beni Sakhr then charged on camel-back round the foot of the ridge and their appearance from an unexpected direction caused a panic among the Turks that produced their prompt surrender. Over two hundred prisoners were taken for a loss of two lives. A couple of trains in the station were looted thoroughly and damaged less thoroughly—because of the distracting delicacies, destined for the officers at Medina, with which they were loaded.

On the next day, and the two following, there were heavy falls of snow and hail, and the cold was so intense that ten of Nasir's men died in one day from exposure. This caused them to fall back on their tents at Jefer; the desire of storing their booty was doubtless an additional incentive. But the news of Jurf's capture was the signal for a fresh rush on Shobek by the hill Arabs around Petra. The bleak weather failed to stop them—and the Turks were no more successful. The news of Shobek's capture unleashed Nasir again, and after a swift night ride through the snow he arrived at dawn on the cliff overlooking Tafila, summoning the inhabitants and the small Turkish garrison (150 men) to surrender on pain of bombardment. It was an empty bluff, as Nuri Said's regular detachment was not with him. And his bluff might have been called if Auda had not suddenly ridden forward alone to the edge of the town and cried— "Dogs, do you not know Auda?" The defences of Tafila collapsed before his trumpeting voice as those of Jericho had once collapsed before Joshua. The town had surrendered long before Mastur's Motalga arrived from the westward, from the Wadi Araba.

Capture was easier than retention. The clans had old feuds and began quarrelling among themselves. Auda as usual was the storm-centre. The rumbles hastened the arrival of Zeid, who had been given charge of these Dead Sea operations by Feisal. Ja'far and Lawrence accompanied him, and a small force of about a hundred Arab regulars with two mountain-guns followed as fast as the bad roads allowed. Zeid did his best to compose the troubles with the ointment of gold. Auda was treated according to the principle of the street vocalist who is paid to go away. But harmony was hardly attained before the Turks introduced fresh discord.

Lawrence, valuing Tafila only as a step in the ladder towards the Dead Sea, had not imagined that the Turks would place a value on it sufficient to draw them away from opposing Allenby's advance. Thus he was taken by surprise when a Turkish force, hastily collected at Amman, was rushed south to regain Tafila. It comprised three weak battalions, a hundred cavalry, two mountain howitzers and twenty-seven machine-guns, and was led by Hamid Fakhri Bey, the commander of the 48th Division. Marching from Kerak on January 23rd, it fell next afternoon upon the Arab pickets guarding the Wadi Hesa, a gorge ten miles north-east which separates the land of Moab from the land of Edom and formed the apparently impregnable approach to Tafila. The sudden onset, however, rolled the pickets back before they could be reinforced.

THE "BATTLE" OF TAFILA

In view of a possible attack Ja'far had chosen a defensive position on the overhanging heights behind the great ravine of Tafila. Lawrence had disagreed with this plan both on tactical and on political grounds. The precipitous slopes offered dead ground for an attacker, who could push past the eastern flank and turn the position while himself immune from fire. And the abandonment of the town would throw its people into the Turks' hands. Nevertheless, the sudden emergency gave no chance for reconsideration, and about midnight Zeid gave the order to fall back to the chosen position behind the town. This created a panic in the town as Lawrence had foreseen.

He stayed behind with his bodyguard after the rest of the force had left. "It was freezing hard, the ground all over ice and snow, and in the dark narrow streets the crying and confusion were terrible. I went out and walked about, listening. The men were in a passion of fear, nearly dangerous, but not to me, for I was wrapped up in a dark cloak and not distinguishable and my guards were all around in case of accident. It was important to know the real public opinion, and soon we saw that they were in horror of the Turks, ready to do all in their physical capacity to support against them a leader with any fighting intention. This was satisfactory."

So he took the initiative of sending twenty of the Motalga forward to help those of the peasantry who were still opposing the Turks' advance. He went himself to find Zeid, whose calmness in the crisis seemed a good omen. Lawrence profited by it to offer the germ of a battle plan. This was to culminate in a victory of which most generals would have been proud, but of which Lawrence himself, in retrospect, professed to be thoroughly ashamed. He blames it on a fit of Berserker rage. And his explanation is as enlightening as it is delightful.

"The Turks should never, by all rules of sane generalship, have returned to Tafileh at all. It was simple greed, a dog in the manger attitude unworthy of a serious enemy, just the sort of hopeless thing a Turk would do. How could they expect a proper war, when they gave us no chance to honour them? Our morale was continually being ruined by their follies, for neither could our men respect their courage, nor our officers respect their brains. Also it was an icy morning, and I had been up all night, and was Teutonic enough to decide that they should pay for my changed mind and plan."

"They must be few in number, judging by their speed. We had the pieces and could checkmate them easily. Only in my wrath I went too far and determined to play their kind of game, to deliver them a pitched battle such as they intended, on the pigmy scale of our Arab front, and to kill them all. I would rake up the old maxims and rules of the military text books, and parody them in this action. It was a wanton step, for both the strength and the ground were on my side, and I could have won by refusing battle, beat them in manœuvre as on twenty similar occasions before and after. Somehow bad temper and conceit together made me not content just to know my power, but anxious to display it openly to the Arabs and to the enemy."

As a military apologia it is a gem. So was the battle that followed, by any "military" test.

Zeid had realized the disadvantages of the chosen position and readily accepted Lawrence's proposal to send forward Abdulla, the chief of his bodyguard, with a few men on mules and a couple of light automatics, to test the Turks' strength and dispositions. The reinforcement stimulated the Motalga and the villagers, who drove back the Turkish cavalry screen on to the main body, just moving out after a cold night in bivouac. Lawrence and Zeid could hear the distant bursts of machine-gun fire. But while Zeid wished to wait for definite news from Abdulla, Lawrence was anxious to force the pace, and so went forward himself. In the streets of Tafila he found some of his bodyguard rummaging among the goods there strewn; he

MAP 8

BATTLE OF TAFILA

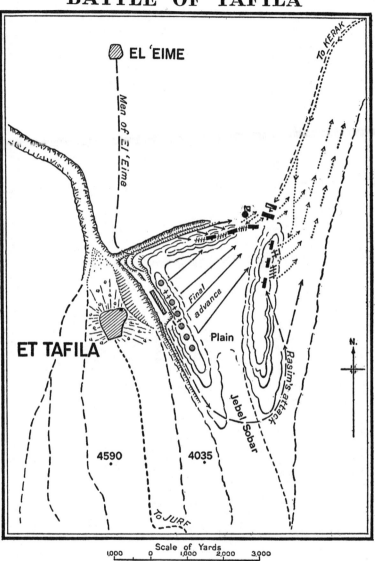

EL 'EIME

Men of El 'Eime

To KERAK

ET TAFILA

Final advance

Plain

Rasim's attack

Jebel Sobar

N.

4590

4035

To JURF

Scale of Yards
1,000   0   1,000   2,000   3,000

ordered them to recover the camels and bring up their light automatic.

Crossing the Tafila ravine he climbed on to the plateau beyond, and there found a ridge—"a low straight bank with some Byzantine foundations in it, a very proper place for a reserve or ultimate line of defence." This low ridge formed the base of a triangular plain, some two miles across, bounded by low green ridges along each side. The apex pointed north-east and through it ran the road from Kerak along which the Turks were now pressing.

Lawrence, by dint of forceful persuasion, collected some of Zeid's personal camel-men whom he found hiding, and made them sit along the skyline of the "reserve" ridge. "They looked important, from a distance (there were some twenty of them) like the points of a considerable force. They were to add all newcomers to their display till further notice, and particularly my villains with their gun. I gave them my signet for authority."

Then he pushed on across the plain and met Abdulla coming back to report to Zeid. His ammunition was exhausted and he had lost five men from shell-fire; but he was still full of fight and was only intent on persuading Zeid to come forward. Leaving him to do this, Lawrence walked on. Shells were now bursting on the plain and to add to his discomfort the stalks of wormwood scored his bare feet. When he reached the apex he found about sixty men holding the corner of the western ridge, while the Turks were pushing down the eastern ridge to outflank them. He came first upon a cluster of peasants. They said they had finished their ammunition and it was all over. "I assured them that it was just beginning and pointed to my populous reserve ridge." Telling them to withdraw there and collect fresh ammunition, he mounted the ridge where the Motalga were still holding on, "quoting to them the adage not to quit firing from one position till ready to fire from the next."

"In command was young Metaab, stripped to his skimp riding-drawers for hard work, with his black love-curls awry, his face stained and haggard." "My presence at the last moment, when the Turks were breaking through, was bitter; and he got angrier when I said that I only wanted to study the landscape. He thought it flippancy, and screamed something about a Christian going into battle unarmed. I retorted with a quip from Clausewitz, about a rearguard effecting its purpose more by being than by doing; but he was past laughter, and perhaps with justice, for the little flinty bank behind which we sheltered was crackling with fire. The Turks, knowing we were there, had turned twenty machine-guns upon it."

Lawrence asked Metaab to try to hold on for another ten minutes, while he, having no horse, set off on foot at a run. As he ran he did not forget to count his paces to help in ranging on the position when the Turks occupied it. "This Motalga ridge was going to be the province we would lose to win the battle, a death-trap for the enemy ignorant of our game; and so I ran away in good spirits." Before he reached the ridge the Motalga horsemen caught him up, but Metaab lent a stirrup to help him along—to Lawrence, with his fondness for inversions, this Waterloo stirrup-charge in reverse may have had a pleasing piquancy.

Safely reaching the reserve ridge he found some eighty men now distributed along it, and more arriving. "We had the automatics put on the skyline . . . with orders to fire occasional shots at long range to disturb the Turks, after the expedient of Masséna in delaying enemy deployment." One feels that Lawrence's wrath must now have evaporated under the rays of his humour, and that he had entered with zest into his parody of orthodoxy. His two hundred men deterred the Turks from advancing by showing themselves generously, until about 3 p.m. Zeid came up from the old position with some fifty of his men and two hundred villagers. He also brought nine machine-guns and light automatics and a mountain-gun to strengthen the fire-defence.

"We remembered just in time that movement is the law of strategy and started moving." Rasim Bey, an Arab regular, was dispatched with about eighty mounted men—horse, camel and mule—and five light automatics, "to make a circuit round the eastern ridge and envelop the enemy's left wing, since the books advised attack not upon a line, but upon a point, and by going far enough along any finite wing it would be found eventually reduced to a point of one single man." "Rasim liked this, my conception of his target. He promised, grinningly, to bring us that last man."

The remaining Arabs paraded about the reserve ridge, at Lawrence's instigation, to cloak the departure of the "cavalry." Meantime the Turks on their opposite ridge "were bringing up an apparently endless procession of machine-guns and dressing them by the left at intervals along the ridge, as though it were a museum. It was lunatic tactics. The ridge was flint, without cover for a lizard." Thanks to Lawrence's pacing the Arab guns had the range (3,100 yards) and were only waiting to sweep the Turks' ridge.

While they waited a fresh reinforcement arrived, about a hundred men from the neighbouring village of El 'Eime, or Aima. "Their arrival decided us to abandon the precepts of Marshal Foch, and to attack from at any rate three sides at once; so we sent the Aima men, with three automatic guns to envelop the enemy's right or western flank." As they happened to arrive on the scene from this direction it might seem that geography had as much part as strategy in deciding the form of their attack. But the facts—which Lawrence does not disclose in his book—are that Zeid had called on the Aima men to reinforce his main body according to the orthodox principle of concentration, when Lawrence intervened and sent them back to work round the flank that the Turks had so conveniently exposed to enfilade. His flair for the weak spot, here the right spot in a double sense, found an apt response in the Arab peasants, his instruments. Primitive men, who know not Marshal Foch have a sound instinct for finding the enemy's rear, especially when, as here, it offers a covered approach.

While the four automatic weapons on the reserve ridge swept the Turks' position and occupied their attention, Rasim's five light automatics (which, for invisibility, were handled by only two men apiece) were pushed forward unseen until, with a sudden burst of fire, they crumpled the Turks' left wing. The "cavalry" then charged in to exploit the disorder. The men of El 'Eime also crept to within a few hundred yards of the machine-guns on the Turks' right flank and thence shot down their unsuspecting crews. As soon as this was seen the Arab reserve charged across the central plain, with crimson banner flying, to complete the victory.

Lawrence's thoughts outpaced them, and ran on to the Wadi Hesa gorge. "It was going to be a massacre, and I should have been crying-sorry for the Turks, but after the angers and exertions of the battle I was too mentally tired to go down into that awful place and spend the rest of the night saving them. I knew that by my decision to fight I had killed twenty or thirty of our six hundred men, and the wounded would be perhaps three times as many. It was one-sixth of our force gone on a verbal triumph, for the destruction of a thousand Turks would have no effect on the issue of the war. Had I manœuvred, I could have worn them out and ruined them, losing perhaps only five or six men in doing so."

One may question, however, whether there was time for manœuvre to take effect without losing Tafila, with its potential train of political ill-effects. Nor were Lawrence's other self-reproaches fully justified. Although the Turks fled in confusion, leaving their commander dead and abandoning two howitzers and all their twenty-seven machine-guns, as well as their baggage, their cavalry combined with the Arabs' tiredness to check the pursuit when the Wadi Hesa was reached. But over two hundred prisoners were taken, and many more killed, while the retreat was harried by the Bedouin from the Kerak district. The exact loss is uncertain. Lawrence heard that only fifty fugitives returned, whereas a Turkish report puts the figure at about four hundred; a German, although indefinite, suggests that a much smaller proportion escaped. The Turkish report probably includes the garrison of Kerak, as this retired to Amman with the fugitives.

Heavy snowfalls and a wind of razor-edge extinguished the Arabs' flickering impulse to follow up their success, and even Lawrence was constrained to recognize that the effort placed too high a tax on human capacity. The clumsy helplessness of camels in mud would also be a tactical danger.

But although his force was chained to Tafila, his mind was projected towards his Dead Sea objective, and there succeeded in exerting a strategic influence. He bethought himself of Abdulla el Feir, camped down in the sunny, snow-free plain on the southern shore of the Dead Sea. He could operate if they could not. So Lawrence got through to him, told him of the victory and moved him to seize the chance of raiding the little lake-port near El Mezra, on the eastern shore, whence the grain of the Kerak district was shipped north to feed the Turkish armies.

Abdulla el Feir picked out some seventy Bedouin horsemen and rode thither along the narrow track between the hills of Moab and the water-edge. At dawn on January 28th, only three days after the battle of Tafila, they reached the cove and found a motor launch and six dhows anchored. Like the Athenians at Ægospotamoi the crews were resting on the beach. Inverting Lysander, Abdulla el Feir charged them from the land side, and thereby achieved a far rarer feat, the capture of a fleet by cavalry. Ten tons of grain and sixty prisoners were taken. After scuttling the ships and burning the huts the expedition returned, without a casualty.

This attainment of his strategic aim, the interruption of the Turks' line of supply, pleased Lawrence far more than his own tactical victory It helped to wipe out the regretted stain of blood, and put him in a good mood to write his report of the Tafila operation for the staff in Palestine. He made the report a fuller parody of orthodoxy than the battle, phrasing it in the impersonal tone and professional jargon that soldiers have loved since Caesar wrote that masterpiece of official deception, *De Bello Gallico*. Thus, as Lawrence has said, his professional superiors might take him for a reformed character, an amateur humbly following in the footsteps of the masters instead of a clown making fun of the professional procession that, with Foch their bandmaster at the head, went drumming down the old road of blood into the house of Clausewitz.

His jest was crowned by the award of the Distinguished Service Order. When he next saw Allenby he suggested that a naval D.S.O. would be more appropriate, a retort that showed his sense of values no less than his sense of humour. A few months later he had a fresh opportunity. When out on an expedition two British aeroplanes sighted his camel party and gave chase; and although Lawrence made his men ride round in a ring—the customary signal to show that they were friendly troops—the aeroplanes continued to pelt them with bullets, luckily without effect. Lawrence's way of reporting the incident to Sir Geoffrey Salmond was to recommend himself for the Distinguished Flying Cross "for presence of mind in not shooting down two Bristol fighters which were attempting to machine-gun my party from the air."

In the weeks that followed his success at Tafila he had need of his humour. The continued hard weather frustrated his further object, of occupying all the corn belt and linking up with Allenby at the northern end of the Dead Sea. The tribes ahead promised their support but the tribesmen with him were held fast by the snow, and the longer they stayed the more they lapsed from his idea of activity.

They were still more definitely immobilized by having to send their camels down to warmer pastures in the valley.

Sick of being cooped up in his unsavoury and verminous quarters at Tafila, Lawrence decided early in February to return to his base and collect more money ready to nourish the spring campaign. It was hard riding on the soft ground, with the camels continually slipping in the slush while their riders were nipped by a wind that, exasperatingly, froze them without freezing the path under foot. They passed Maulud's post at Abu el Lissal without anyone hailing them—his unfortunate Arab regulars, provided only with British khaki drill of summer pattern, had lost half their strength in toll to the bitter weather which alone prevented the Turks from overwhelming the remnant. At last Guweira was reached and there Lawrence found not only Joyce but Alan Dawnay, head of the newly-formed Hejaz Operations Staff—known as "Hedgehog"—that had been formed at Cairo in November for closer liaison with, and the greater organization of, the Arab operations. Lawrence stayed three nights and then, receiving thirty thousand pounds sent up by Feisal, set off back to Tafila, which he regained alone after a still more trying ride. There he found a young Arabic-speaking intelligence officer, Kirkbride, who had come across from the Palestine front.

Movement forward was now practicable and Lawrence made a reconnaissance to the Dead Sea with that idea. But when, on returning, he urged it on Zeid, he met difficulties, due still more to Zeid's entourage. The chief excuse was a pretence that Zeid had spent all the money, intended to subsidize the advance, in payments to the local tribesmen who had simply been sitting still. Finding argument vain, Lawrence told Zeid that if the money was not returned he would leave him.

The shock of this disappointment, coming after a long period of strain, seems to have given Lawrence a desire to be quit of the whole business. And he felt that he had now an excuse. The frustration of his military plans was a reflection on his power over the Arabs, on his judgment of men, and it nullified the very purpose for which Allenby was employing him. With the thought of offering his resignation, he set out westward to see Allenby.

After a ride of nearly eighty miles he reached Beersheba, where he was greeted with the news that Jericho had been captured. Then

LAWRENCE'S "GHAZALA," AND FOAL

JA'FAR PASHA AND SHERIF NASIR AT SHOBEK

THE "BLUE MIST" IN WADI ITHM

"TULIPS" EXPLODING ON THE RAILWAY NEAR DERAA

he went on to Allenby's headquarters and luckily met Hogarth on the station platform. Here was a man to whom he could relieve himself. He blamed himself for Zeid's moral failure. He declared that he was sick of responsibility. He complained of the free hand he had been given—and taken. By offering him a choice, instead of giving him an order, his chiefs in Cairo had put on him the moral responsibility for buoying up the Arabs with promises that might never be fulfilled, and that if fulfilled militarily might be hollow politically. Worse still, small as was his faith in British promises, he had lost his faith, through experience, in the Arabs' power to consolidate in peace the goal to which he had led them in war. Thus, for his own part, he wanted to go back and become a cog in the military machine, with things comfortably arranged for him. The harness of obedience was better than the self-applied spur of command.

The state of his body partly explained this attitude of mind— "I was a very sick man: almost at breaking point." But there was more behind it. Undoubtedly the few days he had spent with the armoured cars, in ordinary British soldier company, had shown him the attractions of this carefree, subordinate existence. Even its comforts made appeal to his racked body—cars were better vehicles than camels for the fighting spirit to preserve its energy. The impression of those days, reinforced by later experience, was to affect his postwar choice of occupation.

Hogarth did not attempt to argue with Lawrence, but took him to breakfast. Over breakfast Clayton made a new call on his services, sweeping aside his protests on the score of necessity. General Headquarters had been trying for days before his unwarned arrival to get in touch with him, and aeroplanes had been sent to fetch him.

This call for Lawrence was the sequel to a fresh call on Allenby from the West. And by a paradox Lawrence's double shame at Tafila had done far more towards answering it than he realized, now or later.

CHAPTER XVI

MORE AND MORE REGULAR

March–July, 1918

The next stage beyond Jerusalem—Lloyd George's vision of Aleppo—Allenby's shorter-range aim is upset by the British disasters in France, which drain his strength—The Turks' weakness
A call to Lawrence—The Arabs are to follow up a British move into Trans-Jordan—The British failure reacts on the Arab cause—The Arab Regulars, in Lawrence's absence, suffer a check at Ma'an, but the effect is redeemed by Dawnay's stroke below it which permanently severs the rail connection with Medina—The British, in Lawrence's absence, go into Trans-Jordan again: to chase a shadow
This fresh failure paralyses them for the time and exposes the Arabs at Ma'an to danger —The Arabs avert the danger by breaching the railway above Ma'an—Allenby's gift of 2,000 camels inspires Lawrence to his boldest design—The need for it is forestalled by the rapid recovery of Allenby's offensive power

IMMEDIATELY after the capture of Jerusalem, Allenby, in practical reward, received the promise of a further reinforcement. He was asked in return to outline his further plans. His reply emphasized the handicap of the wet season, but intimated that during it he would operate against the Hejaz railway to isolate the 20,000 Turks south of Amman. Later, after pushing forward his left gradually, he would prepare another large-scale offensive with naval co-operation.

These designs seemed far too narrow to Lloyd George, when he saw them. His desire was to see Turkey knocked out of the war. To this end he would like to see Aleppo gained, cutting off the Turkish forces in Mesopotamia, or at the least Palestine fully occupied. Allenby was asked what extra force he would need for the alternative goals.

Allenby replied that he hoped to achieve the lesser task by mid-summer with his present force, but for the larger he would require at least sixteen infantry divisions—more than double his present force. And, even if he had them, he doubted whether he could supply them. He made it clear to the Government that he preferred to continue the steady step by step advance previously outlined than to follow Lloyd George in airy flights of imagination. And his reply makes it clear to the historian that his horizon was still bounded by

MAP 9

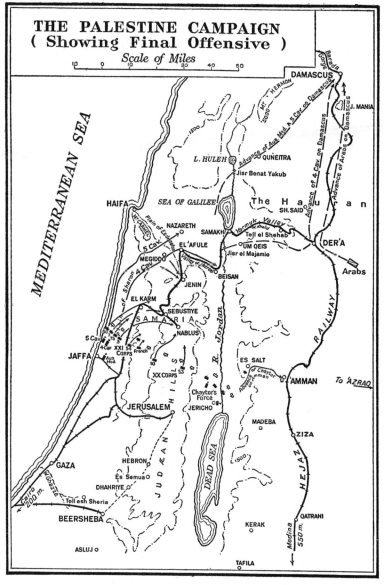

THE PALESTINE CAMPAIGN
(Showing Final Offensive)

siege-war views of mobility, strategic and tactical. He was justified in so far as mobility is dependent on its instrument.

Robertson was, naturally, strong among the spokesmen of "impossibility." But his influence was waning, his supersession coming, and on January 21st the Military Representatives on the new Supreme War Council of the Allies took the decision, under Lloyd George's pressure, to stand on the defensive in France, Italy and the Balkans, and to "undertake a decisive offensive against Turkey with a view to the annihilation of Turkish armies and the collapse of Turkish resistance."

To arrange it, the British Government sent out General Smuts, an old exponent of mobility at Britain's expense, on a mission to examine the position of the Palestine and Mesopotamia forces. In the consultations that followed Smuts found that he had to adapt Lloyd George's desires to realities: of which perhaps the grimmest were not concrete obstacles—Turkish or geographical—but ideas. He had to descend from Boer to British conceptions of mobility.

The final scheme was that Allenby should be reinforced with one British and one Indian infantry division from Mesopotamia, and an Indian cavalry division from France. Thus he would have ten infantry and four mounted divisions. With this Allenby promised to make an offensive as vigorous as the progress of his railway would permit. His plan was to begin with the steps he had already suggested, and then extend them northward, up the coast, keeping step with the advance of the railway. A smaller column would try to advance inland on Damascus and occupy the Hauran with the aid of the Arabs and Druses.

Only the first part of the plan was ever put into operation, because of the break in the Western Front that followed the German offensive of March 21st. The crisis in France led not only to a cancellation of Allenby's instructions but to the draining of his force. Two complete divisions were taken away, while nine yeomanry regiments and twenty-three infantry battalions were also drawn out of the remaining divisions. Their places were filled by Indian troops, who were fitted into the original framework as far as possible, and despite the difficulties the result reflected great credit on those responsible for the organization and training. The reconstituted force had seven infantry divisions, as in the original, and four

mounted divisions instead of three. Ultimately, these disturbing re-
ductions proved the proverbial blessing in disguise, for they compelled the British command to develop both its means and ideas of
mobility, while freeing them of the threatened incubus of numbers
too large for supply while in movement. And in September that force
achieved a rapid and sweeping triumph that the double-sized force
proposed in January would never have attempted.

To quote the verdict of the Official History, Allenby's spring plan
was "sound, but stiff and mechanical, and it made transport
master instead of servant. By reflection during the summer Sir Edmund Allenby so transformed it that it achieved in less than a fortnight what its original would have taken many months to perform."
An unofficial historian might dispute the plan's claims to the qualification "sound." For history has many lessons to tell us that a plan
which seeks security at the expense of surprise and mobility is the
depth of unsoundness.

In view of the reasonable excuse that the conditions, of enemy
resistance especially, had changed vastly by September, it is interesting to have a look on "the other side of the hill." Liman von Sanders,
the successful defender of Gallipoli, who took over the supreme
command of the Turks in Palestine in February, was informed on
arrival by von Falkenhausen that "the British were so superior along
the entire front, that they could pierce the front at any time and
place they might select." Liman von Sanders agreed after inspecting
the front.

Falkenhausen was chief of staff of the so-called Seventh "Army"
in the inland sector facing Jerusalem—according to Liman von
Sanders it had only 3,900 rifles available for the defence of a sixteen-
mile front. The Eighth "Army" held the coastal sector. The Fourth
"Army" east of the Jordan comprised all the troops guarding the
Hejaz railway down to Ma'an. The ten divisions of the two armies
facing the British between the Jordan and the sea were reduced to an
average strength of about 1,300 rifles. Ration strength was about
three times as large. But in the fighting strength should be included
the machine-gunners, who averaged about 800 a division. The
Turks, indeed, had a higher number of machine-guns than the
British—60 to a division—and here lay their real defensive strength.
Mobility was the means to overcome it. And here the British had

long handicapped themselves.

Another significant point is that the Turkish strength was actually weaker in the spring, when Allenby was to have attacked, than in the autumn when he wrought their collapse. In September eight fresh Turkish battalions had arrived as well as ten thousand men as drafts to fill the gaps caused by casualities. In addition three picked German battalions were added to the three already there. But these as well as four of the Turkish battalions were sent to the Fourth Army, the Arab zone. Indeed, when Allenby's blow fell in September there were almost as many Turks pinned down inactive east of the Jordan as faced the British west of the Jordan.

The visit from Smuts was the cause of the call to Lawrence in February. Allenby wanted to know what aid the Arabs could give in the large offensive plan which he had now been encouraged to undertake. If he was to push northward he needed the Arabs to cover his eastern flank by drawing off the attention of the Turkish Fourth Army. This meant that instead of the creeping paralysis over the widest possible area of Lawrence's strategic theory, Feisal's army would have to concentrate on producing a more sudden local paralysis in the Amman area, in order to fit in with Allenby's plan. To do this it would itself have to be relatively concentrated—another violation of irregular principles.

Thus out of loyalty to Allenby, Lawrence was now drawn to propose what he had hitherto opposed—the capture of Ma'an: "We should have to take it before we could afford a second sphere." With more transport—he asked for seven hundred baggage camels—as well as more firepower, they "could take a position some miles north of Ma'an and cut the railway permanently, so forcing the Ma'an garrison to come out and fight them; and in the field the Arabs would easily defeat the Turks." It was a highly regular conception—of the highest quality.

To attempt it the Arab army would need assurance against the Turks coming down the railway from Amman, and catching them between pincers. Allenby replied that this would be fulfilled by his own coming preparatory move against Amman, during which he intended to put a garrison in Es Salt. He also sent to Aqaba two camel transport units which enabled the Arab Regular Army to maintain itself eighty miles from its base.

At a conference on February 28th it was settled that the Arab army should move at once to the Ma'an plateau, to take Ma'an, and that the British should move across the Jordan, occupy Es Salt, and destroy the railway south of Amman. Allenby's Chief of Staff, Bols, wanted the Arabs in the north to help in the British advance, but Lawrence did not regard such close co-operation as practical—it was too much "like mixing oil and water." He argued that it would be better to wait until the raid on Amman was over and Es Salt permanently occupied, as the deliberate retirement from the railway might easily be misinterpreted as an enforced retreat, and so cause a reaction among the Arabs.

"Chetwode, who was to direct the advance, asked how his men were to distinguish friendly from hostile Arabs, since their tendency was a prejudice against all wearing skirts. I was sitting skirted in their midst and replied, naturally, that skirt-wearers disliked men in uniform. The laugh clinched the question, and it was agreed that we support the British retention of Salt only after they came to rest there."

It was also decided that when Ma'an was captured, the Arab Regulars would be moved up and based on Jericho. Thence they would act on Allenby's flank in the intended drive to the north.

But all these plans were doomed to go awry, although the path to success had been cleared by Lawrence's self-despised success at Tafila. By it he had achieved a strategic effect that he seems neither to have calculated nor subsequently appreciated at its due value.

For the Turks, who could understand a smack in the face better than a creeping paralysis, were stirred by their defeat at Tafila to avenge it. For this purpose they dispatched the bulk of the garrison at Amman on an expedition to regain Tafila—just as the British were preparing to advance on Amman! From that moment everything turned on time.

The expedition was dispatched by the Hejaz railway. One column detrained at Qatrani, thirty-five miles to the north-east of Tafila, and another at Jurf ed Derawish, seventeen miles to the south-east. Both converged on Tafila, and although Zeid seems to have put up a stout fight against heavy odds he was forced to evacuate the town on March 6th. The Turks followed him up and drove him back again next day towards Shobek, but he avoided the loss of any guns or material. After this empty parade, the expedition set off on its return journey a fortnight later, and the Arabs promptly reoccupied Tafila.

But before the bulk of the expeditionary force was back the British had begun to cross the Jordan, on the night of March 21st, for the raid on Amman. The Turks had barely a thousand rifles to oppose the British 60th Division, Anzac Mounted Division and Imperial Camel Brigade.

Unfortunately heavy rains confronted the British with Jeremiah's question—"How wilt thou do in the swelling of Jordan?" And the answer was not a happy one. First, the British postponed the attempt for two days, until the 21st, hoping for an improvement. Then a check at one of the crossings caused a long delay while arrangements were made to clear it by a flank attack from the other, so that the passage was not completed until the morning of the 24th. Further time was lost in the advance across the great plateau, owing less to the enemy's resistance than to the badness of the routes—and to a failure to obtain previous information about them. Es Salt was not occupied until the evening of the 25th, and Amman, about 25 miles from the Jordan, was not reached until the morning of the 27th.

The delays had allowed time for a German battalion and a mule-mounted Turkish battalion to arrive back from the Tafila expedition, and also for Liman von Sanders to hurry down larger reinforcements by rail from Damascus. For the next four days vain attacks were hurled against the Amman defences. Eventually by a finely executed night approach the New Zealanders captured Hill 3039, a dominating height south of the town, early on the 30th, thus gaining what according to the textbooks was obviously the "key of the position." But the Turks, sadly ill-educated, refused to recognize the fact, and so the key was not turned in the lock. Reluctantly, and perhaps rather late, recognizing the force of impregnable facts, the British began their retirement during the night. And they had done little damage to the railway during the four days it had lain in their hands. Lawrence called it "unpardonable carelessness." "They went to Amman, not to take the beastly village, but to smash the railway. Miles of the line, from Amman, southward, was in their hands—and they hardly broke a rail."

The retreat across the muddy plateau, amid crowds of wailing refugees, was as depressing as it was exhausting. And under these conditions the original intention of holding Es Salt permanently was apparently forgotten, the garrison joining in the general reflux—on April 1st.

Economically, the "raid" had not been too unprofitable, the capture of nearly a thousand prisoners nearly balancing the British casualties. Morally, the effect was as damaging to the British as it was enheartening to the Turks. The British had not only forfeited the opportunity created by a handful of Arabs at Tafila, but had exposed their numerous Arab supporters around Amman to the Turks' vengeance.

Lawrence had ridden north ready to take advantage of Allenby's occupation of Es Salt. He left Abu el Lissal on April 3rd with a convoy of two thousand baggage camels, carrying ammunition and food. The scale of the convoy shows the scale on which he had prepared to act in the Madeba area—"it was equipment for 10,000 irregulars for a month."

In the passage across the railway he had an amusing little adventure, for as he climbed the embankment a sleepy Turkish soldier suddenly stumbled out of a culvert, saw Lawrence, pistol in hand, found that he was separated from his own rifle, and resigned himself to his fate. He seemed hardly to believe his luck when he heard Lawrence's cryptic words of reprieve:—"God is merciful." But his reaction was like that of a London gutter-snipe after a narrow escape from being run over, for Lawrence, glancing back, saw him cocking his fingers to his nose.

On April 6th, after four easy stages, the convoy reached the well-watered Atara district south-east of Amman and here found some of their Beni Sakhr allies encamped. The intended plan was that as soon as the British had taken Es Salt the Beni Sakhr would move westwards across the railway to Themed, the main watering place of the tribe, and then, covered by Allenby's cavalry, establish their headquarters at Madeba. But all these ideas were dispersed by the British failure at Amman.

Desert news seems for once to have travelled with curious slowness. For according to Lawrence's account it was nearly a fortnight after the British had reached Amman that the Beni Sakhr, in their

LAWRENCE, AT AQABA

camp less than forty miles distant, heard of it and began moving towards Themed. Then, however, messages seem to have multiplied quickly, first to say that the British were retiring from Amman, and then that they had "fled" from Es Salt. These reports were like a cold douche to the Arabs, who were not comforted by Lawrence's hopeful denials. He himself "grew seriously disturbed in the conflict of rumour, and sent Adhub, who might be trusted not to lose his head, to Salt with a letter for Chetwode or Shea, asking for a note on the real situation." This precautionary search for information seems to have been rather belated. "Very late at night Adhub's racing horse-hooves echoed across the valley and he came in to tell us that Jemal Pasha was now in Salt, victorious, hanging those local Arabs who had welcomed the English. The Turks were still chasing Allenby far down the Jordan valley. It was thought that Jerusalem would be recovered. I knew enough of my countrymen to reject that possibility; but clearly things were very wrong. We slipped off, bemused, to the Atatir again."

"This reverse, being unawares, hurt me the more. Allenby's plan had seemed modest, and that we should so fall down before the Arabs was deplorable. They had never trusted us to do the great things which I foretold; and now their independent thoughts set out to enjoy the springtide here." The arrival of a band of gipsies gave them an opportunity to exchange the dubious prospects of war for the immediate pleasures of woman.

The presence of these gipsy women gave Lawrence a different out-let of his unexpended energy. He hired three of the women as companions on a reconnaissance of Amman, dressed up himself and Farraj in similar clothes, and walked through the town. The visit convinced him that the defences of Amman did not invite attack, but he also found that the appearance of himself and his companions was too inviting for some of the Turkish soldiers, so that they had to take to their heels to escape these unwelcome advances, doubtless to the surprise of the Turks. The adventure persuaded Lawrence that he would in future, as apparently on his Baalbek ride the previous June, wear British uniform when visiting enemy quarters—on the ground that it was too brazen to be suspected.

Seeing that prospects in the north were clouded for the time he now determined to rejoin Feisal, and also to send back the Indians from Azrak, where the garrison had spent a trying winter. One of those who had died from the cold was Daud. His bosom friend, Farraj, did not survive him long, nor had he the wish to linger when shot through the body in a scuffle with a Turkish railway patrol on the way back. Finding him mortally wounded, Lawrence made an attempt to carry him away in a blanket, but he screamed so pitifully from the pain of his wound that they put him down. Then, rather than leave him to be tortured by the Turks before death, Lawrence forced himself to put a bullet through Farraj's head.

More ill news greeted Lawrence when two days later he came in sight of Ma'an. This time it was due to the folly of Arabs, but Arabs who, unlike the Bedouin, were steeped in a regular tradition of warfare. Feisal and Ja'far had accepted Lawrence's plan of indirect approach to Ma'an, but it did not satisfy most of the officers of the new Arab Regular Army. Instead of being wise enough to lure the garrison out into the open by placing the Arab Army astride the railway, they clamoured for a direct onslaught. Joyce had argued in vain against blunting their untried weapon, whereat Maulud, eager for an assault, had complained to Feisal of English interference with Arab liberty—liberty in this case to imitate Western military follies. Then Joyce had fallen ill and been taken back to Egypt with pneumonia. By the time Dawnay arrived to reason with the Arab officers the chance for reason had gone because of their feeling that they must justify their boasts.

Dawnay had therefore devised a plan adjusted to their desires while still retaining indirect moves. The available force [1] was distributed in three parts; a centre column of Arab Regulars under Maulud's command together with Auda's Abu Tayi horsemen; a northern column also of Arab Regulars, under Ja'far; and a southern

[1] The "Arab Northern Army" now consisted of:—
i. *The Arab Regular Army,* under Ja'far Pasha.
   A Brigade of Infantry, a battalion of mule-mounted infantry, a battalion of Camel Corps, and about eight guns.
ii. *British Section,* under Lieut.-Colonel P. C. Joyce (sick at the moment).
   Hejaz Armoured Car Battery (of three Rolls-Royce cars mounting machine-guns and two 10-pounder guns on Talbot lorries), a company of Egyptian Camel Corps, a flight of four aircraft, and transport and labour detachments.
iii. *French Detachment,* under Captain Pisani.
   Two mountain-guns, four machine-guns, and ten automatic rifles.
iv. *Bedouin and Arab Peasant Irregulars,* raised in variable quantity for cperations in their own areas, under Major T. E. Lawrence's direction.

column under Dawnay's direct control, which comprised the armoured cars and the Egyptian camelry, together with some Bedouin. Maulud's centre column opened the ball by storming Ghadir el Haj, the next station south of Ma'an, on the night of April 11th. It then moved up to attack Ma'an. On the night of the 12th Ja'far's northern column captured Jerdun station, the station immediately above Ma'an, taking two hundred prisoners and two machine-guns. After burning the station the column moved down the line during the day and destroyed three thousand rails. But the inherent weakness of the plan was that it allowed too little time for this railway bait to be swallowed by the Turks before the Arab Regular Army was committed to an assault on Ma'an.

When Lawrence arrived on the scene, early on April 13th, the centre column had just succeeded in capturing Jebel Semna, the low hill which overlooked Ma'an from the south-west, but Maulud himself had been badly wounded. Lawrence hastened up to his litter and in response to his inquiries the old fighter muttered, like an Arabic version of Nelson at Trafalgar—"Yes, indeed, Lurens Bey, I am hurt; but, thanks be to God, it is nothing. We have taken Semna." More happily, he recovered. But the attack made little further progress.

The success at Semna encouraged the hot-heads, and Feisal received a petition signed by all his officers in which he was "implored to allow the sons of the Arabs to hurl themselves against the Turkish trenches." He and his British advisers felt that it was useless to expostulate. Where reason had already failed the Arab officers could only be cured by experience.

Ja'far came down to Ma'an to direct operations, and on the 16th Nuri Said led an assault on the station covered by the artillery. But as they reached it the French guns ceased fire. Lawrence, who was following the advance in a Ford car, hurried back to find the cause of this ominous lapse of artillery support, only to be told by Pisani that every round had been expended. Pisani bitterly added that he had begged Nuri Said not to attack when there was such a deficiency of ammunition.

Thus the Arabs, who had taken seventy prisoners in their coup, were compelled to relinquish their hold on the station and, as so often happens, lost more heavily in their retreat across the open than in their successful advance. It was the more disappointing because of the fighting spirit they had shown and the skilful way they had used ground-cover in this first serious test of the new army. Auda's Abu Tayi, however, had not lived up to their Abu el Lissal reputation, doing little to help Nuri's attack. Even allowing for the difficulty of working regulars and irregulars together, the Abu Tayi had been disappointing, and when Auda came into Feisal's tent and said—"Greeting, Lurens," Lawrence retorted—"Greetings for yesterday evening, Auda."

On the 18th Ja'far withdrew to the Semna position and attempted to procure Ma'an's surrender by invitation. The Turks' reply showed an inclination to accept but regretted the necessity of complying with superior orders to hold out until the last cartridge. Ja'far signified his readiness to facilitate this process of exhausting their ammunition, but in the interval Jemal Pasha, relieved of British pressure at Amman, was able to send down a force to reoccupy Jerdun station and pass a pack convoy of ammunition and food across the railless gap into Ma'an.

Meantime the British-Egyptian-Bedouin southern column had been breaking the railway south of Ma'an. Dawnay had organized this himself on what Young terms "the most approved Staff College lines." On April 12th a party had gone out by car from Guweira across the mud-flats to reconnoitre the ground near Tell esh Shahm station just above Mudauwara. Leaving the cars under cover, Dawnay took his subordinate commanders and liaison officer by a covered route to the top of a rocky hill from which they could observe the objective. The "gun sites, times for aeroplane co-operation, lines of approach for armoured cars, successive positions for the E.C.C. [Egyptian Camel Corps], even the general direction of the Beni Atiya camel charge were planned out in the utmost detail." Young, seeing the mere twenty Turks who formed the garrison, "could not help feeling that it was really not quite fair of Dawnay to make such up-to-date and elaborate plans for their destruction."

On the return of the reconnaissance party to Guweira they found that this beautiful structure had already been chipped, as a message from the Beni Atiya announced that they had decided to attack Tebuk on their own and so would not be able to fill their destined part in the Tell esh Shahm plan. The vagaries of the Arab irregular were a trial to the Regular mind, if also refreshing to it. It was fortunate that Dawnay, for all his immaculateness of inward conception and outward appearance, possessed a sense of humour that made adjustment possible.

In the process Lawrence also had opportunity to exercise his humour. Immediately after the check at Ma'an he had driven down to join Dawnay, feeling "uneasy at a regular fighting his first guerrilla battle with that most involved and intricate weapon, the armoured car." He was dubious also whether Dawnay, who did not speak Arabic, would realize the possibilities of friction latent in the mutual antipathy of Bedouin and Egyptians, or be able to smooth it over. So he decided to offer his services "delicately, as interpreter."

Dawnay had no false pride and welcomed Lawrence gladly when he arrived on the 18th at the camp, now established north of Tell esh Shahm. Lawrence marvelled when he saw it. "The cars were parked geometrically here; armoured cars there; sentries and pickets were out, with machine-guns ready. Even the Arabs were in a tactical place behind a hill, in support, but out of sight and hearing: by some magic Sherif Hazaa and himself had kept them where they were put. My tongue coiled into my cheek with the wish to say that the only thing lacking was an enemy."

Lawrence's delicate irony had been stimulated by the sight of the sentries marching up and down—"they were giving us away across the quiet of the night." So he took the liberty of posting them in concealment, telling them to listen and keep still. The comedy of "sentry go," a costly production, has been many times performed in our irregular campaigns, and delights a hostile gallery even more than the Whitehall crowd. Subsequent performances in Ireland were greatly appreciated by the Sinn Feiners.

Still more impressive were the operation orders, "orthodox-sounding things with zero times and a sequence of movements." Each unit had its appointed duty and time at which to perform it, all perfectly dovetailed so as to avoid hitches and ensure that each move was covered by proper fire support. The one difficulty was that Sherif Hazaa could not synchronize his watch, having none, but Dawnay overcame it by arranging that he should time his move by that of the cars. The first step would be to take the post which Joyce and Lawrence had engaged on New Year's Eve; the second, after lunch, to take "South Post"; the third to converge on and capture the station.

At dawn on the 19th the armoured cars, which had "taken station" in the dark, rolled silently forward on top of the sleeping Turks in their trenches, and the astonished occupants promptly came out with their hands up. Hornby then dashed up with the Talbots, laden with explosives, and demolished "Bridge A," which went up with a thunderous roar. Lawrence was shocked not only by the force of the explosion but by the lavish way guncotton had been used, so he ran forward with Dawnay to show Hornby his more economical method of stuffing guncotton into the drainage holes which he thus converted into mine-chambers, a use unintended by the bridge-builders. Subsequent bridges were dealt with more cheaply, but no less effectively, in consequence.

The program of attack on "South Post" was disturbed by the irregular behaviour of Hazaa's Bedouin. While the Egyptians were advancing soberly according to the customary method of alternate section rushes, the Arabs instead "thought it was a steeplechase and did a camel-charge up the mound over breast-work and trenches. The war-weary Turks gave it up in disgust."

The third and final step followed. Operation orders had said "the station will be taken at zero 11.30." But "the Turks, ignorantly and in haste, surrendered ten minutes too soon, and made the only blot on a bloodless day." The Egyptians were coming down from the north, the guns covering them with a bombardment, the aeroplanes dropping bombs, the armoured cars working forward—when, through the haze, the Turks were seen waving the white flag in token of their desire for premature surrender. A race for the station followed. Lawrence won it and gained the station bell, the next man took the ticket punch, and the third the office stamp. The Turks looked on in amazement.

"A minute later, with a howl, the Bedouin were upon the maddest looting of their history. Two hundred rifles, eighty thousand rounds of ammunition, many bombs, much food and clothing were in the station, and everybody smashed and profited." Egyptians and Bedouin came almost to blows over the food, and a camel suddenly set off a Turkish trip-mine, to its own demolition and the momentary distraction of the looters. He has told me that anticipation of such friction was the real reason that had impelled him to come down. "The antipathy of the Egyptians and the Bedouin were intense and the Egyptian effort to save some of the loot from private plundering nearly started a fight. I had a very near call, but just managed to keep the Arabs in hand. Otherwise all the regulars might have been killed." But this explanation needs to be completed by the evidence of other eye-witnesses. They have told me that the way Lawrence stilled the tumult was uncanny—"like the hypnotic influence of a lion-tamer."

The booty was so vast that the structure of Dawnay's plan now broke under its burden. For in the morning most of the Arabs had gone off. The faithful remnant were repaid when the armoured cars occupied Ramleh station, which was found empty of Turks but not of their goods. But next day the cars alone went on to explore Mudauwara, which they found too strongly held for assault. However, Dawnay persevered so energetically with his railway destruction, helped by a contingent of Arabs sent down by Feisal, that eighty miles of line between Ma'an and Mudauwara was utterly wrecked together with its seven small stations. As the Turkish reserves of rail were now used up, the Hejaz line was permanently severed and Medina isolated.

If Dawnay had learnt the necessity of adjustment he had also shown the value of thoroughness. Lawrence's tribute to him deserves quotation—"Dawnay was Allenby's greatest gift to us—greater than thousands of baggage camels. As a professional officer he had the class-touch: so that even the reddest hearer recognized an authentic redness. His was an understanding mind, feeling instinctively the special qualities of rebellion: at the same time, his war-training enriched his treatment of this antithetic subject. He married war and rebellion in himself; as, of old in Yanbo, it had been my dream every regular officer would. Yet, in three years' practice, only Dawnay succeeded."

While Dawnay went back to Cairo, Lawrence discussed with Young, his newly appointed "double," what further operations could be set on foot. It was decided that while a small part of the Arab Regular Army should be left to contain the Ma'an garrison, the bulk should move north under Nuri Said to attack Jurf ed Derawish. Young was to go with Zeid, get in touch with Mirzuk and induce the

Beni Sakhr to join in the attack on Jurf, co-ordinating their movements with those of Nuri. After the capture of Jurf the operations would be extended if possible so as to produce north of Ma'an another eighty miles breach in the railway.

After obtaining Feisal's approval for the plan, Lawrence sailed for Egypt to gain fresh light on Allenby's intentions, Dawnay accompanied him to Allenby's headquarters, and when they arrived there on May 2nd they heard more bad news; or, rather its augury. For Bols greeted them and blissfully remarked, "Well, we're in Salt all right." He went on to say that the chiefs of the Beni Sakhr had come to Jericho to offer the assistance of their "twenty thousand tribesmen" at Themed, and that in consequence he had worked out a new plan of operation against the Amman plateau. In the early hours of April 30th the British had advanced from the Jordan and that same evening the Anzac horsemen, slipping northward, had entered Es Salt.

It sounded well, but Lawrence saw its hollowness. "I asked who the chief of the Beni Sakhr was, and he said 'Fahad': triumphing in his efficient inroad into what had been my province. It sounded madder and madder. I knew that Fahad could not raise four hundred men; and that, at the moment there was not a tent on Themed; they had moved south, to Young. We hurried to the office for the real story, and learned that it was, unfortunately, as Bols had said. The British cavalry had gone impromptu up the hills of Moab on some airy promise of the Zebn sheikhs; greedy fellows who had ridden into Jerusalem only to taste Allenby's bounty, but had there been taken at their mouth-value."

Actually, there was more excuse for Bols than Lawrence suggests. For Mirzuk, Feisal's representative in the north, had sent the sheikhs over the Jordan and had given them a letter for Allenby in which he said that he only needed a little assistance from the British to finish the Turks in Trans-Jordan. His vivid imagination thus shares responsibility with Bols' credulity—but does not excuse it. The neglect to consult Lawrence before chasing this bubble may perhaps be explained by the fact that some of the staff at General Headquarters were still sore from Lawrence's comments on their neglect to blow up the railway bridges during the previous advance to Amman If so, their attempt to score off him proved a costly revenge.

Allenby was certainly led astray by his staff over this renewed move into Trans-Jordan. Guy Dawnay had left him for France, and Bartholomew, who was to work out the final operation of the war, had not yet left Chetwode's staff for Allenby's. Moreover, this operation is incorrectly described, even in the official history, as a "raid." According to his subsequent dispatch his object was "to cut off and destroy the enemy's force at Shunet Nimrin, and, if successful, to hold Es Salt until the Arabs could arrive and relieve my troops." But beforehand he wrote to Chauvel, who was entrusted with the move, "As soon as your operations have gained the front Amman-Es Salt you will at once prepare for operations northwards with a view to advancing rapidly on Deraa." It becomes clear that the operation was inspired by a vaulting ambition, and it is also one more instance of the difference, so familiar to the historian, between a commander's intention and his subsequent explanation for history.

The Turkish forces had increased since the previous attempt, and the bulk of them, some six thousand, were now holding an immensely strong position at Shunet Nimrin astride the main route to Amman. It lay on the escarpment of the great plateau which, abandoned by the British in their previous retreat, now formed a barrier across their path. To overcome this increased resistance the British force, otherwise the same as before, had the Australian Mounted Division added.

The 6oth Division, reinforced by part of the Anzac Mounted Division, was destined for the forbidding task of frontal attack on the position, while the rest of the mounted troops were to ride north up the Jordan valley, climb the escarpment and gain Es Salt, held by only a few companies of Turks. Thence they were to sweep south against the rear of the main position. The supposed representatives of the Beni Sakhr had promised meantime to block the tracks to Amman by which the Turks were supplied. Thus, in promise the Turks were completely bottled.

The men of the 6oth Division soon had cause to realize the difficulty of their task. Despite repeated efforts their attack was stopped by machine-gun fire. Meantime the cavalry rode a dozen miles north to the Es Salt-Ed Damiye track. Here a brigade was dropped astride the track to cover the flank, but the bridge was left in the Turks' hands. The rest of the cavalry now turned east by two tracks and scrambled up on to the plateau, becoming strung out in the process; Es Salt was not occupied until the evening. The 5th Brigade, composed of English Yeomanry, which had been still more delayed, staged an attack on the place next morning only to be greeted, not with Turkish bullets, but with Australian chaff.

That morning also the 60th Division had a more seriously hurtful reception when it attempted to renew its attack on Shunet Nimrin. What of the cavalry who should have saved them this vain effort by descending on the enemy's rear? The 5th Brigade pushed down as far as a little bridge at El Huweiz where they were halted by shells from a single Turkish gun sited on a cliff beyond. They seemed to have shown an irregular aversion to casualties without the irregular's capacity for finding a way round. The brigadier "proceeded with the plan which to his mind was the only one possible; to take up a strong position astride the road and await the attempt of the Turks to force a way back," if and when they were driven to retire by the 60th Division. As these are the words of the Official History, one cannot suspect them of irony. But they apparently mean that the brigadier, instead of coming to the aid of the infantry, preferred to let the infantry help him. Eventually, in the afternoon, the brigadier rode back to see the divisional commander, who, accepting his estimate of the strength of the Turkish position without going to see it for himself, decided to postpone further action until next day, when a second brigade would be employed. This was a fatal decision. As time trickled away, opportunity ebbed.

For Turkish reinforcements had been brought from the northwest across the Jordan by the Damiye bridge and were being driven like a wedge down the eastern bank towards the British line of retreat. It now became a race between the British cavalry move against the Turkish rear and the Turkish infantry move against the British rear. The cavalry proved the less capable of progress and the more sensitive to danger. Despite vigorous messages from the higher command they did little next day, May 2nd, save detach units to cover their own rear, while the unfortunate infantry of the 60th Division continued to attempt hopeless frontal attacks. By the 3rd the situation of the cavalry, who had exhausted their rations, certainly became awkward, if not so dangerous as they believed. That afternoon Allenby came down to see Chauvel and, confronted with "a somewhat exaggerated report," decided to cut his loss and order the abandonment of the whole enterprise. The withdrawal to the Jordan was skilfully executed and achieved without serious interference from the enemy.

The apparent danger had caused an urgent summons to Lawrence. He was "asked to be ready to fly over to Salt, land, and lead the cut-off cavalry via Madeba, Kerak, Tafila, back to safety. It would have been possible, as there was lots of water and some food. The Turks would have been properly flummoxed! The staff thought the Salt force were probably cut off from the Jordan by forces too strong to pierce."

The Arabs on whom Bols had counted had made their contribution to the British failure. In default of the cavalry they might have caused a collapse of the Turks' resistance by cutting off supplies. The Official History suggests that they "appear to have been bought off," taking a double profit for their deliberate inaction. But the real explanation seems to be given by Young, who relates that, when Mirzuk received a reply from General Headquarters which showed that they had gulped down his offer, he was frightened at the consequences of his unauthorized proposal, and decided not to attempt to move the Beni Sakhr. "He knew perfectly well that the Beni Sakhr would do nothing without guns, and no guns had arrived." Lawrence has commented on this episode, "Mirzuk had not the authority to move them. After the shock of a month before, they would have taken a lot of moving!"

Nevertheless the fiasco of this second attempt to move into Trans-Jordan brought ultimate advantage to the British, which Allenby did not fail to exploit. For it concentrated the mind of the enemy command on this area. The British reputation for pertinacity in "try, try again" strategy encouraged Liman von Sanders to believe they might try it again yet a third time in Trans-Jordan.

From Lawrence's point of view the failure had one advantage in that it made the British staff more patient with Feisal's difficulties. It also strengthened Lawrence's personal position, "they saw that moving irregulars was an art, like moving troops, and agreed to let me know if anything of the sort was ever required." But it complicated Feisal's relations with the tribes in the north who became less willing than ever to stake their fortunes on such insecure support as the British offered as allies. "Our movement, clean-cut while alone with a simple enemy, was now bogged in its partner's contingencies. We had to take our tune from Allenby, and he was not happy. The German offensive in France was stripping him of troops. He would retain Jerusalem, but could not afford a casualty, much less an attack, for months." "For the moment, we must both just hold on."

This was what Allenby told Lawrence on May 5th, which should, according to the original plan, have seen the launching of the great northward offensive. Lawrence felt concern because the relaxation of British effort meant that Feisal's army would be unable to transfer itself to the Jordan, while committed to an uncompleted blockade of Ma'an which the Turks at Amman might now be free to interrupt. Allenby promised to do his best to help by maintaining an air of renewed advance on Amman, which would also help to conceal his own ultimate intentions. The Air Force promised, and rendered, still more definite help to Feisal by repeated bombing raids on the railway which disorganized traffic. The Air Force, indeed, by Lawrence's verdict, "was invaluable now."

Lawrence also obtained an immediate present from Allenby in a way that revealed his skill in turning particular human weaknesses into assets. At tea-time he heard from Allenby that the greater part of the Imperial Camel Brigade was to be disbanded, and went to see Sir Walter Campbell, the Quartermaster-General, in the hope of obtaining their camels for Feisal's use. Campbell, "very Scotch," showed a rooted dislike of the idea of parting with them. They were earmarked for divisional transport.

"I returned to Allenby and said aloud, before his party, that there were for disposal two thousand two hundred riding camels, and thirteen hundred baggage camels. All were provisionally allotted to transport; but, of course, riding camels were riding camels. The staff whistled and looked wise; as though they, too, doubted whether riding camels could carry baggage. A technicality, even a sham one, might be helpful. Every British officer understood animals, as a point of honour. So I was not astonished when Sir Walter Campbell was asked to dine with the Commander-in-Chief that night."

With the soup, Allenby raised the question of the camels. Campbell at once enlarged on what a godsend they were for transport use.

"He over-acted. Allenby, a reader of Milton, had an acute sense of style: and the line was a weak one. He cared nothing for strengths, the fetish of administrative branches."

So when Allenby turned, and with a twinkle asked what Lawrence wanted them for, he received the more heartening reply—"To put a thousand men into Deraa any day you please." Allenby smiled and briefly said to Campbell—"Q, you lose."

"It was an immense, a regal gift; the gift of unlimited mobility. The Arabs could now win their war when and where they liked." From this sprang the idea of the boldest stroke that Lawrence ever conceived. After mooting it to Allenby he went south to prepare the way.

When he arrived back at Aqaba and told the Arab leaders of Allenby's gift, they forgot their dignity in delight. As a further aid towards mobility Lawrence proposed to dispense with the Egyptian camel-transport men, too fettered by their regulations, and replace them with Arabs. The British authorities jumped at his offer so promptly that the transport organization was temporarily dislocated while Arab drivers were being obtained. It was repaired by Young who now took over the "Q" side of the force and found in it a more apt medium for his organizing gifts than in trying to co-ordinate Bedouin operations.

He was glad to be free of them, for he had not enjoyed the part of understudying Lawrence. Nor had the Arabs. The fact that he wore British uniform and carried European tinned food in preference to eating theirs, created an initial prejudice, and his own strenuous comments on their casualness towards synchronized plans were thus all the less well received by them. On his side he had certainly room for complaint—from his point of view.

Auda's increasing sulkiness, Mirzuk's chimerical designs, Nuri's natural unwillingness to lend any of his guns to the Bedouin, created embarrassments which seemed to ruin his hopes of extending the railway attacks northward. The minds of the Arab leaders were set on a fresh attack against Jerdun, and Young had to content himself with a promise that Nasir would move north with the Bedouin and four guns as soon as this was achieved. But when he saw Feisal on the eve of the appointed day, he was apologetically told—"It is most unfortunate, but there has been a mistake in the day. To-day is really the first of the Arab month, as last month had only twenty-nine days in it, but the Bedouin are convinced that there were thirty days in last month, and that to-day is, therefore, the 30th." The battle was postponed accordingly, and his own departure in consequence.

On May 12th the attack on Jerdun was delivered by the Arab Regular Army, helped by the bombs from three British aircraft, and the station was captured with 140 prisoners. The Arab leaders' delight in the victory obscured their recollection of the promises given to Young, and more delays occurred. It was deemed fitting that "as the victorious Sherifian army was on its way to join General Allenby, it would be as well if each man were given a new pair of trousers." But when the Regular detachment was at last on the way the Bedouin failed to appear. Then while Nasir waited for them, the Regular detachment and the guns were borrowed to assist a fresh attack on Jerdun, which the Turks had reoccupied. This attack, on the 17th, was interrupted by the sudden appearance of a train which had not been intercepted, and the Arabs fell back. Worn out by his ceaseless riding to and fro, which had led the amused Arabs to nick-name him the "Shuttle," Young now retired to a hospital with a deepened distrust of all irregulars.

Yet no sooner had he disappeared than Nasir moved north to the Wadi Hesa, with Peake's Egyptian camelry and Hornby as dem-olition expert, and broke the railway so effectively over a fourteen mile stretch that the menace from Amman was kept at bay during the critical weeks.

On the surface, the event seems an example of characteristic Arab inconsistency; and so it may well have seemed to Young. But, on reflection, its scale and importance contradict so simple an explana-tion. Rather does it suggest that Young had failed to adjust himself to the natural conditions of irregular warfare—that his calculations allowed no grace for the political preparation, and no elasticity to compensate for the liveliness of the Ma'an garrison. One of the deeper truths of war, especially of irregular war, has been aptly ex-pressed by Lawrence—"timing in war depends on the enemy as much as on yourself." Time-tables too often enable the enemy to turn the tables on you.

Nasir's move took the Turks completely by surprise. First he destroyed Hesa station, on the 23rd, and next day Faraifra station, without having any men killed. Between his forays he fell back to his hidden valley, rich in pasture and within quick support from Tafila. These were the "intangible ghost" tactics of Lawrence's desire.[1]

The news drew him north, and on the day of his arrival the Turks sent a camel detachment down to reoccupy Faraifra. It was dealt with in a way that pleased him, Nasir's machine-guns pinning down the Turks while Auda cut in and carried off all their camels. Henceforth the only real menace to the Arabs, and the only weapon that could reach them, were the enemy's bombing planes. Their ferreting capacity made an impression on Lawrence which was not without effect on his post-war outlook.[2] Happily for his present designs he was dealing with an opponent who still placed his chief reliance on numbers of ground-troops.

On returning south Lawrence was able to assure Feisal that ample breathing space was assured until the Arabs, with the augmented mobility that the coming increase of camels promised, could renew their offensive at longer range and on a wider scale. In preparation for this he proposed that all the Arab Regulars now in the Hejaz with Ali and Abdulla should be transferred to Aqaba. This would give Feisal a regular force of about ten thousand men. Lawrence's design was to distribute it in three parts. The largest but least mobile would continue to contain Ma'an. Another, of about two or three thousand infantry, would move up to the Amman plateau as a core for the Beni Sakhr and a link with Allenby. The third, a highly mobile camel-force of about a thousand men, should make a long distance move against Damascus to sever the Turkish communications and thus unhinge the resistance facing Allenby. This was the spear-point of the plan—it was more than a raid that Lawrence had in mind.

"'My plan for containing Ma'an, holding the Moab plateau, and

[1] According to Liman von Sanders, who cites the fact as evidence of "how difficult it was to maintain the Hejaz railway in operation," twenty-five bridges were destroyed in just over a fortnight.

[2] On this point Lawrence's own comment is illuminating:

"The war showed me that a combination of armoured cars and aircraft could rule the desert: but that they must be under non-army control, and without infantry support. You rightly trace a cause of the R.A.F. control in Irak, Aden, and Palestine to this experience. As soon as I was able to have a voice on the Middle East, I approached Trenchard on the point, and with Winston's eager support persuaded the Cabinet swiftly into approving (against the wiles of Henry Wilson)—and it has worked very well. The system is *not* capable of universal application."

simultaneously raising the Hauran was actually to capture Damascus and so destroy the Turkish Palestine Army between my hammer and Allenby's anvil. He had assured me that he was immobilised . . . by the drafts withdrawn for France." "This was now 1918, and stalemate across its harvest would have marked the ebb of Feisal's movement. His fellows were living on their nerves (rebellion is harder than war) and their nerves were wearing thin. Also the big war was not looking too well.

"So I made up my mind to take the offensive, encouraged to it by hints from the War Council, who also felt that it was Damascus in 1918, or never. Allenby agreed, unofficially, while not promising to pass the Palestine boundary: but I felt that did I get on to near Aleppo he would come along, too." Lawrence was certainly never more truly Elizabethan than when he formed this plan. And it had, too, an appropriate touch of Gideon.

Feisal accepted the plan and gave Lawrence letters to carry to Hussein. Knowing Hussein's jealousy of his son, Lawrence decided first to obtain leverage upon him from the British authorities. He went to Cairo and expounded his ideas to Dawnay, who saw their value. The two then went together to Wingate, who was also ready to make this further sacrifice of his own power, although the letter he wrote for Lawrence to deliver to Hussein was more gentle than Lawrence liked. They next went up to Allenby's headquarters, on June 19th, where the unexpected awaited them.

Lawrence found a remarkable lightening in the atmosphere. The reorganization of the army was so far advanced, and also the vision of its chiefs, that Allenby was planning not merely to carry out the postponed spring offensive but to execute it on far bolder lines, with Damascus and Aleppo as the geographical goals. The offensive would be launched in September, and the Arabs were wanted, as arranged, to cover Allenby's flank and distract the Turks' attention by striking at Deraa.

This news, promising a more rapid development, reduced the importance of the projected transfer from the Hejaz. Nevertheless Lawrence, having experience of past disappointments, deemed it wise to have an alternative ready if possible, and so, armed with a letter from Allenby, sailed for Jidda. Hussein, however, had apparently been warned of his purpose and frustrated Lawrence by staying securely in Mecca. Conversation over the telephone was an inadequate medium and gave Hussein opportunity for missing what he did not wish to hear. As Lawrence no longer felt the same urge to pursue his project, he rang off and returned to Cairo, there to devote himself to the problem of fitting the available Arab forces into the frame of Allenby's new design. "Allenby would do the big offensive, and my job again became a permeating one. So I didn't need the troops from Hejaz, and was rather glad to leave them alone."

This period was Lawrence's longest absence from the Arab front —he was away until July 28th. It is significant that this was a bad period for the Arab Army. During it they suffered several checks, culminating in the severe repulse on July 21st of a too regular daylight attack on Jerdun station. The Arabs had concentrated eight hundred regulars and a thousand Bedouin, with artillery, machine-gun, armoured car, and air support, against the Turkish garrison of 400 men but were beaten off with a loss of eighty killed. Their recoil not only enabled the Turks to reprovision Jerdun and Ma'an, but produced such depression as to arouse fears for the safety of the Arabs' hold on Abu el Lissal. If this loss of spirit, like the loss of Tafila in March, is indirect proof of how much Lawrence's influence counted it also suggests that indirect tactics and irregular methods were best suited to fulfil the Arabs' strategy—as he had always contended.

CHAPTER XVII

THE FINAL STROKE—PREPARATION

July–August, 1918

Allenby's plan of attack—The need for distraction—A call to Lawrence—A preliminary diversion by the Imperial Camel Corps: Buxton's raid—Lawrence's self-analysis—A "bully beef tin" bluff—Internal complications threaten the Arab plan, but the march to the north begins

ON JULY 11th Lawrence and Dawnay were again at General Headquarters, where they were told the outline of Allenby's plan. At that moment the British Government had received no hint of his intentions, so careful was he to cloak them until his staff had worked out calculations that promised their realization.

Lawrence's experience of British staff calculations had made him healthily critical of them, so that he "took the precaution to go into their offices and assure myself of the exact methods on which they were working." His anxiety was diminished when he found that the chief of the General Staff was on leave, as well as the chief of the "Q" staff, and that in their absence Bartholomew and Evans, their now unfettered right hands, were working out the material factors of the problem, and, better still, were planning to redistribute the transport of the army corps in a way that suited the varying mobility of their roles instead of a stereotyped pattern. Thus the momentum of the advance might be sustained and the pursuit extended. Instead of being tied to a fixed-length chain of supply, the fighting troops of the army were now to be given comparative freedom of movement by the use of an elastic cord that could not only be stretched but quickly attached to fresh points. There was also the definite intention of living on the country except for troops' rations during movement.

The plan of operations was based on a reversal of the Gaza-Beersheba plan. Instead of threatening an advance near the coast to cloak the real stroke inland, every possible ruse was to be employed to suggest an inland move, from the Jordan valley, while the breakthrough was made in the coastal corridor. The mass of the infantry were to be stealthily concentrated near the Mediterranean, and the cavalry concealed behind them in the orange groves near Jaffa. After Bulfin's XXI Corps had smashed a hole in the Turkish front, the Desert Mounted Corps was to ride through. After pushing north for fifteen miles, it was to turn east into the hills of Samaria to seize the rail and road junction at Sebustiye, cutting the Turkish communications. Meantime Chetwode's XX Corps would attack the Turks' front in the hills, in order to pin them down while their bolt-holes were being blocked. It was a finely conceived picture of a decisive envelopment, Cannæ-like in its completeness. A few weeks later it was still further improved by a bold enlargement which cast the enveloping net further to the Turks' rear, and so lessened their chances of slipping out before the net was drawn tight.

But as in all "picture-battles" its perfection was its weakness, by allowing no scope for variation—for developing an alternative if the original design could not be fulfilled. The conditions defined the plan, because it was only in the coastal sector near the railhead that sufficient reserve supplies could be accumulated or the cavalry find a suitable path for rapid advance. Well might Bartholomew express anxiety over the uncomfortably narrow margin between complete success and failure. If the Turks got wind of the intention, and were wise enough to retire in time, the British Army, as Lawrence remarked, would be "like a fish flapping on dry land, with its railways, its heavy artillery, its dumps, its stores, its camps all misplaced."

Everything turned on maintaining the Turks in their state of delusion and keeping their eyes fixed on the Jordan. To this end the British staff were weaving a network of plausible strategic misclues on a wider scale than ever before. As Lawrence truly remarks —"Deceptions, which for the ordinary general were just witty *hors d'œuvres* before battle, had become for Allenby a main point in strategy."

But for actual distraction Allenby must largely depend on his Arab wing. It was with this appeal to their inventiveness and resource that Lawrence and Dawnay travelled back to Cairo.

They were greeted by a fresh complication, in the shape of reports that the Turks were contemplating a new stroke against Abu el Lissal about the end of August. If it came, it would be likely to dislocate the move to Deraa. The Arabs now needed a distraction to secure their own plan as well as providing one for Allenby's. The two purposes, however, might be blended. It was Dawnay who thought of the means—the idea of using the surviving battalion of the disbanded Imperial Camel Brigade. With Bartholomew's aid they obtained the loan of two companies under Major R. V. Buxton for a month on the condition that they should avoid casualties. Lawrence was highly amused that "Bartholomew felt it necessary to apologize for the last magnificent, heart-warming condition, which he thought unsoldierly!"

Dawnay and Lawrence drew up a scheme by which Buxton's detachment would march from the Suez Canal to Aqaba and thence to take Mudauwara station by a night attack. With a second long stride, turning north, it would reach the neighbourhood of Amman, destroy the bridge and tunnel there, and then return to Palestine.

The plan was not well received when it reached Aqaba.[1] Joyce and Young had been hard at work organizing, under manifold difficulties, the transport of the Arab Regular Army for the coming move to Deraa. Young, especially, thought that Lawrence was too airy in his treatment of administrative questions, and apt to assume that the Arab regulars could move as light as his Bedouin irregulars. Young himself, with meticulous care, drew up a scheme by which a well-stored base would be established at Azrak, and intermediate dumps at Jefer and Bair, so that by October a flying column of all arms could be moved to Azrak and operate from there with a ten days' radius of action. It could also be maintained there, through the replenishment of the base by regular convoys from Aqaba at ten-day intervals.

Dawnay's message was a disturbing shock. Joyce feared the effect of a British force intruding into the Arab zone, and could not understand why Lawrence, so long the opponent of such a mixture, should have suddenly changed round. Young's objection was "purely arithmetical." For, according to the new instructions he would have to form a chain of dumps of forage and rations for Buxton's move.

---

[1] Lawrence has given me a significant sidelight on the methods of communication that were used:

"Allenby every morning for breakfast had a log of Turkish signals over the preceding 24 hours: we read their every message—and I presumed they read all ours. To keep our moves secret we used air-mail or word of mouth. To keep the Turks' public, one of my cares was to distribute wire-cutters over their rear, and cut their telegraph at least daily."

"Each camel load given to Buxton was a camel load taken from our own flying column, and we wanted all we could get." Hence, in an urgent answer, while reluctantly accepting the Mudauwara project they protested against the second and longer-range operation. But this, in Lawrence's view, was the chief part, as the means of persuading the Turks that the British were intending yet a third advance into Trans-Jordan. He saw that through it he might redeem the losses of the first two blundering attempts, by converting them into a chain of purposeful strategy. The fact that the Camel Corps had taken part before was likely to help the delusion.

Seeing the wider strategic aspects of the problem Lawrence was equally critical of Young's scheme, when it reached Cairo. Knowing "the muddy impassable roads" of the Hauran in winter, he saw the practical weakness of a scheme which placed a force there so late in the season. More pertinent still was the fact that it did not fit the particular case. For Allenby was going to attack about the end of September. Any sort of force at the right time was better than the most perfectly equipped force that arrived too late.

He flew over to Aqaba to tell Joyce and Young of Allenby's new plan. If his explanation was convincing it did not altogether assuage annoyance. "Relations between Lawrence and ourselves became for the moment a trifle strained, and the sight of the little man reading the *Morte d'Arthur* [1] in a corner of the mess tent with an impish smile on his face was not consoling." Young here would seem to speak for himself, for Joyce's doubts were soon disarmed when Lawrence pointed out that Buxton's force would not come in contact with the Arab Army, while the rumour of its presence would be likely to give the Turks an exaggerated impression of its size and deter them from interfering with the Arab movements. As for Young's objections, Lawrence regarded them as due to that creed of "impossibility" so prevalent among professional soldiers, and he was the less tender because he felt that Young had the ability to overcome difficulties if he wished, or had to.

There was an entertaining passage at arms between them. Taking

[1] Malory's *Morte d'Arthur* with two other books—the comedies of Aristophanes and the *Oxford Book of English Verse*—made up Lawrence's campaigning library. During earlier months he had carried none, but when he set out on his Yarmuk Valley raid (in October, 1917) with the idea of wintering at Azrak, he chose these three for companionship.

Young's schedule for the Deraa raid, Lawrence crossed out the provision for forage beyond the dump at Bair, saying that pasture was splendid this year in the Azrak-Deraa area. This removed the heaviest item. He cut down the allowance for food saying that the men could live on the country. Young sarcastically remarked that the ten days' return journey would be a long fast. Lawrence retorted that he had no intention of returning to Aqaba. So it went on, Lawrence meeting "regular" objections by repeating his irregular maxim that the Arabs lived by their raggedness and beat the Turk by their uncertainty.[1]

If Young was still annoyed, and Joyce still a trifle dubious, all hesitations were forgotten in the zest of achieving more than seemed possible—and it was strange how much more that was. Lawrence's confidence was like the prick of a hypodermic injection—it stung locally but it produced a pervasive effect. As he himself has remarked, it was not due to a belief in his powers to do a thing perfectly, but to a preference for doing it somehow rather than leaving it undone.

The military arrangements for the move were, by comparison, easier than the diplomatic arrangements, which fell entirely on his shoulders. The ladder by which the Arab force sought to reach Deraa and Damascus had to be constructed of a series of tribal rungs, each fitted carefully into its place, and the whole fitted together. Most important of all was it to secure Nuri Shaalan's support, without which the expedition could hardly hope to mount the ladder. To this end he was invited down to see Feisal.

[1] Lawrence's explanation of this episode sheds light on his care for information as a basis of calculation:

"Before making my Deraa scheme I had taken the trouble to look at the country—and before settling to go there in August and September, I had studied the pasture and water. So (*pace* Young) I knew:

(i) Where the pasture was rich enough for 2,000 camels, and therefore the routes we would have to take to.

(ii) Where the flood-pools lay (there is no natural water between Azrak and Mezerib—only rain-pools). These pools are filled by floods down whichever valley runs in the Spring—and they entirely conditioned our halting-places. Had Umtaiye not filled we should not have gone that way—of course.

As for retreat—had we met disaster there was all Wadi Sirhan open to us, and Aqaba afterwards, at our leisure. Sirhan was (in Sept.) full of sheep and dates and flour. Also we had 2,000 camels, each affording a meat meal for 200 men.

I knew my Arab soldiery, in and out, and they were much more self-sufficing and easier to feed than Englishmen. Young was treating them like an army: I wanted to treat them like the uniformed peasantry they were."

An interesting impression of Lawrence at this time is given by Major Stirling, who came from Egypt with a large green Vauxhall car for Feisal's use and subsequently became general staff officer with the Arab force.

"Arrived at Abu Lissal, some five thousand feet up, I found Lawrence, who had just returned from a most successful raid on the railway, sitting in his tent on a beautiful Persian rug looted from some unfortunate Turkish train. He was dressed, as usual, in the most immaculate white robes with the golden dagger of Mecca in his girdle. Outside lolled some of his bodyguard cleaning their rifles and crooning softly to themselves and undoubtedly enjoying the quiet contemplation of some particularly devilish bit of work which they had just perpetrated. They were a remarkably interesting collection, numbering just under a hundred. Most of them belonged to the Ageyl and were hired soldiers by profession. Not one of them but was famed for some daring deed, and for hard living, hard riding and hard swearing, they were the pick of Arabia. This bodyguard was a very necessary precaution, for there was a price of £20,000 on Lawrence's head, and Arabs are treacherous folk—unless they are your sworn and paid men. Any one of his bodyguard, however, would have cheerfully died for Lawrence.

"There was another reason why picked men were necessary. Lawrence's movements were sudden and his rides long and arduous, and few ordinary Arabs cared to cover at a stretch the distances which he did. It is an amazing thing that an Englishman should have beaten all the records of Arabia for speed and endurance.

"What was it that enabled Lawrence to seize and hold the imagination of the Arabs? It is a difficult question to answer. The Arabs are notable individualists, intractable to a degree and without any sense of discipline, and yet it was sufficient for almost any of us to say that Lawrence wanted something done—and it was done. How did he gain this power? The answer may partly be that he represented the heart of the Arab movement for freedom, and the Arabs realized that he had vitalized their cause; that he could do everything and endure everything just a little better than the Arabs themselves; that, by his investment with the gold dagger of Mecca, he ranked with the Ashraf or the descendants of the Prophet, and the Emir Feisal treated him as a brother, as an equal; that he seemed to possess unlimited gold—for the average Arab is the most venal of all people. But chiefly, I think we must look for the answer in Lawrence's uncanny ability to sense the feelings of any group of men in whose company he found himself; his power to probe behind their minds and to uncover the well-springs of their actions."

That power was often put to the test, but never perhaps more hardly than when, in this last summer of the War, Lawrence discovered that Feisal was negotiating with the Turks in the belief that the British were a broken reed. Feisal had an excuse not merely in the defeats that the British had suffered but in his own prior discovery that the British themselves had been carrying on negotiations with the Turks—and with the section of Turks most inimical to his hopes. The conversations between Aubrey Herbert and Talaat in Switzerland came to Feisal's ears within a week of their occurrence, and his alarm made him receptive to Turkish overtures. Then, after the British abandonment of Es Salt, Jemal Pasha sent down Mohammed Said, Abd el Kader's brother, from Damascus, and the outcome of their discussions was that Feisal offered to forsake the British side if the Turks would evacuate Amman and hand over the province to the Arabs. The negotiations had not before been disclosed to King Hussein in Mecca; he was aghast when he heard of them, and sent a vehement telegram of protest, to the effect that he would never countenance such a pact and that the Turks should be told—"only the sword lies between us."

Naturally, the British representatives at Aqaba and in Egypt were kept in the dark. But despite Feisal's discretion Lawrence was quick to gain an inkling of the truth; while his sense of duty to the Arabs led him to see the necessity of keeping open a way of escape for the Arab fighting men in case of necessity, he decided to check these moves when they reached a point dangerous to the common cause. The manner of his intervention was characteristic. Gently disclosing to Feisal his knowledge of the negotiations, he pretended to regard them as a clever piece of political tactics, designed to throw the Turks off their guard, and he suggested that Feisal should develop it. This was done and the game of bargaining continued for a time. For Lawrence realized that Feisal would be constrained to change it from a purposeful policy into a harmless diversion once its existence was known to his allies.

AZRAQ

Another example of Lawrence's art in handling Arabs was seen in the way he guided their natural instinct for dispersion of effort, so as to extract its full profit while checking its dangerous extravagance. His aim was to hit without being hit, yet to hit where it would hurt. Left to themselves the Arabs, as he once remarked to me, "would have chopped the tree all round," instead of cutting at the roots. Hence while stimulating Arab activity along its natural channels, he found means to avoid unpromising moves. Sometimes he did this by going to Feisal and saying—"We won't pay for this show." At other times, with more subtlety, he discouraged such plans by causing a momentary upset among the leaders who were arranging to take part.

His methods of combining the Arabs for strategy were closely related to his methods in strategy, and as carefully thought out. Concentration of thought produced concentration of force—in effect if not in appearance. His outward air of dispersion may deceive the historical student as completely as it deceived the Turk. For the dispersion was on the surface, and the concentration lay in the current. He had not studied Bourcet in pre-war days without profit—he knew that a concentrated effect could only be gained through an air of dispersion that caused the dispersal of the enemy's would-be concentration. The art of the strategist lies in reconciling these two opposite conditions. Here it is worthwhile to quote a couple of reflections that Lawrence once made on this difficult art: the first was that one should seek "to pass around obstacles, yet avoid branching the main stream"; the second that in using distractions to this end one should "leave an air space between them and the main stream to prevent 'ruffling.' "

On July 30th Buxton arrived in Aqaba with the two Camel Corps companies, three hundred strong, after a seven days' march from Kubri (162 miles), on the Suez Canal. Feisal had been warned privately of their coming, and Lawrence went down to meet the force at Aqaba, where the few Bedouin who saw them were amazed, having scarcely believed that there were "so many Englishmen in the world." To minimize possible friction Lawrence delivered a precautionary address that many remembered. Stirling gives the fullest account one has heard:

"After supper Lawrence had the men collected round a large

central blaze and gave them the straightest talk I have ever heard. He explained the general situation to them, told them that he was going to take them through a part of Arabia where no white man had ever set foot and where the Arab sub-tribes were none too friendly, that there was no need to worry about the Turks but every need to worry about our allies the Bedouin. They were mistrustful folk, he said, and would most certainly think that we had come to take their grazing-grounds. The essential thing was to avoid any cause of friction. If any were offended or insulted he begged of them to turn the other cheek—both because they were better educated and therefore less prejudiced and also because they were so very few. The men were delighted and retired for the night, thinking that they were about to embark on the greatest rag in the history of war —as perhaps they were!"

On August 2nd they set out by the Wadi Ithm for Rumm. Lawrence himself guided them over this first critical stage through the Howeitat country because of the importance of surprise, if casualties were to be avoided. If they encountered some of the suspicious tribesmen his presence might help to calm them and also prevent warning being passed on to the Turks. It was fortunate that he went, for when the contingent reached Rumm the Howeitat who were encamped there showed themselves most resentful of this English intrusion. Although the efforts of Lawrence and Sherif Hazaa allayed trouble with the chiefs, odd tribesmen frequently sniped the party during the hours of darkness. When morning came diplomacy had a better chance, and by midday Lawrence felt that it was safe for him to go back, while Stirling, who had attained a remarkably quick influence with the Beni Atiya, helped by their common love of horses, was left with Buxton.

It had been a strange experience for Lawrence to be among a body of English soldiers, typical of their simple and friendly kind, and it brought on a sudden homesickness, making him feel an outcast. By reaction it made him more conscious of the way he was playing England's tune upon the Arab keyboard.

A fresh reminder came when, after riding back, he found an aeroplane waiting to take him to Jefer, to meet that Nuri Shaalan who had taxed him a year before with the difference between England's pledges to the Arabs and those she had given to the French.

Thus as the aeroplane barely scraped over the mountain-ridge, Lawrence found himself almost hoping that it would crash and wipe out in his blood the shame of those promises with which he excessively tortured himself.

However, the interview with Nuri Shalaan and his Ruwalla sheikhs was not so difficult as in Lawrence's anticipations. Momentarily suppressing his qualms of conscience, he joined with Feisal in a subtly moving appeal to the idea of Arab nationality, emphasizing the mystical enchantment of sacrifice for freedom, until "the Rualla melted in our double heat" and Nuri Shalaan committed his tribe to the cause. It was a moment of triumph that like others would yield Lawrence aeons of introspective torment. After it, Lawrence flew back to Guweira and then rode to Aqaba, where the news of Buxton's success at Mudauwara brought a thought-quenching exhilaration.

After a preliminary reconnaissance by car, which showed that all was quiet, Buxton's force had converged on the station in three parties during the early hours of August 8th. This, the "black day" of the German armies in France, proved equally black for the Turkish garrison of Mudauwara. The British plan was inspired by the idea of an indirect approach to come round between the station and its guardian redoubts, and attack both from the inner side. White tapes had been laid before midnight to the jumping-off point, but as no one knew the ground save from air photographs it proved extremely difficult to lead the parties into position. Thus the time margin became unpleasantly narrow and faint streaks of daylight were coming when at last the assault was ready. Another ten minutes delay and it might have been a surprise the wrong way round. Happily, the bombing parties stole in and caught two of the redoubts unawares, and the station also. The northern redoubt, however, offered a hot resistance for an hour until it was battered into surrender by shells from the motor-guns, and 150 prisoners were taken for a loss of seven killed and ten wounded. After destroying the station, with its water-tower and steam pumps, and also the wells, Buxton's force marched north to Jefer at dusk.

There Lawrence and Joyce greeted them on the 12th, and went on with them, combining a dual purpose—that of reconnoitring an armoured car road for the Deraa move as well as smoothing the way for Buxton. They travelled by car, with an armoured car as escort; it was the first time such a strange mechanical beast had been seen in these northern deserts, and it startled the Bedouin. But it also induced among them a more friendly manner than they often showed to unarmoured travellers. The virgin voyage was a triumphal passage, the Rolls-Royces making light of the desert route. They reached Azrak on the 14th, and came back still quicker, sometimes roaring along at forty miles an hour, so that at dusk next day they sighted Buxton's camp-fires at Bair.

Here they found trouble. Young had duly sent fourteen days' rations thither, but only eight days' supply had arrived, the unwilling camel-drivers having apparently asserted their independent will when they got out of reach of Young's. It meant an alteration of plan. "Buxton purged his column of every inessential, while I cut down the two armoured cars to one, and changed the route."

Once more the fact of being among British soldiers brought Lawrence a sense of mixed ease and unease. He felt proud of his fellow-countrymen; they were so kindly and homely, and fitted so naturally into so strange a setting. But it made him feel the stranger. It was his thirtieth birthday and he used it to take mental stock of himself. Four years earlier, when he plunged into the war, a queer spasm of ambition had made him decide to be a general and knighted by the time he was thirty. Now the opportunity lay within his grasp, if he survived, but he had lost the taste for such childish trappings. The one ambition that survived was to be held in respect by men he could respect. This desire made him sensitively quick to question his own self-truthfulness. He thought of the way Allenby and the Arabs trusted him, and how his bodyguard were ready to die for him. He was too clear-sighted to regard himself as superman. He did not fully realize the ordinary man's craving for idols—perhaps because he was not free from it himself—or the power of legend to create them. So he inclined to ascribe it to his actorship, and to wonder whether all fame was built on fraud.

He was the more ready to criticize himself because he had an instinctive shyness born of a sense of difference. That shyness often led to the abhorrent imputation of modesty, which in its conventional sense implies blindness. In trying to rid himself of the charge Lawrence has often shown an assertiveness which has led to the equally foolish charge of conceit. His intense consciousness of his own thoughts and actions produced an exceptional power of self-analysis, which became habit, incessant save when it could be submerged in violent effort. From it sprang a curiosity as to himself which was the mainspring of much of his action. He was perhaps not so different from other thinking men as he imagined.

He was conscious that he enjoyed the fame he had gained, and because of his excessive sense of remoteness from other men he had the more fear of this enjoyment becoming known to them. This led him to reject the honours he had first desired, until eventually his pleasure was to come within reach of his object without actually grasping it. One may perhaps see here an instinct allied to his desire for friendship that shrank from the touch of friendship, physical or mental. Like a number of men who truly stand out from the herd he had a sense of loneliness deepened by an instinct of friendliness, and had disencumbered himself, too freely for his own peace, of the common ties and pleasures that help others in laying bridges across the gulf. Nor like others could he drown doubts in the joy of creation, for his reason disapproved the attempt. Even independence had an unwanted flavour, for his instinct was to find a worthy master, while reason working on experience warned him that all idols were discovered to be hollow if approached too closely. So reflection led him not merely to more doubt but to more distaste for himself.

When movement was renewed he obtained release, and a passing gratification of his military instinct, in noting Buxton's quick adaptability to irregular warfare. For Buxton broke up the stiff column formation into a cluster of groups, each moving at its own gait, suited to the variations of ground. The camel-loads had been lightened and rehung, the system of clock-hour halts abandoned, and the halts devoted to grazing rather than grooming. All these changes pleased the connoisseur of irregular war. "Our Imperial Camel Corps had become rapid, elastic, enduring, silent," although even now Lawrence's camels, brought up to walk in Arab style, averaged more than four miles an hour, instead of three, and so gained extra time for grazing.

On the 20th they reached Muaggar, fifteen miles southeast of Amman, whence they intended to strike at the great bridge. Unluckily, as they approached, a Turkish aeroplane flew over the column. And from villagers they heard that several parties of Turkish mule-mounted infantry were quartered in the villages near the bridge, guarding the tax-gatherers. This force was not sufficient to prevent success, but it might make success expensive. In view of the ban on casualties, Lawrence regretfully decided to abandon the attempt, to the still greater disappointment of the Camel Corps.

"To gain what I could, I sent Saleh and the other chiefs down to spruce their people with tall rumours of our numbers, and our coming as the reconnaissance of Feisal's army, to carry Amman by assault in the new moon. This was the story the Turks feared to learn: the operation they imagined: the stroke they dreaded. They pushed cavalry cautiously into Muaggar, and found confirmation of the wild tales of the villagers, for the hill-top was littered with empty meat-tins, and the valley slopes cut up by the deep tracks of enormous cars. Very many tracks there were! This alarm checked them, and, at a bloodless price for us, kept them hovering a week. The destruction of the bridge would have gained us a fortnight." By thus playing on the Turks' fears for Amman, Lawrence interposed a distraction to their concentration of forces—for an attack on Ja'far's force before Ma'an. "I wanted Jaafar not to be actively engaged with an offensive enemy when we marched off his mounted men towards Deraa."

But it was not merely the coming Arab move that profited from this preparatory bluff, for it would appear to have led the Turkish command to divert newly arriving reinforcements to the Fourth Army at Amman, at the expense of the British-menaced coastal sector.

At dusk on the 20th Buxton's force set off towards Azrak, where they enjoyed a brief rest, marred by the death of Lieut. Rowan—due to the carelessness of an Arab with his rifle. "We buried him in the little Mejaber graveyard, whose spotless quiet had long been my envy."

At Azrak Lawrence also buried the guncotton ready for use in the coming Deraa raid. On the 26th they were back at Bair,[1] where Lawrence took leave of them and raced on to Abu el Lissal by armoured car.

[1] Buxton's force rejoined the British at Beersheba on September 6th, having covered over 900 miles in 44 days, of which 6 had been rest days and the equivalent of 14 had been spent in watering. The difficulty of the conditions increases the significance of this feat of mobility and endurance.

Here trouble greeted him—he should have learned to expect it by now. The Meccan official newspaper which had come up by mail was found to contain a proclamation to the effect that fools were styling Ja'far Pasha the general commanding the Arab Northern Army, whereas there was no such rank among the Arabs. This seems to have been published by Hussein out of spite, after hearing that Ja'far had received a British decoration. Its outcome was that Ja'far tendered his resignation to Feisal, and was followed by all the senior Arab officers. Feisal and Lawrence did their best to allay the resentment, but when Feisal telegraphed a protest to his father he received a vitriolic answer. Thereupon Feisal telegraphed back offering his own resignation, and Hussein sent a further telegram appointing Zeid, who promptly refused the post. For a few days the wires vibrated with indignant messages and counter-messages.

The trouble could not have come at a more awkward time, because it threatened to upset an operation, composed of a series of moves, in which for once everything turned on time-table. And not merely the military issue. Allenby might still win his battle without the Arabs' aid at Deraa but the Arabs could not stake their claim to independent sovereignty unless they not only helped Allenby but gained Damascus.

Sacrificing the lesser to the greater, Lawrence's first act was to send off a messenger to warn Nuri Shaalan that he could not, as he had promised, come to address the gathering of the Ruwalla tribes. By arousing Nuri's doubts, this failure to appear might lose the services of the Ruwalla in the Deraa operation, but without Feisal's army there would be no operation.

Then Lawrence turned to oil the machinery at Abu el Lissal. Nuri Said, who in later years was to become Prime Minister of Iraq, gave invaluable aid in proving that his political gifts were as marked as his military. So did Stirling. Taking the lead from Nuri the Arab officers agreed to move to Azrak pending an apology from Hussein. "If this was unsatisfactory, they could return, or throw off allegiance."

On Lawrence's own methods of internal diplomacy Stirling sheds an amusing sidelight—"It was an education to listen to Lawrence at one of the Arab Councils. When in debate some sheikh became a little difficult, Lawrence, from his amazing knowledge of the past life and inner history of every leading Arab, would let drop a hint or reference to some small disreputable incident in the sheikh's past which was generally enough to silence the man in question and put the rest of the Council in a good humour." Quite as often, however, Lawrence gained his way by a timely reference to some reputable achievement—"I could flatter as well as flutter."

He showed an equally subtle wit in the process of extracting an apology from Hussein that would satisfy Feisal's honour and restore his position among the Arab officers—a matter that Lawrence deemed vital not for the military but for the political need. The attack on Deraa could be delivered without him, but he alone could seal their success at the occupation of Damascus. Before he could play the part of the Prophet resurrected, his prestige must be revived. Allenby and Wilson were helping by verbal pressure on Hussein, but the old man was recalcitrant. His telegrams, however, came to Lawrence for delivery to Feisal and, penetrating the cipher, he "had undesirable passages mutilated by rearranging their figures into nonsense, before handing them in code to Feisal. By this easy expedient the temper of his entourage was not needlessly complicated."

Finally Hussein sent a long telegram, opening with a lame apology and then repeating the offence. Lawrence suppressed the second part before handing the message to Feisal in council. Feisal read it aloud and then decisively said—"The telegraph has saved all our honour." The Arab officers burst out into a chorus of joy, under cover of which Feisal whispered to Lawrence—"I mean the honour of nearly all of us." Lawrence pretended not to understand, whereat Feisal said to him—"I offered to serve for this last march under your orders: why was that not enough?"

"Because it would not go with your honour."

Feisal murmured—"You prefer mine always before your own."

But the crisis was resolved. And from other witnesses it is clear that personality played as great a part as "personalities" or suppressions in making the Arab leaders follow Lawrence's lead.

Already on August 30th, by dint of Young's exertions, the first convoy of six hundred laden camels had started on its 300 mile march to Azrak with an escort of thirty Gurkha machine-gunners and thirty-five Egyptian camelry. On September 2nd, the trouble among the Arab soldiers was sufficiently settled to allow the second convoy of eight hundred camels to follow, only one day late. The fighting force comprised 450 Arab Regular Camelry with twenty Hotchkiss guns, two British armoured cars and five tenders, two air-craft, and Pisani's French mountain battery. On September 4th Lawrence himself left in a Rolls-Royce tender, in the hope of being in time to rally the aid of the Ruwalla. He was accompanied by Nasir and a new assistant, Lord Winterton, who had stayed behind as a welcome relic of Buxton's force. Feisal and Joyce were to follow.

Thus the desert had become a military highway, dotted with northward-moving columns that headed steadily for Azrak, bringing a message of menace to the unsuspecting Turk. It gave a justifiable sensation of pride to the British soldiers, of difficulties overcome, of a creation achieved. But to Lawrence it brought mixed feelings as, in a Rolls-Royce, he raced past the plodding columns, so slow compared with his Bedouin. It seemed to him a shamefully comfortable form of desert-travel, although Nasir, in the back, smothered in dust, did not seem to share his view, especially when the tender hit the bumps at the end of a mud-flat at over sixty miles an hour. The desert, too, seemed shamefully populous, its familiar emptiness de-filed by the unending sight of marching troops. It was some con-solation to hear a report that while they were moving north, the Turks were launching another expedition south into Tafila. The news was a reminder that, strategically, the concourse was not so conspicuous, to the Turks at least, as it seemed to him. "Our formidable talk of advance by Amman had pulled their leg nearly out of the socket, and the innocents were out to counter our feint. Each man they sent south was a man, or rather ten men, lost."

Against his regrets Lawrence could set a sense of assurance that gave him a restful enjoyment such as he had not known before. "For on this march to Damascus (and such it was already in our imagina-tion) my normal balance had changed. I could feel the taut power of Arab excitement behind me. The climax of the preaching of years had come, and a united country was straining towards its his-toric capital."

This remark may suggest that the romantic in Lawrence had re-asserted itself after long suppression. For in the back of his own car he had almost the only Hejaz Arab in the force—Nasir. But in Lawrence's mind the Hejaz was a page turned over, a tool discarded.

His thoughts had turned to Damascus when the thoughts of others

were still fixed on Mecca and Medina. His sense of realism had long
since rejected the notion that the Hejaz, barren and isolated, could
rule or even share the future of the fertile and populous lands in the
north. The Hejaz revolt had served its purpose as a lever by which
to raise an Arab Revolt. And now "by a momentary miracle we had
truced all the feuds for this month, so that from Akaba up to Damascus all was clear going." He had removed the obstructions and paved
the way. The rest would depend on his success in exploiting the opportunity. Already there was enough of reality, of individual accomplishment, to warrant a mood of exultation.

CHAPTER XVIII

THE FINAL STROKE—EXECUTION

September, 1918

Allenby's plan is enlarged—Lawrence's plan of distraction in aid of Allenby—The Arab move begins—By successive strokes the Turkish communications are cut around Deraa—The Turks' attention being drawn to Trans-Jordan, Allenby's attack up the coast is launched—Two Turkish armies are destroyed, but the Fourth Army remains —Its Arab foes are interrupted by a menace from the air

THE great British offensive was to be launched on September 19th. Lawrence had promised Allenby that the Arab force would envelop Deraa on the 16th and cut the railway on which the Turkish armies depended. Since the promise was given, Allenby had enlarged his plan and so reduced the risk of hitches. It was still, by force of circumstances, rigid in initial aim, but elastic in potential development. Lawrence's had more initial variability but was more rigid in ultimate aim.

Returning from a ride one day in mid-August, Allenby sprang upon his staff the announcement, more dramatic because of its crisp directness, of his decision that the cavalry should sweep straight up the coastal plain, cross the Carmel Range near Megiddo, descend into the Plain of Esdraelon and seize the road and rail centres of El Afule and Beisan. Thus they would be astride the lines of retreat of the Turkish Seventh and Eighth Armies, and so far to their rear that there would be little chance of their escape. The only outlet would be the extremely difficult one across the Jordan eastward, into a desolate region where the Arabs would be buzzing like wasps and now armed with a sting.

Deraa was an even more vital point, for there centred the rail communications of all three Turkish armies, and the line of retreat of the Fourth. But it was beyond the range of any cavalry bound, even as now extended. Only the Arabs could reach it. Upon them much depended if the Turkish dispositions were to be paralysed before Allenby's stroke descended, and while it developed.

Lawrence's plans were "a feint against Amman and a real cutting of the Deraa railways; further than this we hardly went, for it was ever my habit, while studying alternatives, to keep the stages in solution." Lawrence had studied to his profit the teaching of Bourcet who, from the practical experience of twenty campaigns, had taught Napoleon so well that this pupil's first campaign had been his best.

Lawrence shrewdly calculated that by the mere fact of establishing the Arab force at Azrak, dead opposite Amman, "the first part of our plan, the feint, was accomplished." "We had sent our 'horsemen of St. George,' gold sovereigns, by the thousand to the Beni Sakhr, purchasing all the barley in their threshing floors, begging them not to mention it, but we would require it for our animals and for our British allies, in a fortnight. Dhiab of Tafileh . . . gossiped the news instantly through to Kerak."

This brief account does not unfold the full subtlety of Lawrence's measures to persuade the Turks, for Allenby's benefit, that Amman was the target of the coming offensive. He had sent several buyers to the threshing floors, and had bought for hard cash all the piles of feed-barley for horses that the Beni Sakhr could spare. The terms were that they should hold it for Lawrence until warned at what camp, within a day's march, it was to be delivered. Also he had had a census taken of all available sheep and, through four local agents, made provisional contracts for the sheep, "delivered to camp." On these he paid commission but bought none outright.

Furthermore, he himself visited the Madeba area shortly before the offensive, and there marked two large landing-grounds for aircraft, hired Arabs to camp by them on watch, and left smoke signals and landing signs, with instructions for use. "Of course I chose people sitting carefully on the fence for my confidence." He also took advantage of being in touch with Arab staff officers of the 4th Army. "I warned these of a thunderbolt shortly to fall on them at Amman, from east and west, and conjured them to so dispose their troops as to be ineffective on the day, both ways."

The same deep note of double-bluff had inspired him in composing a project of attack on Madeba by Hornby with the Zebn tribesmen. "I had put all my influence behind Hornby's push, personally attaching to him all the Beni Sakhr sheikhs, and telling them that he would roll up Moab from the south while I cut it off from the north and east. I had also given him Dhiab of Tafileh, an old windbag, and two of the Majalli sheikhs of Kerak, who notably had a foot in each camp." But while thus ensuring that its purpose as a distraction should be fulfilled, Lawrence took care that it had the power of conversion into a reality, by endowing it with guns, money, troops, explosives, part of his own bodyguard—even Sherif Zeid.

For, underlying the distraction, lay the idea of *variability*. A feint in the event of Lawrence's success at Deraa, in the case of failure it could be converted into "the old second string to our bow," through the Deraa force moving south to reinforce it. The fact that the Turks had now forestalled this move by their new move against Tafila not only showed that they had swallowed the bait, but was an indirect testimony to the value of having alternatives. Moreover, the alternative could be revived, for as soon as the Deraa force struck, the Turkish Tafila force was likely to be withdrawn hurriedly northward. Lawrence's attack on the Hauran would then be Hornby's opportunity. A plan so beautifully fitted and yet so flexible must wring an ecstatic sigh from the most jaded connoisseur of military art.

The Deraa plan also comprised an *hors d'œuvre* and three alternative courses.

"As preliminary we determined to cut the line near Amman, thus preventing Amman's reinforcement of Deraa, and maintaining its conviction that our feint against it was real. It seemed to me that (with Egyptians to do the actual destruction) this preliminary could be undertaken as a night operation by the Gurkhas, whose detachment would not distract our main body from the main purpose."

"This main purpose was to cut the railways in the Hauran and keep them cut for at least a week; and there seemed to be three ways of doing it. The first was to march north of Deraa to the Damascus railway, as on my ride with Tallal in the winter, and cut it; and then cross to the Yarmuk railway. The second was to march south of Deraa to the Yarmuk, as with Ali ibn el Hussein in November, 1917. The third was to rush straight at Deraa town."

"The third scheme could be undertaken only if the Air Force would promise so heavy a daylight bombing of Deraa station that the effect would be tantamount to an artillery bombardment, enabling us to risk an assault against it with our few men. Salmond hoped to do this; but it depended on how many heavy machines he received or assembled in time. Dawnay would fly over to us here [at Azrak] with his last word on September the eleventh. Till then we should hold the schemes equal in our judgment."

It would be difficult to find a more masterly plan, or one as well expressed, in the records of war. Quality of art does not depend on size of canvas. One may also find finer picture-battles reflected in history's mirror, where flaws of execution are not easily visible. But as a conception adjusted by consummate calculation to the uncertainties of foreseen reality, this plan is a masterpiece, and none the less for being a miniature.

The expected aeroplane from Palestine duly landed at Azrak on the 11th. But instead of Dawnay, who was sick, it brought another staff-officer whose air-sickness seems to have affected a memory that can hardly have been good at the outset. For having left behind the notes he had been given to bring, he now forgot to mention the important change in Allenby's plan—the extension of his encircling move to El Afule and Beisan.

Perhaps his confusion may have been aggravated by the shock he suffered when he inquired, in a highly professional tone, about the defence scheme for their "advanced base." With the irritatingly casual air that covered an impish depth Lawrence replied: "We haven't any; you see, the Turks will never come and look for us here." The Staff Officer did not linger. Winterton remarks that "he retired gracefully on his 'plane, escorted by another 'plane, fully convinced, I feel sure, that the 'whole outfit,' as Australians say, would inevitably end in prison at Constantinople."

From the pilot, however, Lawrence and Joyce discovered obliquely that Salmond's resources in bombing-machines would be inadequate to cover an assault on Deraa. Hence this alternative was dropped. They decided to adopt the northern move, above Deraa, to make sure of cutting the "trunk" line to Damascus.

Next day Peake was dispatched with his Egyptian detachment and the handful of Gurkhas to make the preliminary break near Amman.

At dawn on the 14th the main body, about twelve hundred strong, marched forth from Azrak, heading for Umtaiye, a great pit of rain water fifteen miles below Deraa and five miles east of the railway to Amman. Round the Regular core was now woven a gathering force of picked Bedouin, Auda with some of his Abu Tayi, and the sheikhs of the Zebn and Serahin. Nuri Shalaan, cutting his ties with the Turks, had brought 300 Ruwalla horsemen; he had also offered the services of two thousand camelry, but had been asked to hold them in reserve in the Sirhan, lest they scare the villagers of the Hauran before the supreme moment, for the Arabs, had come.

Lawrence had stayed behind in Azrak, settling affairs with Nuri and Feisal, but next morning he came racing after them in a Rolls-Royce most appropriately named the "Blue Mist," which was henceforth his super-mobile headquarters. Bad news, as usual, formed his greeting. Peake had returned with his mission unfulfilled. His party had run into a large encampment of local Bedouin who were being paid by the Turks to protect the railway. As he had neither Lawrence's persuasive tongue nor gold-bags to induce them to transfer their allegiance he had been forced to turn back.

Lawrence was bitterly annoyed at the news. If Deraa was to be cut off from the north and west as arranged, it must, for the security of the operation, be previously cut off from the south. Also, he wanted Amman to be "the nervous place" for the next two days. But it was too late to send another detachment from the slow-moving Regular force, which had no time to spare if it was to reach its objective in time. Quickly he summed up the points of the problem—and decided to execute the task himself, with motor mobility.

He had pushed on to Umtaiye ahead of the force and had made a preliminary reconnaissance of the railway on camelback before dark, discovering not only a good motor-route but a suitable bridge for demolition. After his return to camp he told the others of his plan, and suggested that this solo effort would be rather amusing. As Young remarks—"To one at least of his hearers it did not sound at all amusing, it sounded quite mad. But this was again the Lawrence whose madness had taken Akaba, and his madness on this occasion cut the Deraa-Amman railway."

Next day, the 16th, while the main body continued its march toward Tell Arar, north of Deraa, Lawrence ran down westward to the railway near Jabir in a tender "crammed to the gunwale with gun-cotton and detonators." Joyce and Winterton accompanied him with a second tender and an escort of two armoured cars. On reaching the cover of the last ridge before the railway, Lawrence transferred himself and 150 lbs. of guncotton to an armoured car. In this he drove down to the bridge, while the other car moved to engage the defending redoubt. The Turks surrendered after a brief resistance and Lawrence set to work while Joyce hurried down in a tender with more guncotton.

That particular demolition gave Lawrence great joy of craftsmanship—"In the drainage-holes of the spandrils six small charges were inserted zigzag, and with their explosion all the arches were scientifically shattered; the demolition being a fine example of that finest sort which left the skeleton of its bridge intact indeed, but tottering, so that the repairing enemy had a first labour to destroy the wreck, before they could attempt to rebuild."

As they finished, enemy patrols were approaching. The demolition party drove away hurriedly and then, to their horror, Lawrence's tender broke a spring at a bad bump when they had only gone a few hundred yards. It was peculiarly bitter that their first structural accident in eighteen months of desert travel should have occurred at this moment. "A Rolls in the desert was above rubies," yet there seemed no choice between losing one and losing all. The driver's ingenuity, however, proved equal to the emergency, and by a high-speed improvisation with wedges of wood, lashed together, they got out of range and then made a more secure repair.

Next morning, the 17th, they caught up the main body just as it was launching its attack on the redoubt that guarded the bridge at Tell Arar. The Ruwalla raced for the line but neglected the redoubt, and then stood in the middle of the permanent way in the attitude of conquering heroes, until bullets suddenly began to spurt about them. Then, however, one of Pisani's guns was brought up and under cover of its fire the Arab Regulars quickly stormed the redoubt. "So," as Lawrence wrote, "the southern ten miles of the Damascus line was freely ours . . . It was the only railway to Palestine and Hejaz and I could hardly realise our fortune; hardly believe that our word to Allenby was fulfilled so simply and so soon.

"I wanted the whole line destroyed in a moment but things seemed to have stopped . . . I rushed down, to find Peake's Egyptians making breakfast. It was like Drake's game of bowls and I fell dumb with admiration." However, with some energetic encouragement, the process of demolition got under way, only to be threatened with interruption by the appearance of eight Turkish aeroplanes, hastily sent up from Deraa. Although untrained in air precautions the Arabs' instinct taught them the right action, and they scattered so effectively that after an hour's rain of bombs and bullets there were only two casualties. Then, providentially, the Arab Army's one surviving aeroplane, an obsolete B.E.12 piloted by Junor appeared on the scene and drew off the attention of the Turkish machines, although at the sacrifice of itself. The pilot had a lucky escape and celebrated it by borrowing a Ford to carry out a ground-raid on his own against the railway.

Advantage had already been taken of the air diversion. Collecting 350 of the Arab Regulars Nuri had started them on the way to Muzeirib station on the Palestine branch, some five miles west of Deraa. The peasantry trickled after them.

Lawrence now set off with his bodyguard to follow, while Joyce stood on guard at Tell Arar and covered the Egyptian demolition party with the remainder of the force. On the way Lawrence was hit in the arm by a splinter from an air bomb, but happily the wound was slight. As he drew near Muzeirib it looked as if the whole country-side was running to join in the attack, and when the station garrison surrendered, after a few point-blank shells from Pisani's guns, the Haurani peasants had their fill of loot. There was a light interlude when Nuri saved a case of bottled asparagus from their clutches by crying out "pig's bones" in affected horror. Meantime Lawrence and Young had cut the telegraph, thus severing the main communication between the Turkish armies and their home-base, before proceeding to dynamite the rails and points and wreck the station and its rolling stock.

The question now arose whether they should prolong their westward move and attempt to blow up the bridge at Tell el Shehab in the Yarmuk gorge, the target of Lawrence's long desire. While they were discussing the problem, the young sheikh of the neighbouring village arrived and told them that the Armenian officer commanding the bridge guard was willing to betray his charge, and his loyal subordinates. The officer himself arrived about an hour later and confirmed the offer. He proposed that a few strong men should hide in his house and that he would then summon his subordinates one by one, to be knocked unsuspectingly on the head. To Lawrence "this sounded in the proper descent from books of adventure," and he agreed with a delighted chuckle. Young's reaction was different —"it shocked me to have melodrama brought in to reinforce military operations." However, he was asleep when the plan was adopted, and so could only fall in with the decision.

The force crept down a winding track to the village in the dark, Lawrence with his pockets filled with detonators. Suddenly they heard the sound of an engine in the ravine below. After a long wait the sheikh came to tell them that his plan had failed through the arrival of a train laden with German reserves on their way to Deraa. Nuri suggested an attempt to storm the bridge with the bayonet, but Lawrence now demurred. "I was at the game of reckoning the value of the objective in terms of life, and as usual finding it too dear. Of course most things done in war were too dear, and we should have followed good example in going in and going through with it. But I was secretly and disclaimedly proud of the planning of our campaigns: so I told Nuri that I voted against it. We had today twice cut the Damascus-Palestine railway; and the bringing here of the Afuleh garrison was a third benefit to Allenby. Our bond had been most heavily honoured."

Nuri, after a moment's hesitation, agreed with this argument and the force groped its way back to Muzeirib, which it reached about two o'clock. Lawrence now began to feel the irk of his forbearance, perceiving the danger to Allenby's plan if these enemy reinforcements went back to Afuleh, and to his own retirement across the railway, if they pushed on to Deraa too early. To detain them, by playing on their minds, he sent off two small parties to cut the line at deserted spots on the far side of the bridge. He also sent a message to Joyce asking for the balance of Nuri's regulars to join him here, saying that on the morrow they would move back across the south face of Deraa, thus completing the circle. He suggested that Joyce should return to Umtaiye and await them. For at Umtaiye they would be well placed to menace the Turkish Fourth Army's line of retreat and also to renew their demolitions as often as the enemy attempted repairs.

When dawn came the peasants trickled off to their various villages while the Arab troops filtered towards Nisibin, south of Deraa, the whole so dispersed that the Turkish aircraft were likely to be completely puzzled both as to their numbers and as to their direction. Thus they had an unmolested passage back to the Deraa-Amman line, and on approaching it the guns and machine-guns were pushed forward to bombard Nisib station—as a blind. For while the station garrison was kept busy in preparing to resist an assault, the important bridge to the north was blown up.

The manner of this exploit was typically Lawrentian. For it was uncertain whether the bridge-guard had slipped off to join the station garrison, and even Lawrence's bodyguard did not care to face the risk of walking down to the bridge with their loads of blasting gelatine without knowledge of whether the guard was still there while fully aware that if one bullet hit the gelatine they would be blown to fragments. When Lawrence found that neither orders nor chaff would move them out of shelter he began to go forward alone. That sufficed and he was promptly backed up. The bridge, luckily, was deserted. It was a worthy specimen for his seventy-ninth scalp, and Lawrence viewed it with a loving eye before piling guncotton against the massive piers. While he was thus engaged the rest of the force slipped away eastward to the desert, leaving the guns to the last to keep the station garrison occupied. Finally all were clear and in the darkness Lawrence touched off his fuses and himself tumbled into the enemy's deserted redoubt until the stone-shower was over. Those who watched from afar saw, in the lurid blaze of the explosion, the abutment arch "sheared clean off and the whole mass of masonry sliding slowly down into the valley below."

Lawrence's "preparatory" task on behalf of Allenby was complete. By his three-sided cut ——| at the focal point of the enemy's communications he had gone far to hamstring the Turkish armies just as Allenby was about to jump upon them. The stroke had the physical effect of shutting off the flow of their supplies temporarily —and temporarily was all that mattered here. It had the mental effect of persuading Liman von Sanders to send part of his scanty reserves towards Deraa. More significantly still he sent German troops, the precious cement that held together his jerry-built armies. The success of Lawrence's effort may be traced to the way it was precisely proportioned; too small to impose immediate retreat upon Liman von Sanders; too near the date of Allenby's attack for Liman von Sanders to alter his front-line dispositions, which were ideal for Allenby's purpose.

Only a few hours remained before the hidden mass of the British Army would thrust forward like a gigantic battering ram. It was delightfully disguised. Dust columns had gone eastward by day—created by mule-drawn sleighs, while troop columns marched westward by night. Battalions had marched towards the Jordan Valley by day—and returned by night to repeat this march of a stage army. Cavalry, periodically relieved, had been kept in the valley throughout the summer heat—while Lawrence had been purchasing vast quantities of forage for their coming across the Jordan. Under cover of manifold deceptions Allenby had achieved an overwhelming superiority in the coastal sector. Fifteen thousand canvas dummies filled the vacated horse lines in the interior.

Nevertheless "as darkness fell after a hot airless day upon the great concentration of troops massed in the Plain of Sharon, there was at British G.H.Q. one anxiety overmastering all others." "Was the enemy there?" Perhaps he had retired in time. Would the blow smash a weak defence, or would it hit the air and find an intact defence beyond, out of reach of its guns? That anxiety began to disperse when, at the crash of the British guns half an hour before the first streak of dawn, thousands of Turkish signal rockets soared into the air.

Why had the enemy stayed to be pulverized instead of making a timely recoil? We know now that Liman von Sanders had been anticipating a big attack and that at the beginning of September he had thought of frustrating it by a withdrawal to a rear line near the Sea of Galilee. "I gave up the idea, because we would have had to relinquish the Hejaz railway . . . and because we could no longer have stopped the progress of the Arab insurrection in rear of our army."

No clearer or more striking testimony could be given to the decisive value of Lawrence's "intangible ghost." Decisive not in itself but because it alone made possible the decision.

Although Liman von Sanders was uneasy about the coast sector, he feared still more the effect of an attack east of the Jordan, and even at the eleventh hour the warning of the true plan given by an Indian deserter on September 17th was offset by the more positive news of the Arab attacks on the vital railway around Deraa. Deceived by the Lawrentian mirage, Liman von Sanders regarded this deserter as a tool of the British Intelligence, and his story as a blind to cover Allenby's real purpose. Thus he offered up his forces to destruction.

At 4.30 a.m. on September 19th three hundred and eighty-five guns rained shells upon the Turkish trenches with brief intensity. Soon the infantry swept forward like an avalanche, submerging the stupefied defenders of the two shallow trench systems. Then they wheeled inland, rolling the Turks back like a door on its hinges. The wreckage of the Eighth Army poured through the defile to Messudieh, and upon this hapless mob the British aircraft dived with bombs and bullets.

Meantime, through the open doorway the cavalry had passed, riding straight up the coastal corridor for thirty miles before swinging in to cross the Carmel Range. They were over the passes by the next morning, and not only seized El Afule but temporarily occupied Nazareth, where the enemy's General Headquarters lay, still ignorant of the disaster that had overtaken their troops—because aircraft and agents had cut all the telegraph lines. Liman von Sanders himself barely escaped. By the afternoon the cavalry were in Beisan —to reach it the 4th Cavalry Division had ridden nearly seventy miles in thirty-four hours. The barrier had been lowered across the Turks' lines of retreat.

The one remaining bolt-hole was eastward, over the Jordan, and this the Air Force sealed. Early on September 21st the British aircraft sighted a large column winding down the steep gorge from Nablus towards the Jordan. Four hours' continuous bombing and machine-gunning by relays of aircraft reduced this procession to stagnation, an inanimate chaos of guns and transport. From this moment may be timed the extinction of the Seventh and Eighth Turkish Armies. What followed was but a rounding up of fugitive "cattle" by the cavalry.

Only the Fourth Army, which yet had been the strongest of the three, remained—east of the Jordan. A broken railway and the Arabs lay along its line of retreat. Its fate was to be a rapid attrition under incessant pin-pricks.

When disaster overtook the other armies, the Fourth had still a fair chance of escape. On its western front in the Jordan Valley it had Chaytor's force, which consisted of the Anzac Mounted Division reinforced by a few infantry battalions. By active demonstrations Chaytor's force had fomented the idea of a renewed British advance westward, and so helped to cloak Allenby's real stroke. Its threat also helped to detain the Fourth Army from retreat, although the Turks' delay was due more to the slowness with which news reached them and to their desire to wait for the 2nd Corps, now retiring from Ma'an and the posts on the Hejaz railway north of it. Not until the 22nd did the Fourth Army begin its retreat. The 2nd Corps, harassed by the plague of Hornby's Bedouin, was then still many miles short of Amman, and Chaytor's force moved to intercept it.

The Fourth Army's chance of making good its retreat depended on whether it could brush aside the Arabs and reach Damascus before Allenby's cavalry made a fresh bound to the aid of the Arabs in barring the way. The broken railway, by compelling the Turks to march, would slow down their retreat, but for some days the Arabs would be in a precarious position as the strategic wedge between the Deraa socket and the recoiling mass.

That problem was Lawrence's concern on the morning after he had closed the railway, the morning when Allenby's distant forces were opening their attack. "Strategically, our business was to hold on to Umtaiye, which gave us command at will of Deraa's three railways. If we held it another week we should strangle the Turkish armies, however little Allenby did. Yet tactically Umtaiye was a dangerous place. An inferior force composed exclusively of regulars, without a guerilla screen, could not safely hold it: yet to that we should shortly be reduced, if our air helplessness continued patent."

Here was the vulnerable side of the Arab force. Because of its mobility and fluidity it ran little risk from the Turkish ground-troops, but against the vastly superior mobility of the air arm only direct protection could avail. Although the British air force in Palestine far outnumbered and outclassed the Turkish, which was "virtually driven from the skies," that air superiority was significantly lacking in the Arab zone, despite this being the most vital zone strategically. The Arab force had only been provided with two machines, and both were now lost, whereas the Turks had some nine machines at the Deraa aerodrome. If the Arab force had been composed mainly of armoured cars the danger would have been slight, but with its great quantity of camels and horses it offered an inviting air target, the easier to locate because it was fettered by its strategic role and the need for water. The enemy's bombing was already beginning to wear the nerves of the Arab irregulars. If it was to continue unchecked they might disperse and go home.

Salvation could lie only in obtaining air reinforcement from Allenby. According to arrangement a liaison machine was due to fly over to Azrak from Palestine on the 20th, and Lawrence decided that he would travel back in it to see Allenby.

Meantime he and Junor carried out a raid with two armoured cars against a Turkish advanced landing ground, where three aeroplanes had been seen to alight. Silencing the engines of the cars they crept down a valley until they came in sight of the meadow where the enemy aircraft lay. Then they opened their throttles and leapt forward, only to find their way blocked by a deep, straight-sided ditch. While they searched for a possible crossing, the aircraft crews rushed to swing their propellers. Two of them took off in time, but the engine of the third failed to start and the armoured car settled its fate by putting fifteen hundred bullets into its fuselage from the other side of the ditch. As the cars drove home the other two aeroplanes pursued and bombed them, one with uncomfortable accuracy. "We crept on defencelessly, slowly, among the stones, feeling like sardines in a doomed tin, as the bombs fell closer." One bomb sent a shower of broken stone through the driving slit of Lawrence's car and cut his knuckles, while another tore off a front tire and nearly overturned the car. The experience moved Lawrence to the remark: "Of all danger give me the solitary sort."

Nevertheless, after a few hours' sleep he was out again that night with the cars, covering a fresh railway demolition by Peake's Egyptians as an interlude on his way to Azrak. T.E. was as averse to killing time as he was adept in killing two birds with one stone. But on this occasion he contributed little to the raid, as the cars lost themselves, perhaps because his sense of direction was suffering from five successive nights without sleep. In compensation, however, he stumbled upon a Turkish train and the encounter produced a running fight in the dark between rail and road machines, a spectacle that was made the more bizarre by the green shower of luminous tracer bullets that deluged the occupants of the train.

On reaching Azrak Lawrence met Feisal and Nuri Shaalan and, after giving them the latest news, seized the chance of a good night's sleep. He awoke to receive still better news. For, soon after dawn, the expected aeroplane from Palestine arrived and brought them the first news, astounding and exhilarating in its completeness, of Allenby's victory over the Seventh and Eighth Turkish Armies. Lawrence now embarked for the return trip to Palestine, but before doing so he urged upon Feisal that the news should be taken as the signal for the long-delayed general revolt in Syria. Joyce, also, decided to return to Abu el Lissal to stimulate the pressure on the Turks at Ma'an.

CHAPTER XIX

THE ROAD TO DAMASCUS

A BARE hour's flight from Azrak carried Lawrence into Palestine, a transition from one world to another, from the desert where individuality prevailed to the legions where organization reigned and hierarchy ruled. If the swiftness of the passage was a portent of the way that the air was abolishing the old terrestrial independences, it was also a reminder of the Arab forces' now inevitable subordination to Allenby's pattern.

On landing at Ramleh, he drove straight to General Headquarters where Allenby outlined the further development of his plan. Damascus was now the next objective, coupled with Beirut. While the infantry, one division immediately, pushed on up the coast past Haifa and Acre to Beirut, the cavalry was to set out for Damascus. The Australian Mounted Division supported by the 5th Cavalry Division would move west of the Sea of Galilee and then turn north-east for Damascus via the road through Quneitra. The 4th Cavalry Division from Beisan would strike east for Deraa, to help the Arabs in cutting off the Turkish 4th Army, and then move due north on Damascus. Meantime Chaytor's force, farther south, would march on Amman, also with the idea of cutting off the Turks' retreat.

Allenby asked that the Arabs should assist these moves, taking the Turkish Fourth Army as their particular target, and he firmly warned Lawrence against attempting any independent coup against Damascus until the British forces were at hand.

The immediate problem of preserving the Arabs from air-borne paralysis was satisfactorily settled. When Lawrence explained the precarious situation, Allenby rang for Salmond, who at once agreed to send two Bristol fighters. Then a difficulty intervened. There was no petrol at Umtaiye. But the difficulty was surmounted by ingenuity —Salmond and Borton evolved the idea of using a new big Handley-Page bomber as an air-tender. It was arranged that its pilot, Ross-Smith, who a year later made the first flight from England to Australia, should accompany the Bristols to Umtaiye next day in order to make sure that so large a machine could use the landing-ground there.

Having settled his business, Lawrence had the rare chance of enjoying a day's rest in comparatively civilized conditions. Allenby's headquarters might have been regarded as bare and comfortless to a sybaritic traveller, but to Lawrence the cool airiness of the whitewashed, fly-proof building, surrounded by trees, appeared like paradise. Yet he did not care for it, for he "felt immoral, enjoying white table-cloths, and coffee, and soldier servants, while our people at Umtaiye lay like lizards among the stones, eating unleavened bread, and waiting for the next plane to bomb them." Nor was his distaste for paradise due merely to this comparison—"after a long spell of the restrained desert, flowers and grass seemed to fidget, and the everywhere-burgeoning green of tilth became vulgar, in its fecundity." His mood yields another glimpse into his mind.

Early on the morning of the 22nd the air reinforcements set out for Umtaiye, only to find that the Arab force had moved back a few miles in the night to escape the constant bombing. The Turkish aircraft discovered this new camp at Umm es Surab soon after the British machines had landed and breakfast was twice interrupted by a sudden exchange of sausage-eating for air fighting. Two enemy machines were brought down in flames and then Ross-Smith reluctantly went back to fetch the Handley-Page while Lawrence flew on to Azrak.

Feisal and Nuri Shaalan came back with him, in the green Vauxhall, to Umm es Surab. There they found that the Handley-Page had already arrived and was unloading a ton of petrol, with oil and spare parts, as well as provisions for the British troops. Young, ever mindful of the Q side, had been growing anxious over the problem of maintaining the force, so that these air-borne supplies had a real as well as a novelty value. Their means of transport was surrounded by astonished Arabs, who reverently spoke of it as "THE aeroplane" and called the Bristol fighters its foals. These had already nullified the enemy air squadron at Deraa, which henceforth ceased to trouble the Arab force, but the appearance of the Handley-Page was none the less of moral value by its visible confirmation to the Arab population of Britain's overwhelming might. The great machine also confirmed the military advantage by dropping a shower of hundred-pound bombs on Mafraq station two nights later, with such effect that the trucks in the sidings continued to burn for many hours.

Here and at Deraa air raids completed that paralysis of railway movement which Arab raids had produced—and were still prolonging. For on the 23rd they made a fresh descent on Jabir and burnt the wooden framing with which the Turks were trying to restore the bridge that Lawrence had destroyed a week earlier. Lawrence himself for once took a rest and left the other officers to share with Nuri Said the credit of this latest stroke.

Lawrence, as ever, was looking ahead, concerned with the next move while to less discerning eyes the present seemed still unassured. In his view—"our work against the Fourth Army was finished. Such remnants as avoided out of the hands of the Arabs would reach Deraa as unarmed stragglers. Our new endeavour should be to force the quick evacuation of Deraa, in order to prevent the Turks there reforming the fugitives into a rearguard."

The facts, as unknown to him as to others, were even then in course of justifying him. The Fourth Army was already retreating northward in a disordered stream. A rearguard kept Chaytor's force from reaching Amman until the 25th, and at the sacrifice of itself frustrated his mission of cutting off the Turks' retreat northward. The last trains left a few hours before the British occupied the town. But they were soon stopped by the breaches that the Arabs had made in the line, and the Turks who travelled on them were forced to detrain. Only the earlier departures got through to Damascus, by changes of train. The bulk of the Fourth Army was a foot-slogging, footsore collection of crumbling units, shrinking hourly under the privations of the march and the harassments of the loot-thirsty Bedouin.

If Lawrence erred on the side of optimism in suggesting that only unarmed stragglers would reach Deraa, his forecast was fundamentally correct in a strategic sense. For effective existence a regular army must preserve its organized formation, and it ceases to be an army when it loses its cohesion, when tactical bodies dissolve into mere masses of men. It is then "unarmed" strategically. By the time Deraa was reached such dissolution had already gone far, but any pause in the retreat might have meant a chance for the floating mass to coagulate round the few solid fragments that remained. To pre vent such a pause was, clearly, the true strategic purpose of the Arab forces, and the most essential service that they could render to Allenby's purpose.

On the 24th a British aeroplane came over to give them news of further successes in Palestine and a warning that the Fourth Army was now in retreat towards them. That same day the Arab force moved back to Umtaiye, where a vitally important council of war was held on the following morning. In fulfilment of his new purpose Lawrence proposed "that we march north, past Tell Arar, and over the railway at dawn tomorrow, into Sheikh Saad village." Ten miles north of Muzeirib on the Pilgrims' Road, and on the flank of the Damascus railway, "it lay in familiar country with abundant water, perfect observation, and a secure retreat west or north, or even south-west, if we were directly attacked. It cut off Deraa from Damascus; and Mezerib also." The advantages of such a move are easily seen; the insurance against its risks requires more understanding—for a retreat "west or north" would have taken the Arabs in the enemy's direction. This fact disquieted some of Lawrence's companions "who did not see that Galilee Lake completely covered the very broken districts into which we should retreat. We could have stood a fortnight's siege in them."

Although Young, in particular, expressed misgivings, the Arab leaders rallied to Lawrence's view, and the force prepared to move. In anticipation of an advance, Nuri Shaalan's camelry had been called up from Azrak, raising the total of the force to over three thousand men, three-quarters of whom were irregulars. As an offset the Bristol fighters now returned to Palestine, and the armoured cars to their base at Azrak. "The country round Sheikh Saad was not possible for cars to fight over; also, very little petrol remained. The aircraft took Allenby our program and promised to visit us at Sheikh Saad."

The movement north began the same day, but had hardly begun before it was interrupted by an alarm. One of the Palestine-bound aircraft flew back and dropped a note which said that a large body of enemy cavalry was approaching. This was disconcerting news, especially now that the Arabs were denuded of aircraft and armoured cars. Lawrence and Nuri Said had a hasty consultation as to whether they should continue or stand. "It seemed wiser to run, since Sheikh

Saad was a more profitable stop-block. So we hurried the regulars away." The irregular horse were sent to delay the approaching Turks. But these, part of the Fourth Army, were in such a condition as to have no thought of making an attack—"they were only making for Deraa by an unencumbered road." They had been sighted by the armoured cars returning to Azrak, and when these intervened it was the signal for a panic that scattered the Turks into a swarm of separate fugitives.

Nevertheless, the interruption had not only delayed the Arab move, but threatened it with a more serious and lasting interruption —from a British source. For in camp that night Young argued that the delay had prejudiced the chance of crossing the line unopposed. He went on to urge that the Arabs had now done enough, and would be justified as well as wise in retiring to a position east of the railway, where the Druses were gathering. Here they could wait until the British forces had taken Deraa.

The suggestion was most unwelcome to Lawrence. Morally, because it seemed to sacrifice the Arabs' honour to their safety, by leaving Allenby's troops to bear the final burden. Politically, because "it threw away the chance to consolidate the terrain for which the Arabs had been fighting two years,"—he never lost sight of the Cairo promise "the Arabs shall keep what they take." Militarily, because it threatened to forfeit the best chance of a quick decision. Sheikh Saad would be a lever on the rear of Deraa, loosening all resistance this side of Damascus, and at present only the Arabs were close enough to exert such vital pressure on the Turks' retreat. As Lawrence has remarked—"Surely if there is one military maxim of universal value, it is to press hard on a rout." Nor was that all, for in Lawrence's view the early fall of Damascus would spell the collapse of Turkey, and the breaking of this weak link would in turn loosen the whole cluster of the enemy powers, now fundamentally interdependent.

While Lawrence based himself on the higher issues and military advantages, Young persisted in emphasizing the immediate tactical risks—of pushing across the path of the Turkish Army now so near at hand. He had a vision of their few hundred slow-moving regulars being crushed between ten thousand Turks. Finding Lawrence unconvinced, he fell back on the line that he was a regular soldier and the senior one present. This familiar refuge of mediocre authority was not suited to the unorthodox "conditions of command" in the Arab zone (Lawrence once, most aptly, remarked: "Command in Arabia was like sovereignty in the British Empire—a power in commission, and very difficult to find"). In taking such a line Young did himself an injustice, for he was a remarkable man in his own way, capable of most things except adjustment to irregular ways. Nor was it likely to carry much weight in an argument with Lawrence, who cut it short by saying that he wanted to sleep as he would have to be up early to cross the railway. For he was going with his bodyguard and the irregulars even if the regulars did not come. And Nuri Said's attitude quietly assured him that they would.

In weighing this discussion one may justly appreciate Young's view that Lawrence, accustomed to think in terms of irregular mobility, was inclined to demand of the rather immobile Arab regulars what was for their own part an undue risk. But one can see that Lawrence was using two-party scales—and weighing the Turks' low morale against the Arab regulars' low mobility. The issue proved one more testimony to his profound insight.

In the morning the march continued and was swelled by an increasing tide of Bedouin and villagers. In the afternoon the flood poured across the railway, unmolested by the enemy but itself leaving a trail of broken rails, blown up and torn up with an enthusiastic spread of energy that was hardly less effective than a more scientific but narrower demolition. After the original demolition, communication along this main line had been interrupted for nine days. The line had only been repaired in time for a solitary train to get through that very morning. And now it was broken again. From this moment the railway remained cut and six trains were penned in Deraa, to fall, subsequently, into the Arabs' hands.

Absence of opposition encouraged Lawrence to enlarge the plan and permitted him to detach forces to enlarge it. A series of offshoots sprouted that night. While the main body pursued its way to Sheikh Saad without having fired a shot, Auda turned aside for El Ghazale station, where he captured a stranded train and two hundred prisoners. Tallal rode farther north and captured the enemy's large grain depot at Izra. Nuri Shaalan pushed south down the road to Deraa and rounded up another four hundred Turks who were billeted in

scattered villages. The Arab main body reached Sheikh Saad soon
after dawn on the 27th, its tardy gait accelerated by Young's anx-
iously energetic spur, and there the various detachments soon collected with their spoils of the night.

Straight into their arms walked a large party of Turks, Austrians
and Germans, with eight machine-guns, and were added to the bag
almost before they had realized that they had escaped one war only
to fall into another.

From their hill-top at Sheikh Saad, the leaders of the Arab force
scanned the country towards the morning horizon. It was dotted
with bodies of troops moving north, evidence that the move to
Sheikh Saad had exerted the intended leverage. The Turks, receiving fantastic night reports of the Arab force's strength, had ordered
the immediate evacuation of Deraa and burned the six aeroplanes
left there—"their last hope of 'seeing' where they stood." Some
bodies were too large or too far ahead for interception, but several
smaller and closer parties were roped in. Altogether, some two thousand prisoners were taken in the twenty-four hours to noon of the
27th, and many more were contemptuously turned loose after being
stripped of their equipment and animals. Beside such intoxicating
successes it seemed little, even to the British officers, when an aeroplane from Allenby flew over and dropped a message saying that
Bulgaria had capitulated—the first news to them that this other
Germanic prop was being attacked.

Events multiplied hourly on the Arabs' front. Another British aeroplane came over to warn them that two large enemy columns were
approaching from the south. One of six thousand men was marching
from Deraa and another of two thousand from Muzeirib. It meant
that the main mass of the retreating Turks was now at hand. And
there was as yet no sign of the British cavalry who should have come
to the Arabs' assistance.

Barrow's 4th Cavalry Division, which had been on the Jordan
around Beisan since the 20th, had not begun its eastward march
until early on the 26th. Its leading brigade had orders to reach Irbid
and if possible find touch with the Arabs that night, but on approaching the village it met an enemy rearguard, and in the ensuing
action suffered a check through lack of reconnaissance born apparently of overconfidence. This check seems to have caused a re-

action towards excessive caution. For on the following day, the 27th, its progress was painfully slow, and ceased altogether after midday, for Barrow himself then ordered it to bivouac, at Er Remta, several miles short of Deraa. Thus he had missed by a wide margin the chance of heading off the Turkish Fourth Army—which was a day out of Deraa when he arrived on the 28th.

His missed opportunity exposed the Arab force to seeming danger. In view of the fact that it comprised a mere six hundred regulars, the air warning that two enemy columns, totalling eight thousand men, were heading in its direction might well have shaken the nerve of a conventional commander. But Lawrence's psychological insight into the condition of the Turks led him to discount the danger of the situation, while perceiving the opportunity it presented.

To launch his force against the column moving north from Deraa would have been reckless, with the other column across his track. And in any case it was too large a mouthful to be swallowed. Part of the Ruwalla under Khalid were, however, dispatched to help the local Arabs in reducing it by snippets to more digestible proportions. The column from Muzeirib was small enough for quick dispatch, and a further reason for haste was that its route would take it through Tallal's own village of Tafas. His anxiety impelled Lawrence to ride at once with his bodyguard to Tafas and delay the Turks if possible until the Arab regulars came up in support.

But the move was too late to save Tafas, if not for the military purpose. Smoke was seen rising from the village as Lawrence neared it and he met a few distraught fugitives who told of the ghastly deeds perpetrated when the Turks had occupied it an hour before. The butchery was now complete and the Turkish columns were seen moving out to continue the march north. Lawrence's men opened fire as a brake on their progress until the arrival of Nuri Said's infantry and Pisani's ubiquitously invaluable guns. When these came up and took position, forcing the enemy to turn east towards Tell Arar, Lawrence slipped into the village behind the Turks' backs, accompanied by Tallal and Auda. From a grey heap a child tottered away as if to escape them, cried out in fright "Don't hit me, Baba," and then collapsed with the effort, blood gushing out of a gaping wound. Then they came on more dead babies and the bodies of women, obscenely killed with bayonet-hafts protruding between their legs.

Tallal gave a moan at the sight, drew his headcloth slowly about his face, and then suddenly galloped straight at the enemy, to fall riddled with bullets. Auda grimly said—"God give him mercy; we will take his price." Taking charge of the battle, he harassed the enemy until their formation split into three parts. The smallest, composed of German and Austrian machine-gunners, repulsed all efforts to overwhelm them, but the other two were gradually worn down and destroyed in a running fight that continued till sunset. In view of the vengeful frenzy of the Arabs, Lawrence's order to take no prisoners was somewhat superfluous. "In a madness born of the horror of Tafas we killed, and killed, even blowing in the heads of the fallen and of the animals; as though their death and running blood could slake our agony."

Even when the killing was complete and the Arabs were back in camp with their booty, Lawrence could not rest, for thought of his dead comrade Tallal. So he called for his spare camel and with a single member of his bodyguard rode out in the night to join the Ruwalla who were harassing the larger enemy column. He traced them by the distant noise of shots and the light of occasional gun flashes. They had clung on to the unwieldy column all day—it had covered only a few miles—and now in the darkness were closing in. At sunset the Turks had vainly tried to camp, but the Arabs had pricked them into movement afresh, and they were now stumbling on in disordered packets which dripped a trickle of stragglers too bemused by fatigue to cling to their only chance of preservation.

The contrasting conduct of the German detachments moved Lawrence to admiration. "Here for the first time I grew proud of the enemy who had killed my brothers. They were two thousand miles from home, without hope and without guides, in conditions mad enough to break the bravest nerves. Yet their sections held together in firm rank, sheering through the wrack of Turk and Arab like armoured ships, high-faced and silent. When attacked they halted, took position, fired to order. There was no haste, no arguing, no hesitation. They were glorious."

When Lawrence at last found Khalid he asked him to call off the Ruwalla and "leave this rout to time and the peasantry." If it was Lawrence's habit to look ahead, he did not jump until his foothold was sure. The Arab horse and camelry might overhaul these toiling foot-columns when they wished, and meantime the situation at Deraa had still to be secured. "I did not know what had happened to Barrow: and some such security as an occupied Deraa, or a junction with him, was essential as a prelude to advance on Damascus." Khalid's brother, Trad, had ridden to Deraa at dusk with half the Ruwalla tribesmen, on a report that the place was empty. But there might well be further Turkish columns coming up and, with Barrow's cavalry still some distance away, the Arabs might be hammered unless they were speedily reinforced.

Khalid accordingly rallied several hundred of his men and turned south, while Lawrence rode back to Sheikh Saad. Reaching it at midnight he was greeted by bad news and good. Discord in the camp was already threatening, for the blood-lust of the afternoon was not easily quietened and under its intoxication the Arabs were remembering their own blood-feuds and tribal jealousies. Internal peace had been preserved with difficulty but happily a diversion had relieved the pressure. For messengers had just arrived from Trad to say that Deraa had been captured, with some five hundred prisoners. Nasir and Nuri set off thither with their men, and Lawrence also, although it was his fourth night of riding, "My mind would not let me feel how tired my body was."

Such, indeed, was his impatience that after accompanying Nuri Said for some way he grew tired of travelling horsepace. "I gave liberty to my camel—the grand, rebellious Baha—and she stretched herself out against the field, racing my wearied followers for mile upon mile with piston strides like an engine, so that I entered Deraa quite alone in the full dawn,"—of the 28th. "This was a crazy ride," he admits, "through a country of murder and night terror."

Nasir was at the Mayor's house, arranging for a military governor and police. Lawrence promptly suggested more comprehensive measures, besides placing guards over the pumps, engine sheds and stores, for his desire was to see the Arabs establish an administration before the British could usurp control in their usual bland way. He was just in time, for Barrow's leading troops were advancing to the edge of the hills above the station in readiness for attack. Lawrence went out to warn them that Deraa was in the Arabs' hands. "This was a difficult situation to carry off. I took one man with me only: I shaved and dressed in clean clothes and behaved with histrionic nonchalance, being treated first as enemy, then as native, then as spy, before I found Barrow."

Barrow seemed rather disconcerted at being forestalled, and Lawrence pressed home the advantage by his air of calm assumption that Barrow's troops were the guests of the Arabs. "My head was working full speed in these minutes, on our joint behalf, to prevent the fatal first steps by which the unimaginative British, with the best will in the world, usually deprived the acquiescent native of the discipline of responsibility, and created a situation which called for years of agitation and successive reforms and riotings to mend."

After finding that he had been forestalled both in his intention to post sentries and to take over the working of the railways, Barrow "surrendered himself by asking me to find him forage and food-stuffs." If he did not find it easy to assimilate the unexpected situation, one reason was perhaps his revulsion at the horrid sights which silently registered the night's sack of the Turkish quarters. But having capitulated, he did it with a good grace, for when Lawrence drew his attention to Nasir's silk pennon which hung outside the government office he saluted it in a way that sent a thrill through the Arab soldiers. The action seemed the vindication of their efforts and sacrifices.

To Lawrence, the pleasure had a salty flavour. Within the past few hours he had had a double foretaste of trouble ahead, both among the Arabs and between them and their allies. And his discomfort was sharpened by enforced immersion in a flood of drilled troops. "The essence of the desert was the lonely moving individual, the 'son of the roads,' [*ibn turgi*—an Arab phrase] apart from the world as in a grave. These troops, in flocks like slow sheep, looked not worthy of the privilege of space. My mind felt in the Indian rank and file something puny and confined; an air of thinking themselves mean; almost a careful esteemed subservience, unlike the abrupt wholesomeness of Bedouin. The manner of the British officers toward their men struck horror into my bodyguard, who had never seen personal inequality before."

His repulsion may have been increased by his recent witness at Tafas of the bestial license to which severely disciplined troops were prone when their curbed instincts were allowed an outlet. To a man of his historical sense, it did not suffice to say that these were Turks—he could not help remembering the British troops at Badajoz. But the excesses of soldiers' passions offended him less than the stunting of their souls and their mergence in a mass. "Our armoured-car men were persons to me, from their fewness and our long companionship; and also in their selves, for these months . . . had worn and refined them into individuals." The newcomers were an impersonal mass, whose obtruding numbers emphasized their stereotyped demeanour.

In the days that followed, as the forces converged on Damascus, he was embedded more deeply into this unaccustomed environment, and with increase of contact revulsion grew, producing the reflection —"It came upon me freshly how the secret of uniform was to make a crowd solid, dignified, impersonal; to give it the singleness and tautness of an upstanding man. This death's livery which walled its bearers from ordinary life, was sign that they had sold their wills and bodies to the State: and contracted themselves into a service not the less abject for that its beginning was voluntary. Some of them had obeyed the instinct of lawlessness: some were hungry: some thirsted for glamour, for the supposed colour of a military life; but, of them all, those only received satisfaction who had sought to degrade themselves, for to the peace-eye they were below humanity." "Convicts had violence put upon them. Slaves might be free, if they could, by intention. But the soldier assigned his owner the twenty-four hours' use of his body; and sole conduct of his mind and passions."

If Lawrence had shared the fellowship of the trenches, in a happy battalion, he might have qualified his judgment and even found extenuating circumstances. For in the approach to the fighting line authority became curbed to the benefit of individuality, which in many cases not merely survived but even grew stronger under the pressure of the experience. The front was a Moloch that consumed bodies but souls were often tempered in its fire—the Moloch that hungered for souls lay at the base. One should remember that Lawrence had only experienced the two extremes of soldiering, the cesspool of Cairo staff offices and the solitariness of guerrilla war in the desert.

Again, in weighing his reflections one must take account of his state at this time, when his will drove along an overtried body that dragged on a depressed mind, apprehensive of troubles ahead and acutely conscious of the double nature of the part he was playing, an unceasing irk to his honesty. His dark mood in these days of triumph made an indelible impression on his companions and, because of their affection, grieved them. It seems to have been "caught" in McBey's portrait of him, now in the Imperial War Museum, which was painted just after his arrival in Damascus—T.E. himself says now "It is shockingly strange to me."

Yet, if allowance should be made for that mood, there is a fundamental truth in his reflection on the nature of armies which holds a lesson even for those who have to create armies. It helps to explain why the best drilled armies have so often become blunt swords, and why soldiers are so often ruined in the making. His reflection, moreover, helps to explain why he himself chose the Air Forces for his later service. "The problem of the ranks in the R.A.F. is to produce the mechanic of individual intelligence."

Lawrence distrusted the type of discipline traditional in Regular armies as being a process of the mass that ran counter to the mobility essential for war—war economically and effectively waged. Moreover, he regarded such discipline as more suited to the conditions of peace than of war. The suggestion that "discipline" is not a military virtue may seem paradoxical, especially to soldiers, but Lawrence's view was that the form of discipline developed on the parade-ground, instead of impressing the idea that the soldier's will must actively second his superior's, tends to make obedience merely a reflex action.

This automatic response, without momentary pause for thought transmission, may increase quickness under peace conditions but it makes no allowance for the friction of war, or for casualties among the leaders. One may here recall that Grandmaison and the French General Staff before 1914 expressly aimed at a discipline of the muscles, not of the intelligence, sacrificing initiative in order, by incessant repetition, "to develop in the soldier the reflexes of obedience." That doctrine—and its consequences—go far to bear out Lawrence's view.

Further, he deemed such unthinking obedience harmful to authority itself. By putting excessive power in the hands of arbitrary old age, it often led to an indulgence that deadened the commander's subjunctive mood—to his own ruination.

From experience and reflection, Lawrence had come to a distrust of instinct, which has its roots in animality. Reason seemed to him to give men something deliberately more precious than fear or pain —the customary agents of "discipline." And this conviction led him to discount the value of peace-smartness as a war-education.

For he had observed that in war a subtle change took place even in the regular soldier, and that discipline as a driving force was blended with or even swallowed by an eagerness to fight. It was the degree of this eagerness which decided the issue in the moral sense, and often in the physical sense. War was made up of crises of intense effort; after each expenditure of effort there was a reaction, while the prolongation of any single effort drained the capacity for renewed effort. Discharges of nervous energy had to be brief, with time to recuperate.

The commander must not only avoid running down the batteries, but exercise care in charging them. Here, it seemed to Lawrence, lay the deeper explanation of smartening discipline. There were obvious dangers in generating the excitement of war to create a military spirit in peace-time. To use his own simile, it would be like the too-early doping of an athlete. "Smartness" serves as a substitute, by which the military spirit can be diverted into a harmless channel.

A price has to be paid, however, when war comes—in loss of individual intelligence and initiative. The straitly disciplined soldier is apt to feel uneasy, if not helpless, unless in a herd. War, even regular war, brings frequent shocks that disintegrate the mass and throw the individual on his own resources. If these have atrophied under restraint he is unable to cope with the emergency. Lawrence once remarked that "lack of *independent* courage" is the root fault of the military system. Analysis of history would suggest that it is the main cause of military failure—in all grades, since even the highest have usually "been through the mill" in their time.

On the morning of the 29th Barrow marched north up the Pilgrims' Road, having asked the Arab leaders to cover his right flank.

Actually, Nasir, Nuri Shaalan and Auda with twelve hundred irregular horse and camelry were already ahead of him, having moved the day before to catch up the main enemy column. And all through the 29th they clung on to it, harassing its steps.

Lawrence himself had stayed behind to see Feisal, who arrived that day from Azrak, and to make sure that the Arab administration took firm hold. He had hopes of a night's sleep, but finding it would not come he woke up Stirling, and set out northward before daylight in the "Blue Mist" on the sixty mile course to Damascus. Finding their progress was blocked by columns of cavalry transport, they turned aside and drove to the disused railway line that ran north from Muzeirib. Climbing the embankment they drove fast, if bumpily, along it over the ballast, and so circumvented the block. By noon they caught up the tail of Barrow's headquarters, which was halted. Lawrence's bodyguard was accompanying it; so, taking one of the camels, he rode to see Barrow and find out the reason for the halt. Barrow, who had stopped to water his horses, showed astonishment when he saw Lawrence on camelback and heard that he had only left Deraa that morning! When Barrow asked where they were going to stop that night, he received the teasing Lawrentian reply—"In Damascus."

Early in the afternoon the "Blue Mist" passed the British advanced guard and through the screen, and, forging ahead, dropped notes at successive villages to await the cavalry's arrival. If the information was appreciated, the veiled imputation was hardly palatable. But Lawrence found relief as well as amusement in rubbing it in— "It irked Stirling and myself to see the caution of Barrow's advance; scouts scouting empty valleys, sections crowning every deserted hill, a screen drawn forward so carefully over friendly country. It marked the difference between our certain movements and the tentative processes of normal war." "It also showed a total ignorance of the air arm"—for British aircraft were flying over this area all day.

The "Blue Mist" drove on towards Kiswe, some ten miles short of Damascus, where Barrow was to reunite with Chauvel and the remainder of the Desert Mounted Corps. In mid-afternoon Lawrence heard firing to the right near the Hejaz railway line. Then he sighted a Turkish column of about two thousand men, moving in ragged groups. Round it, like flies, buzzed the Arabs, and Nasir, riding up, told Lawrence that this was all that remained of the original six thousand. The attrition of this column was entirely the work of the irregulars, for the Arab regulars, like the British cavalry, had been too slow-moving to share in the work. But now there was a chance for the latter to take a hand in finishing off the remnant.

Asking Nasir to block its path and hold it up for an hour if possible, Lawrence turned round and drove to fetch British help. Three miles back he came upon the advanced guard. Stirling relates that the elderly colonel commanding it "was particularly stuffy with Lawrence and evidently resented intensely that our little Rolls should be able to dash about with impunity miles in advance of his cavalry, which was moving northward at the time with infinite and quite unnecessary caution." He reluctantly sent forward a squadron, but when the Turks' little mountain guns opened fire the Colonel ordered a retirement. Dismayed at the risk to Nasir and disgusted at such an exhibition, Lawrence hurriedly drove back to make fresh appeal to the Colonel, but could not move him, and so drove on to find the brigade commander. General Gregory at once sent forward a horse battery and a yeomanry regiment, while another regiment moved wide to head off the enemy.

But time had been lost and darkness was falling when the guns came within range. Nevertheless they were in time to forestall a Turkish counter-attack on Nasir, and their shells spurred the enemy to make for the heights of Jebel Mania, abandoning guns and transport. Auda was lying in wait there, having ridden on to collect the Wuld Ali tribesmen; during the night, tired at last of killing, he captured six hundred Turks. The rest escaped in the darkness only to be rounded up two days later by the Australians. In all the Arab forces had taken eight thousand prisoners and killed a number that were estimated at nearly five thousand, besides capturing 150 machine-guns and about thirty guns. Thus the extinction of the Fourth Army may justly be placed to their credit and dated from this night of September 30th on the slopes of Jebel Mania.

Already in the afternoon the north-western exit from Damascus had been closed by the Australian Mounted Division, which had made good progress along its westerly route through Quneitra, and reached the edge of the Barada gorge just as part of the Damascus garrison was retreating through it. Sweeping the fugitive stream with machine-guns fired from the overhanging cliffs the Australians quickly caused it to coagulate into a fear-frozen mass, of whom some four thousand were taken prisoners.

That afternoon also the Sherifial party in Damascus had assumed power and had hoisted the Arab flag over the town hall while the retreating Turks were still marching out. The Turks had swallowed the insult, making no attempt to tear down the flag.

Ali Riza Pasha himself, who had so long combined the dual function of Turkish commander and head of the Arab committee, was not present to inaugurate the change. He had just previously been dispatched to take charge of the Turks' last line of defence, a duty that he had accepted as a conveniently early chance to join the British. And after reaching Barrow's headquarters he so much enjoyed telling how he "had selected heavy-artillery positions that could not be occupied for lack of water," that in his merriment he upset the table on which their breakfast was laid.

His departure from Damascus might have delayed the rising, but his natural successor, Shukri Pasha, was encouraged to act not only by the sound of the British guns but by the unexpected support of the Algerian brothers, Abd el Kader and Mohammed Said, who had remained obstinately pro-Turk until the last hour. They forced their help on Shukri by the menace of their followers; and Mohammed Said took the leadership of the committee, on the ground that he had been appointed governor by the departing Jemal Pasha.

Although the events in Damascus were unknown to the Arab leaders outside, these had sent the Ruwalla horse forward into the city as soon as the twilight scrap near Jebel Mania was over, and had supported them with the Ruwalla camelry. Lawrence had dissuaded Nasir from entering himself, both because of the risk of a mishap in the dark and because a state entry at daylight would be more impressive.

Lawrence and Stirling finally rolled themselves up in blankets at midnight and lay down on the ground beside the "Blue Mist." For a time they talked—of this culmination of two years' effort. Then they tried to sleep, only to be startled by a series of heavy explosions and a reddening glare in the sky over Damascus. Raising himself on his elbows, Lawrence exclaimed, "Good God! They are burning the town." He felt sick at the thought that this goal of their endeavours might be reduced to ashes at the moment of its freedom, and as the price of its freedom. The possibility was like a symbolical portent—so had his own achievement turned to ashes. Yet to Stirling he showed no other trace of emotion and merely said, "Anyhow, I've sent the Ruwalla forward, and we should soon have four thousand men in and around the town."

The facts fell short of their fears, for the explosions came from the ammunition and store dumps that German engineers were blowing up as a parting act. And at dawn of October 1st, when Lawrence rode forward to the ridge overlooking the city he saw it not in ruins, but shimmering "like a pearl in the morning sun." As he drove down the road a horseman galloped up, and holding out a bunch of yellow grapes, cried, "Good news: Damascus salutes you." He was a messenger from Shukri. Lawrence at once passed the tidings to Nasir so that "he might have the honourable entry, a privilege of his fifty battles."

Nasir and Nuri Shaalan then rode into the city while Lawrence, to give them a fair start, stopped the car beside a little stream to wash and shave. He was interrupted by a patrol of Bengal Lancers who rushed up to take him prisoner.[1] Even when Stirling threw open his cloak and showed his British uniform, he merely received a prod from a lance for his pains, and it was not until they met an officer that they obtained release.

Then they were able to make their entry into Damascus through streets lined with people who at first stupefied at the change became the more deliriously excited the more deeply they penetrated.

The women of the harem leaned out of their overhanging windows, their veils thrown aside, and showered flowers and perfumes on the heads of their deliverers. In strange contrast, there were many

[1] Lawrence has commented to me on this incident as follows: "In the desert I shaved regularly. My burnt-red face, clean-shaven and startling with my blue eyes against white headcloth and robes, became notorious in the desert. Tribesmen or peasants who had never set eyes on me before would instantly know me, by the report. So my Arab 'disguise' was actually an advertisement. It gave me away instantly, as myself, to all the desert: and to be instantly known was safety in ninety-nine cases out of the hundred.

"The hundredth case was always the eventuality to be feared. If I saw it coming, I would get into a soldier's cap, shirt and shorts, and get away with it, or draw my headcloth over my face, like a visor, and brazen it out.

"No easterner would ever have taken me for an Arab for a moment. Only the Bengal Lancers, and similar innocent foreign soldiery, here and at Deraa, and in Egypt, and at Allenby's H.Q. They started the notion of my skill in disguise—which was nil."

Turkish soldiers who watched the entry as apathetically as they waited for capture—over thirteen thousand were found in the barracks and hospitals. "Pellagra—the disease of despair, was killing them by battalions."

At the town hall a sterner task awaited Lawrence. For, having made his way through an exuberantly demonstrative mob into the ante-chamber, he found Mohammed Said vociferously maintaining his right to the reins of office. Before Lawrence could deal with his pretensions a diversion was caused by a sudden wild fight between Auda and Sultan el Atrash, the chief of the Druses. When peace was at last restored and murder averted, the Algerian leaders had disappeared with Nasir for refreshment. So Lawrence, who had already decided in his mind to appoint Shukri governor, took him off in the "Blue Mist" on a ceremonial tour of the city, showing themselves to the populace. On the outskirts they met Chauvel's car. "I described the excitement in the city, and how our new Government could not guarantee administrative services before the following day, when I would wait upon him, to discuss his needs and mine. Meanwhile I made myself responsible for public order: only begging him to keep his men outside, because to-night would see such carnival as the town had not held for six hundred years, and its hospitality might pervert their discipline."

Chauvel did not seem to relish the idea of postponing his triumphal entry, but having no clear-cut instructions as to his course he yielded, like Barrow at Deraa, to the superior authority of Lawrence's "certainty," that quiet but resistless air of assurance which all who know him know so well.

He then went back to the town hall to deal with the Algerian usurpers. They had not returned, and when he sent a summons for their presence he received a curt reply that they were sleeping. He then told a relative of theirs that he would fetch British troops to search for them—"it was tactics only, not meant." When the man had gone back with this message Nuri Shaalan asked him quietly if the English were likely to come, to which Lawrence replied—"Certainly; but the sorrow was that afterwards they might not go." Nuri Shaalan reflected for a moment and then promised him the support of his Ruwalla. Soon the Algerian brothers appeared, full of menace, with their retainers. But they hesitated when they saw the superior weight of armed force that lay ready to do Lawrence's bidding. Then he, as deputy for Feisal, and for the ghost of Cromwell, pronounced their Government dissolved and appointed Shukri as acting military governor. Mohammed Said, violently denouncing him as a Christian and an Englishman, tried to appeal to Nasir, who seemed miserably uncomfortable in this unwonted political issue. Lawrence was unmoved. Then Abd el Kader burst into frenzied curses which Lawrence ignored so contemptuously that, maddened, the fanatical Moslem drew his dagger. But Auda saw the action and leapt forward with such tigerish fury that Abd el Kader hastily recoiled. He and Mohammed now saw the futility of further protest, and swept out of the chamber. "I was persuaded they should be seized and shot; but could not make myself fear their power of mischief, nor set the Arabs an example of precautionary murder as part of politics." Happy the statesman who has an historical sense to curb him.

As soon as the brothers had left, Lawrence turned the meeting to the consideration of constructive policy. "Our aim was an Arab Government, with foundations large and native enough to employ the enthusiasm and self-sacrifice of the rebellion, translated into the terms of peace. We had to save some of the old prophetic personality, upon a substructure to carry that ninety per cent of the population who had been too solid to rebel, and on whose solidity the new State must rest.

"Rebels, especially successful rebels, were of necessity bad subjects and worse governors. Feisal's sorry duty would be to rid himself of his war-friends, and replace them by the elements which had been most useful to the Turkish Government. Nasir was too little of a political philosopher to feel this. Nuri Said knew, and Nuri Shaalan." It is a tribute to Lawrence's historical understanding, and a triumph of knowledge over instinct, that he realized it first and most fully.

Under his urge and direction the frame of an administration was constructed. Sagely, the formation of a police force came first. Officers were appointed, districts allocated, provisional conditions of service determined. An Australian detachment, which had taken the surrender of the Turkish troops in barracks, sent guards to some of the public buildings, and thus helped to bridge the gap until the Arab regulars arrived to take over. If these, because of their relative slowness, had played little part in the defeat of the Fourth Army, they were invaluable for consolidating the position—politically.

The water supply also received attention, and steps were taken to cleanse the conduit, fouled by dead men and animals. The light supply came third, and that evening the streets were lit from the powerhouse, a potent sign of the return of peaceful conditions. Gangs of scavengers were formed by Nuri Said to clear the streets of the débris, material and human, of the Turkish retreat, as a first step towards combating the pestilential conditions that prevailed and restoring sanitation. Parties were also told off to prevent the burning stores from spreading their sparks into the city. And another danger was forestalled by curtailing the display of firearms.

Beyond these immediate dangers lay the shadow of hunger looming over the population. As first aid the food that could be salvaged from the Turkish stores was distributed to the destitute. Then the Arab force converted its transport animals to civil use so that supplies could be fetched from the surrounding countryside. More permanent provisioning depended on the railway, and urgent efforts were made to find and re-engage the staffs so that they might resume running as early as possible. The telegraph, too, was restored. And the currency. Notes were printed and new prices fixed. Another problem was that of finding forage to meet the needs of the Desert Mounted Corps. To this Lawrence was specially impelled by his fear that otherwise Chauvel might seize both forage and government.

By the following day the greater part had been arranged and great things achieved, if those who only saw the city then for the first time were naturally more conscious of the ragged edges. Of his own part Lawrence has told me, simply, "I got the other fellows to take a subject each and put it on its feet. There were three days of rush— with pits of silence intervening, and into them one fell unconscious." Stirling, who saw it from the outset, remarks—"A thousand and one things had to be thought of, but never once was Lawrence at a loss." In setting the wheels in motion Nuri Said's political gifts, Young's power of organization, Stirling's knack in handling men, were all invaluable, but Lawrence was the mainspring. The machinery of government was working, even though it creaked.

Before dawn on the 2nd there was a momentary clatter. Lawrence was awakened to hear the news that Abd el Kader was attempting a revolution with the support of his obedient Algerian followers and a section of greedy Druses, who were angered by Lawrence's refusal to reward their belated assistance and hopeful of compensating the loss of plunder.

Lawrence and the Arab leaders waited for daybreak, wisely preferring not to forfeit the advantage of superior weapons by becoming immersed in dark street scrimmages. At the first streak of light Nuri Said moved armed parties to the upper suburbs and carried out a drive that herded the rioters towards the centre. The Arab regulars swept the riverside parades with continuous machine-gun barrages. Only a few would-be revolutionaries were foolish enough to make contact with this lethal current. The rest broke up and fled along the side alleys. It was an effective way of dispersing a rebel band. Mohammed Said was then arrested and imprisoned; his brother escaped into the country.

Although sporadic looting continued, the attempted revolution was broken—without the need of accepting Chauvel's offer of troops. The consolidation of the new regime was helped by the return of Ali Riza, who took over from Shukri the reins of government.

With the passing of this emergency Lawrence was able to return to the task of organizing the public services. At midday he went, in answer to an appeal, to the Turkish barracks where he found two companies of Australians mounting guard over a charnel house. All the Turks capable of walking had been removed, but on entering Lawrence found the place littered with stinking corpses and with rows of dysentery cases dying in their own filth. Taking vigorous action, with such poor aid as he could muster, he brought a semblance of decency into the place and had the dead sorted out for burial in a trench.

When he returned next day the place and its inmates were in process of being cleansed, yet it was still so unpleasant that an army doctor, who apparently mistook Lawrence for an Arab attendant, abused him vehemently for permitting such an outrage on humanity. Lawrence, seeing the grim humour of the charge, gave vent to a strained laugh, whereupon the medical major smacked him in the face. And Lawrence took the buffet without protest, feeling so unclean from his part in the whole chain of events that one more stain could make little difference, but rather had a symbolical fitness.

His depression was the deeper because of a factor that had nothing to do with politics. In the haunting poem that prefaces the *Seven Pillars of Wisdom,* and again in the brief epilogue, he has confessed to a personal motive that, like a magnet, had drawn him along the road to Damascus. Death had outpaced him on the road, and brought the dissolution of his dream. Damascus was his, but Damascus was an empty pitcher, shattered on the well of his desire. This may explain the feverish energy with which he threw himself into the task of bringing order into Damascus, a work of creation that drowned chilling reflections.

Whatever flaws may subsequently have appeared in the new Arab State that he so briefly constructed, they arose from the nature of the materials rather than from the building. This had to be done quickly if it was to be done at all, and in its rapidity lies the remarkable feature of Lawrence's achievement. Other dictators and State-creators have had a foundation to build upon and time to repair their mistakes, time extending into years. He had twenty-four hours.

Yet on October 3rd when Allenby arrived in Damascus, Lawrence was able, in Stirling's words, "to hand over to him an ordered town purged of almost all trace of war, a government functioning with ease and rapidity, and a population filled with joy and relief at the passing of Turkish rule." His achievement was sealed and his audacious initiative justified when Allenby informed Feisal, who made his entry an hour later, that he was prepared to recognize the Arab administration of enemy territory east of the Jordan from Ma'an to Damascus inclusive.

When Feisal had left, Lawrence turned to Allenby with a personal request—the first he had made and his last. It was for permission to hand over his burden. Allenby demurred, wanting him to go on to Aleppo, but in the end his persuasion prevailed over Allenby's reluctance. On the following day he took his departure for Cairo. With peculiarly deep truth one may say that he shook the dust of Damascus off his feet.

It remained with him as a memory—"one of the clearest memories I have, the silky coolness of the Damascus dust, as it lapped over my sandals and powdered my feet. Those white deep paths, under the trees or shaded by the house walls were heavenly quiet and soft."

As Lawrence was travelling south, the Campaign was rolling on to Aleppo, two hundred miles distant. The 5th Cavalry Division reached the outskirts on October 25th, while an Arab force under Nasir and Nuri Said advanced on its right flank. A combined attack was arranged for next morning, but during the night the Arabs slipped into the town, and the Turks abandoned it. On the 29th the Arabs, by a fresh bound, captured Muslimiya station, the junction of the Baghdad and Syrian railways. The life-line was severed, and the Turkish Army in Mesopotamia isolated. Two days later Turkey was out of the war. Eleven days more, and then, on November 11th, Germany herself capitulated. That same day Lawrence arrived back in England, after four years' absence. It was an aptly timed arrival for the man who had counted for more than an army corps in "knocking away the props."

In the crucial weeks while Allenby's stroke was being prepared, and during its delivery, nearly half of the Turkish forces south of Damascus were distracted by the Arab forces; pinned east of the Jordan by the subtle feints and nerve-paralysing "needle-jabs" that Lawrence conceived and directed. Those Turkish forces comprised the 2nd and 8th Army Corps as well as the garrisons along the Hejaz railway between Ma'an and Amman; these together totalled some 2,000 sabres and 12,000 rifles. The ration strength appears to have been about three times as large, i.e., about 40,000–45,000 out of a total ration strength of 100,000 south of Damascus.

The most remarkable feature is that, with some relatively light assistance from Chaytor's force, these Turkish masses were paralysed by an Arab contingent that counted less than 3,000 men, and of which the actual expeditionary core was barely 600 strong.

As a consequence, Allenby was able to concentrate three army corps, totalling 12,000 sabres and 57,000 rifles, against the other half, approximately, of the Turkish forces. And, in the sector chosen for the decisive stroke, to concentrate 44,000 rifles and sabres, against 8,000—odds of more than five to one. The total British ration strength, including Indian troops but excluding Egyptian labour personnel, required to develop this striking force numbered over a quarter of a million men.

Even as thus expressed in a purely arithmetical form of comparison, it would be difficult to find in the whole history of war as extraordinary a case of economy of force in distraction. Small as was the detachment which exercised this immense distracting power, only a fraction of it was truly a detachment from the main British forces— even counting the Gurkhas and the Egyptians it numbered barely a hundred men. Retained with the army in Palestine this handful would have been merely a drop in the ocean. Sent into the desert they created a whirlpool that sucked down almost half the Turkish army; indeed more than half if, as is just, we count the 12,000 Turks cut off in the Hejaz.[1] And even this reckoning leaves out of account the Turkish troops in Southern Arabia.

What the absence of these numbers meant to the success of Allenby's stroke it is easy to see. Nor did the Arab operation end when it had opened the way. For in the issue it was the Arabs, almost entirely, who wiped out the Fourth Army, the still intact force that might have barred the way to final victory.

But beyond the arithmetical was, to use Lawrence's original classification, the biological factor. The wear and tear, the bodily and mental strain, that exhausted the Turkish troops and brought them to breaking point was applied by the Arabs, elusive and ubiquitous, to a greater extent than by the British forces—both before and during the final phase. The biological factor, however, embraces materials as well as men. And here the Arabs' influence was still greater—while the Turks were more vulnerable. The maintenance of the Turkish armies depended on the railway, and on its maintenance. The Arabs alone, through their elastic radius of action, could operate effectively against this weak foundation of the Turkish resistance. First, they executed a strategy of material attrition that came far nearer to using up the enemy's reserves than the strategy of physical attrition had done in other theatres. Then they severed the line of communication at the moment when it became the life-and-death line, when

---

[1] It was perhaps the crowning jest of the Arab Campaign, from Lawrence's point of view, that the garrison of Medina did not surrender until January, 1919. Even then it was only when Fakhri Pasha fell sick that his starving subordinates seized the chance to hand over to the Arabs the now helpless man whose soldierly spirit in holding on obstinately to Medina had done so much to lose the war for his country.

the fate of the enemy hung on this frayed threat. The Deraa demolitions were the death-knell.

But beyond the biological lies the psychological factor. In the profoundest sense, battles are lost and won in the mind of the commander, and the results merely registered in his men. It was primarily the Arabs, under the guidance of Lawrence's mind, who prepared the mind of Liman von Sanders so that he arranged his forces in the way that produced their defeat. That fateful delusion was not merely the triumph of a detachment but of "a war of detachment"—which created a mirage for the Turks' undoing.

BOOK IV

AFTER

CHAPTER XX

TROUBLES OF A MAN WITH A CONSCIENCE

THE War was won, the Turkish Empire overthrown, an Arab state inaugurated, and the possibility of an Arab Confederacy, even a new empire, created. All this had been achieved by the sword—or, to be more accurate, by the long-range bullet and blasting gelatine. Lawrence's military task was completed. The political task remained, although for his own part he had no desire to participate beyond securing fair play for the Arabs—the freedom to do what they wished with the gift he had done so much to bring them.

The wheels of the machine spatter its servants with grease. Those who serve an organization, whether it be a nation or a firm, can hardly hope to escape staining their honesty, bound to it as they are by ambition or self-preservation. Like the overwhelming majority, Lawrence had become stained in the course of his servitude. But he was different, in being more conscious of the stain. He was too clear-sighted for his own comfort. And he suffered accordingly.

Happy in his freedom from ambition, as commonly conceived; happier still in his freedom from the cares of livelihood, and from the ties that bind others to this concern, his mind was so uncommonly lucent that the stain had an iridescent persistency which he could never escape. I have never known a man more sensitive to the truth, from which mankind instinctively seeks protection in shaded glasses.

Thus for him to fight the Arabs' battle was a forlorn hope, spiritually even more than politically. To wipe out the stain was impossible, because it lay in his own consciousness. But he could at least pursue the atonement that was within possibility, not for his sake but for theirs. To this endeavour he now gave himself, despite his own sense of the ultimate futility of all such endeavour.

The purpose was imperilled by the Sykes-Picot treaty, now to be the insuppressible stumbling block, and by the expansionist ambitions that lay behind it. Those ambitions swayed both French and British action, yet with characteristic differences.

The French were guided by a logical policy emanating from Paris and with its roots in a retentive memory. Their claim to Syria went far back into the Middle Ages, being founded on the Latin kingdoms which the crusading wave had left like flotsam on the Levantine coast. During the World War their dislike of seeing an ally established on this ancestral soil seems to have been as strong a check as their preoccupation with the Germans on their own soil in limiting their contribution to the campaign against Turkey in Asia. This parsimony had cramped their representatives on the spot, although these sought to make up for their weakness by their activity—not merely in the political sphere, for it is just to recognize that Pisani's single battery in the Arab zone had more military influence than a hundred batteries in France.

But despite the apparent indifference which so exasperated poor Colonel Brémond, the directors of French policy never seem to have lost sight of post-war purposes from the moment when, in March, 1915, they had laid claim to Syria as soon as they heard that the Russians had put forward their claim to Constantinople. If the French marked time in the Levant while the war was continuing, they were ready to make their advance directly the victory was won, and to reinforce it both with military forces and with an elaborate development of their traditional claim to be regarded as the protectors of Christendom in the eastern Mediterranean as well as the modern protectors of Islam in the southern. It was, however, unfortunate that the Syrian Moslems regarded them as having been too protective in Algeria and Tunis.

If the French have the longest of memories, the British have the shortest. On the whole this has been an advantage, allowing adaptation of policy to reality. Yet it has certain inconveniences especially when dealing with people who do not so easily forget. Neither French nor Arabs were inclined to forget the somewhat contradictory assurances they had received from British representatives, and victory strengthened their memories as well as their appetites. Thus Britain was impaled on the horns of a dilemma. To satisfy one ally would mean not only breaking faith but also raising trouble with the other.

The dilemma might to a large extent be ascribed to a failure of foresight. For when the Arabs had been given assurances to the effect that they could keep what they conquered there had seemed little prospect of their carrying fulfilment so far. Indeed, it was in the summer of 1918 that the most definite pledge of all was given. For on June 11th, in reply to a Syrian memorial, the British Government announced that, in regard to any areas freed from Turkish rule during the war by the action of the Arabs themselves, they recognized the complete and sovereign independence of the Arabs in them, and supported them in their struggle for freedom. It is strange that so sweeping a declaration, without any of the 1915 reservations, should have been made at so late a stage in the war. Yet in June it may scarcely have appeared possible, especially to anyone who had not been in contact with Lawrence, that the trickle of Arabs then blocked before Ma'an could have spread like a flood through Syria by October, to occupy Deraa, Damascus, Beirut and Aleppo ahead of the British troops.

One may find more than a flavour of irony in the fact that the way to this unexpectedly great achievement, so awkward in its consequences, had been cleared by a British victory, and paved by an Englishman's genius for the leadership of native peoples. In earlier times the export of that kind of genius, which inevitably withers where bureaucracy spreads, had been responsible for bringing many new territories under Britain's imperial sway. But in the latest product a higher power of conscience was added to the old power of command, and it proved an imperial complication.

The position was also complicated by variety of views among Britain's counsellors. That healthy variety is advantageous in the long run, the secret of her endurance, but in the treatment of immediate problems its disadvantages are more manifest. While the British Government's policy had none of the clear-cut definiteness of the French, and carried even to excess its traditional opportunism, some representatives were inspired by the historic aim of extending British control over less civilized lands.

It is just to recognize that certain of these apostles of expansion were guided not by mere imperialism but by a reasoned belief in the benefits of British administration, as a means of assuring to the people as a whole a higher degree of justice than usually prevails in Asiatic communities. This is a point of view which has hardly received its deserts, being overshadowed on the one hand by the liberal idealization of nationalism, and submerged on the other by the hard-dying conservatism that still confuses largeness with greatness. Another factor which influenced the advocates of British control, especially in Mesopotamia, was a belief in the practical difficulties of setting up an effective Arab administration in immediate substitution for the Turkish.

But whatever their motives their hopes were threatened with shipwreck by the gust of "self-determination" which had travelled across the Atlantic and the high waves of nationalism that this was raising. The vessel was kept afloat for a time by strenuous efforts, only to be abandoned in the end. And in these efforts, unfortunately, England's honour had gone overboard. Rescue was delayed not only by the desire to cling on to Mesopotamia but also by the ill-considered step in the Sykes-Picot Agreement whereby the Mosul vilayet was placed in the French sphere. Thus, partly in order to preserve the unity of Mesopotamia, to the Arabs' future benefit, the British Government was drawn to sacrifice her pledge to uphold Arab sovereignty in Syria.

That situation developed slowly. The prospect had seemed bright and the Sykes-Picot treaty no more than a cloud on the horizon, when at the end of October, 1918, Allenby organized the military administration of the occupied territory, and divided it into three areas. "South," under a British administrator, embraced Palestine and tallied with the Sykes-Picot "Red" zone. "North," under a French administrator, was the Sykes-Picot "Blue" zone on the coast of Syria. "East" was a much longer and wider belt from Aleppo past Damascus down to Aqaba. It embraced the old "A" and "B" zones so far as they had been conquered by Allenby's forces. Fulfilling his promise to Feisal, Allenby placed this great belt under Arab military administration. Moreover, in deference to Arab susceptibilities, a small section of the old Blue zone south-east of Beirut was included in the eastern area.

Then, on November 7th, the French and British Governments issued a joint declaration that—

"The goal aimed at by France and Great Britain . . . is the complete and definite freedom of the peoples so long oppressed by the Turks, and the establishment of national governments and administrations deriving their authority from the initiative and free choice of the native population.

"In order to fulfil these intentions, France and Great Britain are agreed in the desire to encourage and assist in the establishment of native governments and administrations in Syria and Mesopotamia. . . . Far from wishing to impose on the populations of these regions such or such institutions, they have no other care than to assure by their support and practical aid the normal working of the governments and institutions which these populations have freely set up."

Whatever doubts there may be of its wisdom, this declaration alone suffices to justify Lawrence's oft-criticized course during the post-war settlement, and to condemn all those who in France or Britain strove for other aims. There could be no other course consistent with Britain's honour than to uphold the clear meaning of his declaration. Yet what a supreme irony it carries in the light of subsequent history!

Lawrence's departure from Damascus as soon as the military victory was secured gave him the chance to fight this battle for England's honour and his own, in the only place where it could be won. But he had not expected that it would come so soon—because he had not anticipated that Germany's collapse would follow quite so quickly on Turkey's. The immediate reason for his timely transition from East to West is best given in his own words, most characteristic —"I had finished—what better reason? The Arab Revolt and the Turkish War were also finished. What was in my mind as I went towards London was to begin again—as a junior officer—in France, learning the new way of war. The East was sucked dry. Never outstay a climax."

To expedite his journey to England he not only accepted but requested what might be called an "honour or reward"—the rank of full colonel. His disregard for such distinctions had become so notorious that his application caused amusement. This increased when he explained that he merely wanted the rank, and as temporary as possible, in order to travel home quickly through Italy on the special staff-train from Taranto. "Sleeping berths were given only to full colonels and upward. I travelled with Chetwode, with the local (Allenby-conferred) rank of colonel: and so was comfortable. I like comfort! Troop trains took eight days, and the *Wagon Lits* Express only three." He enjoyed referring to this brief promotion subsequently as his "Taranto rank." The jest gained further point from an incident which occurred there while waiting for the train. Seeing a major inflict what seemed to him a needless humiliation on two men for their neglect to salute, Lawrence used his own superior rank to give the major a lesson in military courtesy—after icily reminding the offender of the true meaning of the salute he ordered him to return the men's salutes.

After Lawrence's arrival he was summoned to a meeting of the Eastern Committee of the Cabinet to give his views on the future of the Arab countries. He proposed the creation of three Sherifian states, in Syria, Upper Mesopotamia, and Lower Mesopotamia, with three sons of King Hussein as their rulers. The suggestion was telegraphed out to Colonel A. T. (later Sir Arnold) Wilson, the Acting Civil Commissioner in Mesopotamia, who received it somewhat coolly and commented on it more hotly, misliking both the division of Mesopotamia and the removal of British administration.

Still more serious, if less frank, opposition was already preparing in French quarters. Picot had landed at Beirut on November 6th as "French High Commissioner in Syria and Armenia." On the 14th he telegraphed to Paris—"as long as the British Army occupies the country there will be a doubt in the spirit of the population, favouring those who are hostile to us. The only remedy is to send twenty thousand soldiers to Syria and ask England to hand it over to us . . . . If we hesitate . . . our position will be ruined in Syria as it has been in Palestine." Picot was already disgruntled because the Arab administrator of area "East" dealt directly with Allenby instead of through himself.

Then the French heard that Feisal was going to London at the invitation of the British Government—which they attributed to Lawrence's machinations. They sent a stiff message to Hussein, to say that Feisal would be received in France with the honours due to the son of an allied ruler but expressing their surprise that the passage had not been arranged through their representative. Brémond, now back in France, was ordered to meet Feisal. He was told by the French Foreign Office that he was to treat Feisal as "a general, a person of distinction, but not to recognize him in any diplomatic character." "With Lawrence, it is necessary to be very blunt, showing him that he is going the wrong way." According to Brémond's published account, the qualification was added—"If Lawrence comes as a British colonel, in English uniform, he will be welcomed. But we do not accept him as an Arab, and if he remains disguised we shall have nothing to do with him."

Feisal came on a British cruiser and was met by Lawrence. Brémond did not succeed in intercepting them until they reached Lyon, on November 28th. Feisal was promptly notified of the Government's attitude towards Lawrence, who accordingly decided to leave the same evening by train for England. Contrary to Brémond's statement, he had not worn Arab dress, so that Brémond must either have suffered a lapse of memory or have introduced the excuse to cover up the French Government's breach of courtesy.

Here one may add that the frequency of Lawrence's appearances in Arab dress has been much exaggerated. He wore it once to an evening party—for amusement; he wore it to be painted by Augustus John; he wore it when he accompanied Feisal to Buckingham Palace as his interpreter. His appearance shocked a certain person who in rebuke said—"Is it right, Colonel Lawrence, that a subject of the Crown, and an officer too, should come here dressed in foreign uniform?" Lawrence quietly replied—"When a man serves two masters and has to offend one of these, it is better to offend the more powerful. I've come here as interpreter to the Emir Feisal, whose uniform this is." In Paris he did not don Arab dress but wore an Arab headcloth with khaki uniform and British badges on a few occasions—to the Council of Ten, when interpreting for Feisal, and to be photographed with Feisal.

After a tour of the old battle-front, Feisal and his escort reached Boulogne on December 9th. The boat lay alongside the quay, and Lawrence was seen coming down the gangway to meet them. After saluting Feisal he gave Brémond a cordial invitation to accompany the party to England, adding the assurance that he would be well received. One perceives the tinge of ironical humour.

After showing Feisal round England Lawrence returned, like him but independently, to Paris in January for the Peace Conference. This time the French could no longer make objections to Lawrence's presence, as he had been appointed a member of the Foreign Office delegation for Eastern affairs. But they opposed Feisal's, and only gave way, Clemenceau overruling his subordinates, after British and

American intervention. Feisal had asked no more than to be admitted to the Conference as the representative of his father, who was recognized merely as King of the Hejaz. Even to secure this position had been difficult because of Hussein's jealous suspicion of his son's aims; Lawrence had to pull various strings somewhat strongly before, in mid-December, Feisal's nomination was obtained. And it was limited by the fact that Hussein's right to a voice in the future of Syria and Mesopotamia was not openly conceded.

But in reality the voice of Lawrence, who had constituted himself counsel for the Arab cause, carried penetratingly through the antechambers of Versailles, into the innermost chambers. His achievement was the more remarkable because the cause he was representing introduced a complication which no statesmen already enmeshed in a world-tangle could be expected to welcome.

On Lloyd George especially his arguments made an impression, helped by the British Prime Minister's instinctive sympathy towards the rights of small or submerged peoples. Although so different in their mental make-up, the two men came to appreciate each other. In Lawrence's view Lloyd George not only towered above the other statesmen at Versailles, but differed from almost all of them in having a real desire to do what was right, instead of merely playing for national advantage. This comment is the more worth mention because it strikes an unusual note. Again, such incidents as when Lloyd George asked where Teschen was, a question which has often been scornfully quoted against him, made a different impression on Lawrence than on others. For he has remarked to me that Lloyd George was the only man who would have asked such questions instead of pretending that he knew—and remaining ignorant.

On the other side, Lawrence's gift of clear exposition was keenly appreciated by Lloyd George, who had suffered much from official experts who cloaked their own superficiality of thought with diffuse explanations that were no better than ritualistic incantations. To Lloyd George, Lawrence set out not only the Arab problem as he saw it but also the solution he had in mind. If his main concern was to see Feisal established at Damascus as the head of an independent Syrian State, leaving the northern coast and the Lebanon to the French, he regarded the setting up of a similar state in Mesopotamia as the necessary complement, to avoid trouble no less than to render justice. The Arabs of the desert should retain their essential independence—of the new States and the old Powers alike.

But the French desire for control of Syria was the block across the approaches to such a solution, just as the British reluctance to relinquish Mesopotamia was the brake on all our efforts to induce the French to modify their attitude. There was a delusive ray of hope when an inter-allied commission was appointed to visit Syria, Palestine and Mesopotamia to report on the feeling of the people as to their future government. But the brightness of that honourable gesture was soon tarnished. The French took care not to appoint a representative, and although the American members went, their report was allowed to fade from neglect. Their verdict had been that a French mandate would be wholly unacceptable.

Although these were depressing months for Lawrence, they at least failed to wither his sense of humour—the Peace Conference was perhaps too fruitful of opportunities. Even in the thorniest soil shoots appeared. One of the most apt stories relates to Lawrence's meetings with Marshal Foch, who is said to have remarked—"I suppose now that there will soon be war in Syria between my country and the Arabs? Will you be leading their armies?" "Not unless you promise to lead the French armies in person. Then I should enjoy it." Whereupon Foch, wagging his finger at Lawrence, is supposed to have answered—"My young friend, if you think that I'm going to sacrifice the reputation that I've built up on the Western Front by fighting you on your ground, you are very much mistaken."

Unfortunately, the version that I have heard from Lawrence is more plain in its truth, and lacks the undertones of truth that make the other version so apt. Foch said to him in a jocular way, "When I have the pacification of Syria, I'll send Weygand." To which Lawrence retorted: "We'll be all right then—so long as you don't come yourself." This subtle touch of flattery reminds one of the classical story of the meeting between the two Great Captains of the Punic Wars, when Hannibal, asked by Scipio whom he deemed the greatest of all commanders, put Alexander first, Pyrrhus second, and himself third; and when asked "What if you had defeated me?" replied "Then I should have put myself first."

In making his analogous retort to Foch, Lawrence's courtesy or his classical sense suppressed his real impression. For he had doubted the depth of Foch's military knowledge ever since he had discovered, in his own far-reaching studies before the war, that much of the textbook that had made Foch's reputation as a military thinker was an unacknowledged "crib" from a German writer. And personal contact with Foch had completed his disillusionment—"In 1919 he was only a frantic pair of moustaches." Another comment which T.E. made when, a few years ago he heard I was engaged on a study of Foch's career, is too good to be omitted—"He was rather a drab creature, surely, with more teeth than brains. It was irony that made him the successful general of the last phase."

Among the highest military leaders Lawrence's admiration was reserved for Allenby, a tribute to character even more than to ability —"He was so large-hearted and clean-judging a chief that all we varied devils worked hard for him, without hardly leisure to see what a rotten gang we were (or the other fellows were). For actual tactics he depended for success on his staff: Guy Dawnay, first: Bartholomew lastly."

These like their chief had shown a capacity to profit by an experience of war such as no soldier in the standardized slaughter of the Western Front had enjoyed; there were several soldiers in Palestine who earned Lawrence's respect by developing a pre-nineteenth century quality of military art expressed in modern terms. Contrary to the popular picture, he has no scorn of the professional soldier as such; he recognizes the value of a professional technique in regular warfare, although he sees that a commander should also be versed in the higher sphere of war. His contempt is reserved for the regular who professes a knowledge he does not possess—and does not apply himself to acquire it. This outlook gives point to another story, a true story, about Lawrence at the Peace Conference. A certain general who later commanded on the Rhine, and of whom it is fair to say that his bark is worse than his bite, was nettled by Lawrence's assured manner in expressing his views, and burst out with the foolish rebuke—"You're not a professional soldier." Lawrence piercingly retorted—"No, I'm not, but if you had a division and I had a division I know which of us would be taken prisoner!"

The point is enhanced by the opinion that Allenby expressed when asked by Robert Graves if he thought Lawrence would have made a good general of regular forces—"A very bad general, but a good commander-in-chief, yes. There is no show that I would believe him incapable of running if he wanted to, but he would have to be given a free hand."

In Palestine Lawrence had been allowed a free hand by Allenby; in Paris he had to watch others undoing his achievement. To make it worse the right and left hands of British policy were pulling against each other. These internal divergences produced ironical effects. The Foreign Office sincerely desired a settlement that should fulfil our undertakings to both Arabs and French, and still cherished hopes of satisfying both parties. But Mesopotamia, the inevitable bargain-counter, lay under the hand of the Indian Government, and Foreign Office attempts to prompt the setting up of an Arab administration in Mesopotamia met with little welcome and less response. Such indirect and long-range pressure was easy to resist by the man on the spot, especially when he was such a determined personality as Arnold Wilson. Yet he did not perhaps realize that, whatever the practical advantages of his policy on the spot, they could only be secured at the wider expense of England's honour.

With the mill-stone of Mesopotamia round its neck, British states-manship was hopelessly handicapped in trying to obtain a modifica-tion of the provisions of the Sykes-Picot treaty. The French in-sisted on their full pound of flesh not only because of their hunger for new colonies but because they feared the repercussion on their old colonies in Africa if they conceded Syrian independence. The scales were weighted with dishonoured bonds when Feisal made his appeal to the Council of Ten, and he obtained no satisfaction be-yond carrying off the honours of debate. For when Pichon, the French Foreign Minister, discoursed on the Crusading pedigree of France's claim to Syria, Feisal pricked his eloquence with the quiet retort—"Pardon me, Monsieur Pichon, but which of us won the Crusades?" It was on this occasion that Lawrence, present officially as Feisal's interpreter, performed a *tour de force* by addressing the meeting in English, French, and Arabic by turns.

As the French stood fast, the British gave way. The urgency of greater issues afforded a convenient excuse for purposeful pro-crastination over the Middle East, whilst the new device of "man-dates," which the more cynical Arabs spelt "protectorates," served to put a polish on the purpose.

Thus abandoned to his own devices, Feisal postponed the end by coming to an arrangement with the French, or at least with Clemenceau—contrary to popular belief in England the "Tiger" was less rapacious than many of his jackals. In achieving this provisional agreement Feisal was momentarily helped by the difficulties of the French in Syria. They had become engaged in a veiled war with the undemobilized Turks, who were trying to repeat their Balkan war trick of stealing back during the Armistice the territory they had lost in war. And while the French were thus entangled on the Cilician border their position in Syria was becoming more and more uneasy. Even Picot was brought to realize the unpalatable fact, conveyed in a significant telegram to Paris, that "the absence of Feisal is encouraging the extremists." This confession reinforced the arguments which Lawrence had already put to Clemenceau, and produced the turn about by which Clemenceau, after having first repudiated Feisal, now offered to recognize the independence of Syria on condition that Feisal supported the interests of France.

Convinced that British support was no more than a reed, Feisal was constrained to accept this offer, much to the disgust of his father who, when he heard the news, regarded him as having bartered his soul for a mess of pottage.

It was partly in revulsion from this bargain with the infidel that Hussein took the fateful, and eventually fatal, step of proclaiming himself Commander of the Faithful, an act which immediately hardened the Imam and the Idrissi against him, and cause an explosion of wrath among the fanatical Wahabis which Ibn Sa'ud skilfully directed to Hussein's ultimate overthrow. Towards the end of May there was a foretaste of this disaster when Abdulla, reluctantly urged forward by his pride-blinded parent across the borders of Nejd, was taken by surprise at Turabah during the night. Out of a Sherifian force of some 4,000 men, only a handful escaped with Abdulla. The remainder were massacred with a ferocity which at least testified to the superior savagery of the Wahabis, and won them the respect which so many Englishmen are always ready to pay the "noble savage." Henceforth Hussein's tenure of Mecca was but a precarious survival, kept in existence only by Britain's dubious protection of an ally who was no longer an asset, and by Ibn Sa'ud's shrewd restraint. When the moment was ripe and the stem had withered, he would reach out for the apple.

There is a dignity which commands respect, if it leaves a sting, in the address which Hussein delivered to the Bedouin sheikhs at Mecca at the end of the year—"I have come to remark a great change-round of the Allies, and especially of France in favour of Turkey. Asia Minor, comprising Armenia, will remain Turkish, Syria is given to France in spite of our protests; our possession of Damascus is strongly disputed." "I listened to the faithless English, I let myself be tempted and won over by them. I have contributed to preserve their Moslem empire. Thanks to us, the route to India has remained open during the war. Egypt, which was watching our lead, restrained its aspirations and remained quiet. Thanks to us, the region of Damascus abandoned the cause of the Turks. Alas! I have always believed that I was working for the grandeur and unity of Islam. Things have turned out differently. Let us resign ourselves and not lose confidence in the most high God." "Let us unite our efforts and continue to work in common for the peace and security of the Hejaz."

That hope was virtually extinguished when the British discontinued the subsidies that had restrained Ibn Sa'ud from interference. Whatever his errors of judgment, Hussein had set an example of honesty which shines out in contrast with his environment. Perhaps the verdict of history may be that he was too honest to be a successful statesman.

Although Feisal had made his compact with the French from a sense of practical statesmanship that his father lacked, he seems to have had no illusions, when he returned to Syria in May, of the slenderness of his prospects or the strength of the desire which the French privily cherished. He told their representatives frankly, "I will accept your aid, but I will never accept enslavement."

After a year's uneasy grace his forebodings were fulfilled. In September, 1919, on a fresh visit to London, he was notified that the Government had arranged with the French to withdraw the British troops from Syria in November. He was advised to come to terms direct with the French—a course he had already anticipated. Nevertheless, he now realized better than ever the frailty of that arrangement and made one more desperate appeal to the British not to abandon him. It made an impression but produced no satisfaction. Mesopotamia was not only a barrier across the British path but a beam in the eye of Lord Curzon whose imperialism had long been irked by the policy which his own subordinates in the Foreign Office, as well as Lawrence, were advocating for Mesopotamia.

Thus when Lawrence, in a renewed effort on Feisal's behalf, suggested that the British Government should disclose their intentions regarding Mesopotamia, Curzon objected, and diverted attention by pointing out a mote in Feisal's eye—the surreptitious visit paid by certain Sherifian officers from Damascus to the tribes in Mesopotamia. The military authorities there suspected them of attempting to foment anti-British feeling. Whatever the truth in this charge, which Nuri Said warmly denied when questioned, there was palpable truth in the Sherifian officers' counter-complaint that the attitude of the British officers in Mesopotamia was utterly different from that of those they had known on the road to Damascus—the difference between distrustful rulers and friendly advisers.

Affairs drifted on to their sombre conclusion. The question of Mesopotamia's future government was referred to the Interdepartmental Conference in November which agreed that something must be done to meet Arab aspirations and that Sir Percy Cox was the right man to take over the reins from the existing military administration. But the War Office considered that this must continue until the question of a mandate was settled and peace with Turkey ratified. The latter, one may remark, took four years and nine months to conclude—nine months longer than the war had lasted. Sir Percy Cox, for his part, was naturally unwilling to assume charge until he had a free hand. More delays ensued.

In March, 1920, the Allied dovecots were fluttered by the news that an Arab Congress, meeting at Damascus, had proclaimed Feisal as King of Syria and Abdulla as King of Iraq. This move seems to have been inspired by a too flattering attempt to imitate the success of d'Annunzio's coup at Fiume. But the Arabs were soon taught that they were in another category from that of the Great Powers. Curzon promptly responded to the French request for concerted action, and a message was sent sharply repudiating the decisions of the Congress, and inviting Feisal to attend the Franco-British discussions that were to settle the issue. The sop had an unpalatable flavour.

The San Remo Conference in April served as the occasion for what a cynic might term "The Inter-Allied prize-distribution." The mandate for Syria was awarded to the French; those for Palestine and Mesopotamia to the British. The French formally relinquished their claim to Mosul.

There was an essential difference between the recipients in that the British Government was now moving, if all too slowly, towards giving the Mesopotamian Arabs a real share in the government of Iraq, while the new French Government, replacing Clemenceau's, was moving swiftly towards ousting the Syrian Arabs from control of Damascus.

In Iraq the British paid the penalty of delay when early in July the tribes on the Euphrates rose in revolt. The widespread outbreaks were not suppressed until late in the year, and they required the dispatch of large reinforcements from India. In that and the following year the British military expenditure in Iraq amounted to sixty million pounds. There is an interesting reflection in the fact that it cost us roughly six times as much to hold down the Arabs in Iraq during these two years as it had cost us to sustain the Arab Revolt against Turkey during a similar period.

In Syria, Feisal paid the penalty of French haste, when the possessors of the newly awarded mandate seized the first chance of repudiating the agreement that Clemenceau had made, and of installing themselves in Damascus. Even by the admission of the French High Commissioner's staff, Feisal had striven to moderate the bellicosity of the Arab extremists. Yet he was made the target of the ultimatum which the French dispatched on July 14th, at the appearance of armed resistance. It was in vain that he dispatched a message accepting the demands of the ultimatum—another fact confirmed by French evidence. The French forces had been set in motion by Gouraud, whose soldierly simplicity made him an easy lever for political schemers to handle. Once released they could not be retarded—history was given one more example of the familiar plea of military necessity. Gouraud's troops continued their advance, occupying Damascus on the 25th, and Feisal lost his throne. He took refuge in Palestine and thence made his way eventually to England on one more fruitless attempt to seek British intervention on his behalf. But the French soon had cause to regret his overthrow, for they involved themselves in troubles far more costly and prolonged than the British experienced in Iraq.

The expulsion of Feisal was the final draught of Lawrence's cup of bitterness, although long anticipation had in a sense diluted it. That anticipation, blended with his consciousness of personal dishonesty in the past, was the motive that had led him, when he saw the King after his return from the war, to ask that he might be relieved of his British decorations. All his own achievements, indeed, had but woven a crown of thorns that now pressed harder than ever upon his brow.

The fervour with which he fought the Arabs' battle in the Peace Conference was an effort to relieve that pressure. So was the writing of the *Seven Pillars of Wisdom,* the narrative of his physical and mental experiences during the Arab Revolt. Thereby he seems to have hoped to discharge from his mind the gases of his thought, while at the same time raising a memorial to a cause that seemed lost. But the relief from the discharge came later, and in their passage the gases caused a dangerous overheating.

CHAPTER XXI

THE "SEVEN PILLARS OF WISDOM"

HOGARTH had insisted that it was Lawrence's duty to history to compile a worthy memorial of the Arab Revolt. Lawrence yielded reluctantly, but, having once accepted the charge, he carried it through with the same terrific driving force he had generated in the campaign.

Rarely has a great piece of literature been produced under stress of so many distractions. It suffered also two narrow escapes from complete interruption. The first was at Rome, in an aeroplane disaster; the second at Reading, when merely changing trains. One came at the outset, the other when the end seemed in sight.

He had barely sketched the outline when he found the need of referring to his diaries and other papers, all of which had been left with his kit in Cairo. As by this time, the spring of 1919, Feisal's case had been heard and laid aside, Lawrence felt that he might take the opportunity of collecting his belongings from Cairo. General Groves, the British air delegate, offered him a passage in a squadron of Handley-Pages which was about to blaze the trail for future airways of Empire by flying out to the Middle East. Unfortunately the giant machines were in bad condition, suffering from hard usage and unskilled attention. In consequence they left a blazing trail—of casualties. Lawrence wrote the introduction to the *Seven Pillars* while flying down the Rhône valley, but had progressed no further when the advance machine in which he was travelling crashed at Rome, killing both pilots. Lawrence was more lucky than them in having a seat behind the engines, and he had firmly declined invitations to sit in front with them; through this prudence he escaped with three ribs and his collarbone broken. One of his ribs pierced a lung, which has ever since been liable to hurt him after heavy exertion.

It was by no means his only narrow escape from death in the air—he has told me that he was altogether in seven "write-off" crashes in two thousand hours' flying. This was his sixth; the seventh was in Palestine in 1921.

After two or three days in an Italian hospital he rang up his war-time comrade Francis Rodd, who was then at Rome where his father, Sir Rennell Rodd, was British Ambassador. Francis Rodd promptly arranged for Lawrence to be moved to the embassy, but after a few days in these comfortable surroundings he insisted on continuing the flight to Egypt with the remainder of the squadron. He was still encased in plaster when he left Rome, but the many further delays that the squadron suffered before it at last reached Egypt gave him ample time to recuperate.

Midsummer was past when he returned to Paris. Soon after his arrival he transferred his residence to the headquarters of the Arab delegation in a villa near the Bois de Boulogne and here settled down to his task. He has told me that he wrote in great bursts that lasted as long as twenty-four hours, with only a single break for food. During these sittings he averaged from a thousand to fifteen hundred words an hour, and in the longest wrote over thirty thousand words. Between the bursts there were long intervals, employed in revision.

For his writing was a composite process, of three phases. During the bursts he drafted his narrative from memory, writing only on one side of each sheet of paper—he used a large loose-leaf ledger of un-ruled sheets. Then he referred to his diaries and notes, and rewrote his narrative on the opposite pages with the aid of this historical check. Lastly, he undertook a literary revision and "planed it off into one smooth run." The process took almost as many days as the original draft had taken hours.

Yet the book, of ten "books," was almost finished when he left Paris at the end of the summer. He had been demobilized in July, but as he was already attending the Peace Conferences in a civil capacity, it made no difference save by relieving him of the fetters of uniform—which he had always worn lightly. In November he was elected to a seven years' research fellowship at All Souls College, Oxford, for the purpose of writing something on the history of the Middle East. This fellowship was intended as a means of enabling him to complete his book. He did not, however, go into residence but continued to work at it in Barton Street, Westminster, where his friend Sir Herbert Baker had allowed him a room on the top story of his office.

Then, just before the end of the year, he took the bulk of the manuscript with him on a trip to Oxford, carrying it with other belongings in a bag of the kind that bank or government messengers use. Having to change trains at Reading, he went to the refreshment room, put the bag under the table—and forgot it when he went to catch his train. As soon as he reached Oxford he telephoned back to Reading, but the bag had disappeared. No trace of it has ever been found—T.E. hopes now it never will be.

Even at the time of the loss his first reaction was one of relief and he joyously told Hogarth, "I've lost the damned thing." But Hogarth who, together with Meinertzhagen and Alan Dawnay, had read the manuscript in whole or part, was greatly upset at the news and vehemently insisted that Lawrence must settle down to write it afresh.

The demand imposed an ordeal from which any writer might have shrunk—the fear of such a loss is the phobia of many authors—but Lawrence overcame his repugnance and recovered the lost ground rapidly with the aid of his photographic memory, assisted by his outline diaries. Sitting in his attic in Westminster he worked in prolonged bursts as at the original drafting. By the spring of 1920 the eight lost "books" had been rewritten, the surviving two revised, and the book completed.

This stupendous effort was not inspired by the normal cause of such haste—the desire for early publication. T.E.'s primary purpose in writing seems to be the evacuation of his own mind, rather than the nourishment of others—in his own time at least. He has written three books, only one of which has been published. Before the war he wrote a book based on his travels in the Near and Middle East, only to destroy the manuscript. That book, incidentally, was also christened the *Seven Pillars of Wisdom*, a title drawn from the 9th chapter of the Book of Proverbs—"Wisdom hath builded her house: she hath hewn out her seven pillars." The passage continues—"She crieth upon the highest places of the city, Whoso is simple let him turn in hither . . . Forsake the foolish and live . . . If thou be wise, thou shalt be wise for thyself."

The pre-war book was descriptive, with an underlying moral; from the post-war book a philosophy emerged. The first dealt with the life of seven cities; the second was a sepulchre to hold the ashes of a life that was past, but from which wisdom had passed on.

It seems to have been a combination of this memorial sense with his artistic sense that led T.E. eventually to produce the book. But there was a long interval between the second rewriting and production. Still dissatisfied with the style he not only pruned and polished the manuscript but continued a study of literary technique that was characteristic of his thoroughness. He sought to obtain from his numerous literary friends, who included some of the greatest masters of English prose, an explanation of their principles and method of composition. He admits that the result was somewhat barren and that although he found a common "attitude," there was small evidence of a conscious technique, save among amateurs. Thus the technique which he himself developed was evolved mainly from his own theorizing—it gradually became so much part of himself that even his casual letters are artistic productions.

By the light of this self-evolved theory he revised his draft during 1921 and 1922, while in the East and in London. When the new draft was finished he burnt the old, with the aid of paraffin and a blow-lamp, in Epping Forest—a tedious process, he confesses. A few pages, the only relics that remain, were bound up in the new manuscript. Of this he then had eight copies (five of which survive) printed verbatim at the *Oxford Times* Press. He had them printed merely because it seemed as cheap as to have them typed—the total cost for some 330,000 words, two columns on a page, was about eighty pounds. And to guard against any chance of extra copies being preserved, he sent sections to press in "haymaking order"—intermixed. The eight copies, he reckoned, would suffice for his friends who desired to read the complete record. But the circle of friends who had this desire was wider than he had reckoned, and their pressure put a greater strain on his intention than he could resist, when combined with his innate love of beautiful printing—typography had for him no less an appeal than topography.

The decisive impulse came from Gertrude Bell who, having read the book, craved to possess a copy, and urged him to consider printing the book privately for his friends. He consented, not only to oblige them but because such a course would enable him to give the same care to the book's production as to its writing. The price was to be thirty guineas a copy. Thus the term "friends" became enlarged

AQABA

to include the wealthy friends of his friends. And as subscriptions flowed in, his vision expanded. He could produce a volume finer even than he had contemplated, and he arranged that a group of artists under Eric Kennington's direction would illustrate it. Thus the cost rose by degrees to ninety pounds a volume. Rather more than a hundred were printed for subscribers besides those, all imperfect in some small detail, intended for presentation to his friends and wartime comrades, at a total cost of some thirteen thousand pounds.

His own resources were quite inadequate to meet such an outlay, but friends backed the venture, the lead being taken by Robin Buxton, who had commanded the Camel Corps at Mudauwara and was now a director in Martin's bank. To cover the inevitable debt that the limited edition would now incur he arranged with Buxton that a public edition of reduced content should be printed.

All these developments and arrangements consumed time, and Lawrence needed time for the further re-writing he now undertook. While he did not add any fresh material, he made extensive textual changes, guided by the stylistic aim of achieving greater conciseness and a perfected shaping of the sentences. He also cut out one or two stories. The effect was to reduce the book by fifty thousand words.

This hypercritical revision was a lengthy process, all the more so because it had to be carried out in his leisure time as a private in the Royal Tank Corps at Bovington, 1923–24, and subsequently in the Royal Air Force at Cranwell. It was here also that he prepared the abridged version, published under the title of *The Revolt in the Desert*. The task was carried out in a couple of evenings, with the aid of two fellow-airmen, by the simple process of cutting out the more intimate passages of self-revelation and experience, and linking the jagged ends loosely together.

The *Seven Pillars of Wisdom* was eventually issued in 1926. Some of the copies changed hands at extraordinary prices, one at least being offered for sale by a bookseller at £700. *The Revolt in the Desert*, which appeared in 1927, rapidly ran through five reprintings, but as soon as Lawrence heard from his publishers that the overdraft was ready to be cleared, publication of the English edition was stopped. Even so, the sales, swelled by those in America that had still to be credited, brought in royalties that not only recouped the debt on the *Seven Pillars* but left a large balance.

To the regret of his friends, T.E. would not touch a penny. By an arrangement he had made before publication these profits were disposed of by a trust. One may add that in connection with the object his irrepressible sense of humour took a part. So it did also in his original demand that the French translation should bear an inscription saying that the profits would be devoted to "the victims of French cruelty in Syria."

His reason for rejecting all personal profit and honours sprang partly from his fastidious sense of honesty, and partly from an acute sense of policy. The two motives seem so subtly blended that it is difficult to separate them. He had pursued an ideal; he would soil its memory if he accepted any personal recompense. He had also been the paymaster of a people, and he knew well that his bags of gold had served not merely as a maintenance but as a bribe. In such conditions the only way he could feel clean, in motive at least, was to cleanse himself of every particle of personal advantage. And by doing so he would greatly strengthen himself towards achieving his impersonal aim.

I remember him saying that having "posed as a sea-green incorruptible" he must be consistent in maintaining the pose. It was a pose for a purpose. But although he would contend that it was purely practical, in the deeper sense, the explanation does not seem to me to go deep enough. If he has carried his renunciation of profit to what seems a fantastic extreme, it has been because of the keenness of his inward perception. He could see spots that others would miss, and to satisfy himself was far more difficult than to satisfy the world. That personal sense of honour, moreover, was allied to a care for his country's honour. The nearest approach to condemnation of others that I have ever found him make is when he speaks of Englishmen who were not above taking presents from the people they were sent to assist. T.E., in fact, is a "Crusader"—of peculiarly unhistorical purity.

His view of the *Seven Pillars of Wisdom* as literature is affected by this same habit of playing to bogey, of competing only against a self-created standard. Hence the praise that others have bestowed on its splendid prose, as well as on its descriptive and analytical power, brings little or no satisfaction to him. He was both amazed and amused, however, by the comment of H. G. Wells that it was a great human document, without pretensions to be a work of art. T.E. remarks that it had "enormous pretensions." His own criticism is the opposite—that the book is not a human document like Xenophon's *Anabasis* but an artificial straining after art. He also terms it a "depressing" book, without any message.

For my part I would admit that it is depressing in a double sense. It sets a standard of sustained effect, in paragraph after paragraph, that makes another writer acutely aware of his artistic deficiencies. It makes the obscurities of human vision more depressingly obvious than could the bitterest indictment—T.E. is hard only on himself. The clearness of his light not only shows up the dust on the window pane, but makes this seem the irremovable encrustation of age. Thus to a conviction of futility it adds a sense of finality.

The message is there, but it is too painful to contemplate, even for the author. In concluding it he closed his life as T. E. Lawrence. The *Seven Pillars of Wisdom* bears no author's name on the title page. The reason was a characteristic one—that it looked "cleaner" —his name was printed on the original title page but he rejected it in proof. Nevertheless there is a symbolic significance in the omission of his name. So also is there a symbolic fitness in the fact that the copies were initialled "T.E.S." not "T.E.L."

In that symbolism one may find a message of inspiration that is missing in the book. It remains as a graven pillar, but the wisdom has continued life in his new life. That fact refutes his implicit conclusion that nothing is worth while. He is the message, not his book.

CHAPTER XXII

FULFILMENT

"For wisdom is better than rubies, and all the things that may be desired are not to be compared to it. . . ." (PROVERBS VIII. 2.)

"WHY has Lawrence chosen to go in the ranks of the Air Force?" "How can a man of his gifts waste them in such humdrum work—surely he could find a better opening?" "Why doesn't he at least take a commission?" "How can a man of his intellectual interests endure the drabness and discomfort of barrack-room life?"

These are the questions that always spring forth whenever and wherever his name is mentioned. To answer with certainty is impossible, but in the course of discussion as well as through the evolution of one's own thought a perception of the probable explanation has come.

The most general idea—it has the wide currency of a legend—is that Lawrence condemned himself to servitude in the ranks as a kind of penance for his failure to secure the Arabs what he had promised them; that he sought by this degradation to wipe out the stain on his honour, or, quixotically, to make a personal atonement for his country's breach of faith. His friends usually scout such a suggestion. I do not, entirely. There may be a masochistic strain in him, liable to gain strength as he loses strength in periods of abnormal strain. But if so, I am convinced that it is only a minor part of the explanation, and that if it had any influence on his original act of enlistment, it has none on his continuance in the ranks of the Air Force.

I believe that his renunciation is predominantly due, not to an idea of atonement, still less to a sense of failure, but to a sense of fulfilment, reinforced by a sense of futility.

His remarkably developed sense of proportion, and sense of humour—the second implies the first, but may go further—were, I conceive, blended elements in his decision. For the first, by giving a clear view of real values tends to produce an extreme disdain of worldly values, and the second finds exercise in correcting them—by means the more subtle as the sense of humour is the more profound.

One aspect of T.E.'s sense of proportion is a love of real power that, with nourishment, produced in reaction such a passionate repudiation of the pomps and vanities of power as to become itself almost a vanity.

There was a further element that should not be overlooked in analysing the sources of the step that has surprised the public. I am sure that T.E. himself did not overlook it when weighing his future in the scales of his judgment. His self-perception was too sensitively acute for him not to be aware that the strain he had undergone had over-strained the delicate balance of his mind. The finer the adjustment, the finer the margin.

This compound explanation may become clearer if one briefly sketches the course of his career from 1920, subsequent to the expulsion of Feisal from Damascus.

It was not until after he had finished the second re-writing of his book in 1920 that Lawrence took full advantage of his fellowship and went into residence at All Souls. Then, unfortunately, in his case the disadvantages became more apparent. He has always been able to command good talk, but only in solitude could he work, and this he could no longer command at Oxford. The mysterious undergraduate who shunned company in pre-war days had now the magnetic attraction of a legendary figure—for visitors to Oxford, even more than for members of the University. He says that the only thing he succeeded in writing during his months in residence was the introduction to the new edition of Doughty's *Arabia Deserta*.

Moreover, he could better afford the time that these visitors occupied than the money their entertainment cost him. The slender stipend of a research-fellowship—it has since been improved—might be a useful supplement for a young graduate of private means, but it was inadequate for the unavoidable expenses that Lawrence had to meet. Two hundred pounds a year did not enable him to show hospitality and keep a decent appearance. For the first time since boyhood, lack of money became a burden. The debit margin was not large, but it made all the difference between ease and inconvenience. He has several times remarked to me that the ideal, for a single man of his tastes, is to have an assured income of £300 a year—"enough for a place in town and country." But Oxford was neither, and even if the margin had been covered I doubt whether he would have chosen to remain there. It did not offer the variety of humanity or the simplicity to suit his taste. His idea of a town and a country residence was a secluded attic in a pleasantly active quarter of London, and a primitive cottage in the rural depths of England. Residence at Oxford overtaxed his income without fulfilling his needs.

Relief came through a new opportunity of service to the old cause. Materially it was temporary, spiritually, it was lasting.

As the year 1920 drew to its close, events were vindicating Lawrence's repeated warning of the dangers of playing fast and loose with national aspirations in the Middle East. A too inelastic adherence to our old Imperial policy and a too supple interpretation of our assurances had involved us in widespread trouble. At home the post-war boom was followed by a slump that, in reaction, raised an outcry to cut our loss and "clear out" of the new mandated territories.

At a meeting with Lloyd George, Lawrence discussed the mess and Curzon's responsibility for it, suggesting that the only way to straighten it out was to relieve Curzon of responsibility. As Lloyd George made it clear that he could not remove Curzon from the Foreign Office, the alternative was to remove the Middle East from him. This possibility, once planted in Lloyd George's fertile mind, soon fructified. The Colonial Office was a suitable department to take over control, if provided with an adequate head—the man counted more than the Ministry.

Winston Churchill, then the occupant of a post-war War Office, was offered the Colonial Office with an extension of its responsibilities. He consulted Lawrence on the problem of the Middle East. Lawrence, while anxious to see him accept the charge, frankly warned him that success would depend on a readiness to take risks—in particular to make an Arab King in Mesopotamia, and evacuate the British troops, handing over its defence to the Air Force, a less obtrusive and more economic type of foreign garrison than an Army. On such conditions Churchill might hope for success—a success, although Lawrence did not say it, that would not only ease Britain's troubles and safeguard the future, but enhance Churchill's prospects of attaining the Exchequer, the goal of his dreams. A chance to wear his father's robes.

As history relates, Churchill accepted the office and attained both goals. The old division of responsibility between the Foreign Office, India Office and War Office was superseded by a single control of Middle East affairs, centred in the new Middle East Department of the Colonial Office. Here Churchill gathered round him a picked band of assistants, drawn both from within the Civil Service and from outside. Among them were two prominent participants in Allenby's campaign—Meinertzhagen and Young. And Lawrence was made Political Adviser.

He accepted the post on the understanding that the wartime pledges made to the Arabs on Britain's behalf would now be honoured as far as lay within Britain's power. He also asked and was promised free access to the Secretary of State, with permission to give up his post when he wished. When the question of salary was raised, he suggested £1,000 for a year, at which Churchill remarked that it was the most modest thing he had ever been asked, and made it £1,600—Lawrence, however, did not spend it on himself.

The agreement was completely fulfilled, and the unity of action attained. Only once was there even a surface breeze—when Churchill's cherished bust of Napoleon provoked T.E. to a laudation of Lenin's supreme greatness that successfully "drew" his master. The happiness of their personal relations, the keenness of intellect that was common to both, and Lawrence's freedom from all personal ambition, helped to make their official relationship a partnership. And in little more than a year, the partnership achieved their public ambition.

Syria had been swallowed by the French, but Trans-Jordan remained, and more important, Mesopotamia. Even before the war, Lawrence had come to the conclusion that the ultimate focus of Arab nationality, and its future, lay in Mesopotamia, potentially richer and greater than Syria. He could thus more easily adjust his immediate aims to his long view.

The new Department came into existence in February, 1921, and in March, Churchill, Lawrence and Young went out to Cairo for a conference which was attended by the principal political and military officers of the Middle East territories, as well as by prominent representatives of the War Office and Air Ministry. The vital issues, however, were all arranged before the conference was staged. Under Churchill's masterly handling, the conference served to confirm the decisions, and fill in details.

Feisal, thrown out of one kingdom by the French, was given another in Iraq by the British. His election by the people was as free as elections in England. He arrived in Iraq in June, and was crowned in August, his own charm and Sir Percy Cox's tact smoothing the passage. The British Government gave formal recognition to what they had privately decided. It had previously been settled that after Feisal's enthronement, a treaty should be framed, by which Iraq's sovereignty should be reconciled with Britain's mandate.

This treaty, duly negotiated, paved the way for Iraq to attain a state of independence friendly to the interests of Britain and fulfilling the conditions of civilized government as stipulated by the League of Nations. The wisdom of Sir Percy Cox in placing himself from the outset in the position of an adviser instead of a controller, smoothed the way for theory to become fact in the progressive transfer of administration from British to Arab hands. And Feisal's honourable observance of the spirit of the original agreement made possible the progressive realization of the bold conception. If there have been losses in the process they are outweighed by the solid fact that Britain has been enabled to redeem her honour and to give a shining proof that the idea underlying a mandate could be fulfilled both in spirit and letter.

Lawrence's honour was also redeemed and his sense of failure replaced by a sense of fulfilment. He had gained for the Arabs more than he had originally hoped—then he had scarcely expected that the British would part with Baghdad, still less Basra. He had gained the Arabs the chance to stand on their feet; to use their opportunity according to their lights and their talents. He could do no more. Only responsibility could develop a sense of responsibility—so profound a psychologist had no need to learn by experience this elementary truth.

His satisfaction was not due to an anticipation of early perfection. He expected that the new-born Arab State would have to suffer its growing pains. Indeed, he knew so well the essential individualism of the Arab that he had no great confidence in the ultimate issue, although he saw possibilities that encouraged him in forwarding them. Twelve years' experience had at least gone further to justify his hopes than the prophecies of early disaster in which others indulged. But, above all, there was "a promise to be kept." If there was a risk in fulfilling it, there would be more lasting evil for Britain in dishonouring her bond.

The creation of an Arab state in Iraq, sympathetically linked with Britain, was his main aim, but not the only achievement. It was an additional satisfaction that the same stroke of the pen which secured the Arabs their opportunity, presented the Air Force with its opportunity. Political wisdom is best produced when historical and psychological knowledge are blended—as they were in Lawrence. If responsibility was the way to maturity for a person or a people, so it might be for the service with which he believed the future lay.

Another achievement was unpremeditated—the establishment of Abdulla in Trans-Jordan. The Arabs there were already restive, and a looming threat to Palestine, when a further complication was introduced by Abdulla's initiative in moving up to Amman with a view to repaying the French for his brother's expulsion. The news caused alarm in Jerusalem and Cairo. The difficulties of turning him out by force were manifest—the Trans-Jordan tribes might rise in his aid, and the British had no troops to spare. Yet if he were allowed to pursue his purpose, and to conduct operations against the French from the British Zone, the French would have serious grounds for complaint. A solution was found by improvising a principality—a solution that reversed the decision of the Cairo Conference.

From past knowledge of Abdulla, Lawrence judged that he could easily be persuaded into the paths of peace if it was obviously expedient. With Churchill's approval, Lawrence flew to Amman and brought Abdulla back by car to Jerusalem, whither Churchill had come to meet Sir Herbert Samuel. In half an hour's talk on the Mount of Olives Churchill received so clear an impression of Abdulla's good sense and political sagacity that he forthwith took the momentous decision to leave Abdulla in Trans-Jordan, as head of a semi-independent Arab State, on condition that he refrained, and restrained his future subjects, from interfering with the French in Syria. Thereby, yet another plank in Lawrence's original platform was put in place, if in a different order to the original plan.

That same summer of 1921, Lawrence also made an effort to keep in place the parental trunk. In June he went to Jidda to offer Hussein a treaty that would serve as a life-buoy, to secure him the Hejaz, on condition that he renounced his perilously provocative claim to overlordship of the other Arab lands. But Hussein clung obstinately to his self-conferred prerogatives and thereby sealed his own fate. Lawrence relieved the tedium of indefinite arguments in Jidda's summer heat by occasional cables phrased with a Shakespearean pungency that shocked Curzon's highly developed sense of diplomatic dignity.

A story has been published that when Hussein failed to get his own way he threatened a drastic solution of the deadlock by calling for his sword and saying—"In these circumstances, Colonel Lawrence, there is only one thing for an honourable man to do." To which Lawrence is supposed to have replied, with a bow of profound respect: "In that case, Your Majesty, I shall carry on these negotiations with your successor." Unfortunately it is another of the many stories that are apt without being true. The truth is less extreme as well as less picturesque. Lawrence has told me—"King Hussein used to threaten to abdicate. I wished he would, but was never funny about it. The old man was a tragic figure in his way: brave, obstinate, hopelessly out of date: exasperating."

Hussein's politically suicidal self-determination to interfere with other Arabs was the one blemish on Lawrence's satisfaction. Otherwise, he felt that the utmost had been secured, not only for the Arabs in general, but for those Arabs who had been his comrades in war. He had, too, the conviction that what had been settled would free his own country from the millstone that shortsighted ambitions had hung round her neck. In salvaging her honour, her money also was saved—sixteen million pounds in the first year.

In gaining for the Arabs the free disposal of their future, Lawrence had gained this also for himself. The settlement was his "outlet"— there is significance in the term which he habitually uses. It let him out of public affairs and out of the life of "Lawrence."

By early 1922, it seemed to his clear sight that the critical stage was safely passed. So, on completing a year of service in February, he asked for his release. Churchill protested strongly, and in grateful deference to his wishes, Lawrence agreed to stay on until he could be spared, and in the meantime, declined any further salary. At last, in June, tired of waiting for the word that would release him, he announced his definite decision to leave, telling Churchill— "There'll be no more serious trouble for at least seven years." The prophecy caused scornful laughter in several quarters when reported, but time justified it.

On leaving the Colonial Office, T.E. spent a few weeks in doing "nothing at all except tramp London." Then he took the step that has amazed the public more than his war achievement.

For in August he enlisted in the ranks of the Royal Air Force. And for this purpose he took the name of Ross—it was casually suggested by an officer in the Air Ministry, who was in his confidence. It had the practical convenience of being late in alphabetical order, so that he did not have to hurry for pay parade!

There is a palpable irony in the fact that, after such determination to free himself from government service, he should have promptly re-entered it. But it may seem less strange if we remember that he had left a position of high responsibility to return in a status of irresponsibility. Low-grade employment in civil life may offer equal freedom from ruling other men's fate, but not from material cares. Nor does it offer the same interest that Lawrence found in Air Force work. The monastic life may offer equal freedom from both material cares and mental decisions, but it circumscribes the freedom of the critical spirit. Allowing, however, for the difference between the modern and the mediæval mind, it may be near the truth to say that T.E. went into the Air Force for the same reason that some of the most thoughtful men of the Middle Ages went into a monastery. It was not a sudden decision, but had been his intention since the last year of the war. He had been delayed in fulfilling it because of the three years' delay in settling Arab affairs. Back in 1919 he had told Sir Geoffrey Salmond of his desire to join the Air Force, whereupon Salmond had suggested that he should become his assistant in Egypt. To this, T.E. had quietly but emphatically replied, "I mean to enlist."

His mediæval forerunners went into a monastery, not only in search of a refuge, but in support of a faith. T.E. had the same dual motive in entering his modern monastery. In his belief, the utilization of the air was "the one big thing left for our generation to do." Thus everyone "should either take to the air themselves or help it forward."

At first glance, this attitude is not easy to reconcile with his constant refusal to accept any promotion. "Why doesn't he take a com-

mission?"—is a frequent question. The answer he once gave me was
that he did not mind obeying foolish orders, but that he had an
objection to handing them on to other men, as he would have to do
if he took any commissioned or non-commissioned rank. The remark
despite its flippant ring had a serious basis. In war such orders often
result in the useless sacrifice of men's lives. In peace, they often contribute to the sterilization of men's reason. And they inevitably make
the man who transmits the order an accomplice in the crime, however unwillingly. Fortunately, few of the transmitters have the sensitiveness of perception to feel their responsibility. But T.E. has. Thus
for him there are only two suitable posts—the topmost or the
bottom-most. Of the two, he prefers the latter, because of his strong
dislike of interfering with other men's freedom. There is, however,
a third position—that of counsellor unseen, and this, I think, he has
a reviving readiness to fill, now that he has recovered from the exhausting strain from which he was suffering at the time of his enlistment. But how far he is used in this capacity depends on those
who hold power, for he will never force his advice on them.

I think there is no doubt that he welcomes, and enjoys, the opportunity of influencing the course of events, of deciding policy and
directing action without the appearance. His dislike of the pomp of
power is due not only to its waste of time, but to its hypocrisy. He
has a horror of the conscious sham that outward authority entails on
all its holders who are sufficiently intelligent to realize their hollow
insincerity. He perceives how much of the time of the rulers of mankind is consumed in social and ceremonial exercises, time which
might be spent in gaining the knowledge on which to take their
fateful decisions. Also the subtle poison that such exercises spread
through their systems. Ceremony may be a necessity in dealing with
the ignorant and superstitious masses, but it is a moral cancer in the
man who performs it. The rites of civilized authority differ only in
degree from the witch-doctor's incantations.

Lawrence had the chance of filling one of the most important
posts in the British Empire. He did not refuse outright, but proposed
a condition that made his appointment officially impossible—a freedom from living in formal state. He would have left his official residence empty and, taking a quiet room somewhere, would have run
to and fro on his motor cycle, circulating among the people as much

as possible. In his opinion the value of pomp is greatly overrated in our imperial system—Haroun al Raschid is a better guide than Curzon.

His original spell of service in the Royal Air Force was spent at the Uxbridge depot. For months he hid his identity successfully—if he had to use his wits and his wit to throw questioners off the scent without actually violating the truth. Thus at the first inspection by the Commanding Officer he was asked what he had been doing before enlistment; he replied that he had been working in an architect's office. He had, at Barton Street. Then came the more awkward question as to why he had joined the Air Force; to this he replied— "I think I must have had a mental breakdown, sir." This was not so adroit, for he had some difficulty in persuading an offended superior that he was not implying that enlistment in the Air Force was an act of insanity. But as an explanation, it contained a profound truth, although not the whole truth.

In accounting for his proficiency with a rifle his sense of humour came to his aid, when he stated that he had done some big-game shooting. Turkish officers of high rank, such as Jemal Pasha's Staff, might reasonably be so described. The educational test was another fence, and here he took the instructor into his confidence—up to a point. T.E. was not the first man of University education to be driven by circumstances to enlist later.

To this Education Officer's consideration, T.E. owed some of his more pleasant hours at Uxbridge.

It was not a pleasant place at the time. The note that was sounded at the top, echoing downwards, did not tend to produce a good state of morale, as he emphasized at the time in a diary which he maintained throughout the experience. These notes were added to later, at Cranwell, where the atmosphere was happy; but they remained notes without any attempt at formal composition. Incidentally, in reproducing barrack-room conversations they "out-joyce" James Joyce.

Mr. Jonathan Cape years later learnt of the existence of this manuscript diary, which T.E. prefers to the *Seven Pillars of Wisdom* as writing, and suggested that it might fulfil a clause in his contract for *Revolt in the Desert,* giving the firm an option on the next book. The author agreed immediately and submitted the notes for approval, with a statement that his terms for them were a million pounds down in advance, and a 75 per cent royalty. Mr. Cape was not able to raise the million before his option expired.

Despite the difficult conditions at Uxbridge in those days, T.E. succeeded in keeping free of trouble and earned a good character by his unhesitating submission to discipline, as well as by his readiness to do any job, however distasteful, for which he was detailed. But this did not save him, when, after half a year's service, an officer who had known him during the war sold the news to the press. The price paid for this information is said to have been thirty pounds—the figure looks almost too apt for it to be true.

But the effect was serious. For the subsequent publicity caused disquiet as well as distaste in the Air Ministry, so strongly assailed in its fight for existence as to be apprehensive of anything that might give rise to criticism. Thus T.E. was turned out of the Air Force in February, 1923, despite his strenuous protests. They might have availed if the decision had been left with the Chief of the Air Staff, Sir Hugh Trenchard, who became a second Allenby in his relationship to T.E. With him T.E. discussed the situation and received the hint, which he regarded as a promise, that his readmission to the Air Force might be arranged if he obtained a good character after service in the Army.

Through friends in the War Office the way was smoothed for T.E.'s enlistment in the Tank Corps. He now assumed the name of Shaw. Contrary to rumour, the choice was not due to his friendship and admiration for Bernard Shaw; he took it at random from the Army List Index while waiting in a room at the War Office. It had the same convenience for pay parade as "Ross."

In March he joined the Tank Corps Depot at Bovington Camp in Dorset. After completing his recruit training and "passing off the square" he was employed in the quartermaster's stores, where his work was mainly to mark and fit clothing. It was, on the whole, "a cushy job" and had the advantage of giving him the privacy of an office in which he could work at night on the final revision of the *Seven Pillars*. He fulfilled his allotted tasks so punctually and effacingly that he was rarely troubled by the myrmidons of authority, although on one occasion he was punished by three days "confinement to barracks" for leaving his overalls on his bed. On another occasion he punished a pompous corporal for unjust treatment of

FULFILMENT

another man by throwing the corporal's suitcase in the dustbin, but escaped the consequence of this act of insubordination.

The Tank Corps was in several ways a disappointment to him. With certain exceptions, the senior officers and N.C.O.s whom he found at the depot seemed to him too military-minded and too little mechanically-minded to be suitable for training a technical corps. Button-cleaners were the most advanced form of mechanical tool that they could understand, and he carried away from his two years' experience a profound impression of the waste of time and intelligence. It is only fair to add that there has been a marked change for the better since then, in the Tank Corps.

If the conditions during his service were depressing to his real military sense, he found compensations elsewhere. Some of his most restful hours were spent in Thomas Hardy's Dorset home. He also created a home of his own there, a cottage in which he intends to settle down when his service in the Air Force is finished. It lies in an oasis of rhododendrons on the bleak moorland that no reader of *The Return of the Native* can forget.

His one extravagance is motor-cycling, and here he has always had luxurious tastes—because of his love of speed, not of comfort. The man who rides or drives at thirty miles an hour moves too fast to appreciate details, yet too slow to gain a sense of the whole as one does at sixty. Travel faster still, at eighty or ninety, and instead of travelling uphill and down dale, one has a sense of moulding the hills and dales. To T.E. this sensation of supreme speed is entirely exhilarating, because it seems to free the spirit from the bondage of human weakness, and also, I think, because it suggests the power to overcome impediments that nature and human nature place in the way of all achievement.

Such speed as T.E. desires—an ability to do ninety to a hundred miles an hour on any open stretch—costs money to secure. He has diminished the expense by favour of George Brough, the manufacturer of the Brough-Superior motor-cycle. Almost every year he has thus obtained the use of a new demonstration model at small cost to himself, save for petrol and oil—which is a considerable item. For both the horse-power and T.E.'s mileage are high. He averages from four to six hundred miles a week; if duty prevents him from going out one week he usually makes it up at the next opportunity, for the joy of motoring becomes keener with abstinence, although it never palls.

"To explain the lure of speed you would have to explain human nature; but it is easier understood than explained. All men in all ages have beggared themselves for fast horses or camels or ships or cars or bikes or aeroplanes: all men have strained themselves dry to run or walk or swim faster. Speed is the second oldest animal craving in our nature, and our generation is fortunate in being able to indulge it more cheaply and generally than our ancestors. Every natural man cultivates the speed that appeals to him. I have a motor-bike income."

But he scoffs at those of his friends who indulge their love of speed at the wheel of a car, an unresponsive and insensate vehicle compared with a motor-cycle, to which, in his opinion, only a motor-boat is superior. He admits, however, the advantages of a car in wet weather as one grows older, and says that if rich enough he would go touring with both, exchanging to the car when it rained and leaving the chauffeur to bring on the motor-cycle.

Air Force uniform, with its puttees for the calves and easily un-hooked high collar, seems to him an ideal kit for motor-cycling under normal conditions, and for this reason he often travels in uniform rather than in plain clothes.

This practice sometimes produces embarrassments. I have heard from several quarters a delightful story that when, some years ago, Feisal was staying at a house in London, T.E. called on him, only to be refused admittance and then pushed down the steps by the butler, aghast at this mere "Tommy's" impertinence; whereupon Feisal, hearing the commotion, came out and gave the butler a second, and worse shock, by embracing the disreputable intruder. When I asked T.E. about this episode recently, he said that he had no recollection of it, but admitted that he had frequently been kept waiting on a friend's doorstep with the door shut in his face while an unbelieving servant made inquiries within. The "Air Force blue" uniform also lends itself to a different form of misunderstanding. I remember that when T.E. came round the north coast of Cornwall a few years ago in my car we had difficulty, as well as entertainment, in persuading one or two hotel-keepers that he was not "the chauffeur."

When at Bovington, he used to make frequent trips to London on his motor-cycle—the undulating but straight stretch across the downs from Blandford to Salisbury was his favourite speed-track; he rarely crossed it without coming close to the hundred mark. He never grew tired of revisiting Corfe Castle; more recently the town walls of Southampton, unique in England, have been a constant attraction during his Air Force service in the neighbourhood. On many of these trips he took a soldier-companion on the pillion—it gave him an animate as well as an inanimate object to study and savour.

After he had completed a year's service in the Army without spoiling his conduct-sheet, he passed the news indirectly to Trenchard in the hope that he would be readmitted to the Air Force. But no sign came, and T.E. was reluctant to force the issue, imagining that the objection might lie with Trenchard himself. Then he received from Lord Thomson, the Air Minister in the new Labour Government, a proposal that he should complete the unfinished history of the Air Force in the War.

T.E. did not view the task with relish—"the History was an appalling job which had killed Raleigh and daunted Hogarth"—and he found difficulty in picturing himself as the compiler of an Official History. Nevertheless, he was willing to consider it as a passport towards his purpose, and accordingly, offered to undertake it and even to do it without fee, if the authorities would agree to allow him back into the Air Force when the book was completed. This, he calculated, would take two years. But the Air Ministry were unwilling to concede the point, and his proposal fell through.

The early return of the Conservative Government brought an early and unexpected turn for the better in his personal prospects. For, as a result of John Buchan's intercession at Downing Street, the political objections to his re-enlistment were smoothed away, and in August, 1925, he was transferred from the Tank Corps to the Air Force for the remainder of his engagement—seven years active and five on the reserve from March, 1923. This solution not only gratified his desire, but tickled his sense of humour, since he was back in the Air Force far quicker than if his own offer had been accepted, and without the labour of writing the History.

To add to his pleasure, he was sent to a station which went far towards fulfilling his conception of what Air Force life should be. This was Cranwell, in Lincolnshire, where the new Cadet College for the Air Force had been established. Here he was "an aircraft-hand (general purpose unskilled man) in B. Flight. Each Flight had half a dozen training machines for the cadets to learn flying: and three or four instructors, and a dozen or fifteen airmen (one-third fitters, one-third riggers, one-third aircraft-hands) to look after the machines. We did anything there was to do." The one threat of trouble arose not from his superiors but from his fellows. At this enlistment there was no secret about his identity, and the other aircraftsmen were divided between curiosity and suspicion. Was he an official spy?

One can understand such doubts, as well as their sublime irony. They were as natural in these humble aircraftsmen as the perplexity which leads men of higher position and ambition to ask—"Why does he waste his talents in this way?" No one can hope to approach an understanding of T.E.'s choice until he has himself reflected long on a philosophy of life. The drab mind instinctively seeks a colourful explanation of the simple—hence the immense popular appeal of Secret Service tales, that romanticize the often sordid and petty realities of spying and conspiracy. The aircraft-hands who pictured T.E. as the spy of authority were no more gullible than the official heads abroad who pictured him as the spy of British imperialism. It is a delicious breakfast-table dish to read some inspired report in the foreign press, that he is engineering a vast conspiracy in the depths of Asia, when one knows that he is scrubbing a barrack-room in the depths of rural England.

At Cranwell, T.E.'s irresistible naturalness soon overcame the doubts and the diffidence of his fellows. He has a knack of getting on with such men, because he genuinely likes them instead of merely tolerating them. In consequence his "leg-pulling" humour was not only accepted with a good grace, but became a means of pulling them together and pulling them along, so that he became an asset whose value both officers and N.C.O.s have freely acknowledged.

Now as an airman of the lowest grade, he exercised the same power of "command" by pure radiation of personality, as he had formerly, when adviser, nominally, to the Arab forces. Thus, in a different sphere, he gave one more proof that to work *through* men is more potent than to stand *over* them. The achievement is hardly more remarkable than its admission, by those who held the titular authority. It is a light on the progress that would be attainable if only the other leaders of mankind would free themselves from personal ambition—

the rock on which most human efforts split and crumble.

T.E. found as much pleasure in straightening out the clerical work of his "Flight" office at Cranwell as another would find in administering a department or a dominion, and more than he himself had found in running the Arab campaign. In his spare time he completed the final revision of the *Seven Pillars of Wisdom*. For recreation, he sipped the varied company that his collection of friends offered—with friends, as with food and drink, he thinks that the flavour can best be appreciated by a taste and is drowned by a repast.

His motor-cycle continued to be his means of access to the outer world, and the frequency of his excursions was assured by the opportunities that the Great North Road offered. On one run from Durham to Cranwell he averaged 54 m.p.h., his record run, I believe. From these excursions he usually came back laden with good things for his roommates to eat—he was as generous in spending his own scanty means in this as he was adept in "scrounging" more substantial articles for their comfort. His disarming impudence in such foraging would assuredly have won him the respect of Sherman's famous "bummers" who went "marching through Georgia."

It was during this time at Cranwell that he had his two narrowest escapes from serious accident since he had become T. E. Shaw. One night, bringing back sausages for supper, he struck a patch of ice in the dark at 45 m.p.h.—and the next moment found himself lying on one of the grass borders of the road with his cycle, when he found it, on the other. The second mishap was when riding up Highgate Hill; he skidded on the wet tramlines and sheared one side of his motorcycle. Yet the only time he hurt himself seriously, was when swinging the starting handle of a car that he came upon by the wayside. The driver forgot to retard the ignition, and the result was a back fire that broke T.E.'s arm. He rode back to camp with his arm dangling, waited until next morning to get the arm set, and then refused to go into hospital while it was mending.

In December, 1926, he was sent out to India. He was anxious "to dodge the publicity that would follow when *Revolt in the Desert* appeared." He travelled in the troopship *Devonshire* and on arrival went to the Drigh Road depot of the Air Force at Karachi. Here he remained during most of his time in India, and judging by some of his letters, he found life far less attractive than at Cranwell. One reason was that he found that his pay did not go so far as in England towards providing the type of amenities he liked. The greater reason was the restriction on his freedom of movement. To the Indian Government his presence, if known, was likely to be an embarrassment, because of the wild rumours it might generate, and as Indian official-dom viewed him as the arch-disturber of their war-time policy, he deemed it wise to avoid cause for complaint. In consequence he was voluntarily "confined to barracks" throughout his time in India. By contrast with the tedium of life at Karachi, it was a relief when, after eighteen months, he was posted to the frontier. He spent a week-end, only, at Peshawar, and then went on to join a flight at Miranshah Fort, an isolated frontier post that to the ordinary man would have seemed more like a sentence of confinement. He used to call himself "aircraft-hand adjutant"! It is my impression that this two-year spell in India during which he never went out of camp except occasionally when flying, retarded rather than hastened his recovery from the mind strain of the past. Bodily, he was never sick, nor did he feel the heat. While in India he extended his service to do the five reserve years on the active list.

His service in India was cut short by an indiscretion, despite his own precautions. "Aircraftman Shaw's" presence on the frontier leaked into the American papers and produced lurid charges in the Russian papers that "Colonel Lawrence" was spying in Afghanistan, as the agent of British imperialism in a vast conspiracy against the Soviet. It is said that the Afghan Government issued a proclamation that, if seen, he was to be at once arrested; and then another, that he was to be shot on sight. Relations between the Afghan and the Indian Governments were so delicate at the time that, in deference to re-peated appeals from the British Minister in Kabul, Sir Francis Humphrys, T.E. was sent back to England early in 1929.

He was flown direct to the coast, where he embarked on the *Rajputana*. His quiet arrival home in February coincided with some amusing outbursts from friends of Russia. Members of the Inde-pendent Labour Party, particularly Mr. Thurtle, had just put chal-lenging questions in Parliament about his supposed activities in Afghanistan. Mr. Saklatvala was prominent in a Communist demon-stration, wherein T.E. was burnt in effigy on Tower Hill! These in-cidents were crowned by a contrasting joke the next month, when the "news" was announced that he had been received into the Independent Labour Party by Mr. Maxton. The foundation for this delightful report may have been the fact that, on his return, T.E. had strolled down to the House of Commons and presented himself to Thurtle and Maxton. If his visible presence convinced them that he was not spying in Afghanistan, he seems to have left them still mystified as to why any man, with freedom of choice, should elect to serve in the ranks.

While in London he saw Trenchard who asked him where he would like to go, and suggested Scotland as being well out of the way, but this sounded a chilly prospect to T.E., who much prefers heat to cold, and instead he was posted to Cattewater on Plymouth Sound, a flying-boat station. If it was far from London and from most of his friends, he found many compensations. When he had a few hours to spend outside the fenced camp, Lady Astor's house offered a variety of company, although he could not resist teasing her with the suggestion that Cattewater had been named after her. Incidentally, the name, which had the military defect of rhyming with "backwater," was subsequently changed to "Mountbatten." I have heard that T. E. had a hand in "wangling" this change, which was suggested by his Commanding Officer. In doing so he put aside his own preference for the historic Danish flavour of the original name.

For he found at this station an atmosphere that approached his Air Force ideal, and a Commanding Officer, Sydney Smith, who won his enthusiastic regard. Now, for the first time since his enlistment, he began to be utilized in work that accorded more with his capacities, if not with his rank. The post of clerk in an air station office does not sound much, even though the particular clerk's competence may elevate him in practice to the role of secretary. But in this case, it happened that the Commanding Officer was playing a prominent part in the arrangements for the Schneider Cup Race of 1929, wherein Britain, the holder, had to meet a formidable challenge from Italy, the late possessor. Thus T.E.'s role in turn received enlargement. Before long, his utility infiltrated itself into acceptance in its habitual way, so that he found himself acting as clerk to all the three Committees who shared the responsibility, Sydney Smith being the only member who was common to all three. These activities meant frequent motor runs to London and flights to Calshot, on the Solent, where the Schneider Cup course was laid out. He was even loaned the use of a privately owned light aeroplane.

The zest he developed in this work made perceptible cracks in the shell of his weariness. Only a few years before when a friend asked him why he did not use his knowledge of photography and take up work in air survey, he had revealingly replied—"I feel like a beggar, starving in the gutter, who sees a loaf of bread on the other side of the road yet can't be bothered to go and fetch it." Now, in the summer of 1929, it began to seem that this inertia of self-determination was passing.

Unfortunately, there was also a new cloud rising on the horizon, with the advent of a new Air Minister, or, rather, the return of an old—Lord Thomson. Despite his gifts, and his proved readiness to risk his military prospects for a political conviction, he was one of the many who could not hope to understand T.E.'s attitude; even in adversity, he had been buoyed up by ambition. In a conversation soon after he came into office he showed a marked prejudice against T.E.'s retention in the Air Force. It was not a personal objection, but it was clear that annoyance at T.E.'s rejection of his original offer of the History had made him more susceptible to the adverse opinions which various officers had injected into him.

Trenchard had the vision to perceive the moral value of T.E.'s presence in the ranks of the new service he had striven so hard to create and maintain, and some of the best of his assistants shared his views. But smaller men, always apprehensive of what they cannot comprehend, disliked the idea of a critical intelligence in the ranks. Such men, unsure of themselves, become acutely uncomfortable in face of a subordinate who makes them feel inferior, and instinctively seek relief by charging him with indiscipline, or if that be impossible, suggesting that his presence is "bad for discipline."

One may sympathize with their feeling, even if one despises their feebleness. T.E.'s scrupulous correctness can be devastating. I shall not easily forget how once, when he was with me in uniform, at a country hotel, a somewhat "bouncing" person, an officer who had newly joined his station, recognized him and tried to improve the opportunity by displaying a patronizing familiarity. At his intrusion T.E. rose to attention and to all his conversational gambits replied with a chilling deference that even the hardened intruder could not long withstand. The incident was highly entertaining, and instructive, to the observer.

The Schneider Cup Race, and the attention it drew, inevitably gave an opportunity to those who resented T.E.'s normally invisible presence. The Italian Air Minister, General Balbo, was the unconscious prime cause of the cloudburst. An R.A.F. working party was put on to clean the slipway for the British machines, but the Italian one was left slippery with green scum. Balbo, who knew T.E. of old, came up to ask his aid. T.E., as careless of formality as Balbo when a job was to be done, promptly secured a party of aircraftmen to clean the Italian slipway. But neither the conversation nor the intervention had passed unnoticed.

Then on the day of the race, various political personages, prominent members of the late Government, noticed him, and paused for a talk. They could scarcely have done otherwise in view of past association.

But a few days later the storm broke. T.E. was served a sentence of expulsion from the Air Force—by the original arrangement, his contract of service could be terminated at any time on either party's initiative. Various influential friends, however, pleaded his cause, to which Trenchard himself was not unwilling to listen. Still more effective, perchance, was the dropping of a hint in Foreign Office quarters that if T.E. was discharged from the Air Force he might take the opportunity of paying a visit to Iraq.

The sequel, after a few anxious days, was that on September 30th —a fateful anniversary—he had a fresh interview with Trenchard, who told him that a reprieve would be granted on certain conditions. They were that, henceforth, he was strictly confined to the routine duties of an ordinary aircraft hand; that he did not fly; that he never went out of the country, even to Ireland; that he neither visited nor spoke to any "great men." Upon asking for examples, the names of Winston Churchill, Austen Chamberlain, Lord Birkenhead, Sir Philip Sassoon, and Lady Astor were mentioned—all members of the political party then in opposition. When he inquired if Bernard Shaw came among the forbidden great, he was told "No." Bernard Shaw, when told of the exclusion from this category, seemed slightly hurt!

T.E. accepted these hard conditions rather than leave his cherished service, although feeling that the Air Force was acting uneconomically in neglecting to get more than a daily three and sevenpence worth of work out of him.

Its loss was at least his monetary gain. The enforced abstention from intelligent work for the Air Force enabled him to continue, if still in fits and starts, a prose translation of the *Odyssey*, which had been commissioned from an American source and afforded him far higher rate of pay than he has ever received for an original piece of literature.

He had originally hoped to deliver it by the end of 1929, but had laid it aside for his Schneider Cup work with no regrets—"I'd rather do R.A.F. stuff than private work, that's the truth of it; and so I gladly let everything slide when they press me." But now, shut out from mechanics, he returned to the classics. He had leeway to make up. Although that Christmastide he "sat in a lukewarm office and slaved at Homer," the work was still short of half-way when 1930 arrived. At the end of that year he had afresh to record—"I'm working at the *Odyssey* like a tiger, in great hope of finishing it next spring; it takes all my nights and half-days, and I have promised myself to have no holiday till it is over. Barring business interruptions, it should be over in April: and then for a lazy summer, with full pocket and no liabilities." If he grew weary in the labour, he at least found that reading the Greek so carefully was good mental exercise. Six months later he was writing—"I have that *Odyssey* to finish by September, and no heart for it."

It was finished soon after. The last lap had been obstructed by a fresh call to do real service for the air—and the sea! For two years he had been striving through various channels to interest the Air Ministry in the need for, and possibility of, new types of motorboats, suited to attend seaplanes—to race out to their rescue when in trouble, rescue the crews, and buoy up the machines before they sank. In this campaign, his technical knowledge and new-found enthusiasm were equal assets, and at last, early in 1931, they bore fruit. Experimental boats were produced by contractors, and T.E. was employed to test that which had been designed by Scott-Paine. In the process, T.E. acquired an extensive knowledge of the coast of England. As a result of the trials, a large batch was ordered. They can travel 30 m.p.h., twice the speed of the old boats; they are excellent in a rough sea, carry a normal crew of two men, have a glass-roofed cabin fitted for stretchers, and the stern is designed to slide under and hold up the wings of a sinking seaplane. The comprehensiveness, simplicity and accessibility of the internal fittings have been thought out with astonishing calculation and common sense—or, rather, they would be astonishing, if one did not know that T.E. was partly responsible.

The Air Ministry, too, showed a most creditable sagacity—as well as humanity—in detailing him to watch over the building of these new speed boats, and then to test and tune them before delivering them to their stations.

One had long felt that the way to reconcile T.E.'s reviving desire for real service with his sustained refusal to accept any rank, was to employ him in an independent job, where graded authority was out of place. Even in the hierarchically minded services, the principle has long been recognized that Chaplains should hold no actual rank. T.E. might have been tacitly accepted, as he essentially served, in the role of "Chaplain Extraordinary" to the Air Force—working among the members instead of preaching to them from a pulpit, he was a greater spiritual force than the whole board of Chaplains, in raising the standard of decency, fair play and unselfish comradeship. His inspiration again might have been utilized in the development of the Auxiliary Air Force.

But it was perhaps less of a wrench to tradition to recognize that the hierarchical principle has no relation to those of mechanical engineering, and that rank confers no superior authority over a refractory carburettor. The fact that speed-boats were an extraneous element in the Air Force made it easier to stretch the service rule that ability is linked to rank. In reaching this sensible solution of the problem of T.E.'s employment the credit was largely due to Sir Geoffrey Salmond, his ever-ready helper in the Arab Campaign.

The work caused T.E. to transfer his base to Southampton Water, and from here he made long sea-excursions to the East coast and Scotland in delivering the boats, as they were built, to their future stations—"I have web feet now, and live on the water." In this work he has continued, save for one unfortunate break in the autumn of 1932, when a Sunday paper published a story of his new activities. It shook the Air Ministry authorities so severely that it temporarily shook him from his niche. They have a fear of publicity that is palpable except to the Admiralty or the War Office, and in connection with "Aircraftman Shaw" it is morbidly acute. It has long blinded them to the psychological value of "Colonel Lawrence's" choice of their service, and also to the obvious answer to any Parliamentary critics that no other service has succeeded in saving the taxpayer's pocket by securing a mechanical expert for the pay of an aircraft hand.

Happily, Geoffrey Salmond's good sense soon restored T.E. to his chosen work, and one of Salmond's last acts before his untimely death was to promise T.E. the means of experiment for further progress, a promise duly fulfilled by his brother, Sir John Salmond. If the direct purpose is to provide still more prompt first aid to seaplanes, the results may have an important indirect bearing on future security against a submarine campaign.

It marks a change in T.E. that he should be so keen to achieve the goal of this experiment. A few years ago, his sole ambition seemed to be that of lasting out his engagement, which comes to an end in 1935; and he doubted whether he could do it, saying that he felt old and found the life increasingly hard. But since then, I have marked a rejuvenation, both of body and spirit. He recognizes it himself. By his own judgment, it was the exaltation of writing the *Seven Pillars of Wisdom* even more than the strain of the war that brought him perilously close to the border line. Gradually, he has come back, becoming "more human" in the process. Whether it be true as he suggests, that "virtue has gone out" of him, to my eyes wisdom seems more firmly established on her seven pillars.

Withal, he retains that puckish humour whose attractive fragrance Auda labelled so aptly in calling him "the world's imp." Puck may not lie at the roots of his being but is never far below the surface. Thus, not long ago, when he reported for duty at a new station and was asked in stereotyped form for the name and address of his next of kin in case of accident, he replied—"Oh, report it to the Editor, *Daily Mail*—and mind you get a special rate!" Still more recently, when Feisal died, T.E. received a telephone warning that several reporters were on their way from London by train to interview him; he jumped on a train for London, passing theirs in the opposite direction, as the most effective way of evasion. To add zest to their pursuit, however, he left behind a false trail which led them to embark on an undesired, if short, sea-trip to the Isle of Wight.

His intention is still, when he completes his service, to settle down in his Wessex cottage, a hermitage with a window to the world, through which he can emerge whenever inclined to visit friends, concerts, theatres, or merely to take a sip of the London scene. As for work, his idea is to do translations—they can be done to time table—to pay for his luxuries, but otherwise to do nothing. He knows how to enjoy doing nothing, and thinks that he has freed himself from the need of activity to anæsthetize the sense of futility. It is left for the future to show.

He certainly diffuses an atmosphere of contentment such as I have rarely felt in meeting men of active intelligence, and never among those who are actively pursuing the bubbles of what the world calls success. That feeling has grown stronger at recent meetings with him, and it led me not long ago to challenge him with the direct question—"Are you really happy?" After a moment's reflection, he replied, "At times. No one who thinks can be really happy." He went on to say that he had learnt very early the truth that happiness lies within, not in externals, but had also learnt later that those who did not think could be happy, the kind he lived among now. With himself, he found that happiness was intermittent—it came in "absorption."

That reflection would seem to bring in question his present intention for the future after 1935. But I wonder whether, in ascribing greater happiness to the unthinking, he has taken account of variations in the quality of happiness—or of the value of freedom from the desires that produce active unhappiness. He may also overrate the happiness of others by ignoring the contentment he diffuses among those who come in touch with him.

CHAPTER XXIII

POSTSCRIPT

T. E. SHAW, sometime Lawrence, and now for all time "Lawrence of Arabia," passed into unconsciousness on May 13th, 1935. That afternoon, when riding back to his cottage on "Egdon Heath," he shot over the handlebars of his motorcycle after a sudden swerve to avoid a butcher's boy who was cycling that way. On the 19th, he died. It was, I imagine, the way he would have chosen to go: for on his motorcycle he seemed to find the outlet from harassing thought and sense of futility. Also it was an end foreseen.

One August evening in 1933 I tried in vain to keep up with him on a run to Otterbourne along the Wessex roads. My car was fast, but "George VII" was faster, and far quicker off the mark. The way T.E. shot through traffic led me to chide him about the risks he ran, to which he retorted with a humorous defence of its essential safety, helped by an immense power of acceleration. The argument ran on, but ended suddenly when, changing to a pensive note, he said that he knew it would "end in tragedy one day."

About a year later we came back to spend an evening in that quiet garden at Otterbourne; this time he was in my car. On the way, our talk reverted to the question of safe driving; bantering me, he remarked that only on a motorcycle was the man in charge compelled to take a fair proportion of the risk. In a big car one could hit anything, save another car, with impunity, whereas on a motorcycle one was almost certain to be killed—which was a just penalty for carelessness. He said that he would like to see all cars fitted with a backward projection from the bumper, ending in a spearhead just in front of the driver's chest—so, that, if he hit anything, the point would pierce him. If expressed extravagantly, the idea corresponded with what I knew of his personal attitude—he would try to avoid running over a hen even, although to swerve was a serious risk on such a heavy machine as he rode.

The first of those two conversations, not alone by the words but by the way they were said, seemed at the time a communicated vision.

The second strengthened it by implanting the conviction that at the moment when an accident appeared inevitable he would throw away his own life on the chance of saving the other party. Thereafter I had remained in anticipation of the news that came to me over the telephone on that Monday afternoon in May.

If a fitting end, it was a tragic waste—at least for his generation. It cut short a rest from service, and servitude, that had been hardly earned and keenly awaited. By making that rest permanent it left unsolved questions that perplexed him and his friends. For it came when he was floating in the trough of a wave.

So high was the wave that had carried him through the war and its aftermath—casting him in the ranks of the Air Force as it broke— that the fact of a second, and its height, is easy to miss. The later years of his service as an aircraftman saw a resurgence which, if unobtrusive, may itself carry further. He came perhaps to value it more. When I showed him what I had written in the previous chapter about his pervasive influence as "Chaplain Extraordinary" to the Air Force, he questioned its validity: but in a way that led me to surmise that the thought coincided with his inner wish. That was confirmed when after his death I read in a letter he had written, just before it, to Robert Graves—"I have convinced myself that progress today is made not by the single genius, but by the common effort. . . . The genius raids, but the common people occupy and possess. Wherefore I stayed in the ranks and served to the best of my ability, much influencing my fellow airmen towards a pride in themselves and their inarticulate duty. I tried to make them see—with some success."

In that self-submerging effort, self-rejuvenation came, producing a fresh effort towards concrete achievement—the development of speed-boats for the service, immediately, of the Air Force, and ultimately, of the Navy. He believed that such boats, equipped with torpedo-tubes and depth-charges, would make it impossible for another power to conduct a submarine campaign in the narrow seas against our shipping. A hostile battle-fleet would have a still poorer chance against such boats, for their own range of several hundred miles could be indefinitely extended by carrying them on ocean-going ships. I remember him, when showing me Scott-Paine's record-breaking *Miss Britain III*, predicting that from it would be evolved the predominant naval weapon of tomorrow—for half the price of a 15-inch shell. In his vision of future naval warfare, a fleet would loose off several hundred of such craft, each carrying a torpedo and controlled by wireless. Only a direct hit could stop them, and no gun was likely to hit such targets—almost flush with the water and travelling at 60 miles an hour. But beyond this effect on naval warfare was the revolution foreshadowed in ship design; for he held that the basic idea of these speed-boats had a wider application, and that the ships of the future would likewise run over the surface of the sea instead of pushing through it.

Still more than in his Arabian phase, he viewed his own part as the creation of opportunity for others. To his powers of influencing thought and action was due, he felt, the acceptance of the idea. He gave himself to the service of those who had the power of invention —to ease their path by turning the flank of entrenched conservatism.

Among the by-products of this new development was one that when first rumored caused some sensation. Late in 1933 stories appeared in the American Press that "Lawrence of Arabia" had been playing the part of a human target for aircraft dropping live bombs, whereupon certain London papers, dismissing the stories as fantastic, referred to them as an example of the too active transatlantic imagination. But they had a foundation in fact. Since July 1932 the Royal Air Force had been using unsinkable speed-boats, with armour over the crew and engines, as mobile targets for bombing practice. The bombs employed were the ordinary 10-lb. practice bombs of cast-iron with a smoke-compound filling, and they were dropped from as high as 15,000 feet down to under 1000 feet in diving bomb attacks. These practices took place off Bridlington on the North Sea coast, and here T.E. spent several months each summer. His connection with these armoured target-boats came through his service under the Boat Department of the Air Ministry, by whom he was employed "to consider design, to watch construction, and then to test, report and tune the finished articles." Previously, the only mobile marine target had been the old battleship *H.M.S. Centurion,* which was expensive to run and limited in the practice it could provide. These drawbacks led the Director of Training to ask if the Boat Department could produce a towed or wireless-controlled target-boat. Whereupon, to tell the story as T.E. told it to me,

"We said, 'Why not an armoured boat,' and produced the required article in three or four months. Its design betrays the vices of haste, but they are cheap, safe, and afford wonderful practice. The finance people refuse the crews extra-pay, which we are pressing for —not that we think it dangerous, but damned uncomfortable! Hellish hot, smelly, and noisy. They wear ear-defenders, crash helmets and gas masks. Little else!"

But danger had overhung the experiment until experience proved the contrary No one could be sure what would be the concussive effect on the crew when one of these bombs fell with great velocity on the head-cover. Hence the crews were all volunteers from the Marine Aircraft Experimental Establishment at Felixstowe. And in the first summer's bombing practice, T.E. himself drove the boat on several of the earliest runs "to show the crews how." If characteristic of him, the risk was less than on many of the trips he had earlier made in rough seas round the Atlantic and North Sea coasts in proving the seaworthiness of the original "crash-boats." But all who were engaged in the tests had cause for relief when a bomb eventually fell on the armour-plate and had no ill effect; those that hit the unprotected wooden parts of the boat went straight through the hull, which was compartmented and filled with a compound of expanded rubber ten times lighter than cork; the crew then ran out and plugged the hole. "Wet feet" were a minor discomfort compared with the normal ordeal of being penned under the armour and close to the engines for two hours at a time, while under bombing attack, and of being at sea, often in rough seas, for twelve hours a day. But the practice given to the Air Force by these small and nimble targets brought such a great improvement in bombing accuracy that T.E. was led to predict that "in a few years aircraft will deal infallibly with ships."

This statement was the more significant because T.E. rarely allowed his vision to outrun his analysis of the practical conditions. Thus, although he had done so much to create the opportunity for the Air Force to prove its powers in the Middle East, I found him more cautious in tracing its limits than many who had been late converts to the idea of air control. He remarked that as aircraft needed room for manœuvre, and had such a wide turning circle, they were not so effective in "narrow as in wide waters." "Until they can hover, air control is not applicable to a crowded district." Having spent eight months flying and driving over the North-West Frontier, he had come to the conclusion that air control was "applicable to Waziristan, not to the Mohmand country, and becoming less and less effective as you approach to Peshawar." He went on to say that although a strong supporter of "air" he would have reservations over the North-West Frontier Province—"I would take over bits, evacuating Razmak tomorrow."

His interest in affairs, as in the rest of his extraordinarily wide range of interests, seemed to be renewing itself in these last years. He was certainly less apt to strike his old note, that he had "cut completely out of the active world." Even then, for a man self-confessedly out of touch, the way he kept in touch was amazing: and amusing. During one of his brief visits to London he would often see more of its leading people in a day than anyone else might have met in a month. It was a habit of his to make such a round; and an idiosyncrasy, to let you know whom he had seen. Piquancy was added by his other habit of spending the nights at the Union Jack Club, the hostel for the men of the services, where he could hire a cubicle for one and ninepence. In some degree, however, he became more luxurious as he grew older; whereas he had formerly travelled with no more than a toothbrush, in his pocket, he now carried a small *attaché* case. Also, for motorcycling, he had a special black oilskin overall suit made to his own design. Likewise, in the furnishing of his cottage his appetite for good things, and even for comfort, seemed to increase. But his indifference to the pleasures of the table remained; indeed, I came to feel that his readiness to eat a normal meal when in others' company was due mainly to a desire to put them at their ease; that he preferred, if he knew that they would allow it without fuss, to sit and talk while his friends were eating. He felt he was fortunate in escaping "the bother" which the burden of taste or habit was imposing on them. If it may seem curious that one whose senses were so acute should find no pleasure in food or drink, his explanation was that with him sensation came mainly through the eyes.

This may be applied to cover the effect of things read as well as things observed. Reading to him was food, to be enjoyed for its flavour and not merely taken for nourishment. His sensations in reading were very acute and very subtle. They came from the texture of prose, from the shape of a sentence, from the choice of a phrase. And he found the typography no less exciting. No man I have known

McBey's portrait

LAWRENCE ON ARRIVAL AT DAMASCUS

could so extract the whole flavour of a book—from the thought to a punctuation mark, and from the binding to the printer's ink. During the years of his service as an aircraftman he ranged far and wide through contemporary literature—especially poetry, plays, and novels. One class of novel was excluded, however, for when I acclaimed the virtues of the detective novel as the best relief after heavy bouts of work, he retorted that they were "literary golf"—that they "wasted brain concentration on imaginary problems." He read for enlightenment and not for exercise. If one heard a book beginning to be talked about by lovers of literature or pursuers of novelty, one was often reminded thereby of having heard it mentioned first by T.E.

The variety of his taste, in search of something fresh in thought or expression, was matched by his generous eagerness to fan any fresh little flicker of light. Many young authors owed a debt to his help in making known their existence; some might have profited more by his criticism. For despite his assiduous watch on what the younger men were producing, he complained that too many seemed merely "to write for relief, as an ape scratches itself." He wanted books that would provide a "square meal." Among writers of established fame, his admiration for Bernard Shaw and, more qualified, for Thomas Hardy is well known; less known perhaps that for such as W. B. Yeats, Eugene O'Neill, Theodore Powys, E. M. Forster and James Joyce— whose "Ulysses" he regarded as a compendium of literary technique, to be studied if not enjoyed. Memory strives unsuccessfully now to recall all those of whom he spoke in conversations with me, where such talk was only an aside. Thus what comes back can only be an odd fragment, of interest for itself but not as evidence of his judgment's proportions. I remember that it was he who sent me hurrying to see Sean O'Casey's "Silver Tassie," for the sake of that inspired second act, just before the untimely end of its run in front of puzzled London audiences. It was from him that I first heard glowing praise of Henry Williamson. The names of the Garnetts, Edward and David, were often mentioned; they were friends in the flesh and not merely in print. No friend received more attention from him, from high hope of the fruits, than Robert Graves; there was criticism too, and I took it to imply the measure of his expectations. When I dwelt on the merits of "I, Claudius," T.E., while admitting its skill, expressed dislike of it because "all the characters were painted too blackly."

But for "Claudius the God," which followed, he did not stint his praise. He hailed O'Flaherty's gifts but then suffered disappointment —which inspired his comment that "Irishmen usually begin with a great rush and then die away. G.B.S. and Yeats are exceptions, and Swift, I think. But no Irishman goes much further, after he is thirty."

For modern satire he cared little—"the satire that fetches me is Quixote, or Gulliver, or Rabelais, which deals more with nature than with manners." My own deficient taste for poetry deprived me of hearing much of his views on modern poets, but I was struck once at the accent of near-awe which he used in mentioning the name of W. H. Auden. Of war books none appealed to him more than "Her Privates We." When, after reading it, I asked him if he could tell me anything about the anonymous author, he replied—"Frederic Manning . . . an exquisite, and an exquisite writer. I wonder how he really got on in the ranks. Too fine a mind, I think, for real contact: but he has drawn a wonderful picture of the other ranks as I know them." A few years later, Arthur Osburn's "Unwilling Passenger," coming on the ebb-tide of War books, attained a fresh high watermark in T.E.'s judgment.—He admired its photographic quality, and remarked that it had "a beauty of candour that was wonderfully restful . . . I don't think the candour was innocent either."

The influence of his study of photography is to be seen in a theory of literature which he set forth in one of his letters to John Brophy, another friend whose work he followed with interest. "I want a diary, or record of events to be as near slice-of-life as can be. Imagination jars in such instances. In novels, however, slice-of-life jars, because their province is the second remove, the sublimation of the theme. One is eyewitness, the other creative mind. In the first the photograph cannot be too sharp, for it's the senses which record: in the second you need design. Any care for design renders the record infect." That classification may seem too black-and-white for truth; if it justly rules out imaginative retouching, it ignores the part that digestive interpretation inevitably plays in any record. But one must here remark that T.E.'s views were not always consistent, nor his action consistent with these views.

There was an interesting sidelight on both the "Lawrences," T.E. and D.H., in their views of each other. To judge by various aspects of T.E. that seem to be incorporated in several of the characters in

"Lady Chatterley's Lover," D.H. seems to have been strongly impressed with T.E. as a person, if respect and doubt were intermingled. T.E., for his part, thought poorly of D.H. as a man, but had an immense respect for his work, especially his poems. To me, he several times said that D.H. was the Lawrence who would last, and he demurred to my intended title for his book, "Lawrence," on the score of "D.H.L.'s ownership of that name." Whether that objection simply represented his esteem for D.H.'s literary stature, I was not sure.

His own he certainly rated too low—and this may explain much. For his highest admiration was reserved for the creative artist: and to be one was the ambition he had pursued after the War. To quote his own words—"I had had one craving all my life, for the power of self-expression in some imaginative form—but had been too diffuse ever to acquire a technique." Literature seemed to him the art least dependent on a long apprenticeship, and his experiences in the Arab Revolt had offered a ready-made theme. The "Seven Pillars of Wisdom" was the sequel. Reflection should vie with description. In style, in form, in printing, too, he aimed at perfection. But the result to him was dissatisfaction. Suffering from the divine discontent of the artist, but not recognizing the state, he came to the conclusion that he was no artist.

That feeling was reinforced by the results of a too severe test, if also by reaction from the excitement generated in writing his book. Unwilling to draw help from his fame, he submitted a number of anonymous contributions to various editors in the years immediately following the War. They came back, not unnaturally. Many great writers have suffered a similar fate in their early days and often with their best stuff. T.E. too readily jumped to the explanation that the fault lay with him. He deemed himself too imitative.

Once, as we stood at the end of a Cornish headland, watching the waves surge over the rocks, we drifted into talk of writing. He remarked that he had no difficulty in expressing the picture that he saw: words rushed in like the waves. It was otherwise with me, I replied; often hard to find the exactly right words to fit ideas that took shape gradually, the more so because these were themselves remodelled in the process of definition. T.E., however, contended that his own aptness with words was offset by difficulty in bringing ideas into relation. He remarked that he had the power of description and analysis, but not of synthesis or creation. I think there was some truth in his judgment; but the fuller truth was that he had too high a standard, and was so constituted that he suffered too great a strain. In a letter to Kennington from Karachi, in 1927, he remarked, "I've bust all my head's blood vessels in an abortive effort to create, and am condemned not to exert myself in future. What would you do in such a case. Say ha ha and blow your brains out? Too messy. If only it were all over." That awareness of his own overstrain he confirmed to me later, saying that he was "nearly dotty" at the time of his enlistment. And his service in India was, I thought, a hindrance to the process of recovery, which only became marked some time after his return.

Seven years later, writing to a friend, he said, "in 1922 I decided not to go on writing" (a statement which ignores his fresh attempt, this time at supreme realism, in that record of daily life in the Air Force which he christened "The Mint"). With characteristic humour he added, "I think I did write better than the average retired military man: but between that and 'writing' there is a gulf." A further proof to him, of his artistic deficiency was that, instead of "joy in the creation," he "had never anything but weariness and dissatisfaction." Once again I question his judgment: for it is difficult to believe that anyone could produce more than a thousand words an hour for twenty hours on end without being possessed by the urge that is the mainspring of writing, and without the absorption that, in his own recognition, is the secret of happiness. The fecundity and felicity of his letters increases my doubt. Through them, he may even live longest in literature, taking rank as the supreme letter-writer. They are works of art, unforced: if consciously pursued. He wrote them with purpose; each was aimed at his picture of the person to whom he was writing, and strove to make touch with the individual there seen. While he wrote with a care that is rare in these days, he only wrote when the impulse came—for writing. It was an urge for expression, in general, rather than duty to an individual. And when one reads the letters, and takes account of the number that were written in a batch when the periodical impulse came, one can hardly credit that the writing of them was unmitigated labour. There is significance, too, in the fact that he used Indian ink—"it lasts for ever"—in his fountain pen. That at other times he used pencil may have been due not merely to chance but to a revulsion of feeling—against the prospect of endurance. To such changes he was peculiarly liable.

His complexity became more manifest to me during the course of the writing of this book. In October, 1929, I was approached to undertake a book that should attempt to put the Arab Revolt, and Lawrence's part, into historical perspective. The time had come, it was urged, to estimate the significance of that achievement, to bring it into relation with the war as a whole and the course of events subsequently. My initial doubt whether the episode offered adequate scope was not by the contention that here, above all, was a case where the growth of legend threatened to obscure the real outlines. Even so, I had a further ground for hesitation. I had found too much interest in my contact with T.E. to be willing to risk its growth by embarking on such a book if he were unwilling—as I thought was likely. But when I mentioned the suggestion to him, his reaction was more favourable than I had expected; he seemed to like the idea of such historical treatment, and only questioned the possibility of finding enough material for it.

However, as further reassurance to myself, and to give him a chance of changing his mind after reflection, I wrote him on his return to Plymouth. His reply showed signs of a reaction that I came, later, to regard as characteristic—although in this instance the Schneider Cup storm that had just burst over his head may well have accounted for it. Because of this, as he pointed out, he could not associate himself with any book that dealt with his career, although he would do what he could, privately, to help me avoid errors. If I could find sufficient material elsewhere "to get the other side of the story, then it might well be the subject of a military thesis of some value. If not—and I haven't the time, or the inclination, or the heart, to dig very much into my own memories of those times for anyone's sake. Sorry not to be explicit: but it's as explicit as I feel. I don't care a bit, either way." This dubious attitude damped my own; while I did not want any kind of direct authorization that might limit my freedom of criticism, I foresaw difficulty in prosecuting my research adequately unless I could call on his knowledge of events. So I put the project on a backshelf, although continuing to browse in the subject and collect material as opportunity offered.

Three years passed before, freshly prompted, I took up the study in earnest. Decision was clinched by practical evidence of T.E.'s fresh change of attitude. He gave me much more help, and took a far greater interest in the progress of this work, than I had ever conceived that he would: submitting to an immense load of questions, and to continuous cross-examination on points that arose in the evidence. He covered the typescript draft of my chapters with supplementary notes that made invaluable additions to the historical narrative. By the end of the year he was well justified in recalling "how many hours and pages I have spent on your next-appearing book." I could, however, retort that during those months he had caused me disturbance, if also amusement, by his intermittent reactions. He would follow up an elucidation of his personal attitude or action by the complaint a little later, that my narrative was becoming too biographical. He would often express indifference to what was said about him, yet protested that certain criticisms in my draft were too hard upon him; and took pains to furnish the evidence that I required to satisfy me before modifying them. When the draft was at last ready to go to the publishers, he went through it again and approved it; a few weeks later, after reading it afresh he had a sudden qualm that it was too personal, and came to see me; he began by suggesting that the biographical part should be drastically curtailed, and ended by deleting only one insignificant passage. Pure kindheartedness may have been the explanation—he had it, and gave it, in abundance to help others. Or a reluctance to damage what someone else had created. Or an inward recognition of the justice of my complaint of his oscillation. Possibly a combination of these influences. Yet during these months I had a growing feeling that in him a desire for historical recognition and perpetuation struggled perpetually with his nihilism.

That feeling was strengthened in dealing with his collection of wartime photographs. He had several times told me that he thought they had been burnt in a fire at Lionel Curtis's house near Oxford—"a good job too." Later an historical point arose which one of his photographs, he said, would settle; he offered to find out if the photographs had survived. Soon afterwards they were sent to me, and instead of the few dozen I had expected, they ran to over two thousand; I saw signs of the care with which they had originally been arranged and classified, although they were now jumbled. When I wrote to tell him of the state in which they had come, reproaching him for his deficient sense of a duty to history, he retorted with his usual "ha ha"; but he turned up himself a few days later to help me in sorting and identifying them, completing the task the next time he had some days to spare on leave in London. Once engaged on the job, it was amusing to see how immersed he became, down on the floor amidst the piles of photographs. Often they would take him back step by step on journeys he had made, and incidents which he had never disclosed were now related to me. One large packet of negatives was found to comprise those he had taken of churches and castles in France and Syria during his youthful wanderings: they were still in amazingly good condition, and when printed off, were testimony not only to his skill but to his gift for choosing unobvious angles. When I asked him what he wished me to do with this war-collection, he expressed complete indifference—I could keep it if I wished or, if it irked me, throw it back on "the long-suffering Lionel Curtis." But when I went on to argue that it ought to be preserved for the nation and suggested various alternatives for its disposal, he began to show interest, and gave reasons for rejecting the others in favour of the Imperial War Museum, my first suggestion.

In the course of our work I had been often astonished by the way he could fix the place and date of a desert photograph which looked to me indistinguishable from any other tract of the desert. His photographic memory served him well in the process of identifying, and describing on the back, these hundreds of scenes. My surprise led him to expound the theory that memory was like a film; everything was recorded on it and could be "seen" over again if one could get it running; his own memory had improved since he had passed thirty. As I hold that memorizing power is apt to decrease as creative power increases, I noted this comment as a possible corroboration of his own belief that he was unable to create.

Those days brought some other sidelights. Among the photographs we found an attractive engraving, and my wife put it aside for him to take away. But he said that he did not want it—if she liked it, she might as well keep it. When she chided him for such recklessness, he retorted—"I'd give everything away if I could—it's too much bother to keep things—you're more free if you have no possessions." And added—"Besides, I like giving." At this time also I had a letter about a crippled boy who had found in his hero-worship of Lawrence the inspiration to carry him through nights of suffering. I showed the letter to T.E., who writhed at such adoration, exclaiming that he wished it were possible to stop "this sort of folly." Yet when I said that, moved by its genuineness, I had thought of sending the boy a copy of my book, just about to appear, T.E. at once agreed to my tentative suggestion that he might sign it, and wrote a "tonic" inscription.

Shortly before the publication of the book, he had written me—"Everything in your book seems to me very good, except the parts about me. I shall be glad when it's out (and therefore passed by). We can then meet each other happily, as free men." From then on, he overflowed with impish jibes that the book would not sell, that the public were suffering from a surfeit of him, and that I had thrown away its chances by not tearing him to shreds in Lytton Strachey fashion—"aha, that would have been a spectacle." Yet when he dropped in to see me a few days after its publication, I was amused to find how thoroughly he had read the reviews, including some I had not yet seen. It seemed to me a sign that he was still striving to penetrate, through the aid of the impression made on others, the mystery of his own personality. It brought back to me that poignant confession of his—"The eagerness to overhear and oversee myself was my assault upon my own inviolable citadel."

One of the reviews was by a talented soldier who had served with Lawrence in Palestine; it regretted that the book should be "spoilt at times" by a tendency to gird at professional soldiers, so different, the reviewer remarked, from Lawrence's own attitude towards them. T.E. chuckled over this comment, saying that I was far more tolerant towards them than he had been. Dwelling on their limitations he remarked, "They do their best—not their fault, perhaps, it's such a rotten best." But such charity could not be extended to their "trades-unionism" which hindered the growth of knowledge and understanding—"They are dreadfully dishonest to each other, yet rally as one man against outside criticism." He cited Winston Churchill's sketch of Haig in the *World Crisis* as the most "deadly," if subtly veiled, indictment of the best professional product.

T.E., however, hated what he called "niggling" criticism. A book of this kind upon Napoleon stirred him to a defence of Napoleon's greatness which hardly tallied with his own rejection of the "great man" myth—besides being historically questionable. You could "pick holes in Napoleon at every point," yet the fact remained that he had "remade Europe." "He was like a structure in which every brick was cracked, yet the whole hung together"—and had grandeur. "How awful it must have been for him at Waterloo—to be beaten by a Wellington." Another time, discussing modern dictators, T.E. remarked that Mussolini suffered from lack of an intellect—"You have only to see his books and plays!" "A lot of practical sense but no capacity for abstract thought"—I understood T.E. to imply that this deficiency set a limit to Mussolini's practical achievement, and its lasting value. "Lenin was far the greater man"—the only man who had evolved a theory, carried through a revolution, and constructed a state in accord with his ideas.

The suggestion that a successful dictator needed a capacity for abstract thought struck an unusual note, if it seemed to accord with Plato's view that the affairs of mankind were not likely to improve until the rulers became philosophers, or philosophers became the rulers. Pondering it, I recalled a previous conversation in which I had asked T.E. if he had any views on religion, to which his reply was that although brought up in conventional religion, he had long since discarded it, and did not notice the loss. He had gone on to say that speculation and meditation brought one no nearer the solution of abstract problems, although they were good as "an intellectual exercise." His implication, as I conceived it, was that abstract thought might serve a purpose in developing the mind to deal with the complexities of practical problems—over which the purely "practical" man stumbled.

Another straw in the wind caught my attention one evening in June, 1934. He had come up to London to meet his old ally, the Emir Abdullah at the Newcombes'. Afterwards, I drove him back to Waterloo and on the way he complained of the way the newspapers hunted him. I told him that he had himself to blame; that when a man who had achieved a measure of reputation refused his normal share of publicity, he was bound to get much more than his share. T.E. laughed, and remarked that he might still want this—and even more than he had. For it was possible that his greatest activity might still lie ahead.

After some talk of approaches that had been made to him, and of the signs that there was a growing demand for a new lead, he swung back when I put the direct question whether he contemplated taking a lead in any movement. "No"—he still kept the intention of settling down in his cottage, to taste the joys of leisure. If he grew tired of it, however, there were many things he might do. This discussion strengthened my feeling that his outlook, if not his attitude, was changing more than he realized.

There were moments in this last year when I wondered whether the depths of his thought were as clear as they had been. Although I was accustomed to discount the extravagances of his humour, there were things said in apparent seriousness that seemed to conflict with the light that he had shed. I had to remind myself that his mind was too cosmic to be consistent. But it seemed, also, to be suffering from some growing pressure. Was a new urge to action disturbing the wisdom gained in reflection? Such a positive urge might cause the greater disturbance because reflection had carried him too far in negation.

The previous December I had shown him the final passage of my book, ending "He is the Spirit of Freedom, come incarnate to a world in fetters." T.E. thereupon suggested that he did not so much respect the freedom of others as insist on his own—he was the "essential anarch": the very opposite of a Socialist. I questioned this view of himself, asking how it could be reconciled with his immense understanding of others. To this, he retorted that such understanding was easy for him because of the conditions in which he lived—with most people it was clogged by wealth, possessions, houses, families, conventions. Taking a sheet of paper he wrote what he suggested I should insert as a postscript to my concluding note—"This paragraph, seeming to me very personal was shown to the object of it who remarked that probably he more resembled a very agile pedestrian dodging the traffic along the main road." The jest was good, and had more than a flavour of truth. But I recalled a longer talk one night in October when we had discussed Hogarth's view of him. Where Hogarth imputed callousness to him, T.E. suggested the impression was largely due to his manner; he dwelt on his profound "shyness," and his dislike of giving himself away—surely a flaw, I suggested, in one so clearsighted. I went on to speak of Hogarth's comment that if

T.E.'s will decided on the end there was no morality about the means. To this T.E. demurred, saying that he "liked to appear careless of morality, but was not really so." He agreed with my view that the means governed the end, ill means distorting the end.

If there were some things in his behaviour, and more in his talk, which did not tally with such a view, I believe that it was truer to his fundamental nature than what sometimes flashed on the surface, or the currents that moved just beneath it. He was as the sea to a pond compared with many simple natures, and the storms were proportionately rougher.

His attitude was more consistent than his words, or even than his action—and safer to trust. He was the *Spirit* of Freedom, but his spirit was incarnate in a complex physical organism. His mind was abnormally free from the conventions of the society into which he was born: it could not get free from the abnormal tensions of the body with which he was born. As he was all too conscious.

One may find some significance even in one of the lighter episodes of that last summer—produced by a man who had been representing himself as "Colonel Lawrence." Such impersonations were not infrequent; sometimes they brought him letters from injured women who had succumbed too easily to the reflected attraction of mystery. But this one was of wider extent and longer duration. When it was brought to my notice I passed the news on to T.E., whose reply opened characteristically—"If you see the blighter do rub into him that I have never signed myself as Lawrence since 19 twenty something. He is years out of date. In fact he doesn't sound the right sort of man at all." After complying with his request to consult a legal friend of his, I had no further connection with the affair; but I heard the sequel from him a month later. In company with the lawyer and two detectives he had gone to a meeting that had been arranged. "We interviewed my imposure and persuaded him that he was not me. To my relief, he agreed at once. Had he stuck to his statement I should have begun to question myself." As no money had actually passed, the impostor was let off, after he had written letters of explanation and apology to his various victims. After seeing the man T.E. did not find the impersonation flattering to himself, or to the intelligence of those who had been taken in. Among his achievements the man had persuaded a firm to publish some of his poems, and had condemned some of the camels at the Zoo as mangy. But "the unkindest cut of all," as T.E. remarked, was that he had been "under observation as a case by the specialists of a mental institution, still under my former name." What a safety valve was T.E.'s sense of humour.

To find unity in this medley of memories is hardly easier than to find it in such a manifold man. But as I look back, I seem to trace a thread running through that last year—the resurgent desire for creation. The philosophical negation that had formerly led him to say "I could not approve creation," was itself denied by his self-confessed desire to be a creative artist, and by his efforts at its fulfilment—which had extended to the plastic and the pictorial as well as to the literary art. It was in depression with his failure to attain his own standard, or to find that ideal standard itself, that he had turned about abruptly and become "a cog in the machine." But the creativeness he had sought to attain was "to carry a super-structure of ideas upon or above anything I made." I thought he threw a further light on his ambition when one evening we talked of Freud, and he argued that, as in all new developments, the style itself passed but the thread remained—thus producing a difference in all thinking henceforward. He instanced Cubism—now past, yet its influence had permanently affected art. We could only see a facet at a time, but with each new facet seen there was enlargement of man's thought.

Thus it was that he came to feel, I think, that the military art was one in which he had attained creativeness: perhaps the only one. To this realization I may have helped him, and if it was a sphere not large enough, a plane not high enough to satisfy him, he seemed to find a contentment within its limits that was beyond him elsewhere. Certainly, he showed a balance in discussion of it that contrasted with some of his talk of other spheres. And the last time we met he told me that the job he would take if offered was that of co-ordinating our defence system. But he did not deem such a chance likely, knowing that this is a sphere where the creative mind is viewed with more than normal distrust; so that it may be able to influence ideas but has rarely been allowed to take a hand in rebuilding the structure on which a super-structure of ideas can be consolidated. As a consequence the evolution of warfare has remained through the centuries no more than a "swing of the pendulum"—as he often reminded me.

To those who have a hunger for creation, architecture has a

specially strong appeal: for which reason I have come to find significance in its long-standing appeal to T.E. It was almost his earliest passion, and remained with him throughout. Thanks to it, he found a channel of expression, and also another safety valve for the surging forces within him, in the rebuilding of his cottage in Dorset. It was "half a ruin" when he first rented these few acres of land from a distant kinsman; he set to work to slate the roof himself, and travelled round the country on his motorcycle, making acquaintance with builders from whom he "scrounged" slates—it surprised him that no less than nine thousand were needed. In the years that followed, he continued his work for its improvement inside and out, until he had created a little gem of domestic architecture, essentially unique, which most aptly expressed the nature of the occupant. Likewise did its location—lying on a remote heath, starkly bare, it was tucked away in a cluster of rhododendrons, secretive yet friendly, beneath the shoulder of a ridge whence one could see for miles in all directions; from the cottage itself there was a single vista—westwards to Dorchester Cathedral and the setting sun. Apt was its name, Clouds' Hill.

As the term of his service drew to a close, T.E.'s thoughts seemed to focus increasingly on the prospect of rest in this quiet spot,—"my very beloved cottage." Here he had the sense of community with the soil. Here he hoped to find balm for the soreness of the feeling that he was "just not good enough"—by a standard that found no consolation in comparisons.

At the end of August the last target-boat of the year's program was finished, although he had still to deal with a new Diesel marine engine that was being installed for experiment. Its possibilities still kept alive an interest in his work on speed-boat developments that was palling now that he once again had the sense of a mission accomplished. His dominant note became one of tiredness, mental and physical: a tiredness, I think, increased by consciousness of new stresses within. In September he wrote me:

"Tired, very: and at the end of my motor-boat knowledge. Determined to work in these last six months to tie up all loose ends and so ensure my successor i/c Boats a fair start, without commitments—and after that six months no plans at all. What I feel like is a rest that should go on and on till I wanted no more of it—or wanted nothing else.

"The last thing desirable is activity for the sake of activity. I hope I have enough mind for it to be quietly happy by itself. So I shall not do anything until it becomes necessary: or at least that is my hope. Not a plan in my head, not an ambition, not a want: but a doubt that my saved capital may not be enough to keep me in peace.

"Enough or not enough, I'm going to have that rest, anyway!"

In October, after telling me of his task with the Diesel, he finished, "Clouds' Hill, in the background, is the best part of the picture. How bored I'm going to be! Think of it: a really new experience, for hitherto I've never been bored."

In a letter on New Year's Eve, after urging me to pursue certain paths of study we had travelled together, he ended:

"For myself I am going to taste the flavour of true leisure. For 46 years have I worked and been worked. Remaineth 23 years (of expectancy). May they be like Flecker's

a great Sunday that goes on and on

If I like this leisure when it comes, do me the favour of hoping that I may be able to afford its prolongation for ever and ever."

Yet as the time drew near, spelling the end of the service that like all other pursuits he had felt as a servitude, a feeling of unease grew. Loosing the chains came to seem like casting adrift. The prospect perplexed and disturbed him.

He took his discharge at Bridlington, and rode south on a "push-bike," visiting old haunts and friends in this old way. Thereby he hoped to tast the first sweet flavour of leisure, besides eluding the reporters and photographers who were in wait for a man on the famous motorcycle. Pat Knowles, his faithful retainer and friend, meantime laid a false trail at the cottage until the first wave of news interest had subsided. The ruse partially succeeded but some "free lance" photographers still hung about after T.E. came home, and continued to intrude on his privacy until ejected from the garden in a "rough and tumble" scrap. In revenge, they came back and threw stones at his roof, smashing some of the slates. He told me of this when he came to see me a few days later in London, where he had taken refuge from such annoyances. He also said that he had now taken to a "push-bike" for good, having come to the conclusion that, with an income of two pounds a week, he could no longer afford to run a high-powered motorcycle. I heaved a premature sigh of relief. Not many months before he had suffered another narrow escape —skidding on a tramline in Bournemouth the cycle fell over and a car had run over it, but he had jumped aside in the nick of time.

But the resolve palled after his return to Clouds' Hill, where the strain of leisure became greater as it released the activity of his mind. In a letter to Eric Kennington early in May, he wrote "Days seem to dawn, suns to shine, evenings to follow, and then I sleep. What I have done, what I am doing, what I am going to do puzzle me and bewilder me. Have you ever been a leaf and fallen from your tree in autumn and been really puzzled about it. That's the feeling."

If he could not solve the puzzle, he might ease the strain by recourse to a familiar outlet—his motorcycle. That tried friend still lay there, mutely appealing: he answered the call. And thus his last call came. On the morning of Monday, May 13th, he rode into Bovington Camp to send a telegram: on the way back he was seen to swerve suddenly in passing a couple of boys who were cycling the same way and the next moment the motorcycle was "twisting and turning over and over again along the road." The only independent witness declared that T.E. had just passed "a black car" before his swerve to avoid the boys, but these were certain they had not passed any car— a conflict of evidence which gave a final tinge of mystery to the accident. T.E. lay in the road, unconscious, his face covered with blood. He was picked up by an army lorry which happened to come along, and taken to the military hospital—which might seem a final touch of irony. But no effort was spared by those in charge during the days that followed, and meantime a vast public hung in anxiety on the news that filtered through a cordon of privacy.

For six days he lay unconscious, kept alive when most of his functions had stopped by a vitality that amazed the doctors. On the seventh, he passed.

And thus, on a Sunday, there dawned for him the "great Sunday that goes on and on."

THE MAN OF REFLECTION

In attempting to sum up T.E. as a man—his *personal* achievement—there is something to be added to what has emerged in the course of this book. The idea I have formed of his character is, inevitably, no more than what I could see by the dim light that is one man's understanding of another. But what I saw looked more like gold and less like brass the closer I came. Contact with many who are acclaimed by the world as great men produces disillusionment, or at least a consciousness of the limitations that encompass their powers. The same is true of a close study of their careers. In contrast, lengthening acquaintance with T.E. brought explanation of certain reservations I earlier made, while closer study of his career served to enlarge my appreciation of his achievement, personal and public.

There is a passage in the Book of Proverbs which might have been coined for him—"Wisdom is the principal thing; therefore get wisdom: and with all thy getting get understanding."

For this he lived. He was essentially a "Crusader," dedicated to the pursuit of an ideal. It began with the dream of freeing a race from bondage: it became, as his reflection developed, a philosophical crusade. Although formal religion did not touch him, I have come to view him as a man driven by an intense *religious* urge—in the deeper sense.

Through the pursuit his power grew. In dealing with men he had what Stirling has aptly described as an "uncanny ability to sense their feelings . . . ; to probe behind their minds and to uncover the wellsprings of their actions." It was uncanny. I have never known a man who seemed to have such power to read one's thoughts. Deception seemed a vain indulgence—and only the stupid attempted it. Happily for them, sympathy was blended with his insight, so that he was filled with understanding. Only when he looked inward was his sight less sure, and his attitude unforgiving.

He knew others: himself he did not know. He saw too many facets to see himself whole. And his senses were an impediment to his mind, thus creating a drag on his spirit. Nevertheless, his wisdom kept pace with his knowledge well enough to restrain him from the abuse of his power, and to guide him in using it, as far as he would use it, for others' benefit. If his humanity baffled him, he came nearer to fulfiling that passage in Proverbs than any man I have met or studied.

A study of history, past and in the making, seems to suggest that most of mankind's troubles are man-made, and arise from the compound effect of decisions taken without knowledge, ambitions uncontrolled by wisdom, and judgments that lack understanding. Their ceaseless repetition is the grimmest jest that destiny plays on the human race. Men who are helped to authority by their knowledge continually make decisions on questions beyond their knowledge. Ambition to maintain their authority forbids them from admitting the limits of their knowledge, and calling upon the knowledge that is available in other men. Ambition to extend the bounds of their authority leads them to a frustration of others' opportunity and an interference with others' liberty that, with monotonous persistency, injures themselves or their successors on the rebound.

The fate of mankind in all ages has been the plaything of petty personal ambitions. The blend of wisdom with knowledge would restrain men from contributing to this endless cycle of folly, but only understanding can guide them towards positive progress.

T.E., by contrast, was rare among men of influence in adjusting his opinions to his knowledge. He was rarer still in avoiding abuse of the power that knowledge brings, in freeing himself from the desires that commonly divert this power into channels harmful to other men's gifts and growth. Understanding was the explanation, the sympathetic understanding of other men and the more critical if less complete understanding of his own nature—the deficiency here was in synthesis rather than in analysis. There was less dust on his windowpanes than on those of any other man I have known.

That is the Lawrence (or Shaw) one knew. But there was always a Lawrence (and Shaw) who remained elusive. His actions were so baffling sometimes, and his attitudes so variable, as to be exasperating even to friends familiar with his ways—how much more provoking must they have been to men of prejudice! But when one was tempted to accuse him of being unreasonable the echo of his own comment on the Arabs came in answer—"Their minds work just as ours do, but on different premises. There is nothing unreasonable, incomprehensible, or inscrutable in the Arabs." T.E. could not have played the Arab so well unless he had made his mind Arab. And the Arab in him survived, even though it faded.

So did the actor. He had been too long, for the sake of a cause, "an actor in a foreign theatre, playing a part day and night for months without rest, and for an anxious stake." On his art great issues had depended, and to it was largely due his extraordinary success in handling Arabs, and others—soldiers, civil servants, and politicians. What diversity of type and purpose there was among these human elements in the Arab problem—only by suiting his appeal to each had he been able to harness such a team to his end. After playing so many parts for so long, how could he shed the habit of acting? Doubtless, the gift was inborn. Probably, the circumstances of his early life had developed it. In boyhood he had been painfully self-conscious, and even when achievement had removed cause for it he remained too conscious of fate's first injustice. This was an addition to the usual buffets suffered by those who are aloof from the herd, and from which sensitive individuals are apt to seek a shield in pose and pretension.

What man, or woman, does not act—in their contacts with others? The difference is only one of degree. If the tendency was greater than normal in T.E., it was not only from capacity, but because necessity forced its cultivation. And his own awareness of it made it more difficult to discard. Rather, it egged him on, as he confessed, to "embark on little wanton problems of conduct, observing the impact of this or that approach on my hearers, treating fellow men as so many targets for intellectual ingenuity, until I could hardly tell my own self where the leg-pulling began or ended." His fundamental honesty made this uncomfortable for him. And all his activities likewise. "They were intensely conscious efforts, with my detached self always eyeing the performance from the wings in criticism." One may say of him that his worst failure was his inability to become natural. It was reduced, and its dangers redressed, by his quickness of self-perception. The recoil, however, was too quick for his comfort. It was far easier for friends to overlook his faults than for him. "I was a standing court-martial on myself." All motives are mixed, as none saw more clearly than he. Charitable to others, he was hard on himself—too ready to exaggerate the less worthy elements in the mixture.

That acute self-perception and excessively sharp recoil may explain much. The more one came to appreciate his wisdom the more surprising seemed his failure to free himself from trivial inconsistencies. One wondered that a man so powerful in reason could take refuge in small irrationalities. That a man so truthful was apt to indulge in needless mystification. That a man so honest was prone to little deceits of a harmless kind; also to self-justification, even though he affected to disregard it and certainly despised it. His self-depreciation, like his rejection of distinctions, had a vein of vanity.

The further one probed the more one realized the immensity of his knowledge; yet one noted a knack, conscious or not, of circling round the gaps; and of masking the movement by producing some rare fragment of knowledge that was likely to have a surprise effect. One noted, too, that he was less ready to make a direct acknowledgment of ignorance over a specific point than to admit a more general limitation. Then there was his chameleon-like tendency to adapt himself to his surroundings; and one sometimes caught him saying different things to different people. Few of us are devoid of this tendency, and in some measure it may be a practical necessity. If it was more marked in him than was to be expected that may have been because his standards and his stature made him more of a mark; perhaps also the tendency is inherent in the indirect approach which he so effectively applied.

Inconsistency also marked his attitude to public acclaim. Perhaps one may come near to an explanation thus—he saw its falsity, felt its glow, despised himself for feeling pleasure, found pleasure in abasement, saw falsity in his feeling—circular motion along an endless coil. He had a genuine distaste for publicity, not only, I think, because it was contrary to his sense of values, but because it clashed with his self-veiling tendency. Yet it attracted as well as amused him. Also he found momentary pleasure in exercising its attraction. The frankness with which he uncovered many aspects of himself was accompanied by intermittent coyness in concealing others—like a woman hiding her ankles while exposing her bosom. Perhaps in far more than normal measure he was both masculine and feminine.

So powerfully charged with contrasting currents, there was continuous war within him—"reason strong enough to win, but not strong enough to annihilate the vanquished, or refrain from liking them better." Yet there was also a wonderful blend, in the depths below the level of consciousness, so that in the content and in the effect the good vastly predominated. His faults were near the surface, his virtues profound. In contrast to one's experience with others, the deeper one penetrated the more difficult it became to gauge his limits —until one was forced to admit that here was a man bigger in personality and intellect than any other one had known. His greatness can be judged to some extent by his works, if examined, and by the impression he made on others, in close contact.

But it was his fundamental goodness, less expected, which impressed itself still more as acquaintance extended. Such goodness, unlike the near-surface faults, does not lend itself to analysis. But we know it when we feel it—if responsive. So far as distinction is possible, one may say that his positive virtues embraced an intense kindliness, an unstinted generosity, an essential fairness, a compassion which was the truer for being free from sentimentality, a purity of motive so fine that it vomited at any flavour of impurity, a scrupulousness in honouring any promise even when merely an agent, a thirst for truth, and a high courage that could carry him on when the spirit quailed and the flesh weighed down. Negatively, his goodness lay in subduing the temptations to which his supercharged faculties and senses impelled him.

In that never ending struggle he suffered sorely. It was easier for others, who felt the outward radiation, to appreciate the predominance of his virtues. He was too conscious of the conflict within. And because of this also, he may have underrated, even while confessing, the pleasure he obtained "between the walls of living." His life had more harmony than his thought. If this was a turmoil, it was travelling in a state of contentment—like a typhoon in the Pacific.

It may have been to the loss of the age he lived in that his sense of futility imposed too strong a check on his activity. I cannot see, if perhaps because of my own limitations of vision, any sufficient justification for the way he abstained from contributions to knowledge for which he was peculiarly fitted. His balance tipped too far on the negative side: perhaps because he took the sins of the world on himself in a too grand gesture of atonement: perhaps because of a tendency to adjust his philosophy to his inclination when the two did not fit yet did not directly clash.

But the loss to his age may be far outweighed in time to come if what he contributed to the current of thought—not least by living his ideas—continues its radiation. The message is more positive than the man.

THE MAN OF ACTION

No man has come so close to equal greatness in action and reflection. The perfect balance may be unattainable. T.E. himself came to this conclusion. His progress in the reflective sphere caused him to forgo the prizes that were within his reach as a man of action. Perhaps it is better so for the world.

Without the fullness of understanding he attained, his public achievement would have made him a public danger, of the Napoleonic order. On the other hand, without that understanding it is questionable whether his performance would have been so great, for his resources were far less and his circumstances more difficult than those of most men who have carved history with the sword. The legend that has grown up round his personality has obscured rather than enhanced the significance of his military achievement. What the Arab campaign meant to the course of the World War I have already brought out. What it means in the evolution of war is a question worth pondering.

There is an essential difference between the Arab campaign as it was guided by Lawrence and the normal irregular campaign of the past. It was waged against an enemy who, however backward in civilization, was as dependent as any Western State on the lifeline of modern civilization—the railway. An enemy, too, who had been compelled by the unmilitary march of progress to adopt the mechanical tools of modern warfare, and was thus bound to forfeit the value of his man-power, if his material became exhausted. Against this enemy, the Arab campaign was conducted on an applied theory which inverted the conventional military doctrine in such a way as to convert Arab weaknesses into strength and Turkish strength into a weakness.

At first glance the very completeness of this inversion would suggest that it widens the past gulf between regular and irregular warfare. But on reflection one can see that its success turned on new material conditions which are even more marked in modern regular warfare. No civilized nation can maintain itself long without the railway, or maintain war without munitions. What the Arabs did yesterday the Air Forces may do tomorrow. And in the same way— yet more swiftly. Mobile land forces such as tanks and motor guerrillas may share in the process.

Moreover, this new exploitation of the changed "biological" conditions of war may be coupled with a more calculated exploitation of the psychological conditions—to which Lawrence also showed the way. To disarm is more potent than to kill. And in this process of disarming, materially and mentally, the old concentration of force is likely to be replaced by an intangibly ubiquitous distribution of force—pressing everywhere yet assailable nowhere.

Here is the wider lesson that Lawrence's campaign offers. And it is a supreme tribute to his military insight that in developing his theory of irregular warfare he was conscious of its application to all warfare—although he left this to the perception of those who could read between the lines.

To remove any doubts on this point I add an extract from a letter he wrote me in 1928.

"The logical system of Clausewitz is too complete. It leads astray his disciples—those of them, at least, who would rather fight with their arms than with their legs. There is, in studying the practice of all decent generals, a striking likeness between the principles on which they acted—and often a comic divergence between the principles they framed with their mouths. A surfeit of the hit school brings on an attack of the run method; and then the pendulum swings back. You, at present, are trying (with very little help from those whose business it is to think on their profession) to put the balance straight after the orgy of the late war. When you succeed (about 1945) your sheep will pass your bounds of discretion and have to be chivvied back by some later strategist. Back and forward we go."

That letter is a further light not only on his military ideas but on his post-war career—on the withdrawal from activity which puzzled the world he lived in. A man of such historical sense could not fail to see the truth that underlies the cynical epigram—"History teaches us that we do not learn from history." It helped him to quench his desire to contribute to what could only be another swing of the pendulum. And he thought in periods too long to make it a matter of much importance that for a time—hypothetically 1945—the pendulum might be near the mean.

But we are left with the fact that in conception his theory had a general application. That fact brings him into relation with the whole of war, and gives a new meaning to his exploits in Arabia and Syria. Military history cannot dismiss him as merely a successful leader of irregulars. He is seen to be more than a guerrilla genius—rather does he appear a strategist of genius who had the vision to anticipate the guerrilla trend of civilized warfare that arises from the growing dependence of nations on industrial resources.

He has thus a claim to historical consideration among those we call the Great Captains. Quality of art, not quantity of force, is the true standard. Napoleon's genius is far clearer in his masterpiece of 1796, executed with 30,000 men, than in his grandiose failure with 450,000 in 1812.

If the mere size of the armies they commanded were to be the gauge we should reach the palpable absurdity of counting Joffre greater than Napoleon, and of ruling out altogether such great commanders as Cromwell and Stonewall Jackson, or even Marlborough and Turenne, by reason of the comparative puniness of the forces they handled. No one would challenge their position on this ground, so that one cannot question Lawrence's because his forces were on a still smaller scale. Indeed, they bore a far closer relation to Cromwell's 11,000 men at Dunbar or Stonewall Jackson's 6,000 in the Shenandoah Valley, than did these to the army that Moltke commanded, or than the latter itself bore to the march of millions that Foch directed.

And if we reckon force in terms of fire power, as we should, Lawrence's forces were more considerable than their numbers appear—in his operative bodyguard, normally about thirty men, every other man was armed with a light automatic, so that this handful possessed more fire power than battalions of a thousand men in 1914.

If smallness of force is no ground for excluding Lawrence from the roll of great strategists, largeness of area is a strong ground for his inclusion. To quote his own dictum, historically just—"Range is more to strategy than force."

There are few of the Great Captains whose operations have ranged over a thousand miles of territory, and in his the geographical extent was magnified by the racial content. Another possible objection which shrivels on examination lies in the fact that his strategic independence was qualified by its relation to the British campaign in Palestine. If such be counted a disqualification, we should have to rule out Marlborough because of his closer ties with Eugène, and Wellington for his relationship first to the Spanish in the Peninsula and then to Blücher in 1815. Turenne and Condé would likewise come under the guillotine, and Bonaparte would be severed from Napoleon.

Can we, however, go further than admit Lawrence's claim to consideration on this roll? His strategy was so much an inversion of tradition that comparison with his forerunners may seem difficult. In method it certainly is, yet hardly more difficult than to compare the strategy of Hannibal or Marlborough with that of Napoleon, who profited by the revolutionary change that the advent of the "divisional system" had brought. There was an immense gulf between the strategic manœuvre of armies that moved as a single unit and that of the Napoleonic army, distributed in separate and self-contained "divisions"—as well might one compare tennis and football. And there was a fresh gulf between Napoleon's road-moves and modern rail-moves.

The true line of comparison between the strategists of different ages lies through their art and not through their mechanism. It is possible to make a comparative study of the use they made of the means at their disposal to achieve their effects; particularly the use they made of surprise and mobility to upset their opponent's mental and physical balance, and thereby change the balance of the campaign in their own favour. By this test Lawrence comes out high.

It is even possible, with such as have disclosed their conception of strategy, to gauge how far their effects were a matter of calculation. Few have done so as fully as Lawrence, yet by this severe test he comes out still higher.

Moreover, by general recognition the supreme art of the strategist is to convert his opponent's advantages to their disadvantage, while minimizing his own disadvantages. By this test Lawrence has no peer. For the dominant idea in his strategy was to turn the weakness of the Arabs into an asset, and the strength of the Turks into a debit!

Even from the point of view of orthodox strategy, which seeks a decision rather than a creeping paralysis, there is rare value to be gained from a study of the Arab campaign, especially in its later phase. For the possibility of a decision depends on the success of the preliminary distraction. This fundamental truth of war has been under-emphasized, and its importance grossly underrated, by military historians—to the recurrent cost of their countries in war. Distraction is far more than "half the battle"; nine-tenths would be nearer the mark. And nowhere have I found in the records of war such subtly conceived and skilfully gauged distraction as that developed by Lawrence in aid of the Arabs and Allenby. If it offers a lesson for soldiers to study, it offers a proof of what he had learnt by having studied the eighteenth century masters—the last who gave due attention to this vital subject. Similarly, in Lawrence's invariable care to provide his plan with variants, or alternative courses, we may trace his debt to Bourcet, the first military thinker to enunciate the principle that "every plan ought to have branches."

As a tactician, there is less cope for comparison between Lawrence and his forerunners. Not merely because his tactics were mainly irregular but because his strategy went so far to minimize the need for tactics. Rightly, strategy is put before tactics in judging commanders even in regular warfare, for the better the strategic prelude the more assured will be the tactical issue. Few of the Great Captains can offer more than three or four battles for examination. Lawrence can only offer one. But that is a gem. His own mockery of his achievement cannot hide the fact that at Tafila he displayed a tactical artistry, based on consummate calculation, in the purest classical tradition. It was Cannæ, or still more, Ilipa, adapted to modern weapons.

Here also, but not here alone, Lawrence revealed what he himself has so aptly described as "the irrational tenth" which is "like the kingfisher flashing across the pool." It is the flair which makes the great executant. Lawrence can bear comparison with Marlborough or Napoleon in that vital faculty of generalship, the power of grasping instantly the picture of the ground and situation, of relating the one to the other, and the local to the general. Indeed, there is much to suggest that his topographical and geographical sense was more remarkable than theirs.

He generated too, the same electric current of command, and one might justly argue that he generated a stronger current than theirs.

For in contrast to them he was not in command, yet there is over-whelming witness to the fact that, in reality, he exercised command. His power of command triumphed over a double handicap such as no other general of fame has borne. Like Bourcet, who certainly deserves to be counted among the masters of war, Lawrence had to give directions under the disguise of advice, yet his personality rose above his handicap more successfully than Bourcet's. Like Marl-borough, he had to combine the operations and reconcile the dis-cordant aims of allies, yet suffered fewer set-backs. It is true that he received an unwavering support from Allenby such as Marlborough did not receive from Anne, but while Marlborough had to deal with several allies, Lawrence had to deal with a multitude.

This raises a further reflection. The more one studies Lawrence's military career the more points of resemblance one finds with the man who is justly regarded as England's most representative military genius. In Lawrence, as in Marlborough, one finds the profound understanding of human nature, the power of commanding affection while communicating energy, the knack of smoothing out troubles, the consummate blend of diplomacy with strategy, the historic English instinct that there is more in war than the winning of battles, the sense of ground combined with the wider sense of geog-raphy, and perhaps above all, the uncanny calm that acts like oil on a turbulent sea.

To Lawrence, by the verdict of those who have seen him in crisis and confusion, may aptly be applied the words with which Voltaire depicted Marlborough—"He had to a degree above all other gen-erals of his time that calm courage in the midst of tumult, that serenity of soul in danger, which the English call a cool head, and it was perhaps this quality, the greatest gift of nature for command which formerly gave the English so many advantages over the French in the plains of Crécy, Poitiers and Agincourt." It was repeated in the wider plains of Arabia.

There is a further likeness between Lawrence and Marlborough —in one of the means they employed to assist their strategy. Igno-rance of the way Marlborough used money to maintain the alliance against France may explain much of the ignorant disparagement of Lawrence's military achievement on account of the bags of gold at his disposal. It would be difficult to find in our history a coalition

war where Britain's subsidies have not played an indispensable part
in the victory and equally difficult to find one where so great effects
have been produced at so small an expenditure.

The explanation, and the fairest verdict upon Lawrence, has been
expressed by the one among his companions in arms who was the
most regular in outlook.

Sir Hubert Young has written—"Lawrence could certainly not
have done what he did without the gold, but no one else could have
done it with ten times the amount."

If Marlborough also made good use of the gold he handled there
is a profound difference between Marlborough's venality and Lawrence's incorruptibility: as also between Marlborough's use of his
allies as pawns in the game of war that took increasing possession
of his soul, and Lawrence's sensitive regard for their interests and
his country's honour, as well as his own honour. So many military
senses had these two in common, but there is an unfathomable gulf
between their sense of honour. The difference is to be explained
not so much in terms of character, but of thought.

Lawrence plumbed depths over which Marlborough was content
to sail by the chart of his age. If this habit of taking deep surroundings
was an increasing hindrance to Lawrence's progress towards personal success, it was of inestimable service to him in avoiding the
unknown reefs on which generalship has so often been wrecked. He
profited not only from the experience of his forerunners through
the ages, but from his own deep reflection. To their instinct for war
he added a reasoned theory of war more profound than any of the
Great Captains have revealed. If this statement be questioned I
can only refer the reader to Chapter IX of this book, and pose him
the counter question as to where among the writings, dispatches,
and recorded utterances of the Great Captains there is to be found
an "appreciation" of war that can compare with this for breadth
and depth. When I first read it in 1920 it made an instant impression, but I am forced to confess that it was only when I came back
to it after another twelve years spent in continuous study of war
that I came to realize how far Lawrence's thought had travelled, and
how much I had originally missed. It is only now, if even now, that
I appreciate its full significance.

One of the most common experiences when men converse on a

subject that they have studied is the sudden jolt of finding that one of them is out of his depth. It is quite a different feeling from that of disagreement—indeed, it more often comes when men are exploring a subject in unison than when they are arguing opposite views, for then they are making the debating points they know. The relevance of this phenomenon of human intercourse is that it helps to explain both the impatience which Lawrence often showed towards opinionated generals and the respect in which he was held by some of the most exalted in rank but humble in mind, who had worked with him. What the depth of his understanding of war may be I do not know, and may never discover, but I know that almost every other man I have met would be out of his depth long before.

The power of Lawrence's personality is generally recognized, but its radiance has obscured the deeper power that his knowledge gave him. Yet here lies the main message that his war achievement bears for the world, and especially the military world.

For the truth is that Lawrence was more steeped in knowledge of war than any of the generals of the last war.

At first sight this statement may seem startling, but it is essentially matter of fact. Many of the generals of the last war certainly knew more about the working of the military machine than Lawrence, but in all else that counted he had the advantage. His youth helped him. They had spent so many years in rising to command that, naturally, they could not hope to have his intimate experience in using the weapons on which tactics are based. As young officers some of them may have been musketry or gunnery experts, but that experience had inevitably lost much of its value through the evolution of weapons and the methods of handling them. The machine-gun which dominated the battlefields of 1914–1918, was a new development since their youth, and the light automatic, scarcely less important in its influence, had only been introduced since the war began. All these he mastered, showing an aptitude rare even in receptive youth, and adding something of his own to their tactical use. Aircraft were another novelty that he came to understand through actual flying experience that no other commander of land forces enjoyed. He also overrode the barriers that in former days prevented infantry and cavalry soldiers from intruding into the sapper's or gunner's field; thus he added to his equipment an expert grasp of demolitions and a working grasp of gunnery.

This first-hand knowledge of the tools of command, if not essential, was at least invaluable. In the light of history we can perceive that if other high commanders of 1914–1918 had possessed a similar knowledge it would have saved them from their most fatal errors, and would also have shown them how to gain full value from their new tools. The great commanders of old, when weapons were simple and slow-changing, built up their strategic plans on a personal knowledge of the groundwork. Their modern successors, unfortunately, had exchanged it for a too exclusive knowledge of staff-work. The increasing specialization of warfare is largely responsible for the sterilization of generalship. It is likely to become worse as warfare becomes more scientific. It can only be overcome by wide thought and hard work. But of few can we expect the prodigious capacity for both that Lawrence revealed, helped by a remarkable sense of proportion and a still more remarkable ability to free himself from social distractions.

It was through this that in youth he had acquired his knowledge of the history and higher theory of war—I have never known a general who had read as widely. In particular did he profit by having studied those eighteenth century thinkers who paved the way for the revolution in strategy that began on the eve of the French Revolution, and of whom Napoleon was the pupil. This profound knowledge of historical experience, enriched by a general knowledge of many subjects that indirectly concerned war, formed an intellectual equipment such as no other commander of his time possessed.

When checked by personal experience it gave him a theoretical mastery of war that was also unique. His personality transmitted this into a practical mastery. The real message of his astonishing war career is best given in his own words—the explanation with which he confirmed the impression that had grown on me in examining the course of the Arab campaign. "I was not an instinctive soldier, automatic with intuitions and happy ideas. When I took a decision, or adopted an alternative it was after doing my best to study every relevant—and many an irrelevant—factor. Geography, tribal structure, religion, social customs, language, appetites, standards—were at my finger-ends. The enemy I knew almost like my own side. I risked myself among them many times, to *learn*.

"The same with tactics. If I used a weapon well, it was because I could handle it. Rifles were easy. I put myself under instructors for Lewis, Vickers and Hotchkiss. I learned about explosives from my R.E. teachers, and developed their methods. To use aircraft I flew. To use armoured cars I learned to drive and fight them. I became a bad gunner at need, and could doctor and judge a camel.

"For my strategy, I could find no teachers in the field: but behind me there were some years of military reading, and even in the little that I have written about it, you may be able to trace the allusions and quotations, the conscious analogies.

"Do make it clear that generalship, at least in my case, came not by instinct, unsought, but by understanding, hard study and brain-concentration. Had it come easy to me I should not have done it as well."

By his own standard he fell short—"The perfect general would know everything in heaven and earth." He must be judged, however, by historical standards. It may be true as he said to me, when regretting the "fundamental, crippling, incuriousness" that he felt among so many soldiers, that "with 2,000 years of examples behind us we have no excuse when fighting, for not fighting well." How few, nevertheless, profit by that experience. Because he did, he not only earns a place among the masters of war, but stands out among them by the clearness of his understanding of his art. To give him priority in such a company is not so high a tribute as it may sound. As one's study has deepened one has discovered their limitations, while one failed to find his—in the military sphere. Legend rising from idolatry fed by tradition, and supported by ignorance, has given most of them a legendary stature for exceeding the reality.

Nevertheless, if his right to enter that company can be conceded with less doubt than attaches to others, he remains incongruous. The reason is that in spirit he transcends them. Whatever be the admiration evoked by the Great Captains, even the finest character among them would hardly be regarded as a spiritual force, more potent as such than as a man of action. Yet this is the deeper impression that Lawrence left. And like the proverbial pebble in the pool, its ripples spread.

THE MESSAGE

NOT long ago the young men were talking, the young poets writing, of him in a Messianic strain—as the man who could, if he would, he a light to lead stumbling humanity out of its troubles. It is possible that the spirit might have moved him—but not probable. And it is difficult to see any way, compatible with his philosophy, in which he could have played such a role: his indifference to "politics" was as marked as his distaste for the arts of the platform. But at least I can say that, so far as I knew him, he seemed to come nearer than any man to fitness for such power—in a state that I would care to live in. For to his extraordinary powers of intellect and practical capacity he added an attitude, developed in self-discipline and reflection, that fulfils the one condition in which any evolution could be more than a swing of the pendulum. He had learnt the folly of the reforming energy that merely rebounds from wall to wall. Free from pettiness, freed from ambition, immeasurable in understanding, his profound respect for others' freedom embodies the wisdom of the ages—the wisdom which reveals that life can endure, and manhood develop, only in an atmosphere of freedom.

The opportunity has gone—with the man. But nothing that he might have done is equal to what he may do—as a legendary figure. Legends are more potent than emperors or dictators. Others who worked with him were outstanding men: he would have been the first to wish their merits due recognition. Legend has made his fame as 100 to 1. Such magnification, which happens to a few men in each generation, is not true to reality. But it is true of this case that legend had a solid basis, of far greater content than usual. There will be nothing but good in it, if his real message is remembered, and not merely the romance.

For he was a message to mankind in freedom from possessiveness. In freedom from competitiveness. In freeing oneself from ambition, especially from the lust of power. His power sprang from knowledge and understanding, not from position. His influence is a living growth—because it is a spiritual message transmitting a spiritual force. The man was great: the message is greater.

In him the Spirit of Freedom came incarnate to a world in fetters.

INDEX

Aba el Naam, 141
Abbasid Empire, 42
Abd el Kader, Emir, 193, 194, 198, 199, 200, 201, 254, 295, 298, 299
Abdul Hamid, 26, 34, 43
Abdulla (of Zeid's bodyguard), 216
Abdulla el Feir, Sherif, 182, 220, 221
Abdulla el Nahabi, 207, 208
Abdulla, Emir, 42, 43, 60, 61, 81; character, 82, 88, 99, 101, 103, 114, 117, 122, 123, 127, 131, 140, 142, 174, 245; attacked by the Wahabis, 318; proclaimed King of Irak, 320, 335
Abu el Lissal (Aba el Lissan), 154, 155, 156, 157 *note*, 158, 160, 165, 179, 180, 211, 222, 230, 234, 247, 249, 253, 260, 261, 278
Abu Obeida, 168
Abu Raga, 145
Abu Tayi, The, 159, 232, 234, 269
Abu Zareibat, 103, 105
Abyssinia, 50
Acre, 8, 48, 279
Adana (Antioch), 8, 62
Aden, 45, 51, 245 *note*
Adhub, 231
Ægospotamoi, 221
aeroplanes, Arabs' reverence for, 280
Afghanistan, 79, 346, 347
Afuleh, 272
Ageyli, the, 59, 96, 100, 104, 123, 144, 145, 146, 207, 253
Agincourt, 129, 360
Ahad, the, 46
Aigues Mortes, 5
Aima, 219
Ain Kadeis, 18
Aintab, 8
"Air Force blue," 342
Akaba—*see* Aqaba
Aleppo, 8, 17, 35, 38, 48, 55, 120, 155, 171, 186, 224, 246, 302, 309, 310
Aleppo-Damascus railway, 152
Alexander the Great, 315
Alexandretta, 31, 36, 37, 38, 44
Alexandria, 80, 81
Algeria, 308
Algerians, 295, 297, 300

Ali, 58, 59, 60, 63, 65, 81; character, 82, 88, 99, 117, 174, 245
Ali Haidar, 63, 88
Ali ibn el Hussein, 193, 267
Ali Riza Pasha, 153, 193, 194, 203, 204, 295, 300
Allenby, Gen. Sir Edmund, 8, 163; meets T. E., 167-8; character and position, 168-9; 174, 175, 177, 184, 187; in Palestine campaign, 188-209; adopts Chetwode's plan, 189, 191, 192, 193, 194; official entry into Jerusalem, 206, 222, 223; plans for 1918 campaign, 224; his reinforcements taken away, 225; advantage of reduced force, 225-6; plans for taking Ma'an and Es Salt, 228, 238; his discrepant versions, 239, 240; gets camels for T. E., 242-3
—plan for gaining all Palestine and taking Damascus, 248-50, 251; dependent on Arabs, 261, 265, 272; by feint on Amman, enabled to make coastal attack, 274, 276; defeats Turkish armies, 278; arrives in Damascus, 301; recognizes Arab administration, 301; strength of his forces, 302-3
—organizes military administration of occupied territory, 310, 311, 312, 316, 317, 333, 358, 359
Amanus Mountains, 35-6
Amman, 155, 156, 170, 215, 220, 224, 227, 228, 229, 230, 231, 234, 238, 239, 242, 244, 245, 250, 259, 260, 263, 265, 266, 267, 268, 269, 276, 279, 281, 302, 335
Anatolia, 35
Anazeh, The, 114
Anglo-Russian agreement, 25
Angora, 35
Anne, Queen, 359
Antioch—*see* Adana
Anzac Mounted Division, 229, 238, 239, 276
Aqaba, 17, 18, 19, 48, 77, 78, 108, 115, 118, 119, 143, 150, 151, 153, 154, 155, 156, 160, 161; captured by Arabs, 162-3; effects, 162, 164, 165, 166, 167, 168, 169, 172, 174, 175, 176, 177, 179, 180, 181, 184, 186, 193, 194, 204, 206, 207,

208, 227, 243, 245, 250, 251, 252, 254,
255, 257, 264, 269, 310
Aqaba Gulf of, 164, 165
Arab Bulletin, 95
Arab Bureau, 46, 49, 60, 67, 75-6
Arab character, 84, 109-13, 117, 178, 253,
254, 255
Arab Congress, **320**
Arab Councils, 262-**3**
Arab Northern Army, 210, 232 *note*, 261
Arab Regular Army, 213, 222, 227, 228,
232, 233, 237, 244, 245, 250, 251, 263,
268, 269, 270, 271, 294, 298, 300
Arab secret societies, 20, 44, 46, 49, 70
Arab State, 298, 301, 307, 334, 335
Arabia, physiography of, 84
Arabs, 9, 11, 12, 15, 17, 20; revolt planned,
40-1, 42, 43-51, 58; attack on Mecca, 59-
60; on Jidda, 60-1; mode of warfare,
62, 63-4, 172-3; their mobility an
asset, 64; military and naval help from
British, 65-7; distribution and strength,
81; attitude toward purchasing aid at
cost of independence, 84; munitions,
84-5, 93, 94; surprised at Bir Said, 95-6;
their camp routine, 96-7; guerrilla
methods, 97-8; defense of Yanbo, 98-9;
move north, 100; attack south of
Medina, 101; independence of transport, 103; capture of Wejh, 103-6; its
effect on the course of the revolt, 106;
on relations with British, 107-9; support of fresh tribes, 114-16; blow up
railway at Toweira, 116; other raids,
116-17; raid on El Arish, 121, 130,
131; their ultimate aim, 132; character
of their problem, 137-8; raid on Aba el
Naam, 141; march toward Aqaba, 143 *ff;*
raids on railway, 141-2, 145-6, 155-6,
157; attack at Abu el Lissal, 158-9; don
tunics of dead foes, 160; take Kethira,
161; and Khadra, 161-2; 165, 167, 168,
172, 173, 175, 176; "treachery," 177,
179, 180; loot at train-capture, 183-4;
rewarded at Aqaba, 184
—in Palestine campaign, 191-209; co-
operate in 1918 campaign, 210-48; enter
corn-belt, 210; start move on Tafila,
213-14; "battle," 214-20; in move on
Amman and Es Salt, 228 *ff;* dismayed
by reports of British failure at Amman,
231; foolish attempt to attack Ma'an
directly, 232-4; success at Semna, 233;
their irregular methods, 234-5; their
share in Shunet Nimrin failure, 241;

how handicapped by British aid, 242;
delighted by gift of camels, 243; bad
period during T. E.'s absence, 247, 252,
253-5; in bombing raid at Mudauwara,
257; dissension among chiefs, 261-2,
268-9; their vulnerable side, 276; respect
for British planes, 280, 282, 285, 286;
take Deraa, 288; pleased by Barrow's
capitulation, 289; march toward Damascus, 293-4; take the city, 296-7
—assured by Great Britain of recognition, 308-9, 310-11; representatives at
Paris Peace Conference, 313 *ff*
Arfaja, 146, 147, 150
Armenia, 319
Armenians, 20
armoured cars, 212, 232 *note*, 235, 236,
258, 263, 277
Ashraf (Sherif), the, 253
"Asia Corps," 190
Aspern, Battle of, 126
Asquith, H. T., 77, 87
Astor, Lady, 347, 349
Atara, 230
Atatir, the, 231
Ateiba, the, 59, 100, 141
Atwi, 156
Auda, 114; character, 115, 143, 144, 145,
146, 147, 148, 150, 154, 158, 159, 165,
177, 178, 179, 181, 182, 194, 205, 214,
232, 245, 269, 284, 286, 287, 293, 294,
297, 298, 352
Australian Mounted Division, 194, 239,
279, 294, 295, 298, 300
Auxiliary Air Force, 351
Ayas Bay, 37, 56
Ayubid dynasty, 171
Azrak, 114, 150, 153, 172, 193, 199, 200,
202, 203, 204, 205, 207, 232, 250, 252,
258, 260, 261, 262, 263, 266, 268, 269,
277, 278, 279, 282, 283, 293

Baalbek—*see* Ras Baalbek
Bacon, Francis, 172
Badajoz, 290
Bagche tunnel, 36
Baghdad, 35, 47, 48, 49, 55, 114, 117, 190,
197, 334
Baghdad railway, 15-17, 20, 35, **302**
Baha, T. E.'s camel, 288
Bair, 150, 154, 155, 157, 205, 250, 258, 260
Baker, Sir Herbert, **324**
Balbo, Gen., 349
Balkan War, 27, 70
Barada gorge, 294

Barrow, 285, 286, 288, 289, 292, 293, 295, 297
Bartholomew, 189, 248, 250, 316
Basra, 35, 47, 49, 72, 334
Batra, 157 *note*, 165
Beach, Col., 72
Bedouin (Bedu, *sing.*), 9, 40, 59, 101, 109, 112, 113, 116, 130, 142, 147, 161, 185, 186, 203, 211, 220, 232, 233, 235, 236, 237, 243, 244, 247, 250, 255, 256, 263, 269, 276, 284, 319
Beersheba, 17, 18, 36, 121, 188, 189, 190, 191, 193, 194, 195, 222, 260 *note*
Beersheba Arabs, 165
Beirut, 8, 34, 171, 279, 309, 310, 312
Beisan, 265, 268, 275, 279, 285
Belgium, 69
Belinda, 168
Bell, Gertrude, 146, 326
Ben Ghabrit, Si Kaddour, 80
Bengal Lancers, 296
Ben-my-Chree, 61
Beni Ali, the, 59, 62
Beni Atiyeh, the, 114, 234, 256
Beni Sakhr, the, 153, 172, 193, 198, 201, 202, 213, 214, 230, 238, 239, 241, 245, 266
Bieberstein, Baron Marschall von, 25
Billi, the, 100, 105, 114, 142, 175
bionomics, 135
Bir Abbas, 81
Bir el Waheidi, 101, 102, 103
Bir Said, 96
Birijik, 14
Birkenhead, Lord, 349
Blandford, 343
Blücher, Gen., 357
"Blue Mist," T. E.'s car, 269, 293, 295, 297
Blunt, Wilfrid Scawen, 146
Boers' mobility, 225
Bols, 228, 238, 241
Bolshevik Government, 49
Borton, 279
Bourcet, 126, 127, 128, 172, 200, 255, 266, 358, 359
Bovington Camp, 340, 342
Boyle, Capt., 98, 101, 102, 165
Bozanti, 36
brass band, Arabs' pride in, 82
Brémond, Lieut.-Col., 80, 88, 89, 91, 92, 93, 117, 118, 119, 193, 194, 308, 312, 313
Breslau, 28
Bridge of Lodi, 90

Bristol fighting planes, 279, 282
British Admiralty, 352
British Agency, Cairo, 66
British Air Forces in the Middle East, 180
British Air Ministry, 333, 337, 340
British Army—failure at Gaza, 162; its cost in lives, 163; its aid needed to free Syrian Arabs, 170; officers useful in railway raids, 175-6; in Palestine campaign, 188-?; need to abandon mass method of warfare, 188-9; reinforcements, 190; bombards Gaza, 194; strength in 1918 campaign, 225-6; cross Jordan, occupy Es Salt and Amman, 229; results of raid, 230 *ff*; plans for breaking railway at Ma'an, 234; failure at Shunet Nimrin, 239-41, 249; forces proceed toward Damascus, 282 *ff*; to Kiswe and Jebel Mania, 293-4; into Damascus, 295-6
British Cabinet War Committee, 77, 78, 86, 91
—Eastern Committee, 312
British Colonial office, 332, 333, 337
British Exchequer, 332
British Foreign Office, 26, 44, 47, 66, 78, 79, 81, 91, 313, 317, 320, 332, 333, 349
British General Staff, 56, 66, 68, 74, 75, 78, 79, 86; (in Egypt) 118, 122, 248
British India Office, 333
British Interdepartmental Conference, 320
British Museum expedition, 10
British War Cabinet, 87, 245 *note*
British War Council, 31, 32
British War Office, 17, 31, 68, 70, 81, 128, 320, 332, 333, 340, 352
British Zone, 310, 335
Brough-Superior motor-cycle, 341
Buchan, Col. John, 71, 343
—*Greenmantle*, 71
Bulfin, 249
Bulgaria, 33, 285
Bulgarian Atrocities, 23, 25
Burga, 152
Burmester, Capt., 167
Buxton, Maj. R. V., 250, 251, 255, 257, 258, 259, 260, 263, 327

Cadi, Maj., 80
Cæmerrer, 128
Cæsar, Julius, 221
Cairo, 33, 42, 44, 45, 66, 69, 70, 85, 93, 115, 118, 119, 122, 131, 167, 168, 174, 177, 178, 184, 223, 237, 246, 247, 249, 251, 290, 323, 333, 335
Cairo Conference, 333-5

INDEX

Callwell, 69
Calshot, 347
Cambrai, 198
Campbell, Sir Walter, 242, 243
Cannæ, Battle of, 211, 249, 359
Cape, Jonathan, 339, 340
Caporetto, 198
Carchemish, 10, 11, 12, 14, 15, 17, 19, 20, 71
Carlyle, Thomas, 133
Carmel, 8, 265
Cattewater, 347
Caucasus, 31, 71
Chamberlain, Austen, 79, 349
Chaplains, 351
Chauvel, 121, 194, 239, 240, 293, 297, 299
Chaytor's force, 276, 279, 281, 302
Chetwode, Sir Philip, 121, 188, 189, 194, 197, 228, 231, 239, 249, 311
Chrysostom, St., 166
Churchill, Lord Randolph, 332
Churchill, Winston, 26, 30, 32, 245 note, 332, 333, 335, 336, 349
Civil War, U.S., 64
Clausewitz, Marshal von, 30, 56, 127, 128, 133, 217, 221
Clayton, Brig.-Gen. Gilbert, 67, 69, 70, 75, 76, 94, 95, 122, 152, 168, 169, 175, 223
Clemenceau, Georges, 313, 318, 321
Cobbold, Lady Evelyn, 19
Communications, enemy, how intercepted, 250 note
Composite Forces, 1st and 2nd, 106
Condé, Prince, 357
Conservative Government, 343
Constantinople, 16, 24, 25, 28, 29, 30, 32, 35, 50, 55
Corfe Castle, 343
Council of Ten, 313, 317
Cox, Sir Percy, 68, 72, 320, 334
Coxe, *Marlborough*, 128
Cranwell, 327, 339, 343, 344, 345
Creasy, *Fifteen Decisive Battles*, 128
Crécy, 129, 360
Crimean War, 23
Cromwell, Oliver, 298, 357
Curzon, Lord, 8, 79, 320, 332, 336, 339

d'Abernon, Lord, 29
Daily Mail, 352
Damascus, 18, 19, 34, 47, 48, 58, 62, 102, 114, 150, 151, 153, 155, 169, 171, 185, 186, 191, 193, 201, 225, 229, 245, 246, 252, 254, 261, 263, 264, 267, 268, 276; preliminaries of British approach to,

279 ff; 281, 282, 283, 288; forces converge on, 290, 293; exits closed, 294; city entered, 296-7; disorder, 297; new govt. planned, 298-9; cleaned up, 300-1; 309, 310, 314, 319, 320; taken from Feisal by French, 321, 331
d'Annunzio, Gabriele, 320
Dar el Hamra, 117
Dardanelles, 23, 27, 28, 30, 31, 32, 49, 55, 56, 209
Darfur, 50, 66, 92
Daud, 144, 145, 149, 202, 207, 232
Davenport, 85, 95, 117, 176
Dawnay, Alan, 222, 232, 233, 234, 235, 236, 237, 238, 246, 249, 250, 268, 325
Dawnay, Brig.-Gen. Guy, 188, 189, 239, 316
Dead Sea, 48, 92, 164, 170, 198, 207, 210, 214, 220, 221, 222
Delagha, 165, 180
Demetrius Poliorcetes, 128
Deraa, 36, 155, 171, 191, 192, 201, 202, 204, 205, 239, 243, 246, 249, 250, 252, 257, 260, 261, 262, 265, 266, 267, 268, 269, 271, 272, 273, 276, 280, 281, 282, 283, 284, 285, 286, 288, 293, 296 note, 297, 304, 309
Desert Mounted Corps, 194, 249, 293, 299
Devonshire, 345
Dhahriye, 196
Dhiab, 266
Dhuleil bridge, 155
Dhumaniyeh, 157, 158
Dizad, 145
"Djelala," meaning of, 118
Dorset, 341
Doughty, *Arabia Deserta*, 331
Doyle, A. Conan, 70
Drake, Sir Francis, 67, 270
Drigh Road depot, 345
Druse Arabs, 150, 225, 297, 300
Dufferin, 98, 167, 175, 176
Durham, 345

Ed Damiye, 239, 240
Edom, 215
Egypt, 10, 11, 17, 18, 26; during the World War, 31, 32, 33; menaced by Hejaz railway, 36, 37, 38, 46, 56, 60, 65, 71, 77, 108 note, 115, 120, 152, 168, 254, 319
Egyptian Camel Corps, 234
Egyptian troops, 262, 267, 268, 270, 271, 277, 302, 303
Eighth Army Corps, 302
El Afule, 265, 268, 275

El Ala, 116, 175, 193

El Arish, 41, 77, 91, 92, 120, 121, 180

El Atrash, Sultan, 297

El Auja, 36

El 'Eime, 219

El Ghair, 106

El Ghazale, 284

El Houl, 146

El Huweiz, 240

El Jefer, 154, 157, 194, 213, 214, 250, 257

El Kurr, 144

El Mezra, 220

Enver Pasha, 27, 28, 29, 31, 72, 209

Er Remta, 286

Erzerum, 71

Es Salt, 227, 228, 229, 230, 231, 238, 239, 240, 241, 254

Esdraelon, Plain of, 265

Essex Regiment, 209

Eugène, Prince, 357

Euphrates, 9, 10, 14, 15, 16, 35, 48, 321

Euryalus, 179

Evans, 248

Eylau, Battle of, 126

Fabian strategy, 213

Fahad, 238

Fakhri Pasha, 62, 31, 88, 101, 303 *note*

Falkenhausen, von, 226

Falkenhayn, Gen. von, 31, 190

Faraifra, 244, 245

Farraj, 145, 149, 202, 207, 231, 232

Fayoum, 10

Feisal, Sherif, 44, 49, 50, 51, 58, 59, 60, 62, 63, 64; as a leader of the revolt, his difficulties, 65, 81, 82; character, 83, 88, 90, 93, 94, 95, 96, 97, 98, 99, 100, 101, 102, 103, 104, 107, 108, 114, 115, 118, 119, 122, 130, 142, 143, 150, 174, 175, 176, 177, 179, 182, 191, 193, 194, 199, 204, 207, 209, 222, 231, 232, 237, 238, 241, 242, 245, 246, 252, 253, 254, 255, 257; dispute with Hussein, 261, 262, 263, 278, 280, 298, 301; goes to France, 312; and England, 313; at Paris Peace Conference, 313 ff; retort to Pichon, 317; accepts French offer, 318; returns to Syria, 319; proclaimed King, 320; accepts French ultimatum, 321; seeks help in England, 321-2, 323, 331; given Irak by British, 334

Fejr, 145

Fetah, the, 46

Feuquières, de, 136

Field Service Regulations, 130

Fifth Brigade, 240

Fifth Cavalry Division, 279, 302

Fiume, 320

Foch, Marshal, 127, 130, 132, 133, 136, 156, 160, 219; reported conversation with T.E., 315, 357

Fontevraud, 83

Ford cars, 271

Forty-eighth Division, 215

Fourth Cavalry Division, 275, 279, 285

Fox, 60

France—on British plan to attack Syrian railway, 37-8; her interests in Syria, 47, 48, 56, 79-80, 81, 91, 94, 117, 118, 256; historic basis for claim on Syria, 308; her assurances from the British, 308; joint declaration on Arab sovereignty, 310-11; told by Picot to make England yield Syria, 312; opposition to T.E., 313; to Feisal, 313-14; at Peace Conference, 315, 317; compact with Feisal, 318, 319; delivers ultimatum to Feisal and takes Damascus from him, 321-2, 333, 335

Frederick the Great, 126, 133

French Foreign Office, 80, 312

French General Staff, 291

French Revolution, 124

French West Africa, 92

Galilee, Sea of, 48, 274, 279, 282

Gallipoli, 30, 32, 33, 36, 37, 38, 41, 44, 45, 56, 59, 60, 78, 226

Garland, Capt., 95, 116

——mine, 141, 142

Gasim, 146, 147

Gaza, 38, 48, 49, 92, 121, 150, 162, 167, 174, 188; deceptive plan to attack, to mislead Turks, 189-90, 194, 195, 196

General Headquarters, 238, 241, 248, 274, 279, 296 *note*

Geographical Section of the General Staff, 68, 69

George V, King, 209

German East Africa, 50

Germans—on the Baghdad railway, 15-17; on the Hejaz railway, 34, 35, 44; aid to Turks in Palestine campaign, 190, 229; character of their retreat, 287; their engineers at surrender of Damascus, 296

Germany—relations with Turkey, 25 ff; alliance, 27, 55; military and naval assistance, 28, 29; leads attack on Russia, 29; on the sinking of the *Goeben*, 29; ambitions in Arabia, 34

Ghadir el Haj, 233
Ghalib Pasha, 61
Ghazala, Lawrence's camel, 177
Goeben, 27, 28, 29
Goltz, 128
Goslett, 179
Gouraud, Gen., 321
Grandmaison, 291
Graves, Philip, 70
Graves, Robert, 316
Great Britain—relations with Turkey in
19th century, 23-33; policy of compromise, 24; toward Young Turks, 26; at
outbreak of War, 28 *ff*; forced to rup-
ture with Turkey, 29; policy in Gallipoli, 30-3; in Egypt, 31-3
—plan for attack on Syrian railway
balked by French, 37-8; relations with
Arabs, 42 *ff*; pledges support, 46-7, 56;
participates, 60-1, 64 *ff*; its officials in
charge, 65-7; Govt. policy as to Kut,
72-4; British reputation for swallowing
protected territories, 84; pledges to the
Arabs, 256, 308, 309; disagreement as to
these among British officials, 309-10;
imperialism *vs.* nationalism, 310; sacrifices her pledge to the Arabs, 310; joint
declaration with France, 310-11; divided
position at Peace Conference, 317; fails
Feisal and Hussein, 318-19; opposes
T. E., 320; suppresses Irak revolt, 321;
cost of this and of aid in Arab Revolt,
321; gives Irak to Feisal, 334; and Trans-
Jordan to Abdulla, 335
Great Nefudh, 146
Greece, 11
Gregory, Gen., 294
Grey, Sir Edward, 86
Groves, Gen., 323
Guibert, 126, 127
Gurkhas, 262, 267, 268, 303
Guweira, 157 *note*, 160, 161, 165, 177, 181,
211, 222, 234, 257

Habban, 103, 105, 106
Haifa, 36, 191, 279
Haig, Gen. Sir Douglas, 86, 168
Hail, 100, 116
—Emir of—*see* Ibn Rashid
Hallat Ammar, 182-3
Hama, 171
Hamid Fakhri Bey, 215
Hamra, 81, 83
Hanakiye, 175
Handley-Page planes, 279, 280, 323

Hankey, Lieut.-Col. Maurice, 32
Hannibal, 125, 315, 357
Harb, the, 60, 96, 100
Hardinge, 60, 101, 103, 177
Hardy, *The Return of the Native*, 341
Haroun al Raschid, 339
Harran, 8
Hart, *The Ghost of Napoleon*, 138 *note*
Hauran, the, 171, 172, 204, 207, 225, 246,
251, 267, 269, 271
Hazaa, Sherif, 235, 256
Hebron, 195, 196, 197
Hedia, 142
Hedley, Sir Coote, 68, 69, 165
Hejaz, the, 41, 42, 45, 49, 55, 58, 61, 63,
66, 76, 77, 80, 81, 85, 87, 91, 94, 108,
112, 117, 118, 121, 122, 129, 131, 170,
171 *note*, 186, 191, 213, 245, 246, 247,
263, 264, 270, 303, 314, 319, 335
Hejaz Operations Staff, 222
Hejaz railway, 18, 19, 34; its real purpose,
35, 90, 92, 105, 106; raided, 116, 154,
174, 201, 207, 210, 226, 228, 237,
245 *note*, 269-70, 274, 276, 293, 302
Helles, 33
Henderson, *Stonewall Jackson*, 128
Herbert, Capt. Aubrey, 69, 72, 254
Hill, 30, 39, 229
Hittites, 8, 10
Hogarth, Dr. D. G., 8, 10, 11, 46, 60, 67,
68, 69, 223, 323, 325, 343
Holdich, 75, 185
Homer, *Odyssey*, 350
Homs, 171
Hor, Mount, 18
Hornby, 117, 236, 244, 266, 267, 276
Hotchkiss guns, 208, 263, 363
Howeitat, the, 115, 143, 146, 148; eating
customs among, 149, 159, 172, 177, 181,
185, 186, 256
Huleh, Lake, 8
Humphreys, Sir Francis, 346
Hussein, Sherif, 42, 43, 44, 45, 46, 49, 51,
56, 58, 59, 60, 64, 65, 66, 77 *note*, 78,
80, 82, 88, 89, 90, 92, 93, 101, 107, 115,
117; proclaimed King, 118; 174, 175,
176, 177, 193, 246, 247, 254; dispute with
Feisal and T. E., 261, 262, 314; pro-
claims himself Commander of the Faithful, 318; on "the faithless English," 319;
character, 319, 335, 336

Ibn Dakhil, 103, 207
Ibn Jad, 161
Ibn Rashid, 44 *note*, 65, 175

INDEX

Ibn Sa'ud, 44 *note*, 77 *note*, 118, 318, 319
Idrissi, the, 51, 318
Ilipa, 359
Imam, the, 318
Imperial Camel Brigade, 229, 242, 250, 251, 255, 259, 260, 327
Independent Labour Party, 346, 347
India, Government of, 46, 66, 77, 346
Indian Marine, 60
Indian troops, 202, 203, 225, 231, 262, 302
Inland Water Board, 166
—Transport, 166
Intelligence Service in Cairo, 67, 68, 69, 71, 275
Inter-allied Commission to Syria, 315
Iraq, 245 *note*, 261, 320, 321, 322, 334
Irbid, 285
Iskanderun, Gulf of, 36
Isle of Wight, 353
Ismailia, 31, 78, 167
Italy, 26
Izra, 284

Jabir, 269, 281
Jackson, Gen. Stonewall, 357
Ja'far Pasha, 40, 115, 179, 214, 215, 232, 233, 234, 260, 261
Jaffa, 34, 249
Jaffa Gate, Jerusalem, 206
Jauf, 108, 114
Jebel Druse, the, 151, 152, 155, 200, 204
Jebel Faroun, 19, 164
Jebel Harun, 18
Jebel Mania, 294, 295
Jebel Semna, 233
Jebel Shammar, 146
Jefer—*see* El Jefer
Jeida, 175, 176
Jemadar Hassan Shah, 201
Jemal Pasha, 49, 50, 84, 115, 122, 207, 231, 234, 254, 295, 339
Jena, Battle of, 126
Jerablus, 10, 35
Jerdun, 233, 234, 243, 244, 247
Jericho, 207, 214, 222, 238
Jerusalem, 34, 168, 171, 191, 195, 196, 197, 204; British entry into, 206, 207, 224, 226, 238, 242, 335
Jidda, 58, 61, 63, 65, 66, 79, 80, 82, 85, 88, 89, 175, 176, 246, 335, 336
Jihad, 29, 40, 43, 44, 45, 46
Joffre, Marshal, 119, 357
John, Augustus, 313
Jomini, 128
Jordan River, 48, 170, 227, 228, 229, 238,

240, 241, 242, 249, 265, 274, 275, 301, 302
—Valley, 207, 231, 239, 248, 274, 276
Joyce, James, 339
Joyce, Lieut.-Col. P. C., 85, 88, 95, 117, 169, 176, 179, 211, 212, 222, 232, 235, 250, 251, 257, 263, 269, 272
Judea, 196, 197
Juheina, the, 98, 100, 105, 114
— Emir of, 104
Junction Station, 197
Junor, 271, 277
Jurf ed Derawish, 213, 228, 237, 238

Ka'aba, the, 60
Kabul, 346
Kadesh-Barnea, 18
Kannengiesser, Gen., 28
Karachi, 345, 346
Kennington, Eric, 327
Kerak, 210, 215, 220, 241, 266, 267
Kethira, 160, 161
Khadra, 160, 161
Khairi Bey, 50, 58
Khalasa, 18
Khalid, 286, 287, 288
Khalil Pasha, 72, 73
Khamsin, 195
Khartoum, 85, 93
Kirkbride, 222
Kiswe, 293
Kiswa, the, 60
Kitchener, Lord, 18, 25-6, 29, 31, 33, 36, 37, 42, 43, 46, 67, 72
Konia, 35
Kress von Kressenstein, Lieut.-Col., 28, 39, 40, 121, 190
Kubri, 255
Kurds, 11, 15, 16, 20
Kut, 72, 73

Labour Government, 343
Lahaj, 51
Lake, 72
Lawrence, T. E.
Career:
—ancestry and parentage, 3; boyhood, 3-4; social affinities, 4; early schooling, 4; early travels, 4, 5; early military service, 6; undergraduate at Oxford, 6-8; thesis, 8; vacation in Syria, 8-9; robbed by Turkman, 9; demyship, 10; to Egypt, 10; work at Carchemish, 10, 11; jailed as "Turkish deserter," 14; in Baghdad railway dispute, 16-17; expedition to

Sinai, 17-20, 67; at Aqaba, 18-19; report on Turkish communications in Syria, 33, 37, 41, 60, 62-3, 64

—in 1914 at Oxford, working on *The Wilderness of Zin*, 67; assigned to Geog. Section of General Staff, 68; to Egypt, 69; helps Graves, 70; missions to Western Desert and to Greece, 71; to Kut, 71-3; his criticisms of Mesopotamian campaign, 73-5; in Arab Bureau, 75-6; meets Abdulla and Ali, 82; and Feisal, 83; sees Arab forces, 84-5; estimates situation, 85-6; at Yanbo, 88; begins campaign, 90

—opposed to using British troops in Revolt, 93; to Arabs' "protection" by England or France, 94; apptd. liaison officer, 94-5; joins Arab forces, 95-6; dons Arab clothing, 97; suggests move to north of Medina, 99-100, 101; friction with Vickery, 102; co-operates with Newcombe, 104; in attack on Wejh, 104-6, 114; influence with Feisal, 107, 119; ill, but goes to Abdulla's camp, 122-3

—initiates railway raids, 140 ff; humane precautions, 141; march on Aqaba, 143; lays mine at railway near Dizad, 145-6; rescues Gasim, 146-7; council of action with the Howeitat, 148; prefers taking Aqaba before attempting Damascus, 150-1; frustrates Damascus plan, 151; learns of Sykes-Picot agreement, 151-2; undescribed trip alone into Syria, 152; asks Ali Riza to keep Damascus quiet, 153; meets Nuri Shaalan, 153; plan of approach to Aqaba, 154-5; in attack at Abu el Lissal, 157-9; bent on pursuing his strategic design, 160; in capture of Kethira, 161; of Khadra, 161-2; of Aqaba, 162-4

—solves problem of holding Aqaba, 165; of commissary, 164 ff;

—meets Allenby, 167-8; gets money for campaign, 168, 169; assumes direction of Syrian campaign, 170-1; proposes transfer of forces, 174; gets Hussein's assent, 175-6; deals with Howeitat "treachery," 177; his expenditures in the campaign, 179; bombs and captures train, 180-4; his direct leadership, 182; at Aqaba, 184; other railway operations, 185-7

—Palestine campaign, 188-209; estimate of chances, 191-2; attack on railway near Deraa planned, 192; leaves Aqaba, 194; exhorts the Serahin, 199-200; setback in news at Azrak, 200; reduced to attempting attack on Tell el Shehab bridge, 200-1; its failure, 202; escapes capture in first attempt on railway near Minifir, 203; successful second attempt, 204; caught inside the Turkish lines, 204; after torture, escapes, 205; ill, but rides to Aqaba, 205-6; promoted major and made C.B., 206; at official entry into Jerusalem, 206; discusses new projects with Allenby, 206-7; forms bodyguard, 207-8; their armament, 208; his own, 208-9; his alleged titles, 209

—in 1918 campaign—develops mechanized force, armoured cars, etc., 211-13; his aim to entrench the enemy, 212; reason for not wanting the railway completely severed, 213; his Tafila battle plan, 216; its outcome, 216-20; ultimate effect, 228; his self-reproaches, 219-20; urges Abdulla el Feir to raid grain-fleet, 220-1; fired on by British planes, 221; gets funds from Feisal, 222; ill and disappointed by difficulties with Zeid, considers resigning, 222-3; called for fresh action, 223

—proposes taking Ma'an, 227; concerted plans with Allenby, 228; disgusted by British failure to smash railway at Amman, 229; spares unarmed Turk, 230; disguised, with gipsies, inspects Amman, 231; tries to save Farraj, dying, 232; disappointed by results at Semna, 234; marvels at Dawnay's Camp, 235; shocked by extravagant use of guncotton at Ma'an bridges, 236; his influence in preventing fights among looting Arabs, 237; considers new plan for Amman "mad," 238; 241; Shunet Nimrin failure strengthens his position, 241; gets new camels, 242-3; bold design for containing Ma'an, 245-6; not needed, 246-7

—examines plans for Damascus attack, 248, 249, 250; his view of misleading Turks as to British plans, 251; on mixing British and Arab forces, 250, 251; intervenes to halt Feisal's negotiations with Turks, 254; explains situation to his men, 255-6; takes them through Howeitat country, 256; meets Nuri Shaalan at Jefer, 256-7; reconnoitres for Deraa move, 257-8; abandons attempt to attack Muaggar bridge, 259-60; bluff to divert Turks to Amman, 260; diplomacy in quarrel between Hussein and sons, 261; revives Hussein's prestige, 262; starts for Azrak, 263

—purchase of food in plan to fool Turks, 266; alternative courses, 267-8; adopts move of cutting trunk line above Deraa, 268; personal reconnaissance of site, 269; demolishes line, 270; slightly wounded, 271; bombs his 79th bridge, 273; strategical effects, 273-4; finds Umtaiye dangerously weak, 276; gets news of victory over Turkish armies, 278

—flies into Palestine to G.H.Q., 279; settles aeroplane difficulty, 279-80; sees no risk from retreating Turkish army, 281-2; disapproves delay recommended, 283; enlarges plan, 284; at Tafas after Turks' occupation, 286-7; enters Deraa, 288; effects understanding between Barrow's troops and Nasir's, 289; irked by Barrow's cautious advance, 293; fetches British reinforcements for Nasir, 294; fears that Damascus is being fired, 295-6; lets Arab leaders enter Damascus first, 296; makes himself responsible for order in the city, 297; considers conditions of founding Arab State, 298-9; deals with Abd el Kader's rebellion, 299-300; helps to clean up the city, 300-1; depressed, 301; leaves Damascus for Cairo, 301-2

—enters struggle of Arabs against British and French interests, 307 ff; his course justified by Franco-British declaration, 310; to England, 311-12; proposes three Sherifian States, 312; opposed by English and French officials, 312-13; with Feisal at Peace Conference, 313-14; counsel for Arab cause, 314; opinion of Lloyd George, 314; explains his idea of dividing Arab State, 314-15; meets Foch, 315; opinion of him, 316; of Allenby, 316; meets Clemenceau, 318; renews effort for Feisal with Foreign Office, 320; bitter over French expulsion of Feisal from Damascus, 322

—accidents during writing of *Seven Pillars of Wisdom*, 323 (*see* below); other escapes in crashes, 323-4; demobilized, 324; Oxford fellowship, 324, 331; rejects profits from books, 328; writes introduction to *Arabia Deserta*, 331; poverty, 331-2

—discusses Middle East mess with Lloyd George, 332; made Political Adviser to new Middle East Dept. of Colonial Office, 333; relations with Churchill, 333; persuades British to give Irak to Feisal, 334-5; and Trans-Jordan to Abdulla, 335; offers treaty to Hussein, 335-6; deadlock, 336; Arab settlement frees T. E., 336-7; joins R.A.F., 327, 330-1, 337; reasons, 337-8; on taking military rank, 338; first service at Uxbridge, 339; secret of his R.A.F. connexion given publicity, 340; results in his discharge, 340; enlists in Tank Corps, 327, 340-1

—creates a home in Dorset, 341, 353; love of motor-cycling, 341-3; refused admittance wearing uniform, 342; applies for R.A.F. again, 343; asked to complete R.A.F. history, 343; in R.A.F. at Cranwell, 343-5; motives misunderstood—"was he a spy?"—344; motor-cycle accidents, 345; to India, 345-6; further disastrous publicity, 346; at home, challenged by Independent Labour Party, 346-7; his part in changing name of Cattewater, 347; connexion with Schneider Cup Race, 347-9; with Lord Thomson, 348; publicity at Cup Race, 349; expulsion from R.A.F. suspended on conditions, 349-50

—engaged for development of speedboats, 350-2; further publicity, 351-2; his evasion of it, 352-3; his present plans for his future, 353; ideas of happiness, 353

—Summary of T. E.'s achievement, 354-90

Personality:

—Early interest in archaeology, 5, 6, 8, 17-18, 19; in Crusades, 5; in military history, 5-6; attitude toward organized sports, 6, 10; his "dream Crusade" for the Arabs, 5; love of freedom, 6, 7, 12; of solitary wandering, 7, 8, 9; intellectual curiosity, 7; love of reading, 7; attitude toward known and unknown, 10-11; skill on water, 14; at shooting, 15; love of speed, 341-3, 345; of typography, 326

—Charm, 7; perceptive and dynamic, 12-13; strength of character, 15-16; ability to endure hardship, 9, 11-12, 13; temperance, 13; water-drinking habits, 148; many-sidedness, 71; flouting of authority and convention, 74-5, 178-9; detachment, 95, 204; grasp of detail, 170; impish humour, 7, 16, 17, 149, 150, 221, 287, 301, 352; campaigning library, 251 *note*

—Appearance and manner, 13, 205, 291, 296 *note;* clothing, 90, 167, 228, 253, 288-9, 296 *note,* 313, 342; linguistic ability, 317; knowledge of Arabic, 8-9, 11; sympathetic relations with Arabs, 11, 12; influence and authority among them, 15-16, 253-4; tactfulness, 108, 254-5, 261-2; misinterpreted generosity to them, 178; confidence in them, 252

—His unease among British soldiers, 256, 258; shy and self-critical, not conceited, 258-9; enjoys fame but rejects honours, 259; relish of romantic excitement, 263; unique character of his soldiering experience, 290; traits revealed by post-war political struggle, 307 ff; renunciation of profits from books due to sense of honour, 328; authority of his personality in R.A.F., 344-5, 351; recreations, 345; freezes an impertinent stranger, 348-9

—His moral difficulty in matter of British pledges to Arabs—hearing of Sykes-Picot agreement, has doubts of British good faith, 151-2, 256-7; accepts post in Middle East Dept. on understanding that pledges will be honoured, 333; his feeling that Arab focus was Irak, 333; pleased by British transfer of Irak to Feisal, 334-5

—Summary of his character as a military leader, 354-90

—His theory of war, 124 ff; text-book foundations, 124-8; tested in Arabia, 129; plans, 130; tactics and strategy, 142, 143, 150, 152, 153, 155, 156, 158, 159-60, 162, 163; his refusal to waste lives, 156, 163; value of his geographical studies, 165; adaptation required in Syrian campaign, 170-3; ideas on guns, 208-9; on value of mechanized forces in strategy, 212-13; on not completely severing the railway, 213; timing in war, 244; "intangible ghost tactics," 244-5, 274, 275; method of combining Arabs for strategy, 255; variability feature in Deraa plan, 267-8; ideas of discipline, 290, 291-2; on "lack of independent courage," 292; opinion of professional soldier, 316; analysis of differences between historic irregular campaigns and T.E's Arab campaign, 355 ff

—Names and honours—"T. E." and adopted surnames, 3; among Arabs, "Aurans," 198; made C.B. and recommended for V.C., 206; not given rank of Sherif, 209; D.S.O., 221; "recommends" himself for Distinguished Flying Cross, 221; rank among the Arabs, 253; postwar colonelcy, 311; initials used in copies of *Seven Pillars of Wisdom,* 329; takes name of Ross, 337; of Shaw, 340

—Portraits, 291, 313

—Comments on T. E. by others, 15, 251, 253-4, 255-6, 261-2, 269, 299, 301, 316-17

Writings:

—Diary, 339-40

—*Odyssey* translation, 350

—*Seven Pillars of Wisdom,* 152, 301, 322-9; accidents, 323-4; methods of writing, 324; loses ms., 325; rewrites from memory, 325; changed character of book, 325-6; printing, 326; published by subscription, 326-7; revision as *The Revolt in the Desert,* 327, 339; sales of the two versions, 327-8; its literary character, 328-9; bears no author's name, 329, 339, 340, 345, 352

—*The Wilderness of Zin,* 67

Quoted on:

—Schooling, 4; choice of associates, 4; holiday travel in Syria, 8; debt to Hogarth, 10; Arab character, 11; acceptance by Arabs, 12, 13; Saladin and Syria, 18, 64; Intelligence work in Palestine compaign, 75; Pilgrim Road to Mecca, 82-3; Feisal, 83; Arabs as fighters, 84; staff's good opinion of him, 94; his appt. as liaison officer, 94-5; Feisal's influence on his troops, 96; camp routine, 96-7; Arab discipline, 97-8 "The night that the Turks lost their war," 98-9; march to Owais, 101; start for Wejh, 103-4; Arabs' attitude toward British, 107

—"Twenty Seven Articles" on handling Arabs, 109-13; his military reading, 129; the use of regulars, 130-1; equating theory with present problem, 131; "why bother about Medina?" 131-2; his theory of irregular warfare, 133-8; railway raids, 142; the Syrian Arab, 148; attaining perfection, 148; Arab treatment of snake-bite, 149; his

report on trip to see Syrian leaders, 152; the reaction of victory, 160; trouble with the Inland Water Board, 166-7; Allenby, 167-8, 169; using Syrian Arabs, 168; distribution of effort, 170; Arab unity, 171 note; likeness between sea and desert warfare, 172; tactics needed in desert, 172-3; on a "slippery ledge" among the Howeitat, 177; his official version of Auda's conduct, 178; on terrified Turks, 184; Arabs' rewards at Aqaba, 184; own account of the railway hold-up, 185; authority among the Howeitat, 186
—Possibility of taking Palestine, 191-2; his speech to the timorous Serahin, 199-200; nervous reaction after capture, 205; his insensible state on ride to Aqaba, 205-6; reward offered for his capture, 207; choice of bodyguard, 207-8; choice of title, 209; "battle" of Tafila, 215, 216, 217, 218, 219-20; reason for meriting Distinguished Flying Cross, 221; needing more transport, 227; on skirt-wearers, 228; loss of Es Salt, 231; Dawnay's camp, 235; railway attack at Ma'an, 236-7; Dawnay's character, 237-8; impromptu attack on Es Salt, 238; plan to move the Beni Sakhr, 241; his request for camels, 242, 243; on timing in war, 244; his plan for taking Damascus, 245-6; on combining aircraft and ground troops, 245 note; his own "permeating job," 247
—On deceptions in strategy, 249; intercepting communications, 250 note; avoiding casualties, 250; information as a basis for plans, 252 note; playing on the Turks' fears for Amman, 260; tactful tampering with cipher messages, 262; considerate of Feisal's honour, 262; feint against Amman, 265-6; similar double-bluff, on Madeba, 266-7; the Deraa plan, 267-8; taking part of Damascus railway, 270; objectives won at too high a cost of life, 272; contrasts in comfort at H.Q., 280; pressing hard on a rout, 283; command in Arabia, 284; madness at Tafas massacre, 287; busy mind and tired body, 288; a crazy ride, 288; histrionics in a risky situation, 288-9; symbolism of soldier's uniform, 290; intelligence in R.A.F. ranks, 291; cautious procedure

of normal warfare, 293; on apparent burning of Damascus, 295-6; pellagra, 297; disorders at Damascus, 297; on precautionary murder in politics, 298; rebels as bad subjects, 298; coolness of Damascus dust, 301-2
—On his own plans after Arab victory, 311; his "Taranto rank," 312; Foch, 316; Allenby, 316; retort to a general's rebuke, 316; on "enormous pretensions" of Seven Pillars, 329; on income needed, 331; future of air service, 337; on hopes for happiness, 353

League of Nations, 334
Lebanon, 15, 314
Lee-Enfield rifle, 209
Lenin, 333
Levant, the, 308
Lewis guns, 181, 182, 183, 184, 185, 195, 208, 363
Liman von Sanders, Gen., 226, 229, 241, 245 note, 273, 274, 275, 304
Lith, 58
Livy, 199
Lloyd George, David, 87, 92, 119, 120, 190, 224, 225; his opinion of T. E., 314, 332
Lloyd, Capt. George, 69, 92, 194
Ludendorff, Gen., 160
Lyttleton, Maj., 167

McBey's portrait of T. E., 291
McMahon, Sir Henry, 37, 44, 45, 46, 47, 48, 56, 65, 66, 75, 78, 79, 89
M31, 98
Ma'an, 18, 19, 34, 106, 115, 116, 119, 147, 154, 155, 157, 158, 159, 164, 165, 177, 179, 180, 181, 185, 191, 210, 211, 213, 226, 227, 228, 232, 233, 234, 235, 237, 238, 242, 244, 245, 247, 260, 276, 278, 301, 309
Madahrij, 141
Madeba, 210, 230, 241, 266
Mafraq, 281
Magdhaba, 121
Mahan, Influence of Sea-Power on History, 128
Majalli, the, 267
Malory, Morte d'Arthur, 251
Malplaquet, 129
Mandates, 315, 317, 321, 332
Marlborough, Duke of, 129, 357, 359, 360, 361
Masséna, 218

Mastur, 214
Maude, Gen., 79
Maulud, 83, 102, 142, 143, 180, 211, 222, 232, 233
Maxton, Mr., 347
Maxwell, Sir John, 32, 33, 36; plans attack on Syrian railway, 37, 39 note, 46, 75
Mecca, 34, 42, 43, 45, 46, 50, 58, 59, 63, 78, 80, 81, 85, 88, 91, 92, 93, 97, 106, 130, 131, 174, 176, 177, 193, 247, 264, 318, 319
Medain Saleh, 59, 116, 117, 142, 175, 176, 186
Medina, 18, 34, 35, 50, 55, 58, 62, 63, 65, 78, 81, 82, 88, 92, 98, 101, 106, 107, 116, 117, 119, 122, 130, 131, 132, 140, 141, 174, 175, 176, 187, 191, 214, 237, 264, 303 note
Medjiz, 106
Megiddo, 265
Meinertzhagen, Richard, 189, 190, 325, 333
Mejaber, 260
Mesopotamia, 11, 46, 48, 71, 72, 79, 224, 302, 309, 310, 312, 314, 315, 317, 320, 321, 333
Mesopotamian Expeditionary Force, 71
Messudieh, 275
Metaab, 217, 218
Middle East Department, Colonial Office, 333
Mifleh, 198
Milton, John, 243
Minifir, 155, 203
Miranshah Fort, 346
Mirzuk, 237, 238, 241, 243
Mitla Hills, 166
Moab, 215, 220, 238, 245, 266
Mohammed el Dheilan, 177
Mohammed Said, 254, 295, 297, 298
Moltke, von, 128, 357
Monro, Sir Charles, 37
Mosul, 35, 48, 310, 321
Motalga, the, 214, 215, 216, 217, 218
Mount of Olives, 335
Mountbatten, 347
Muadhdham, 176
Muaggar, 259, 260
Mubarak, 95, 100, 102
Mudauwara, 181, 182, 183, 184, 211, 212, 234, 237, 250, 257, 327
Mudge's brigade, 89
Murray, Sir Archibald, 39, 41, 66, 74, 75, 78, 79, 87, 89, 91, 94, 120, 151, 167, 168, 190, 192

Muslimiya, 302
Muzeirib (Mezerib), 252 note, 271, 282, 285, 286, 293

Nablus, 275
Napier, History of the War in the Peninsula, 128
Napoleon I, 23, 24, 68, 90, 125, 126, 127, 128, 130, 133, 266, 333, 356, 357, 358, 359
Nasir, Sherif, 88, 105, 107, 143, 145, 149, 150, 153, 156, 158, 159, 168, 177, 178, 193, 213, 214, 243, 244, 245, 263, 288, 289, 293, 294, 295, 296, 298, 302
Navarino, 23
Nazareth, 8, 275
Nebk, 151, 152, 153, 154
Negab Pass, 161
Nejd, 83, 318
Nekhl, 166
Nelson, Lord, 233
Nesib, 143, 147, 148, 149, 151, 152, 155
Neufeld, Karl, 50
New Zealand Mounted Brigade, 121, 194, 229
Newcombe, Col., 17, 18, 19, 68, 69, 75, 104-5, 108, 116, 117, 122, 169, 176, 193, 194; his "strategic mirage," 195-6, 198
Nicolson, Sir Arthur, 26
Nisibin, 35, 205, 272, 273
Nowasera, 184
Nugent, Capt. Walter, 68
Nuri Bey, 40
Nuri Said, 213, 214, 233, 237, 238, 261, 281, 282, 286, 288, 298, 299, 300, 302, 320
Nuri Shaalan, 114, 148, 153, 155, 156, 204, 252, 256, 257, 261, 269, 271, 272, 278, 280, 282, 284, 293, 296, 297, 298

Odeh, Rev. N., 9
Omdurman, 50
Ommayad dynasty, 171
Owais, 100, 101
Oxford
  —Ashmolean Museum, 8
  —(City of) School, 4
  —University, 4, 6-8, 9, 15, 17, 324, 325, 331, 332; All Souls College, 324, 331; Jesus College, 6-8; Magdalen College, 10; St. John's College, 6
  —Union, 7
Oxford Book of English Verse, 251 note
Oxford Times, 326

Palestine, 36, 37, 39, 48, 120, 122, 151, 162, 174, 179, 186, 250
—Campaign, 188-209; possible points of attack, 188; methods required, 189; the feint against Gaza, 189-90; attack on Yarmuk Valley bridge, 192-4; 198-204; capture of Beersheba, 194-8; Jerusalem gained, 206; operations in corn-belt, 210-13; taking of Tafila, 213-20; capture of grain-fleet, 220-1; Jericho taken, 222; British move into Trans-Jordan, 228-30; breach of railway at Ma'an, 233-7; attack on Jerdun, 244; final plan for approach to Damascus, 248-50; its aim of deceiving the Turks, 249; "ladder" to Deraa and Damascus, 252; attack on Mudauwara, 257; T. E.'s alternative plans, 267-8; Turkish communications cut around Deraa, 269 ff; Allenby enabled to attack coast, 274; defeat of Turkish armies, 278
—approach to Damascus, 279-94; use of bombing planes, 279-81; attack on Sheikh Saad village, 282-4; capture of Damascus, 295-7
Palestine Exploration Fund, 18, 67-8, 69
Palgrave, William Gifford, 146
Palmyra, 152
Passchendaele, 86, 198
Peace Conferences, 313-22, 324
Peake, 244, 268, 269, 270, 277
Pearson, Col., 89
Peninsular Wars, 212-13, 357
Persian Gulf, 25, 35
Peshawar, 346
Petra, 19, 180, 211
—Nabathean, 165
Petrie, Sir Flinders, 10
Pichon, 317
Picot, Georges, 47, 49, 206, 312, 318
Pilgrims' Road to Mecca, 82-3, 282, 292
Pisani, Capt., 185, 186, 232 note, 233, 263, 270, 286, 308
Plymouth Hoe, 67
Plymouth Sound, 347
Poitiers, 360
Poole, Reginald Lane, 128
Port Said, 11
Port Sudan, 60, 85
Procopius, 128
Pyrrhus, 315

Qal 'at Zamrud, 176
Qatiya Oasis, 39, 40
Qatrani, 228

Quneitra, 279, 294
Qunfideh, 58, 88
Quntilla, 180

Rabegh, 61, 63, 65, 77, 78, 79, 81, 82, 85, 87, 88, 89, 91, 92, 93, 94, 95, 101, 103, 117, 118, 130, 131, 201
Rafah, 121
Rahail, 205, 206, 207
Raho, Capt., 140, 141
Rajputana, 346
Raleigh, 343
Ramleh, 237, 279
Ras Baalbek, 152, 231
Rasim Bey, 218, 219
Rawlinson, Sir Henry, 69
Red Sea, 18-19, 34, 45, 55, 60, 77, 85, 116
Remthe, 201
Renaud of Chatillon, 19
Reschadieh, 27
Rhône delta, 5
—valley, 323
Richard Cœur de Lion, 83
Riddle of the Sands, The, 20
Riviera, 90
Riyak, 35
Robertson, Sir William, 39, 78-9, 86, 91, 120, 174, 225
Rocroi, 129
Rodd, Francis, 324
Rodd, Sir Pennell, 324
Rolls-Royce cars, 211, 232 note, 258, 263, 269, 270
Romani, 40
Ross, Maj., 117
Ross-Smith, 279, 280
Rowan, Lieut., 260
Rowanduz, 48
Royal Air Force, 11, 242, 245 note, 267, 275, 276, 291, 327; T. E. joins it, 330, 332, 335, 337, 339, 340
Royal Flying Corps, 95, 189
Royal Geographical Society, 68
Royal Naval Volunteer Reserve, 46
Royal Tank Corps, 327, 340, 341
Russ, Sheikh of, 100
Rumania, 86, 198
Rumm, 157 note, 181, 182, 184, 194, 256
Russia, 198, 308, 346
Russian Revolution, 49
Russo-Turkish relations, 23, 25, 27; war declared, 29-30, 48, 55
Ruwalla, the, 114, 115, 150, 172, 193, 257, 261, 263, 269, 270, 286, 287, 295, 296, 297

Saklatvala, Mr., 346
Saladin, 18, 19, 168, 172
Salammbô, 132
Salem, 184
Salisbury, 343
Salmond, Maj.- Gen., Sir Geoffrey, 180, 221, 268, 279, 337, 351, 352
Salmond, Sir John, 352
Salonika, 32, 33, 78
Salt—*see* Es Salt
Samaria, 249
Samuel, Sir Herbert, 335
San Remo Conference, 321
Sarikamish, 31
Sassoon, Sir Philip, 349
Saxe, Marshal, 124, 125, 126, 127, 128, 133, 139, 156
Schlieffen, Countess, 50
Schneider Cup Race, 347, 348, 349, 350
Scipio, 160, 315
Scott-Paine, 350
Sebeil, 144
Sebustiye, 249
Second Army Corps, 302
Sedan, 129
Senussi, the, 40, 115
Serahin, the, 172, 193, 199, 201, 269
Serbia, 33, 36, 86
Shaiba, 83
Shakespear, Capt., 44 *note*
Shakir, Sherif, 140, 141
Sharon, Plain of, 36, 274
Sharraf, 101, 142, 143
Shatt, 166
Shaw, Bernard, 349
Shea, 231
Sheikh Saad village, 282, 283, 284, 285, 288
Shererat, the, 172
Sheria—*see* Tell esh Sheria
Sherman, Gen. W. T., 103, 125, 345
Shobek, 210, 214
Shukri Pasha, 295, 296, 297, 300
Shunet Nimrin, 239, 240
Sidon, 8
Sinai, 17, 18, 29, 31, 69, 91, 120, 132, 162, 165, 166, 170, 180, 188
Sinai Arabs, 165
Sinai Hotel, 167
Sinn Feiners, 235
Sirdar of Egypt—*see* Wingate
Sixtieth Division, 229, 239, 240
Slaves and servants, their status among the Arabs, 108 *note*
Smith, Sydney, 347

Smuts, Gen. Jan, 225, 227
Somaliland, 50
Somme, Battle of the, 120
South Africa, 168
Southampton, 343
—Water, 351
Stent, Capt., 180
Steuber, Gen., 196-7
Stirling, Col., 74, 253, 256, 261, 293, 294, 295, 299, 301
Stokes mortars, 181, 182, 183, 184, 185
Storrs, Ronald, 65, 66, 76, 82
Stotzingen, Maj. von, 50, 51
Subayyeh, 51
Sudan, 50, 66, 77, 102
Suez, 81, 82, 87, 90, 91, 118, 165, 166, 167, 178, 206
Suez Canal, 29, 31, 32, 34, 56, 162, 166, 250, 255
—Gulf of, 166
Sultan Osman, 27
Sultans of Egypt and Morocco, 118
Supreme War Council, 225, 246
Suva, 98, 101
Sykes, Sir Mark, 47, 48, 49, 56, 77 *note*
Sykes-Picot Agreement, 48, 49, 56-7, 77 *note*, 79, 151, 307, 310, 317
Syria, 5, 8-9, 12, 17, 18, 20, 46, 80, 106, 115, 119, 122, 146, 148, 151, 168, 169, 170; in topography and population contrasted with the Hejaz, 170-1, 309, 315, 317, 318, 319, 333, 335
Syrian Arabs, 148, 150, 152, 168

Tacitus's epigram inverted, 120
Tadmor, 152, 155
Tafas, 286, 287, 289
Talfila (Tafileh), 207, 210, 213, 214; "battle," 215-20, 222, 223, 228, 230, 241, 245, 247, 263, 266, 267, 359
Taif, 59, 61, 62, 83
Talaat, 254
Talbot cars, 212, 232 *note*, 236
Tallal, 267, 284, 286, 287
Taranto, 311
Tarsus, 35, 36
Taurus Mountains, 35, 36, 45, 47
Tebuk, 106, 116, 145, 175, 234
telephone, Arabs' delight in, 82
Tell Arar, 269, 270, 271, 282, 286
Tell el Shehab, 200, 201, 202, 271
Tell esh Shahm, 234, 235
Tell esh Sheria, 188, 193, 194, 196
Teschen, 314
Tigris, 35, 48, 105

Themed, 166, 231, 238
Thomson, Lord, 343, 348
Thurble, Mr., 346, 347
Times, London, 70
Torres Vedras, 180, 211
Toweira, 116, 176
Townshend, 45, 71
Trad, 288
Trafalgar, Battle of, 233
Trans-Jordan, 8, 238, 239, 241, 251, 333, 335
Trenchard, Sir Hugh, 10, 245 *note*, 340, 343, 347, 349
Triple Entente, 25, 29
Tripoli, 26
Trumbull, Dr., 18
Tunis, 308
Turabah, 318
Turco-German treaty, 27
Turenne, 357
Turkey, 8; relations with Great Britain, 23-33, 55-7; with other nations, 23; in 1914, 27 *ff*, 55-7; ships taken over by Great Britain, 27-28; attacks Russia on Black Sea, 29; in Caucasus, 31; Gallipoli campaign, 30, 32, 33; attacks Suez Canal, 31-2; railway systems in Asia Minor, 34-6; menace to British in Egypt, 37-40; partition of Asiatic provinces planned, 47-8; move to crush Arab movement, 49-51, 57. (*See* Turks.) 67; enters War, 69, 70, 319, 320
Turkish Armies—Fourth, 226, 227, 260, 265, 266, 272; its chance of escape, 275-6; retreats, 276, 279; its disorder, 281, 282, 283, 286, 294, 303
—Seventh and Eighth, 226, 265, 275; defeated, 278
Turkish Army Handbook, 75
Turks—attacked at Mecca, 59; at Jidda, 60-1; at Taif, 61; mode of warfare, 62, 63, 64, 65, 70, 71, 72; strength in the Hejaz, 81, 87, 88, 89, 93; failure to attack Yanbo, 98-9; attacked, 100; at Wejh, 103-6; defence of Hejaz railway, 106, 116, 119, 121, 122, 132, 133, 134, 135, 136, 137, 138; their railway mined, 141-2, 145-6, 151, 152, 153, 154, 155-6, 157; at surrender of Guweira, 161; of Kethira, 161; of Khadra, 161-2; of Aqaba, 162-3, 170, 179; concentrate at Ma'an, 179; baulked in advance on Aqaba, 180, 182, 185, 186; in Palestine campaign, their strength, 190; their Yarmuk Valley bridges attacked, 192 *ff*;

deceived by Newcombe's "mirage," 196; its effect, 196-7, 204; set price on Lawrence's head, 207, 253; attack Arabs near Petra, 211; defence of Tafila, 214-220
—strength and distribution in 1918, 226, 227; at Ma'an, 234; at Shunet Nimrin, 239-40, 249; negotiations with Feisal, 254; fooled by feint at Amman, 260, 263, 269; lose redoubt at Tell Arar, 270; their aeroplanes, 271, 272, 276, 280; all bolt-holes sealed, 275, 278, 283, 284, 285; sack of Tafas, 286-7; surrender Damascus, 295
—*See also* Turkish Armies
Tussum, 31
Twentieth Corps, 249
Twenty-first Division, 58, 249

Uganda, 92
Um Keis, 200
Umlej, 101, 104
Umm es Surab, 280
Umtaiye, 252 *note*, 268, 269, 272, 279, 280, 282
Urfa, 8
Utica, battle at, 62
Uxbridge depot, 339, 340

Vahib Bey, 42
Valny, 129
Vauxhall car, 253, 280
Vegetius, 128
Vendémiaire rising, 90
Vickers, 363
Vickery, Maj., 102
Victoria, Queen, 23
Viollet-le-Duc, 5
Voltaire, 360

Wadi Ais, 100, 101, 103, 114, 122, 139
Wadi Araba, 164, 165, 214
Wadi Gharandil, 165
Wadi Ghazze, 174
Wadi Hamdh, 105
Wadi Hesa, 215, 219, 220, 244
Wadi Ithm, 19, 157 *note*, 161, 164, 177, 211, 256
Wadi Jizil, 144
Wadi Khalid, 200
Wadi Musa, 18, 180, 211
Wadi Safra, 83, 88, 96
Wadi Sirhan, 114, 119, 147, 148, 149, 150, 153, 157, 252 *note*, 269
Wahabis, the, 318

Wangenheim, Baron von, 25, 27

War Museum, Windsor, 209

Wavell's history of Palestine campaign, 120, 179, 226, 239, 240

Webb-Gillman, Gen., 73

Wejh, 61, 81, 90, 92, 100, 101, 102; captured by Arabs, 103-6; 107, 114, 115, 116, 118, 119, 122, 130, 131, 145, 150, 162, 165, 172, 174, 175, 176, 179

Wellington, Duke of, 163, 180, 212-13, 357

Wells, H. G., 329

Wemyss, Sir Rosslyn, 67, 85, 91, 167, 179

Weygand, 315

Willisen, 128

Wilson, Sir Arnold, 312, 317

Wilson, Lieut.-Col. C. E., 66, 88, 89, 101, 176

Wilson, Henry, 245 note

Wingate, Sir Reginald, 44, 51, 58, 60, 66, 78, 79, 85, 86, 89, 91, 92, 95, 117, 174, 175, 246

Winterton, Lord, 263, 268, 269

Wood, 193

Woolley, Dr. Leonard, 11, 15, 16, 17, 18, 19, 67, 68, 69

World War, 11, 24, 27 ff, 55, 56, 132, 308

Wuld Ali, the, 294

Xenophon, 136, 329

Yanbo, 61, 81, 85, 88, 89, 94, 95, 96; defence of, 98-9, 100, 101, 102, 103, 114, 117, 129, 169, 174, 237

Yarmuk Valley, 171, 192, 193, 199, 202, 206, 211, 267, 271

Yemen, 34, 50, 140

Yilderim Army Group, 190

Young, Sir Hubert, 15, 16, 161, 234, 237, 238, 241, 243, 244, 250, 251, 252, 258, 262, 269, 271, 272, 280, 282, 283, 284, 299, 333, 360

Young Turks, 20, 26, 42, 43

Zaagi, the, 208

Zaal, 156, 182, 183, 184, 194

Zebn, the, 238, 266, 269

Zeid, Sherif, 60, 65, 96, 99, 175, 214, 215, 216, 217, 222, 223, 228, 237; in dispute between Feisal and Hussein, 261, 267

Zeitun, 181

Zeki, 143, 148, 149, 152

Ziza, 153

Zones in Sykes-Picot agreement, 48, 310

Other titles of interest